D0277165

A SOUL ON ICE

GAVIN HEWITT

A SOUL ON ICE

A Life in News

MACMILLAN

First published 2005 by Macmillan
an imprint of Pan Macmillan Ltd
Pan Macmillan, 20 New Wharf Road, London N1 9RR
Basingstoke and Oxford
Associated companies throughout the world
www.panmacmillan.com

ISBN 1 4050 4738 0

Picture Acknowledgements
BBC Natural History Unit – 32.   BBC News – 6, 7, 8, 9, 12, 13, 20, 21, 22, 33.
Peter Gigliotti – 29, 30.   Jimmy Grant – 27, 28, 31.   George Kochaniec, *Rocky Mountain News* – 23.
Radio Times – 1.   Mike Spooner – 19.   Mike Viney – 4, 14, 15.   Korczak Ziolkowski – 11.
All other pictures are from the author's private collection.

A CIP catalogue record for this book is available from
the British Library.

Typeset by SetSystems Ltd, Saffron Walden, Essex
Printed and bound in Great Britain by
Mackays of Chatham plc, Chatham, Kent

For those who shared history's moments with me

And for those I love – too often left behind

For always roaming with a hungry heart
Much have I seen and known.

'Ulysses', Alfred, Lord Tennyson

Contents

Acknowledgements

Nearly every incident in this book was shared. As a television corres-pondent I have rarely, if at all, travelled alone. Producers, camera crews, sound recordists have always been at my side. They have ridden the waves with me; the exhilaration of witnessing great events, the frustrations, the dangers. We have often laughed together and they have also had to suffer the bad days.

In writing this book I found that we all remembered different detail. Each of us had stored away fragments from the past but they were often not the same. Everyone I approached, some of whom I had not spoken to for twenty years or longer, were generous with their time. These were moments in their lives too and they wanted me to keep writing. For their insight into my early BBC years I want to thank in particular Steve Morris, Mike Viney, Peter Matthews, Bill Norman, John Jockel and Ray Gibbon.

Alister Bell and Mike Sweeney helped bring back to life my years as a Canadian Correspondent. Neville Bolt, an extraordinarily talented producer, remembered details and incidents I had long forgotten when we travelled together for CBC.

Many of my stories on *Panorama* were shot by Lex Tudhope and Mike Spooner and they added colour to the weeks spent together in such places as Sudan and China.

I have also been able to raid the memories of other reporters and producers. Peter Ruff proved an excellent friend and source on my early days at Radio Brighton. Frank Simmonds, Jenny Clayton, Peter Bell, and Dai Richards not only produced memorable *Panorama*s but recalled all the events that never appeared on screen. Peter Molloy was invaluable. He not only helped me with the chapter on the Mafia but was always encouraging, reminding me of stories that I had told him but had long forgotten. There were others; David Sells filled in the gaps from our time in Poland and Robert Fisk took much better notes than I did when we were in Afghanistan and Iraq and I was able to draw on his articles about the trips we made together. For more recent events I was able to turn to Dan Kelly and Thea Fairley.

Peter Gigliotti, an outstanding cameraman, went through the Iraq war with me and stayed sane through appalling conditions and even worse equipment. I owe him and Jimmy Grant special thanks.

Some of the best pictures I have ever had to write to were provided by Hedley Trigge. In 2003 when I had to work my way back to good health after a serious operation he was a real friend.

I have also been fortunate with my editors. I learned much from Mark Starowicz in Canada. On *Panorama* Tim Gardam and Mark Thompson were always challenging. Most recently I have worked with two excellent editors on the BBC's *Ten O'Clock News*, Mark Popescu and Kevin Bakhurst.

I have to thank Richard Sambrook who five years ago brought me back into mainstream news as a Special Correspondent.

I am very grateful to my agent Catherine Clarke not just for her advice but also for encouraging me to believe that amidst all the notebooks and out-takes there was a personal story. I am hugely indebted to Pan Macmillan for their enthusiasm and, in particular, to my editor, Jeremy Trevathan, for his comments and his vision for the book.

And of course love and thanks to Becky, Daniel and Sally who somehow survived the turbulence of my life on the road.

1

A Soul on Ice

I was summoned to the news editor's desk in front of the bay window with its view of Brighton Pavilion and the Corn Exchange. 'There's an author in reception,' the editor said without looking up. 'Do us a three-minute interview.' It was a kind of humiliation. I was trusted to do interviews with authors and academics and not much else.

I was a twenty-year-old, fresh out of university, on £44 a week. In the short time I had been working at Radio Brighton it had been made clear to me in dozens of subtle, and not so subtle, ways that I knew little about journalism – not the grind of daily police calls, magistrates' courts, council meetings, accidents and crime scenes.

My colleagues in this seaside newsroom had all worked on local papers. They had been snarled at by hard-faced editors. Their papers had paid for them to go on journalism courses in places like Portsmouth or Cardiff. They knew how to report from court or tap a policeman for information. I knew no shorthand and had never even stepped inside a magistrates' court.

I was on trial and not yet to be trusted with stories. Authors, however, were a different matter. They were not really news – more, features. You couldn't mess authors up. That was the view. I asked the editor whether he had any more information about the man in reception. 'His name is Green,' he said. 'Has a local connection.' That was often as good a brief as you would get in local radio. I picked up my Uher, a portable tape recorder, and headed down one flight of stairs.

There was only one man in reception and he was looking out of the window. He wore a green tweed jacket and gave the appearance of a university lecturer. 'Mr Green?' I asked. He turned and

I recognized the face immediately. He was older, but there was no mistaking the blue, questing eyes that I had seen staring from magazines and the back of so many novels.

'You're Graham Greene,' I said, unable to mask my surprise. 'Who did you expect?' he asked with a brief smile. I led to the studio the man who at the time was probably Britain's most famous author and who rarely gave interviews. He was sixty-nine, alert and watchful.

I had read *Brighton Rock* at university. Pinkie's world and the racecourse gangs had long gone. They had disappeared shortly after Greene had published the novel in the 1930s but many of the places he had referred to in the novel, like the Aquarium, the Royal Albion hotel and Dr Brighton's, were still there. There was a note of nostalgia about Greene; he felt the town with its shopping precincts and supermarkets had been drained of much of its character and had become indistinguishable from anywhere else.

When the interview was over he asked me what I wanted to do with my life. 'I want to be a foreign correspondent,' I said quickly and with great certainty. He gave a half-smile. 'You will have to learn,' he said, 'to keep your soul on ice.' He paused briefly before adding, 'But don't keep it there too long.'

I returned to the newsroom and wrote down what he had told me. These were thoughts from a man at the other end of his life; thoughts that had had time to oak and mature. I was too raw, too untried to have used much guile and deception to get a story, but I knew enough to suspect Greene was right. It was a chance encounter, but one I have never forgotten on a journey that has taken me from local radio to the BBC's *Ten O'Clock News* on television.

At the time I met Graham Greene I was brimming with ambition but had lived little. I had been born in Penge, south London, in the early 1950s. Over the years the places in our past develop colours, shades, moods. Penge, for me, has always been covered in smog, a dense, sooty soup that trolley buses disappeared into and which swallowed up the pub across the street. Looking back it feels Dickensian, with a bombed church next door, a ruin where the homeless lived amidst the rubble. It was a place to escape from. We did move away but we never travelled. The wider world beyond went unexplored and so it largely remained until I left university.

Even when I sat down with Greene I had been abroad only once and that was a few months earlier when I had stayed for five days at the Hôtel du Lac in Vevey, Switzerland.

A month after I had gone to university in 1968 I was persuaded to get on a bus and join a demonstration against the Vietnam war in Grosvenor Square, London. I was seventeen and had no real opinion about the war. I found myself amidst people with raised, clenched fists chanting, 'Ho, Ho, Ho Chi Minh.' At the time I scarcely knew he was the North Vietnamese leader, but the words shouted through bull-horns sounded dangerous and subversive. A woman close to me screamed 'pigs' at the police line and spat in their faces. I had never found anything to hate so much. I was surrounded by red flags, pictures of Che Guevara and angry men urging us to charge police lines. All I knew was that I was caught up in something, something threatening, and that at that moment the world was watching these streets and I was there. I was on a frontline I little understood, but I felt alive, involved and at the heart of things, and it was a feeling I would never forget.

It was not until my second year at university that I knew with a flash of certainty what I wanted to do. I had been watching a television report from Vietnam when I decided that was how I wanted to spend my life. I never wavered, I never had doubts. I wanted to be a foreign correspondent.

While at university I had been offered a job at Radio Brighton. After my finals I didn't even wait to get my results. I left the day my last exam was over. I wanted to be out there working, to call myself a reporter. I was in a hurry, tripping over myself.

Often at Radio Brighton we relied on 'walk-ins'. These were people who came in off the streets with stories to tell. As long as their tales were about Brighton they stood a fair chance of getting on air. It was one of my tasks to check out the 'walk-ins'.

One day a middle-aged man appeared in reception. He was scruffy, with dirt under his nails, and a little unsure of himself. He had been walking on the Sussex Downs and had found a small clay pot with a Latin inscription on it. He had no idea what it was but wondered whether it was Roman.

I examined the pot. Where the crusted earth had been scraped away I could see a hand-carved inscription underneath. I was convinced by it. A local man had stumbled on an archaeological find. So I got him to tell the whole story on tape. During the interview I asked him to read out the inscription. He broke into an Italian accent, which emphasized the end of the words, and read, 'Iti sapis potan dati none.' On the tape I could be heard apologizing that my schoolboy Latin was not up to translating it.

Only after the interview had been broadcast as the final item on the local news did I return to the newsroom. Every face was creased in a smile. They were all looking at me. I had fallen for one of the oldest cons. There were many variations of this story, but by a little juggling of the letters the code was cracked to reveal 'It is a piss pot and a tin one.' I so wanted to be a reporter but I was giving every impression of being a klutz, a dork, gauche and gullible.

I had a piece of luck. The BBC was looking for trainees who were not just graduates but who had had some experience in local journalism. I was taken on and was suddenly in London close to where I wanted to be. We were a privileged few. As part of our training we had to work in a BBC office outside London. I got Belfast at the height of the Troubles and a chance to report on local television. It was unlike anything I had experienced before. The army patrols with soldiers peering through their scopes for snipers, the sirens of the bomb squads, the shudder of the explosions, the almost daily funerals. It seemed the most important, the most vital place in the world. It sucked you in until you lived and breathed every incident.

One day I was in East Belfast and saw a Protestant mob ransacking a Catholic church close to the Short Strand area. They did not want the cameras there and it was wise to leave. Just as we were walking away I saw a boy – aged about eight or nine – holding a statue of the Virgin Mary upside down and smashing the head against the edge of the kerbstone. In a second I knew this was the shot, this was the one moment that captured the blind tribal hatred. It was his young face, so focused, so concentrated on his task, so convinced that he was engaged in important work. I had to have the picture and I shouted at the cameraman. Even as we lined up the shot, rocks began landing around us. A stone splintered the back windscreen of our car. I jumped into the driving seat and we bounced across the bricks and stones as the crowd kicked out at the doors.

Afterwards the cameraman avoided me. He did not want to work with me again. In my ambition to capture the story he thought I had been careless of those around me. Part of me knew he was right, but I couldn't get the image of the boy out of my head; nor the fact that we had missed it. Even now I still feel some irritation. I wanted people to see what I saw. So I became passionate about pictures, about finding those few seconds of action that take you to the essential heart of a story and make you, in a flash, understand it.

I was changing in a way Graham Greene would have understood. I saw much, but was learning to feel little – to be there but always detached. We would see the injured lying on the streets or watch the pale tear-worn faces at the funerals but rarely, if at all, did they seem to touch us. It was as if we were emotionally immune, inoculated, a breed apart who saw all the world's pain but never felt it.

By the age of twenty-five I was getting my chances on national news. The stories were slight at first but shortly afterwards I was covering the Iranian revolution, the Soviet invasion of Afghanistan, the Iran–Iraq war. At the time a large photo of me was printed in the *Radio Times*. It showed me in an off-white suit heading into Heathrow with an exaggerated and rather improbable stride. I was living a rootless, suitcase existence, driven from place to place by the irregular beat of world events but often disconnected from ordinary life. At the moment my son was born I was locked up in Iran.

In 1981 I left the BBC and went to Canada as a senior correspondent for a Canadian network. Much later I would move to BBC *Panorama* and the BBC's *Ten O'Clock News*.

Early on I noticed that when I returned from covering major events or doing an interview the stories I would tell my friends were rarely what had appeared on television. It was almost as if there was a hidden account, a parallel version, an unofficial history that never got told. Sometimes they were conversations that had occurred when the microphones had been switched off. At other times it was the story behind the making of the film that was of more interest than the report itself.

Some of these stories were comic riffs – how we came to overtake the Pope's body – and others bordered on farce, such as when I was smuggled into an embassy for a secret meeting with Prince Charles. There were moments of fear – detention in Iran, facing a death squad in Guatemala, standing accused of spying for MI6. Sometimes I felt like Woody Allen's character Leonard Zelig, turning up everywhere and then finding myself invited to sit next to Jacques Chirac at dinner or taking puja with Rajiv Gandhi.

I witnessed defining moments in history. I was in East Berlin the night the wall came down. I went undercover into China after Tiananmen Square. I rode into Baghdad with the American Third Infantry Division. I interviewed world leaders: Chirac, Blair, Clinton, Mugabe, Indira Gandhi, Arafat and many others. In all of this there was so much that could not be said on TV.

There were the moments that occurred off camera. In 1985 I was standing at the top of the stairs of the People's Palace in Khartoum awaiting the arrival of American Vice-President George Bush. The Sudanese president at the time was Gaafar Numeiri, a general with nine rows of military honours stitched to his tunic. He was a hard man to make out; a one-time Communist who had recently embraced Islam.

In a fit of zealotry he and his aides had hurled bottles of Scotch into the Nile to mark the banning of alcohol. Sales of Nile perch had soared with the rumour that the fish had absorbed some of the Scotch. Numeiri was not without a sense of humour. When I had interviewed him at the palace he asked me whether I'd had a drink since being in the country. I replied, truthfully, that I had been dry. He then told me that he was improving my health and that I should be grateful to him. 'Look at what I am doing for you,' he insisted with an expansive wave of the hand. It was impossible not to smile.

The reason the Americans were in town had nothing to do with Scotch-throwing by the Nile. Several million people faced famine. A few days earlier I had driven west from Khartoum into the interior of Kordofan. It was as if the country had been visited by a terrible plague. Carcasses of animals littered the desert floor, their distorted faces mortified in the moment of final exhaustion. The wooden frames of deserted huts had been bleached white by the hubbub, the searing desert wind. Thousands of square miles of savannah had been buried under sand. A million people from such tribes as the Kababish, the Beja, the Meidob were starving and on the move.

Sudan was begging for American help. So President Numeiri was pacing up and down nervously as he waited for the American vice-president to arrive. Finally George Bush shrugged off his clinging secret servicemen and bounded across the hall to embrace his Sudanese host. 'Ah, Mr President,' Bush gushed, 'my dear friend.' President Numeiri beamed through the bear hug.

The two men began walking up the stairs towards us. George Bush waved his hand at the window and said, 'What wonderful weather you have here.' There was a brief silence as the Sudanese leader looked out and blinked at the relentless sun which was slowly destroying his country. 'But there's a drought,' Numeiri said, with the bewildered look of a man who feared there may have been some terrible misunderstanding in the planning of this high-profile visit. 'We need water,' he added. Bush realized his gaffe and said, 'Of course and that's why we're here,' and concealed his embarrassment in another embrace.

The cameras were not on the stairs. They were in a separate room waiting for a press conference. If George Bush's remarks had been recorded they may have dogged him during his campaign for the presidency. Of course it had just been a gaffe but, in fact, the Americans did have a different agenda. They were more interested in signing up Numeiri as an ally against his troubling neighbour Mu'ammer Qaddafi.

There have been other moments when I feared I had betrayed everything I stood for, when I felt I had crossed the line from reporting the news to making it. During the war in Iraq I travelled with an American tank company all the way from Kuwait to Baghdad. One day, having been ambushed and fired on, we stopped near an electricity sub-station in the western part of the Iraqi capital. The tanks and Bradley fighting vehicles fanned out and formed a defensive ring.

I was sitting on top of a tank-recovery vehicle idly using my binoculars. As I panned around I noticed a blue truck with men lifting off what seemed like boxes of equipment. They worked at a pace, as if they were anxious about being discovered, and that's what made me pan back to them. As I looked I noticed a man in front of the truck who was studying our unit, possibly with binoculars.

I was suddenly afraid that we were about to be attacked. Part of me wanted to stay silent, to do nothing, to pretend I had not seen anything. After all, this was not my war; but I was there and these were the people I was travelling with. I called across to the captain and said he should check out the blue truck. I thought he might send a tank over to investigate, but he ordered a Bradley to open fire. Tracer rounds flew across the open ground. The captain was shouting to the gunner, 'Keep it low, keep it low,' but the rounds were bouncing off the truck and flying into the buildings behind. I was horrified, sickened. On my word innocent people might be losing their lives.

The blue truck exploded. In the orange fireball I saw what looked like a person flying through the air. Then the truck exploded again, and once again in a final deafening blast. This secondary explosion was confirmation to the soldiers around me that the truck was carrying rocket-propelled grenades. Soldiers high-fived me. One man came up to me and said, 'You saved my life, man.' It didn't feel like that to me. In making television news there have been frequent dilemmas, moral dilemmas, and I wanted to write about those too.

Just occasionally there have been moments when the mask of detachment has slipped. In 1988 I was in Prague with the Communists still in power. We had filmed secretly as the playwright and dissident Vaclav Havel had once again been sent back to prison. We had been to see his wife, Olga, in their apartment overlooking the Vistula. She kept a black scorpion in a jar and remarked how even from jail the words of her husband could frighten the authorities.

A few days later, in one of the main squares, the Communist Party was holding a rally. We had been tipped off that some students might disrupt the speeches. We waited near the platform until we heard some booing and then moved through the crowd to where the trouble was. We were among party members and they did not want us filming any protest. Suddenly two or three secret policemen began pulling at the leads at the back of the camera. Without a moment's thought I was shouting at them to get their hands off the camera and I grabbed one of the men. Having watched the harassment of men like Vaclav Havel I was seized by a fierce, almost irrational hatred of these party thugs. I heard the voice of an old man shout, 'CIA provocation.' The students saved me from a beating or worse. They grabbed us and hurried us to the edge of the crowd and put us in the back of a car, while their friends struggled with the police. There have been other moments, although not many, when I have found it impossible to stay on the sidelines and they, too, form part of my story.

As I looked back over my notes I realized that many of the stories were about the making of television news. In 1966 President Lyndon Johnson had remarked, looking into the cameras, 'All of politics has changed because of you.' Asked what had caused the fall of Communism in Eastern Europe, Lech Walesa, the leader of the independent union Solidarity, had pointed to a nearby TV set and said, 'It all came from here.' Most people get their news from television.

Everyone, it seems, now knows the power of the image, that one shot can echo around the world and change perceptions. Governments kill to stop pictures getting out. In Zimbabwe a cameraman and I had to flee a mob with machetes who had been told to stop any pictures being taken of their attacks on farm owners.

Frequently I have heard the cry, 'Get the cameras.' In May 2002 we were covering an anti-globalization demonstration in Genoa, Italy. We were filming anarchists smashing a car showroom when they spotted the camera. Four youths wearing black masks and carrying sticks attacked us, seized the £30,000 camera and threw it on their bonfire of the modern.

In many different ways politicians, movie stars and royalty all try and control the image. There is a daily tussle over what appears on the nightly news and I have been at the heart of major controversies. Here, too, I wanted to write about some of the arguments off screen, the out-takes, the offcuts.

During the British election in 2001 the Labour Party wanted all controversy, all unexpected moments, drained from election coverage. They were ahead in the polls and gave the impression of just wanting to count down the clock to voting day. From their perspective they were right. The only image that is remembered from that drab campaign is the punch thrown by Deputy Prime Minister John Prescott. It was played, re-played, slo-moded from every angle. For the first and only time the boxer Frank Bruno found himself commenting on an election campaign.

As a special correspondent for the BBC I did several reports on the party leaders. I travelled for a period with Tony Blair in his battle bus and flew with William Hague in his helicopter. During these journeys I would do a short interview about the campaign. One day I was with Tony Blair and the Labour bus on the outskirts of Leeds. My cameraman, Hedley Trigge, and I were the only journalists present.

As we approached the city the bus driver lost his way. I looked out of the window and we seemed to be in the middle of an industrial estate with storage warehouses. We then came to a narrow bridge and the driver stopped. We were sitting a few rows back from him. He was clearly agitated and was looking for some-one on the street to talk to. Rather red-faced he announced that he was unsure whether the bridge could take the bus's weight.

Gradually everyone ended up at the front of the bus discussing this, including Tony Blair, one of his closest aides and a special branch officer. I was immediately struck by how unusual all this was. In the United States this would have been headline news. It would have bordered on the scandalous for the president's motor-cade to have lost its way. Yet here was the prime minister stranded in front of a narrow bridge with no place to turn.

I said to Hedley that we should record this. It was not a significant moment but it was of interest. As soon as we lifted the camera we got into an argument. 'You can't film this,' said one of the prime minister's staff. 'Why not?' I asked. Tony Blair looked irritated and it was made clear that future access during the campaign would be denied unless the camera was turned off.

So – and I regret this – we put down the camera. Moments later the incident was over and the prime minister was transferred to a special branch Land Rover Discovery. In one sense it was all trivial, but in our image-conscious world it mattered enough to argue over. Those incidents, too, formed part of the stories that I told friends but rarely, if at all, told the viewer.

It was after I had returned from covering the war in Iraq that I felt it was time to go unplugged, to unfreeze Greene's 'soul on ice', to sift through the notebooks, the video clips, the memories of colleagues and to tell what happened beyond the eye of the camera. Not just the skein of major events, but the humour, at times surreal, of a life on the road. Nearly every story here was shared and I have been able to raid the recollections of friends and colleagues. There are some confidences that cannot be broken, promises made that must be kept, but, where I could, I have told it how it was.

2

That Was the Pope's Body

All reporters are hustlers; we get alongside people only to open them up, to relieve them of their stories. We circle them, we work them, we befriend them, we use every silver-tongued argument that persuades. We are chameleons of the street, who can identify with everyone; verbal muggers in pursuit of the quote, the fact, the access that delivers the story. And covering all this, like an insurance policy, is our article of faith – the people's right to know.

I left university, aged twenty, my bags packed with idealism. Reporting, for me, was a calling. We were the good guys, truth-seekers, set on keeping the powerful honest. I had never given much thought as to how these nuggets of truth would be prised out. So without having spent a day at journalism school or on a local paper, without even a basic understanding of the law, I began my life as a reporter. I recall making my first phone call, very self-consciously, and saying, 'This is Mr Hewitt from Radio Brighton,' and another reporter taking me aside and saying, 'You sound as if you're chasing people behind on the rent.' Reporters, I learned, always dropped the 'Mr' and used their first names.

I listened with amazement when a colleague described having a drink with a policeman. The idea of drinking with a cop seemed extraordinary, if not downright dangerous or even corrupt. Very quickly I learned that a good reporter was an operator – someone who could talk their way past a police line, cold-call, knock on the doors of strangers, find a side entrance into the local hospital. At the end of most days I would go to the Black Horse and listen as anecdotes were traded. These tales were rarely about the stories themselves, the people involved or the lives affected; the crack was nearly always about how the story had been landed.

Amidst the bragging there was an undertone, an undercurrent; stories were told without names or details, but told nonetheless. There was the reporter who had, while visiting a grieving relative and while her back was turned, removed a photo from her mantel-piece without telling her. Then there was the reporter who had befriended a mother whose daughter had gone missing. Once he had gained the inside story of her return, he had turned to the woman and said, 'Your daughter was nothing but a slut.' This cruel line was intended to poison the well for any rival reporters that might come after him. I never knew if stories like this were true, but over the pints I learned that the world I had entered was more shaded than I had expected, and sleight of hand was often rewarded and celebrated.

There were also snippets of advice, some bizarre, some delivered with drink's late-night sincerity. On one occasion I had waited to be included in a conversation with one of Fleet Street's legendary reporters. Finally, when the evening was past its best, he looked me in the eye and said, 'You should remember this.' He took out his notebook. 'See that,' he said, 'a soft-cover. You got to have a soft-cover. A notebook is no use unless it fits in your back pocket,' he went on. He removed his jacket to show me. 'A notebook must mould with your arse,' he said, as if imparting ancient wisdom. 'You should remember that,' was his final comment before drifting away. And then there was the old-timer who could summon up only one scrap of advice from a lifetime. 'Only drink when you're happy,' he told me.

I did not necessarily want to become like any of these reporters, but I hung on their words, eager to learn anything that might help on my journey towards becoming a foreign correspondent. I soon discovered that local papers, radio, television news, foreign report-ing all had their bag of tricks that were rarely taught, but were either handed down or learned on the street. By my mid-twenties I was getting the occasional chance on the BBC's main news. Just half-chances, stories that others would not touch – like Christmas Day cricket. I shot it from every angle, interviewed almost every player, ran the cameraman ragged who kept telling me it would 'only make a minute on air', but I was young and ambitious and minutes mattered to me.

On 18 September 1977, I was asked to 'doorstep' Rod Stewart at Heathrow Airport. The rock star had not only just split from his girlfriend Britt Ekland but she was threatening to take him to court for a share of his money. It was an unusual story for the BBC to cover and I was told by the editor that we would only run the report if Rod gave a 'news-line', but for me it was another half-chance. This was a 'doorstep'; an ambush where reporters and cameras surround someone and try and get a comment. I had done them before, but not for television.

As with everything else there was a technique to this and I flew around the building getting tips from other reporters and cameramen. Always keep the person in front of you, I was told. Never let him pass. Stand in his way. Once he has passed the camera can only see the back of his head and the moment is lost. Never ask questions that can be answered 'yes' or 'no'. Use his first name. Get his eye and hold it. Make him feel you are the one he can trust. Stick to him wherever he goes. Always have a 'killer' question up your sleeve that will get a reaction.

So, peppered with advice, I headed to Terminal 3 to await Rod Stewart's arrival from Los Angeles. This was an end-of-bulletin story, a 'droppable', but in my mind it had become a challenge. I waited with my camera crew, my eye never leaving the sliding door of the baggage-claim area. I rarely spoke to the cameraman; I just watched, totally focused on a door. There were other cameras and reporters but I was determined to reach Rod Stewart first. Then he was there. The familiar spiky, straggly blond hair. Even as I saw him I heard the shutters and the winders on the stills cameras beside me. Two newspaper reporters beat me to his side. It didn't matter that he was speaking, I threw in my first question.

'How do you feel about the court case, Rod?'

He didn't answer me and so I raised my voice and repeated it.

'How do you feel about the court case, Rod?'

'I'm disgusted by it.'

The reply was so short it threw me but I was now on his right shoulder.

'How do you feel about coming back to Britain? You're a tax exile.'

'I've actually come back to watch a football match on Wednesday.'

My line was not working and other reporters were trying to hustle me off my questions.

'Would you consider living here again, Ron?'

(Ron! How could I have said Ron? My face reddened at the stumble.)

'Yes, one day,' he replied.

The answers were too brief.

'Would the tax laws have to be changed?' I continued.

'Yeah, I think they could be.'

I was getting desperate now. The other reporters felt I was asking the wrong questions, but my left arm clung to him.

'Any chance of you and Britt getting back together again?'

'No chance. It's finished.'

Better, but short again. We were now pressed against passengers who were sitting down and Rod Stewart was looking for the exit, but still I clung to him and, like some shoal of fish, we all moved together, clambering over travellers and their bags.

'Don't you feel you owe her something after two and a half years?' I went on.

'That's a pointed question which, when the case is finished, I'll be able to answer.'

He was now looking me in the eye. I was the man he was having this conversation with, but I still didn't feel I had it and I launched my killer question, the one I had prepared in the car to Heathrow.

'She says she wrote some of your songs?'

'She certainly did not.' He stopped at this and emphasized the word 'certainly'.

'I'm sure,' he continued, 'that the people who bought my records bought them for me. Not her.'

'Hasn't she helped you with your career?'

'No.'

There was a note of anger here and I, at last, felt I had my bite. As I paused Rod Stewart ducked through a door and was gone. And that was it. Television news. This business that I wanted so badly. And that night they ran it all. All fifty-eight seconds of it. What did it all mean? What did it say? I was in too much of a hurry to ask these questions. There was always tomorrow and another story.

For most people ambition grows slowly, unrecognized, until it has taken hold, but I could date my ambition. I had drifted through my early school with moderate grades. Then, when I was thirteen, my bedroom door opened and my mother told me my father had died during the night. I did not cry or feel anything. I just said, 'I will be down shortly.' We were living by the sea at that time and during the afternoon I went for a walk. On a hoarding I saw the headline for the evening paper: 'Local Vicar Dies'. The words were about my father, but I turned away, curiously disengaged, as if the headline had nothing to do with me. And in that moment, staring out at a grey churning sea, I decided 'it was up to me'. There was no one to rely on, no safety net. In the days that followed I hated all the people who came to the house and asked me how I was. I just wanted to be left alone, to get on. In the funeral car I started giggling and, as I looked out of the window and saw people staring at this young giggling face, it made me laugh more. And that was that; I laughed through my father's funeral. And, afterwards, I remember the tension in the house. My grandmother, who had been a dress-designer and who had recently lost her husband, remarked to my mother, 'Now you know what it's like.' And I wanted my escape. Back at school I started working, working for myself, and by the age of seventeen I was gone and at university.

I was curiously without roots. My father had erased his past. Even now the picture is dim. It seems he had grown up near Newcastle, the youngest of nine children. His parents had died and he was brought up by a sister. When he left school he worked down the mines. Sometime later, when he was an older teenager, he and some of his friends went to disrupt a meeting at the Eldon Road Mission. Something happened that night, possibly a religious con-version, but it changed his life. He started to educate himself and eventually became a Bachelor of Divinity and a Master of Theology. He studied Hebrew, ancient Greek and Latin and, much later, was ordained into the church. There was, however, no hinterland. My father, as far as I can remember, never spoke of where he was from. If he was asked about it he left the room. There was no contact with his family. It might have been that he wanted to leave his old life behind him; it might have been class. He had worked down the mines, but the past was an unmentionable subject.

I felt I did not go back. The road just ran out. There was nowhere I felt I belonged, no geographical place that I called home. No town or region where my roots went down. The reporter's life was made for me. A life on the road. A life of loose connections. In and out of people's lives. And always the buzz of getting the story to air. The daily reward; a daily affirmation, in a way, of who I was. It was addictive, caroming from story to story. Always available. I wrote Charlie Chaplin's obituary for BBC News but only because he died on Christmas Day and, of course, I was willing to do it.

What I wanted, above all, was to be a television correspondent and to report the major stories. It was not just about appearing before camera; I was fascinated by the power of the picture. I saw how it moved people, how it changed events. I was helped in this by Dick Ross, a tall Australian senior duty editor. He would stand by the Steenbeck, the editing machine, racking the film backwards and forwards until he found a piece of the action. Sometimes it was away from the centre of the shot but he would declare, 'There's the story.' He told me to hunt for the narrative in the pictures. They were not just a collection of random shots. There was a story in there. Television news was never about the mid-shot, or the top shot. Its power lay in the close-up action, as it did in a photo. Having found that image, the key was to write to it, to bring it to life. He taught me the power of the one line, terse and spare, that, when laid in commentary over the picture, had the force of a commercial. It was like music. A line and then a pause. A silence. The power of a shot could live in the silence. And always television was about people, their testimony, their first-hand stories.

Then chances came and I was out there, a young, raw, breathless reporter hunting for shots. One day in late July 1978 I was asked to go to Orly Airport in Paris. The news desk had been tipped off that a father was planning to snatch back his son who was being taken abroad by his mother. At the time the issue of child custody was in the news. We chartered a small plane from Luton Airport and bounced across the channel and landed in fog. I was with camera-man Bernard Hesketh and his soundman, John Jockel. Hesketh was vastly experienced and believed in high standards. He almost always wore a dark suit and tie. I once saw him standing beside the Shatt-al-Arab waterway in Iraq in the heat and the dust, but he still had not removed his shirt and tie.

Inside the terminal we stood and waited, with the camera hidden. And then I saw men running, heard the cry of a woman's voice, watched a child being carried to a car outside. It was dramatic footage and we sped into Paris to edit it. The next day we were in Brittany to cover an attempt to cross the Atlantic by two British balloonists. And then it was hard driving and back to Paris. There had been a shooting outside the Iraqi embassy in Paris. Two men had walked into the embassy and had opened fire and taken hostages. It was part of an ongoing dispute between the Iraqis and Yasser Arafat's faction of the Palestine Liberation Organization. A peaceful end to the siege had been negotiated, but as the gunmen were being led away guards inside the embassy opened fire and killed a French policeman. A fierce gun battle erupted in a Paris street.

We raced against the time, snatching shots and pieces to camera. I had heard that the Iraqi ambassador, Mr Tawfik al-Wandawi, had been summoned to the Élysée Palace to see the French president. I had also been told that he spoke some English. We tore through the streets, double-parked the car beside the Bristol Hotel and ran across the road to the Élysée Palace. Outside there was a group of journalists huddled around a figure. They were speaking in French but I could not hear what they were saying. All I knew was that our deadline was approaching. We tried to push in closer but the French journalists would not be nudged aside. So, in desperation, I told Bernard Hesketh to stand by. I would break up this news conference with a question in English. I told him that as soon as he could see the ambassador through the lens he should cue me. Bernard squeezed past a couple of reporters and pushed aside a photographer and finally I heard him say, 'OK, Gavin.' At that point, even though I could not see the man, I called out at the top of my voice, 'Mr Ambassador. Mr Ambassador. A word in English.' The reporters all turned around and it was only then that I saw the rather perplexed face of the man in the middle. Even though all the reporters were speaking to me I ploughed on with my question. Finally, it dawned on me what the reporters were saying. 'He's not the ambassador.' 'Well, who is he, then?' I said. 'He's the French trade minister,' came back the reply. I had just broken up a news conference with a French minister. We slunk away and ran back to the car.

I was not done yet. I was caught up in a kind of delirium. It was back to the Iraqi embassy, hurtling through the traffic. I rang the bell and a thickset man answered. I said I was from the BBC and had come to see the ambassador. The man, who wore an open-necked shirt, invited us in and we sat down in an elegant high-ceilinged room. I presumed the ambassador was being called and we chatted away to this man and others who I thought were guards. The man who had opened the door sat threading beads through his fingers. We talked about Paris, about France, about food and then about women. About women's legs. What made a woman's leg beautiful? How did Arab women's legs differ from French women's? And all the time I was burning with impatience.

And then, after about half an hour, I asked him when the ambassador was coming. He replied, 'Who is the ambassador?' I was confused by this and said, 'I don't know.' We all looked at each other. Then the man who had let us in said, 'I am the ambassador.' I said, 'You must be joking,' before I could check myself. 'No,' he insisted, 'I am the ambassador. What do you want?' 'I would like an interview,' I said but, by now, I was totally thrown. This was the man we had been discussing women's legs with. Bernard Hesketh set up his tripod but I could see his faith in me draining away. So I interviewed this man while still uncertain whether he was the ambassador. After he had left the room I asked the other men whether there were any pictures of the ambassador with French officials. They brought out some photos, but they were inconclusive. Outside the embassy Bernard felt we couldn't send the interview to London. He was unconvinced the man was the Iraqi ambassador. So we got back in the car and drove to the offices of the French paper *Liberation* to see if they had any stills of the man. Time ebbed away. We eventually filed a report, but without the interview. Only when it was too late did we discover that we had, after all, interviewed the Iraqi ambassador. Later that evening the three of us sat down at a table just off the Boulevard St-Germain, worn out by the craziness of it all.

Much later in the evening we phoned the news desk to let them know where we would be staying. They had been trying to find us. The Pope had just died and they wanted us to go to Rome. They had booked us on the first flight the following morning. I had never been to Italy and was not a Catholic, but this was a major story and I was on it.

We arrived at Ciampino airport outside Rome when the light was still soft. We were met by a driver, who occasionally worked for the BBC, called Furio D'Ortona. He was a small, squat, thick-armed man with a mound of black chest hair. He was in his early thirties and had a smattering of English. At that time I spoke no Italian. Pope Paul VI had not died in the Vatican in Rome but in his summer palace in Castel Gandolfo in the Alban Hills. We went directly there, all of us, our equipment and bags squeezed inside a Fiat 125.

As we drove I felt the weight of the story. The Pope was the spiritual leader of 700 million Catholics around the world and I would be reporting his death for BBC television. Italy was, at once, both foreign to me and unexplored. Out of the window I could see the remains of ancient viaducts, tall cypress pines, honey-stoned farmhouses with pantiled roofs.

Castel Gandolfo was perched on the edge of a crater about fifteen miles south of Rome. As we started the climb towards the small town people were parking their cars on the verges and walking. They were not stylish, just ordinary people, mainly Italians. There were more women than men. Some of the men looked uncomfortable in their suits, as if they were unused to wearing them, and they fiddled with their collars. A few of the women carried handkerchiefs ready for tears. They all walked in silence as if talking was disrespectful. Near the main square the crowd had thickened into tight knots and they gave way to our car with glances of resentment.

Outside the Pope's palace were long lines of people waiting to file past his body. Every so often they broke into hymns or chanted 'Ave Maria'. The pictures were strong, but I needed to find English speakers who could sum up what Pope Paul VI meant to them. Everyone I approached was Italian and the office had not thought to find us a translator. Bernard kept telling me, 'We must do vox pops.' I was becoming desperate and went to the front of the line and walked down, calling out in a loud voice, 'Does anyone speak English?' Eventually I found a woman who told me the Pope was a good man; but it wasn't enough. John, the sound-recordist, told me that one of the souvenir-sellers spoke English. Initially I recoiled at the idea of interviewing a man surrounded by his litres of *vino sacro*, but finally I gave in. The trinket-seller spoke of Italy's great sadness, his eyes even moistened on hearing his own words, but I suspected he was about as genuine as the keys to St Peter's, which he was selling for $1.20. And that was our first report, full of the colour of the streets but empty of any insight into who this Pope had been.

Overnight a plan formed in my mind: I should concentrate on the priests. It was more than likely that some of them spoke English. So I positioned myself by the palace gates and pestered black-robed clerics as they got out of their polished official cars. And then I had my moment of luck; I met a priest, also dressed in black, but with purple buttons on his coat. We interviewed him and afterwards I asked to film the Pope's body. Just five minutes, I pleaded.

Later that day we were invited inside the palace and walked up some stairs to the Swiss Room where the Pope, robed in red, lay on a catafalque. He wore a white mitre and red shoes. Entwined in his hands was a rosary and I asked Bernard for a close-up. As I looked around I was struck by the attention to detail; it was as if the set had been dressed. At one end of the catafalque was a silver crucifix and at the other was a burning candle. At the four corners stood Swiss Guards in their yellow-and-blue-striped uniforms. Standing there I felt this was more than just about a man who had died, it was also about the power of the church.

The days had been humid and the room smelt of decomposition. I watched the people as they came into the room. Some wept. Some clearly felt that just by being in the presence of the dead Pope there might be a blessing in it. All were moved.

We were given only a few minutes to film and all the time we were being told to hurry up. I suggested to Bernard a piece to camera with the Pope behind me. He was unsure about this. I argued that it put me at the heart of this story. He thought it might be seen as in poor taste. Then there was the battery light problem.

The Swiss Room was in low light and a piece to camera needed extra light. And the officials would not agree to that; they were trying to keep the room as cool as possible. Even so we had filmed the Pope and had picked up a clutch of interviews.

It had been a strong report, but I saw the following day as the real challenge and I was determined to make my report distinctive. It was a Wednesday and the Pope's body was going to be moved to the Vatican. The journey to Rome would provide the best pictures since his death and Bernard, John and I spent hours discussing how we would cover it. The cortège would leave the palace late afternoon and travel along the Via Appia Nuova to the centre of the capital. We faced a choice. We could stand at the gates of the palace and film the departure and rely on RAI, the Italian network, to cover the rest of the journey, or we could try and cover some of it ourselves. Certainly the pictures would be better if we shot it. Bernard was an excellent cameraman and RAI had a different style of shooting. Their shots were rarely steady.

Listening to all this was Furio D'Ortona, the driver. With a smile he said it was possible to film the departure and the journey. 'It is certain,' he bragged. In time his driving would become notorious, but that still lay ahead. He was also a man with mystifying influence with the police; he could drive onto the tarmac at Fiumincino airport and meet BBC reporters at the plane's steps, by-passing customs and immigration. That, too, was unknown. In the end, Furio's confidence persuaded us and we decided to film both the departure and the journey.

It was almost dusk when the cortège drove through the gates of the papal palace. There were eleven cars and police motorcycles. As it passed I recorded a piece to camera and then we jumped into our car. The trick now was to get ahead of the cortège. There was no way to overtake it on the main road down from the hill-town but Furio knew another lesser-known route. We shot through narrow ancient streets with the car almost touching the walls. We clipped tables outside a closed trattoria and they spun away in our wake. We went the wrong direction down one-way streets. The speed was terrifying and dangerous but, somehow, it seemed necessary, even excusable. Furio drove with a half-smile. Getting alongside the Pope's cortège now mattered to him as much as it did to us. His pride was staked on it like a large bet.

After we left the hill-town we found the main road blocked by the police. Furio turned into a lane and vines and olive groves flashed past us. Then we tore through another village with the three of us strap-hanging in the vehicle. Bernard shouted to Furio to slow down but he was beyond restraint. Ahead I could see what looked like an autostrada with no traffic moving. We burst out of the side road almost colliding with a hearse. Furio spun the wheel left and we were all thrown against each other. 'What was that?' I shouted. 'That was the Pope's body,' said Bernard. Almost at once, a carabinieri car herded us off the new Appian Way and we were back in open country.

Someone said, 'This is crazy,' but Furio said there was another exit close by and minutes later we emerged again beside the cortège. We were now riding into Rome alongside the Pope's body. A policeman in the vehicle in front stuck a white-and-red stick, shaped like a lollipop, out of his window, telling us to stop, but Furio ignored him. Bernard wound down the window and began filming the hearse and the simple wooden coffin. A wonderful tracking shot. And then there were the crowds. Not great in number, but they stood on the overpasses and by the edge of the road. Most of them clapped as the motorcade passed. Some fell to their knees and prayed. Some wept. Most just watched impassively. It was enough to be there, to say they had been there. And beside the Pope's cortège an unexplained blue Fiat. And as I sat there watching the people I felt a rush of exhilaration, living in history's eye.

Then unbelievably bad luck. Bernard announced that he was out of film and the spare magazine was in the boot of the car. We all knew that, if we stopped, we would never regain our position, but there was no point in continuing. Furio braked hard and we ran for the magazine. Immediately a police car blocked us. I was certain we would be arrested but the policemen held us there long enough to ensure we could not catch up with the cortège again. Then Furio, angry and brooding, drove dangerously into Rome where we picked up some more shots.

That evening we edited the piece and, of course, included one brief shot that no one else had. Later I walked around Bernini's colonnade beside St Peter's Square. Under floodlights they were building wooden partitions for the crowds expected for the funeral. Part of me was pleased with the day's report, but there were troubling questions that I did not really want to face. What would I do for a shot? How far would I go? What would I do for a moment of television?

A few weeks later I was back in Rome for another Pope's death. Pope John Paul I, the smiling Pope, had lasted just thirty-three days. This time I concentrated on interviews with ordinary Catholics. Some were sad, many more were confused and wondered out loud about what God was trying to tell his church. When I returned to London, Basil Hume, the Archbishop of Westminster, sent a letter. He wrote of the 'extremely sensitive way' the recent events had been reported. 'It really was most impressive. All Roman Catholics, indeed many others,' he said, 'have good reason to be grateful to you.'

It crossed my mind what he would have said or written if he had seen that Fiat alongside the Pope's hearse. 'If only they knew what was involved in getting the story,' I said to myself. And it would not be the last time that I would think this. Over the years I would change, but then I was young with blind ambition.

3

We Consider You a Spy

It was as if the war had ended yesterday. That was my first impression. I had never been to Eastern Europe before nor stepped inside the Communist world. This was April 1977 and Warsaw was frozen in time, another time, the age of austerity – those spartan ration-book years after World War Two that I had seen on news-reels. The country seemed to have missed out on demobilization. Much of the traffic was military and soldiers walked the streets in uniforms as if just back from some frontline.

I lived for these moments. Another country. The unknown. The flood of images and impressions. I had still travelled little, and everywhere was new and alive. I collected the tickets, the hotel brochures, the baggage labels, the bank notes as if I feared memory was not enough. I wanted something concrete to hang on to, to say I had been there. I had already discovered that there was the story and the adventure of making the story and, in the early years, it was the latter that drew me as much as the former. I was an adventurer-journalist.

Warsaw was a washed-out, drab, monochrome place without bright colours. The shop windows either were empty or had small stacks of tins or bottles with fading labels that might have been there for ten years. There was no advertising, no incentive to promote or sell. The older men wore dull, heavy worsted coats over grey suits and sober ties. The older women, too, huddled beneath shapeless coats and woollen hats, with boots worn and scuffed from trudging through the snow. They all carried shopping bags just in case a delivery was made to a store while they were passing. Even the younger girls lacked colour. There were flashes of style, a loosely tied scarf over the shoulders or a splash of lipstick, but little more.

I have never forgotten my first hours under Communism. The long lines, the shortages, the heads down, the resigned faces. I met the *stojacy* – the 'standers' who were paid to keep a place in a queue. All of this was true, yet, as I would find, this was only the surface of things.

We were a team of four. David Sells was a vastly experienced journalist who spoke some Polish and had lived in Warsaw in the 1950s. Peter Matthews was the cameraman and Bill Norman was the sound-recordist. Obtaining visas to film in Poland was difficult but we had tempted the authorities. It was two years since the Communist countries had signed the Helsinki agreement with its clauses on human rights. In a few weeks there was going to be an international conference reviewing whether countries like Poland had lived up to their commitments. We took advantage of this and proposed going to a school to film the changes they were making in the teaching of history. The authorities liked the idea and within weeks we had our visas.

The history proposal was largely a front. We were there to meet a group of dissidents who the Polish authorities both feared and harassed. They belonged to a group called KOR, the Workers' Defence Committee, and had not been filmed before. The committee had been formed the previous year after riots against an increase in food prices. They were mainly intellectuals – lecturers and economists – who had campaigned against the harsh treatment of those workers who had taken to the streets.

What made this group so threatening to the authorities was their links with the workers. In the past the men in the mines and shipyards had been bought off with extra deliveries of sausage and beef. But the dissidents told the workers that their problem was the system and its lack of democracy. KOR's meetings were frequently broken up and its leaders detained. We could not know it, but the men and women we were coming to see would help give birth to the independent union Solidarity, and shorten the days of Communism itself. Whilst we were still in London a message had been passed to them and they had agreed to meet us.

We stayed at the Hotel Europejski, a nineteenth-century hotel that had been destroyed in the war and later rebuilt. Inside it was modern and functional with panels of veneer and plastic flowers that needed dusting. We expected the rooms to be bugged and when we wanted to talk about our plans we sat in the lobby amidst the Swiss-cheese plants and the lurid marine-blue carpet.

By the second day we noticed that whenever we sat down a group of men would come and sit nearby. These were heavy-set men with workers' hands and unsmiling puffy faces. They rarely spoke to each other; they just sat there twirling their car keys through their fingers. These were the men from the UB, the Polish secret police. We had been careful, but not careful enough.

Our difficulty was that before we could film the dissidents we needed to meet one of them to make the arrangements. We decided to try and relax our watchers with a visit to Chopin's birthplace at Zelazowa Wola, about forty miles west of the capital.

It took us about an hour and a half in our rented Polish-built Fiat. The road across the flat Mazovian plain was pot-holed, narrow and muddy from the clumps of soil that had fallen from the horse-drawn carts. They were the farmers' only transport and we crawled behind them. The carts were long, thin and v-shaped with roughly carved side poles. In the fields horses pulled wooden ploughs, while the farmers trudged behind pressing in the furrows. Some beet and cabbage had been planted, but this was a land of toil as it had been for centuries.

Chopin's house was a relief. It was more of a low-slung cottage than a house, but it was white, airy and surrounded by gardens and woods. The first blossom was out and polonaises and mazurkas drifted through the willow trees from concealed speakers. I breathed deeply and relaxed away from the oppressive eyes of the city.

We saw them together. Two men, city men, in dark brown suits, pretending to examine the irises. There was no mistaking them. The secret police had followed us. We all stood there by a stream, unsure of each other, as Chopin's romances played on. In a moment the place had changed for us and we were anxious to leave. There was no point in staying. On our return we were subdued. Every so often Bill would look back and report, 'They're still with us.' On one level this was a game; us pitted against a team of hard-faced goons. As journalists we felt we had a certain immunity, almost a diplomatic status. But always there was that lingering doubt. This was a system where the deniable happened – beatings, random accidents and false charges. As we drove we calculated the odds, but only the secret police knew how far they would go to stop us.

On the way back into the city we had planned to break away and meet Jacek Kuron, one of the leaders of KOR. With a car following us that would be difficult, but on the edge of Warsaw there was an opportunity. We all saw the chance. Two red-and-white trams were about to pass in front of us. There was no time to discuss it. It was instinctive. The risk had to be either taken or avoided. At the last moment David drove across the tracks between the trams, while the tram drivers hit their horns. There was no way the UB could follow us. We had a precious fifteen-second advantage. David raced for a side street, stopped the car and we disappeared into the crowd.

Jacek Kuron, with his crumpled denim suit and open-necked shirt, looked like an academic. He was about forty, with dark receding hair, and the hunted life of a dissident clung to him. He smoked nervously and there were dark patches under his eyes. Kuron was an unlikely rebel. At one time he had been to the left of the Communist Party and had been to prison for that. Now he saw the regime as repressive and was considered by the authorities one of the most dangerous men in Poland.

'They will know everything,' he said; 'the apartment is watched continuously.' The only thing they would not know, he continued, was the date of the meeting. He wrote it on a piece of paper. He had one condition: when we filmed we stayed until the talking was over. On previous occasions when KOR had met, the UB had sent in thugs who had pulled people out and beaten them. The authorities wanted to prevent KOR being able to plan or organize. Kuron saw us as a kind of shield, calculating that the secret police would never attack with us present. He also wanted the world to know that, despite the Helsinki agreement, they were still denied their basic rights.

When we returned to the hotel our watchers were there before us, sitting in the car. It was hard not to smile at them. By the next day it had all become more serious. After we had slid between the trams the UB mounted a major operation. We calculated that they had assigned between twenty and thirty agents to us. When we walked along the street there was a phalanx of three or four of them. Some were women, large and mean faced, who carried their radios in plastic shopping bags. Sometimes we caught them holding these bags in front of their faces and speaking into them. When we sat down at a restaurant the nearby tables were cleared. People eating were moved elsewhere. In their place would be these unsmiling men and women, who never talked to each other and never ordered any food. They just sat there. David was used to harassment in this part of the world, but he had never seen anything like this before and that concerned us.

In the evening we walked to Warsaw's Old Town. It looked like an eighteenth-century market square, but it had been restored after the war. The Germans had systematically destroyed nearly a thousand houses here before leaving the city. The reconstruction had been painstaking, but I didn't like the Old Town. History hung there like a low-lying mist. On the walls there were plaques marking the spots of public execution under the Occupation. And to me, with our minders beside us, it seemed the hand of repression had not been lifted.

There were only a few restaurants. They closed early and the food was all the same. They all had menus, but requests for most dishes were met with 'Niema' – 'There isn't any.' So most nights it was borsch soup with a dab of sour cream and meat balls, if we were lucky. Not many people could afford to eat out, so it was often just the four of us and the secret police. Shortly after the incident with the trams, David got up and asked the goons what they recommended on the menu. It was our way of hitting back. They shrugged, their sullen faces never changing expression. No one had done this to them before. One of them muttered that we should ask the waiter. On the way out I baited them. 'Enjoy the meal,' I said. At first the surveillance was intriguing and a little amusing but it quickly became stifling. I felt boxed in, unable to speak freely, and increasingly nervous.

I had been warned about the girls before I left London. Most hotels in Eastern Europe had prostitutes. They would sit either alone or in twos at the bar or in the lobby, holding your eye for that second too long and in that moment confirming that they were selling. The hotel girls were also informers. That was the price of being able to work the bars where the men with the hard currency sat. I had also been told that girls were used to create embarrassing incidents where the men ended up being arrested.

I was returning to my room when the girl stopped me in the lobby. She was about twenty, with heavy eye-shadow, cropped boyish blonde hair, a short beige skirt and boots. 'Excuse me,' she said in heavily accented English, 'I want to talk.' I smiled and said I was a little busy. She came much closer and I could smell her cheap perfume and the gum on her breath. She was inches from my face when she said loudly, 'I want boy.' The lobby went quiet while everyone stared. I was frightened. I knew that if there was an argument I could be charged with harassing a girl. I tried to appear relaxed and resisted shoving her away. I said to her quietly, and with the trace of a smile, 'I want girl but not this way.' Her red lips were very close and I thought she might kiss me. 'Why not?' she said smiling, her hand moving to the belt of my trousers. I looked around. The secret policemen were watching. A man in the lobby had a camera, but I couldn't tell who he was. 'Excuse me,' I said, 'I need to find a toilet.' It was all I could think of. The girl walked away and the man with the camera lost interest.

I did not know whether this was an attempt to set me up, and that was the point. Everything threatened, and little happened. The stony-faced men sat close, but never spoke to us. The girl approached, but left me alone. Bill detected traces of a mould on his front-door key, as if it had been copied, but we couldn't be certain. One morning, when they placed four jowly-faced men at the table beside us, David snapped and argued with them but, it turned out, they were a delegation of Russian miners from the Urals. Everywhere eyes followed us and we ended up fearing the shadows.

In the midst of this we continued filming. We visited a school and spoke to a class of students aged sixteen and seventeen about history. They were open, friendly and unafraid, even though the teacher hovered close during the interviews. They had new text books that were more honest than the previous ones about recent German history, but there was no criticism of the Soviet period.

Yet, here in the classroom, there were hints of the thawing that the architects of détente had hoped for.

The day after the visit to the school Peter and Bill called us down to the car park at the back of the hotel. This was the only place where we felt free to talk. Their rooms had been broken into and the film cans opened. They were certain of this because around the edge of the cans they had stretched white adhesive tape. At the point where the tape ended they had made the slightest mark with a pen. They knew that if the tape was unwound it would be impossible to put it back in exactly the same place. If the cans had been opened the film would be fogged and unusable.

There was other filming we wanted to keep secret, like an interview with the respected economist Professor Edward Lipinski. He was in his late eighties and a dissident. The police feared harming him. Their favoured tactic was to snatch him from a meeting and to bundle him into the back of an ambulance and drive him home. He said what others still feared to say. We asked him, 'Professor, what is the major problem in Poland?' 'It is very simple,' he replied in a slow resilient voice. 'We have no liberty.'

We developed a plan for our secret meetings. I drove through the city with the secret police behind. I would then drop off Peter. A mile later Bill would get out, and later still David. The police did not know who to follow and it was much easier for us to lose a single minder. In this way we made some contacts, but the UB changed tactics. We soon had four or five lime-green or sky-blue Fiats trailing us. They drove close, jostling us in the traffic. We decided to change hotels to see if we could lose the UB for a while but they found us within hours and took the rooms beneath us. We could only imagine they had some way of seeing into our rooms or listening to us.

On May Day we filmed the annual Communist Party rally. We had arranged this officially and were given a press card, a place on a viewing platform and a man from the Information Ministry. May Day was a holiday but not, it turned out, for the workers. Groups from all the major factories and plants were selected to parade past and wave at the party leaders. This was not a Polish tradition but a ritual borrowed and copied from Moscow. So the old men, the leaders, stood stiffly in their grey coats and trilbies much as the comrades in Russia stood atop Lenin's tomb. A tide of grateful workers from the Ursus tractor factory and the Huta Katowice steelyards flowed before them. That was the fiction, but what I noticed was that within fifty yards of passing the platform the parade dissolved. The workers dropped their banners and ran for the trams, eager to reclaim their day off. I tried to film this but the militia insisted we remain on the press platform.

David got on well with the man from the Information Ministry and asked to speak to his boss. They returned together to his office where David complained about our treatment, that we were being harassed in contravention of the Helsinki accords. The official was dismissive and suggested we had imagined it. David asked the man to come to our car so he could pass on the numbers of the vehicles that had been tailing us. Bill had written down the number of every UB car so that we could be certain when we were being followed. The ministry man thought all this absurd, unworthy of an organization like the BBC, but as we handed over the list we noticed that the last number was the same as the car parked behind us with two men inside. Even outside the ministry we had our watchers. It was a minor victory against an apparatchik accustomed to living a lie. He said he would investigate but we never heard from him again and never expected to.

The meeting with the dissidents was planned for early evening. We took some general city shots during the day. We acted the tourist and by the afternoon the number of our watchers had fallen. We drove waiting for that moment, that pattern of traffic when we could lose the UB. Then it happened, their cars were momentarily caught in traffic and we raced into a side street, losing ourselves and our followers in a strange neighbourhood. There we waited until it was time to go to an apartment on the other side of the river.

We parked near a grimy apartment building and scurried inside with our equipment concealed in bags. The apartment was small, book-lined and cloudy with cigarette smoke. There were about nine or ten people there and a few more came in behind us. It could have been a poetry reading or a recital in a student's room or a faculty meeting. There was Kuron the sociologist and Adam

Michnik, a historian in his early thirties who would not have been out of place on any campus. There was Helina Mikolajski, a grey-haired actress without work. Then Jan Litynski, an underground publisher with wide-rimmed glasses and a white polo-necked shirt. There were others there, older economists and academics.

Kuron spoke a little in English for our benefit, but the meeting was in Polish. I sat there and studied this group. They seemed so unthreatening. Just people with ideas and words. And yet they were feared. There was an earnestness about them as they drew on their cigarettes. They had all given up something, peace of mind, promotions, jobs. Friends were warned off them. They were not on the run, but they were pursued. Some had been arrested half a dozen times, some had been detained. And yet, for all that, I envied them. They had a cause and for us there were no good causes left, or so it seemed. This motley group of intellectuals had few possessions; they lived light, sleeping on different floors, and yet their lives were rich. And that challenged the surface of things. Born in a different place, at a different time, I hoped I would be with them, but I could never be sure of that.

We sat there in the smoke and the dim yellow light as they made their plans. Whenever they heard a noise from the corridor outside the apartment they tensed and fell silent, bracing themselves for an attack by the UB. At any time they expected the door to fly open and the thugs to arrive with their batons and fists. They placed us close to the door. If we were beaten up there would be an international incident and they doubted the authorities wanted that. We stayed like this for several hours until, in ones and twos, they drifted down the stairs into the insecurity of the dark streets. We took pictures of Kuron in front of a horseshoe tacked to the back of the door and left. On the way out we saw the UB. They knew we had been at the meeting and had filmed it.

Our main concern was how to protect our footage. Peter changed the labels on the film cans but that would not stop the police. Whenever he left the room he carried the can with him. The next day we went to the British embassy and dropped off the film. They agreed to store it, but refused to smuggle it out in the diplomatic pouch. Getting our footage out of Poland was up to us.

The mood of the police hardened. That evening, as we walked

to the Old Town, one of our followers nudged Peter into the road as a red-and-white bus came around the corner. Bill managed to haul him back onto the pavement. Shortly afterwards we heard that two of the men at the meeting had been in an accident on their way back to Crackow. One of them had died.

I was called in to see a senior figure at Polish TV who had sponsored our trip. He gave every appearance of being a TV man with his grey checked jacket and black polo-neck sweater, but he was a senior party official. We sat down across a desk that had been cleared of all papers. 'Mr Hewitt,' he said, 'you are not making the film that was agreed.' I misread his mood and talked confidently about May Day and the history class. I did not lie, but as I talked about the special beauty of Chopin's birthplace I could sense his anger rising. The more I spoke the more energetically he rubbed his hands. Then he exploded, close to my face. 'Mr Hewitt,' he said, 'you're treating Poland like a British possession in Africa.' 'Which one?' I replied arrogantly. He slammed his fist into the table. My flippant remark had made an enemy of the man. 'Don't think we don't know about you,' he said, pointing his finger at me. 'You call yourself a journalist. We consider you a spy.' He was ranting, his face taut with anger. 'We know all about provocation,' he said, 'and that's your game.' I was shocked by his accusation and when I replied I spoke quietly. 'None of this is true,' I said. He stood up and left the room.

I walked out to the car where David and the others were waiting. I was pale and that is what the others remember. I had been bold to the man's face, but I was trembling inside. 'No one has ever spoken to me like that in my life,' I said. They all laughed. 'They think I'm a spy,' I said, and David's expression changed. It had become serious. I could easily be detained on some trumped-up charge. We spoke about my leaving the country that day but on balance we thought my arrest would not be worth the damaging publicity. It was a difficult call and one that I would have to make many times. There was pride, reporter's pride, in bringing back the story. There was also the excitement. Car chases. The secret police. The adrenaline flow. So I stayed. What we did do was tell the embassy, and ended up with an invitation.

That evening we drove to a leafy part of the city where a few of the older houses had survived. This was where the British ambassador lived. He had invited us to a drinks party. It had been the idea of the embassy, who thought that seeing us with the ambassador might just make the authorities pause before moving against us. We were followed to the residency by three cars. The secret police seemed to know where we were going because as we stopped they held back, parking on the other side of the street about forty yards away.

The ambassador and his wife were on the steps greeting guests. When I shook the ambassador's hand I said to him, 'You can see we brought our friends with us,' nodding towards the UB vehicles. 'You've got friends here?' said the ambassador. 'Well, bring them in.' I looked blankly at the ambassador and wondered whether or not he had been briefed. 'Well,' I said, 'I don't think we should—' 'No,' interrupted the ambassador expansively, 'I insist. You've got friends. Bring them in.' There were other guests waiting to shake the ambassador's hand. I lowered my voice and said, 'They're not really friends. They're the UB.' There was a slow dawning on his face. 'Oh I see,' he said. 'Very well. Jolly good. Carry on.' And so we sipped drinks, a quartet played, and a woman talked to me about Polish recipes.

The following day we drove south to the city of Crackow. Curiously we did not seem to be followed, but it was an uneasy journey. I could not erase from my mind the dissidents' accident that had happened on this stretch of road. I found myself monitoring every passing truck looking for the slightest twitch that might indicate a wheel turning towards us.

We passed the city of Radom, a hard-scrabble industrial town, where they knocked out telephone sets, sewing machines, fertilizer and much more. The town was ringed with workers' apartments. Block after block of water-stained concrete. There was the occasional red banner or party slogan but even they hung tattered. It was like some giant holding pen. A workers' corral. People came here to work not to live. A few months earlier they had set fire to the Communist Party headquarters. Nothing had been planned or organized. Something had snapped. It was just anger, blind to consequence, sudden and involuntary. 'If I lived here,' I announced to the car, 'I'd get a gun and fight.' They laughed at me. Within days, David said, the Soviets would crush such resistance. There was only one way. The long-suffering, inchmeal defiance of the dissidents and the church wearing down the system from the inside. But I was young and impatient.

We had come to Crackow to film a church service. For most Poles the Catholic Church was their national identity, their sense of who they were, and the services were packed. The Virgin Mary was called the Queen of Poland. The dissidents had links to the church. It was a powerful alliance.

The church was welcoming new seminarians with a procession and an open-air service. Under the massive walls of Wavel Castle they lined up the young seminarians in platoons, as if to say to the authorities that the church had its troops too. We were the only camera crew there as the procession wound through the streets. There were two cardinals present: Stefan Wyszynski, the seventy-five-year-old primate, and a younger man who Peter focused on. There was something about him, his steady smile and his eye for the camera, and the way he said, 'Welcome,' in English. But David went to Peter and said, 'Not the man on the left, we need the cardinal on the right.' So Peter panned across to Cardinal Wyszynski, the senior man, and stayed with him. The other cardinal was Karol Woytila. Within a year he would be Pope John Paul II and the whole Communist world would feel the tremor of his election.

As the open-air service began, a low-flying military transport plane droned overhead, circling and circling, drowning out the Mass. It was petty harassment but everyone was used to it. No one shouted abuse or raised a fist. There was something unifying, bonding, about standing shoulder to shoulder, the engine thrust competing with liturgical chant. The cardinal even joked about it, certain that, on this day, the heavy-handed state was the loser.

While in Crackow we visited the site of the extermination camp at Auschwitz to get some pictures for our report on the teaching of history. It can never be a quick visit, a tourist stop, a photo opportunity. It is too overwhelming, too momentous. Even as visitors walk beneath the gatepost with its obscene slogan '*Arbeit Macht Frei*' – 'Work Will Make You Free' – they fall silent. They remain that way as they walk through the *Badeanstalten*, the bathhouses used for gassing. No one talks because words fail. The mounds of hair. The piles of wire-rimmed glasses. They are still there. A searing indictment on all of human history. The evil clings to you and weighs you down. In the car back to the hotel none of us spoke and we avoided dinner that night.

We returned to Warsaw, collected our film cans from the embassy and prepared to leave the country. We had asked the TV station for a permit to export film, but they refused. The resident Reuters correspondent came with us to the airport. He had agreed to watch from a balcony, so that if we were arrested or our material seized he could report it at once.

As we passed through customs an officer took the film behind the glass and said, 'You don't have a permit for this.' So this was it, we all thought. They planned to confiscate the film. We protested and said that we would camp in the customs hall until the footage was returned. 'The police will come,' said the official. We shrugged. If all our work was going to be seized then at least they could arrest us and there would be an incident. We waited whilst the customs men made their calls. Then the cans were flung back at us. We were free to leave. We could only guess at what had been said. Perhaps the police assumed the film had been fogged and was unusable.

In London we discovered that some of the rolls had been exposed, but, ironically, they were the ones of the history class. They had believed the labelling on the cans.

After the story ran, David Sells was not allowed back to Poland for ten years. Six members of KOR were detained. I returned the following year when the Pope was elected. At the TV station I ran into the official who had called me a spy. He recognized me at once and asked the guards to remove me from the building. 'Do you really want to do this,' I asked him, 'when the country is celebrating the election of a Polish Pope?' 'Stay,' he said, 'but don't return.' Already the party was losing some of its certainty. Later, during the years when the independent union Solidarity was occupying the shipyards at Gdansk, another BBC correspondent was taken aside and shown transcripts of my conversations. It was, he was told, proof that I worked for MI6. I was a man with a file, and over the years when I reported from the Soviet Union or elsewhere in Eastern Europe I was often watched.

Jacek Kuron later became a minister. Adam Michnik rose to edit a leading Polish daily. Solidarity formed a government. Its leader, Lech Walesa, would point to a TV set and say the fall of Communism 'all came from here'. I could never quite believe that a regime could divert so many secret police to us but, time and again, I would find that governments feared the camera and the images it captured.

4

Locked Up in Iran

I was commuting to and from a revolution. Three weeks amidst the fist-clenched mobs, the noise, the slogans, the anger. Above all, the anger. Then three weeks home. Towards the end of 1979 and into 1980, my life had assumed a routine and I was reporting on my first major international story.

Every time the plane dipped over the Elburz mountains and revealed Teheran below, there was a bracing, a steeling of myself, a certainty that I would be afraid. The Islamic Revolution was a fact. The Shah had gone, but Iran was an unsettled country, dangerous in its unpredictability. Power had shifted to the mullahs, to komitehs, to zealous, bearded young men on edge for spies and enemies.

You met them on arrival. Revolutionary guards examined the passports. They leafed through the document slowly, examining each page, each stamp. In November 1979 a guard had been suspicious of the letter I had from the Iranian embassy in London. The date was wrong. It was a simple error made by an official and I offered to go to the Ministry of Islamic Guidance in Teheran to change it. I explained that the letter still gave me permission to visit Iran. The more I spoke the less he trusted me. He took me and the cameraman I was travelling with into a bare room with just a table and a few chairs. Other guards came to inspect the letter. They held it up to the light. They argued amongst themselves.

After some hours I was told that the British Airways plane I had arrived on had been prevented from leaving. It was sitting on the tarmac with its passengers on board. The decision had been taken to remove me from the country and the plane would be cleared to depart only when I got on it. I demanded to speak to whoever was in charge but the man, who was about twenty, told me the komiteh had decided. He gave a slight shrug as if to say further protests were pointless. Then two guards with rifles insisted we walk across the tarmac to the plane.

On board, the captain announced that I was the reason for the delay and the passengers scowled at me. Whilst in the air back to London my expulsion from Iran was the lead story on the BBC's World Service.

Two days later I returned to Iran and was allowed into the country. I had changed the date myself and the guard on duty did not even look at it. Whether you were stopped, waved through, detained or threatened came down to a revolutionary whim.

Before we returned to Iran there was always a discussion about alcohol. It had been forbidden since the revolution but, for a period, journalists would bury a bottle or two inside their cases. By the end of the year none of us did that any more. The guards not only inspected every bag, they kept a hammer under the table in the customs hall. If they discovered a bottle, they would place it among your clothes and then smash it, close the case and hand it back to you with a smile.

In November a group of students had seized the American embassy in Teheran and taken over fifty diplomats and staff hostage. They demanded that the Shah, who was receiving medical attention in New York, be returned to Iran for trial. The students had the backing of Ayatollah Khomeini, the leader of the revolution. This was more than just about the Shah. It was about stirring up the people, giving them the anger to fuel the revolution.

Khomeini called America the 'Great Satan' and the embassy was its 'nest of spies'. It was made easy for the less educated to understand. Here, in the midst of their city, was a place of evil. To protest outside became almost a religious duty. Each day tens of thousands of people would parade past the embassy walls shouting, 'Death to America.' This was a casting out, a cleansing and the mullahs grew powerful on it.

We worked in a team of three: myself, a cameraman and a sound-recordist. Most days our local driver would take us from the Intercontinental Hotel to as close to the embassy as he could get. This was the only major story in the world and we filed a report every night. Each day we went hunting for pictures. There was always the chance of something happening at the embassy. The gates were padlocked but there was a gap between them. We would line up the camera and wait and sometimes we would glimpse one of the students who were holding the hostages. If we were lucky they would come to the gate and we would ask a question.

There was never a quick visit to the embassy. In the first few weeks the crowds outside were immense, often hundreds of thousands. They were packed in tight, squeezed up against the walls. We had to thread our way through them holding the camera and tripod above our heads. The men and women were kept apart. The men would file past first and then came the women in their chadors. A tide of black stretching back down Taleghani Avenue.

Just occasionally we would be trapped against the gates when the women arrived and we had to push through them. We never liked doing this. We could never be certain that we were not offending some custom. The women made it difficult for us. They never gave ground or opened up space for us to pass. It was as if they dared us to physically touch them. I tried a friendly smile without making eye contact. Once I caught a woman with our tripod. I immediately apologized, but the women around her hissed and circled us. On two occasions I felt a sharp jab. Some of the women carried knitting needles inside their chadors and poked us as we passed. When I wheeled around to look at them they did not turn away. They were certain of the rightness of what they had done. A jab for the revolution. A blow against the unbeliever.

On 18 November 1979, there was an expectation that the students were going to release some of the hostages. Ayatollah Khomeini had ordered that women and black Americans who had been working at the embassy should be freed 'if spying was not proven'. During the day the students promised that for the first time we would be allowed inside the embassy compound and that we could talk to the hostages about to be released.

We waited at the gates, a large crowd of reporters and cameramen. Our names and the organizations we worked for were passed inside. The students were nervous and argued with each other. There were factions. Some were convinced that we, too, were 'spies' but others wanted their wider world, the Islamic world, to see their compassion in releasing some of the hostages.

It was early evening by the time our names were called out and we filed into the 27-acre compound. We were taken to a courtyard where they conducted a lottery to see who would ask the first question. Very rarely have I won from any spin of the wheel, but on this occasion I got to ask the first question.

Three hostages came out. There were two marine sergeants, Ladel Maples and William Quarles, and the embassy secretary, Kathy Gross. They sat on chairs while guards stood behind them cradling G3 rifles. I knew there was only one question, even though I doubted the hostages could answer it truthfully. So I asked them how they were being treated. 'We are tied to chairs sixteen hours a day,' they replied, but they had not been physically harmed. Only a year later would another story emerge.

Even though the embassy was the focus of the drama, power lay eighty miles to the south of Teheran, in Qom. This was a holy city of Islamic learning and the spiritual capital of the revolution. It was a dry place, dust-blown from the hard wind that whipped in from the surrounding desert. I felt the mullahs and the teachers wanted it that way. There were no distractions here. It felt cut off, inward-looking, with only a flat landscape beyond. There was no advertising, no pictures of anything. No colour except for the neons above the boarding houses and the Golden Dome that rose above the Holy Shrine Mosque. In the alleyways, the talabahs, earnest young men in turbans, clutching books, walked to and from the seminaries. They never smiled and they never said hello. It was as if by acknowledging me they risked contamination.

In December we drove to the city to see two ayatollahs. One was Ayatollah Khomeini, the stern face of the revolution. The other was Ayatollah Shariat-Madari, an Islamic scholar of great standing, and the more moderate of the two men. We had an appointment with Shariat-Madari, but we decided to try our luck with Khomeini.

He had moved to the city after returning from exile. It was not difficult to find where he was living. Each day a crowd went to the house in the hope of glimpsing him. We followed until we were stopped by a line of revolutionary guards. We would not be allowed into the house, they told us. Khomeini would not see us, but we could stand with the people.

There must have been several hundred people outside a modest house of mud-and-straw brick. Some tattered posters hung on the walls. The people did not want us there. This man belonged to them. They had prior claim, and we found ourselves pushed to the back. Everyone faced what looked like an open window. Occasionally they would break into a chant of 'Khomeini is the One.' I saw a white turban moving inside the building but this was not who they had come to see.

Then all the hands around me were raised as if waiting to be touched or blessed. Through the outstretched hands I saw one of the most famous faces on the planet: the man who had launched a revolution which would be as far-reaching as the Soviet Revolution sixty years before. It was impossible for the cameraman to get a clean picture but, for once in my life, I gave up caring. This was a moment for myself. It was an immense privilege to be there. It was like seeing Lenin in 1918. I just wanted to study this man who was shaking the world. His face was expressionless. He saw the crowd but never acknowledged it. He just stood there with a forbidding glare. Dark beetle brows under a black turban. I never saw a trace of a smile and neither was it expected. The men around me wanted an ascetic. The sterner the face the more they trusted him.

The modern world, carried in on a tide of oil revenues, had come too suddenly. Customs and traditions had been uprooted and swept away. The ayatollah, in his utter simplicity and his unbending beliefs, promised to lead them back to safety, to a past where they recognized themselves.

Khomeini stayed only a few moments and then withdrew into his unfurnished room with its rugs and bare walls. As we walked away I looked into the faces of those around me. They spoke little, as if not wanting to break the spell of having been in the presence of their spiritual leader. Khomeini was not charismatic in any Western sense but I knew that those who had stood with me would die and kill for him.

I saw Ayatollah Khomeini a few weeks later when he went to vote. He sat in the passenger seat of his four-wheel-drive car. The crowds pressed against the vehicle. Some stroked the window just in front of him – gentle, pleading movements. Khomeini raised his right hand in a slow almost imperceptible gesture of acknowledgement. When he got out he was surrounded by people chanting, shouting and struggling to touch him. They were certain that to brush his robe was to receive a blessing. Hands lunged from the crowd. They would not give him space and he had to leave; his vote was cast for him. When he passed me I detected an old man's fragility, a momentary recoiling from the passion of the revolution he had launched. I tried to catch his eye, to make human contact, but he looked through me; his face was impassive, inscrutable and severe.

Ayatollah Shariat-Madari did not live far away. There was a much smaller crowd and there were fewer guards. He was accessible to outsiders in the way Khomeini was not. Shariat-Madari was propped up by a red cushion that rested against bare grey walls. With his dark-rimmed glasses he looked avuncular, a friendly scholar. We sat on the floor and gradually moved closer to him as those in front finished their brief conversations. I asked him about the American hostages. This was not the issue, he told me. He was more concerned with power, with the absolute power that would be Khomeini's if the new Islamic Constitution was passed. The people should be sovereign.

It was easy to like Shariat-Madari, with his smile and his message of justice rather than revenge. But this was not a time for the moderate voice. It was a time for anger, for righteous anger, for tearing up, for tearing down. Other outsiders and I were often looking for moderates in whom we could invest some hope, but we were always disappointed. We wanted Iran to conform to our world, but it stubbornly refused.

In January 1980 Kurt Waldheim, who was the UN Secretary General, visited Teheran believing that he might help resolve the crisis over the hostages. It was a doomed visit. Waldheim had previously met with the Shah and his family and the crowds had the pictures to prove it. They did not want this man negotiating the hostages' release. I had heard that Waldheim was going to visit the martyrs' cemetery at Behesht-e-Zahra. Many of those killed during the revolution were buried there and he intended to lay a wreath. It was only a rumour but I gambled it was true. My cameraman and I were the only news team there.

The visit was supposed to be secret but other people, ordinary Iranians, also seemed to know. I noticed them at once. Groups of people studying the field of black-and-white funeral photos of young men, but in fact watching and waiting. Waldheim arrived by helicopter and got into a car for his visit. The cemetery erupted and a crowd emerged. They shouted, raised their fists, and forced his car to stop. Waldheim was terrified. At one moment he looked at me, almost pleading to know what to do. Through the closed window I could see him gesticulating at the driver and shouting, 'Go, go, go.'

Later that day he went to a club that had been used by officers of the former regime. It was packed with people who had been tortured and disfigured by the Shah's secret police. They waved crutches at him, they removed their false eyes in front of him, they unstrapped their artificial limbs and held them above their heads. Stumps were thrust in his face. And all around him was the noise. The chanting. The anger. 'Why hadn't he negotiated for them during the Shah's time?' they demanded to know. Waldheim's face was clenched tight, just holding on until the ordeal was over. Shortly afterwards he left the country.

The hostage crisis dragged on. Intermediaries came and went but there were too many factions within Teheran for it to be resolved easily. The country remained dangerous and unsettled. In early April 1980 we decided to take a road trip, to travel west. There was tension on the border with Iraq and in the previous days there had been skirmishes between the two countries. Iraq was expelling Iranians and, to the north, Kurdish rebels were fighting the Islamic revolutionary guards and the Iranian army. I thought I would get a couple of stories from the trip.

There were five of us crammed inside an ageing white Renault: me, the cameraman Oggie Lomas and the sound-recordist Ray Gibbon. There was also a radio reporter and his translator, a young woman called Roshan. We left Teheran early and drove south-west towards the Iraqi border. The landscape was flat, empty, interminable, dirty-grey, two-parts desert to one of soil. Only the storks assembling their improbable nests on the top of poles held my interest.

We drove 300 miles to Qasr e-Shirin, a small border town, and stopped at a mosque. Roshan and I went inside to ask where we might find the people who had been expelled from Iraq. Both of us removed our shoes and Roshan put on a headscarf. The conversation began badly. Men surrounded us. Why did we want to know this, they asked. What was it to do with us? One of them particularly disliked Roshan. They could see she was not a traditional woman. She wore jeans and she was travelling with men she was not married to. I could see we made them angry and the anger built like a storm cloud, feeding off itself. They all talked at once, anxious not to be outdone in their outrage. Roshan turned to me and said, 'Let's go.' There was an urgency in her voice and I tried to walk to the door calmly. We picked up our shoes, but before we could put them on I felt something hit me in the back. A crowd gathered on the mosque steps and started stoning us with shoes and shouting 'Whore' at Roshan.

We half ran to the car without stopping to put on our shoes. Roshan was shaken. She felt an enemy within her own country. Again the anger. The anger towards outsiders. The paranoia. The suspicion. It was as if by casting us out they were cleansing themselves.

We debated returning to Teheran. Roshan felt safer in the capital but, having come so far, we decided to continue the short distance to the border. We found a bluff from where we could see inside Iraq. There was no line of refugees, just a few people walking with the possessions they could carry. I used the backdrop to record a piece to camera and it was then that I heard a shout.

A young man ran up the path towards us waving a pistol. He wore an olive-green army jacket and was shouting. He said he was arresting us as spies. Roshan tried to calm him by saying we were accredited with the Ministry of Islamic Guidance, but he did not want to listen to a woman. At gunpoint he told us to get back into the car and said he was taking us to the local headquarters of the revolutionary guards.

Inside the car it was impossibly cramped. I was sitting on top of Ray Gibbon and next to the man who was pointing his gun at those in the front seat. We were all scared, scared by the man's intensity, the blankness of his stare, the certainty of his belief that he had found a group of spies. I had already learned to fear young men with guns. In my experience they could kill casually. As we bumped along the pot-holed roads I said to the others that if we stopped and it looked as if this man might carry out some roadside revolutionary justice, I would attack him. There was nothing brave about this. I closed my eyes and tried to summon up the hate and the anger that would overcome my fear. Without the man understanding what we were talking about, we all agreed we would fight.

We stopped beside a dull yellow building on the edge of town. There were a couple of guards outside with rifles and never was I so pleased to see them. This was the local headquarters of the Pasdaran, the Revolutionary Guards. The young man paraded us like a prize, but the commander was educated and thoughtful. We explained why we had come and that we had told the ministry of our plans. He thanked the young man and then dismissed him. He explained with a smile that the young man had tried to join the guards but was considered too unstable. We were invited to lunch and we sat cross-legged and ate a plate of rice and lamb. Later we were taken to meet some of the refugees from Iraq. The commander then told us to leave.

That evening we stayed in the town of Kermanshah before heading north into the hills and Kurdistan. We stayed in a dusty hotel and were the only guests. In the morning I sat on the toilet, and as I sat there I noticed the lines and hair-cracks in the porcelain. I slightly shifted my weight and the toilet disintegrated beneath me. It splintered into small fragments and left me on the floor, with a pungent smell of old sewage rising from the drains.

I went down to reception and told them the toilet had broken. One of the hotel staff was sent to my room and a short while later reported back to the receptionist, who became angry. I had damaged his hotel, he claimed. I apologized but said I had hardly done it deliberately, but the receptionist was not satisfied. 'You cannot leave,' he said. He was going to send for a mullah so this matter could be judged. Incredible as it was, it began to dawn on me that I might face an Islamic court on charges of destroying a toilet. I decided I did not want to meet the mullah and said I would pay for the damage. I gave the receptionist $50 and told him I needed to get a document from the car where the others were waiting. When I got outside I said, 'Let's go,' and we drove for Kurdistan.

Once I was certain we weren't being followed I relaxed and laughed at the absurdity of it all. I imagined what the papers would make of a BBC correspondent going before an Islamic court for breaking a toilet. We passed an hour choosing the headline.

The road climbed and the hills grew steeper. Kurdistan was part of Iran but in places was controlled by rebels who wanted self-rule. We did not want to meet the Iranian army or the revolutionary guards who might arrest us. Fortunately we arrived in the capital, Sanandaj, without passing any roadblocks.

This bustling city, with its dun-coloured sandstone buildings, was largely untouched by the Islamic Revolution. The people were open and friendly. A man asked us with a smile whether we wanted a beer. I hesitated, but it seemed safe to drink here. Immediately, the man shouted into the market, 'The BBC wants a beer.' It was not quite the discretion I had imagined, but a short while later cans of Swan lager arrived at the hotel. I was on edge, frayed from the paranoia of the streets. I needed the beers to relax me, to take me away for an evening from the heat of the revolution.

I fell into a light sleep but soon woke again. I had felt something crawl across my face. I switched on the light and there were about thirty cockroaches on the floor and on the bed. I attacked them with my shoe but they were nimble and retreated into the crevices by the toilet. Some I caught, crunching their thin shells with my shoe. Most of them withdrew, waiting to return when the light went off. Several times I lay in the darkness for a few minutes, turned on the light and charged the cockroaches. It was a game I could not win and I got no sleep for the rest of the night.

In the morning a guide took us further into the hills, down rocky treeless paths where the shale crumbled beneath us. Beside a track and under an outcrop we found a group of men with rust-stained ammunition boxes and rifles wrapped in cloth. They were selling G3s, AK47s and other weapons I did not recognize. Kurds were buying. Some wore the traditional pantaloons, cummerbunds and brocaded jackets. They were willing to give radio interviews but they did not want close-up pictures taken, so we had to drive back up the hill for a long shot. I was disappointed, but this was evidence that the Kurds were being smuggled weapons for their fight with government forces. I was also impatient to leave, aware of how serious it would be for us if we were caught there by the Revolution-ary Guards.

We said goodbye to our guide on the main road. We then had a difficult journey. We had arranged to meet some of the Kurdish leaders and perhaps witness the fighting. To reach them we had to drive through disputed territory and pass towns controlled by the Iranian army.

The road was empty and the hills cold and barren. After a couple of hours we drove into a town for petrol. The mood of the people was different from that in Sanandaj. The man who served us was wary and unsmiling. The plan was to fill up and leave immediately, but we had been up since dawn and it was cramped inside the car so we all got out and stood around eating biscuits in the weak sunlight. Soon, an army jeep drove up and parked beside us and soldiers asked us who we were. We tried to sound casual; we said that we were returning to Teheran having been to the border, but the soldiers insisted we follow them to their base. I was angry. Angry with ourselves. We knew the risk of the towns and yet we, a group of foreigners, had stood around eating.

At the base we were taken from the car and locked inside an empty room. There were bars on the windows and the door. It might have been a cell for holding or questioning prisoners. We sat on the floor and talked in low voices. We were most worried about the arms dealing we had filmed that morning. If we had been seen there they might accuse us of supporting the rebels. The hours passed and the conversation dried up. Outside the window soldiers and revolutionary guards came and went.

Then the door opened and a soldier said that the colonel wanted to see one of us. I agreed to go. As we walked across the yard, I was hopeful that I could persuade him to release us. The colonel was in his mid-forties, overweight and with a wide moustache. He did not get up from behind the desk and he refused to shake my hand. His English was good and he asked me what we were doing in Kurdistan. I told him that we had been to the border and thought it would be interesting to return to Teheran via Kurdistan. He said it was illegal to be here. I said we had not been told that in the capital. He demanded to see written permission but, of course, we did not have the papers.

As his questioning continued I began to think he suspected us of being arms dealers. Out of nowhere he said he had always hated the British and still did. I asked him why. 'Look,' he said, gesticulat-ing with a wide sweep, 'what they have done to Iran.' I said I was not responsible for the past, but he wouldn't be deflected. He burned with resentment. 'Why,' he said, 'did you sell us faulty Chieftain tanks?' He demanded an answer. I said I was a journalist and had nothing to do with this. 'But you are BBC,' he said, pointing at me, 'you are government.' I tried to explain that although we were funded by government we were independent from it. He was unimpressed and returned to the question of the tanks. 'You sold us tanks with engines that smoked.' He believed the British had deliberately offloaded flawed tanks. I was now frightened of this man and told him that people in Teheran knew where we were. I wanted him to know that we could not simply disappear. He said his men would search the car and I was taken back to the holding cell.

Again the anger. The hurt. The resentment. My colleagues knew at once the meeting had not gone well. I told them we had a colonel who deeply resented the British. The radio reporter had recorded interviews with the arms smugglers and feared the tapes would be found. Time passed and little happened. Occasionally a guard would lean against the grilled door and just stare at us. We each had low moments when we would sit on the floor, draw up our knees, cross our arms and stare at the ground.

Ray devised an Iranian version of the game Battleships. The aim was to take your opponent's holy city. He drew a board on the stone floor. Each player had one ayatollah and five mullahs. There were revolutionary guards and students. Each piece was given a value. We noisily threw ourselves into this. The guard craned his head against the grille to see what we were doing. The game was not just a distraction, it was a little way of fighting back.

Roshan talked to the guard and reported back that they had found the tapes. There was little we could do but wait. Sometime afterwards she said that they might let her go and fly her back to Teheran. I was against this. I said that we should stay together rather than negotiate separate deals. I was also very reluctant to lose our translator. I was angrily insistent and rather insensitive to the fears of a young woman locked up in a country where women were losing their voice.

There was a strained silence in the cell as darkness came and the hours grew longer. At one point they backed up an American-made tank to the window. The fumes from the exhaust filled the room and we could not talk above the sound of the engine. It might have been just another piece of petty harassment. It might have been nothing, but it increased our anxiety.

I was called back in to see the colonel and asked about the tapes. I said we had been told in Teheran that weapons were being brought into Kurdistan and this proved it. Nothing I said moved or persuaded him. There was something deep down, almost visceral, something he had absorbed in his past that made him mistrust the English.

Back in the cell we heard nothing for a long period. Roshan spoke again to the guard and I could tell from her tone that there was news. They had found hashish in the car, she said. All of us knew what the Islamic regime did to drug dealers. There had recently been pictures in the papers of dealers, tied to posts, being shot. I was scared. I had no doubt that the drugs had been planted to justify sending us before an Islamic court. I felt it was now urgent that we contact our embassy in Teheran. The mood was strained. Then the radio reporter said quietly, 'The hashish is mine.' It was a small amount in an envelope, he told us. Inside I was furious, and I struggled to remain calm. He had put all of us at risk. I knew that I was not prepared to pay the price for this. 'We will do everything,' I told him, 'to get out of here but ultimately you will have to take responsibility for the drugs.' I wanted him to face that and, although he was frightened, he agreed.

We were left like this with our thoughts and our fears. I could not sit still. I paced up and down, unnerving the others. I went over in my mind every strategy, every argument, every angle that might help us. Sometime later – I do not know how long – I noticed activity in the yard. Men were running. Military vehicles were starting up. Roshan called over the guard. Kurdish rebels had been sighted and an attack was expected. We had a new fear that the base would be attacked with us locked in a cell.

Then the door opened and we were told to go. It was as quick as that. A soldier said we must return to Teheran immediately. We had to take the direct route, and within minutes we were leaving the base. The colonel had more serious matters to think about than us. We did briefly consider resuming our journey to see the rebels but our nerve had gone.

Eight hours later we arrived back at the Intercontinental Hotel in Teheran. A colleague handed me a folded yellow telex. I did not read it immediately but someone had written in bold black letters the word 'Congratulations'. When I got to my room I opened it. The heading was 'Urgent Urgent for Gavin Hewitt. Room 636.' The message read: 'It's a boy . . . mother and child about seven and a half pounds doing well. Birth natural all send love. Birth at 0830 hours Sunday.'

On reading the words 'it's a boy', I was momentarily baffled as if I had been delivered the wrong telex. It took me that half second to realize that this was the baby we had been expecting. Daniel had arrived early and had been born when I was in a grubby cell.

As I sat there all the events of the previous days fell away. They were mere incidents. A sideshow. I had missed a moment, a real moment that defines a life, any life. And it could never be reclaimed. So it was a moment of celebration and a moment of loss.

I decided to return to London at the end of the week when my replacement would arrive. The next day I was called to the British embassy to see the ambassador, Sir John Graham. We had not met before and he had suggested a chat over lunch. We sat on the balcony overlooking the gardens and the summer house where the Teheran conference had been held and Churchill, Roosevelt and Stalin had discussed the future of the war.

I had a gin and tonic and I spoke about my recent trip. He said he thought the situation was becoming more difficult and less stable. He then told me that on the Wednesday he was leaving Iran. I was surprised by this and asked whether we could film him going to the airport, but he said that would not be possible. He then looked at me and said, 'I think it would be a good time for you chaps to be leaving too.' We talked on through the second gin and tonic. As I stood up to leave he said again, 'Listen, I really think it's a good idea if you get out of the country for a while.' I thought about his advice on the way back to the hotel. I knew Iran was dangerous, but I had become accustomed to it and in any event I would be home by the weekend.

On Friday, 25 April, I joined the thousands heading to Friday prayers. It was something of a ritual for us. A senior cleric would give the sermon and sometimes talked about the hostages. We found a position near the front. A man excitedly jabbed me in the chest and said, 'The Americans are all dead in the desert.' I took no notice but there was a ripple in the crowd.

Something was happening. A driver found me and gave me a note from our office that we shared with the American network NBC. It read: 'Washington says there's been a rescue mission. It failed. Be careful.' Soon the crowd were told that the Americans had been defeated in the desert. They rose as one and shouted, 'Death to America.' Men beat their chests with their right hands.

The Americans had sent in Delta Force to rescue the hostages. Helicopters and planes had reached a staging-post in the desert. On the way they had lost too many helicopters to fly on to Teheran. As they abandoned the mission, a helicopter and transport plane collided. There were American casualties. It was a tragedy and a humiliation for President Carter.

Everyone was talking. Talking to each other. Talking to strangers. Spreading the word. The streets were fevered, intense. Cars drove fast in different directions with guns pointing from their windows. Horns blazed as young men waved traffic and people aside. Road-blocks sprang up. The city was caught up in a delirium, a hunt for spies and Americans.

We were stopped by guards, by passers-by, by boys. Each time we had to show our Iranian press cards. 'You are lucky,' said one young man in an olive-green jacket. 'If the Americans had taken the hostages, we would have taken you.' The crowd were with him. And that is, of course, what would have happened. We would have become hostages. And amidst all the noise and the horns I remembered the ambassador's words. He had known what was coming but had been unable to explain. And in those swirling uncertain moments I realized that if the rescue mission had succeeded I might never have seen my son.

Back at the hotel we edited our report. The BBC had been barred from filing from the television station but in a piece of professional charity Jon Snow, who was working for ITN at the time, offered to feed our report on his satellite.

My office in London was keen to get us out of the country and we wanted to leave. Later that day I got a call. The editor of BBC News and the editors of the three main American networks had agreed to charter a plane to Teheran to fly us to safety. I had never heard such a bad idea and said I would refuse to get on the plane. I could just imagine how the revolutionary guards would view an American charter landing at Teheran airport. All of us preferred to take our chances and stay, and the charter plane never flew.

The Iranian leadership revelled in America's defeat. We were taken to see the charred remains of the American servicemen. They were paraded as a kind of ghoulish trophy. The plastic bags were opened and the burned bodies and dog tags displayed. Presiding over this was Ayatollah Khalkhali, who was known as Judge Blood or the revolution's chief executioner. He held up a limb with a wristwatch on it.

Initially, I had had sympathy with the revolution – the Shah's extravagance, the brutality of his police. But as I watched this religious man poke around inside a body bag for a limb to be displayed, I turned away sickened. Nothing justified this. It seemed then, as with other revolutions that had come before, that in purging the past they would exceed the barbarity of their predecessors.

A short while later Ray, Oggie and I withdrew to a hotel in the hills above north Teheran. I knew from other assignments that one has only a certain amount of courage at any given time. When it runs out it's time to withdraw, to break away, to breathe freely, to reconnect with normal life. As for me, I wanted to see my son.

We stayed in the hills a few days and then went to the airport to catch a regular flight to Zurich. Leaving was the last, unpredictable hurdle. The Revolutionary Guards searched every departing passenger for cash and, particularly, for dollars. They believed that all such money was either stolen or earned corruptly and should be confiscated. Most of it, I am sure, ended up in their pockets.

Usually we spent the night before departure soldering rolled dollar bills inside tape recorders or other pieces of equipment. But on this occasion I had a different plan. Just before we got on a bus to take us to the plane a guard asked me whether I had any money. 'Money?' I replied, looking confused. He repeated, 'Money. Do you have any money?' I said, 'Yes. I have some dollars.' I patted both my breast pockets as if I was searching for them and I then pulled out a wad from my left pocket. It was only $200, but in small denomination bills it looked much more. He took it at once. I protested just enough for him to believe he had found all my money. Looking suitably dismayed, I walked to the plane with several thousand dollars in my right-hand pocket.

I slumped wearily into my Swissair business seat. The flight attendant asked me if I wanted a drink and I said a gin and tonic. She said that would not be possible until we had cleared Iranian airspace. I asked her whether I could have some corn flakes before take-off. She looked at me as if I was slightly unstable but said it was possible. Then with the best smile I could summon up I asked her whether it was possible to pour gin onto the corn flakes. It was such a crazy request that she agreed to it. So as we climbed out of the chaos of revolutionary Iran I enjoyed my gin and corn flakes – and made my small gesture of defiance.

Almost a year later I stood at an airport in Algeria and watched the American hostages take their first steps as free men and women. They had been 444 days in captivity. They had endured mock executions. Some had not seen sunlight for months.

Even so, Iran remained a special place for me. Despite the fanaticism, I liked the people. We backed the Shah because he was a strong man and on our side, but we turned a blind eye to what we did not want to see and reaped the whirlwind – a wounded, angry, humiliated people.

5

The Great Game

It was late afternoon, the first Friday in the new year, and I was waiting in the fading light for a defector. I stamped against the cold and I stamped with impatience. Everything depended on this man. It was 4 January 1980, and I was in Iran but trying to reach the country next door. The Soviet army had invaded Afghanistan. President Carter had called it 'a serious threat to world peace'. It was more serious, he said, than the Soviet invasions of Hungary or Czechoslovakia. Détente was all but dead and the world seemed to be spiralling towards a new Cold War.

That afternoon, in Teheran, we had covered an anti-Soviet demonstration outside the Afghan embassy. It had been full of rage and shots had been fired. While there I had spoken to an Afghan diplomat, who was cowering inside the embassy. He was planning to defect, he told me, in protest at the invasion. It was then that I had the idea. I told him that I wanted to travel to Afghanistan and asked him to give me a visa. He had told me to return with the passports at the end of the day.

In the intervening hours I had found a flight that was leaving for Kabul in the middle of the night, but we needed the visas. Then, just as I had all but given up on seeing the Afghan diplomat again, he was standing beside me. He opened up the embassy and gave me and my camera crew three-month visas. He wanted the world to know that his country was being occupied. It was his last act of defiance. He locked the embassy door, wished me luck, and then walked to the Iranian foreign ministry to claim asylum.

There were three of us travelling to Afghanistan: me, the cameraman Mike Viney and Steve Morris, his sound-recordist. We were flying with Ariana, the Afghan national airline. As we lifted off from

Teheran airport I caught the first, almost imperceptible glow of a new day. This was the biggest story I had covered. Nothing came close to it. All the passengers around me slept, that abandoned sleep where mouths hang open and people fall against each other. I had been up all night but did not have a trace of tiredness. In my mind I went over and over our options at Kabul airport, looking for the one move that might give us an edge. I was obsessive, driven. Getting the story seemed important beyond anything else I knew. I had an almost reckless desire to succeed. It was partly reporter's pride, to beat the competition, but it went deeper than that. These challenges were addictive. The charge of adrenaline. The chase. That heady, rare-aired feeling of being in the eye of history.

It was only then, sitting back in an airline seat, that it struck me how little I knew about Afghanistan. The Soviets claimed they had been invited into the country to protect it from chaos. Two years earlier a coup had brought a Marxist regime to power, but there had been growing resistance from rebels. That much the radio had been reporting. I took out my notebook and decided to list every fact I could about the country. I ended up with a list of two. The people were Muslim and I recalled there had been an Afghan war involving the British. My knowledge was pitiful.

As we started our descent I moved to a window seat. The mountains below were immense, jagged and snow-covered and, for a moment, I imagined we were flying into one of those manicured cities, Geneva or Zurich. Then just beneath me I saw a military encampment: a bivouac with smoking fires, armoured vehicles and Russian soldiers in their winter greatcoats and shapka hats. As we touched down we passed a row of giant Antonov transport planes with troops disembarking. Helicopter gunships stood on the apron with their rotors turning.

The world had not yet seen any of this. I got Mike to snatch what pictures he could from the window while I tried to shield him from the flight crew. We got off the plane last and as we crossed the tarmac I decided to risk recording a piece to camera with the Russian planes in the distance. If we were refused entry at least I would have something. I knew nothing, of course, about the situation in Kabul but I described the scale of the Soviet encampment I had seen from the air.

A red banner fluttered incongruously from the terminal building. 'Welcome to the land of the new revolution,' it read. The invasion was but days old and already the slogans were going up; the same empty words and phrases that I had seen plastered on buildings in Eastern Europe.

There was a line at immigration but those with visas were waved through. The only question the official asked me was whether I had any magazines or newspapers. I had a few papers and cuttings that did not even mention Afghanistan, but he confiscated them. It was the old Soviet way. Send in the Red Army and then isolate the country from the outside world. I did not expect that they would tolerate a foreign television team for long.

Then suddenly we were outside the airport under a winter sun. The mountain air was crisp and smelt of wood fires. We stood there with our pile of camera boxes. None of us had been to Afghanistan before. We spoke no Pashto and did not even have a hotel reservation. In front of us was the airport road lined with pine trees and empty of traffic except for one parked car. Afghan Taxi No. 7. A faded yellow-and-white Peugeot 404. The driver was a middle-aged man with dark hair and a narrow trimmed moustache. He wore a tattered grey suit and an open-necked shirt. I asked him in English to take us to the main hotel. To my surprise he replied, 'Welcome to Afghanistan. I will take you to the Intercontinental Hotel.'

Kabul. A place of bright, vivid colour. A cameraman's city. The sky was crystal blue and the snow clean and fresh. I liked it at once. The men in their turbans. Brilliant whites, pin-stripes, russets, charcoal greys. All worn differently. Some were tightly wrapped; others hung loose with part of the cloth draped over the shoulders; others had the end of the turban sticking up like a cockatoo's crest. Underneath, the faces – craggy, rugged and sun-leathered – all lined with a history I knew nothing of. Some were lighter-skinned. Some Asiatic. Some had long, sharp, curious, intelligent faces. From the tea-shops, from the donkey carts, from the streets, they all stared back at us. They neither smiled, nor turned away. Just inscrutable faces watching, withholding their verdict. And, behind them, squat buildings of sun-dried bricks and mud.

For a while we were all absorbed, lost in the city's vivacity, until one of us asked, 'Where are the Russians?' There were soldiers on the street but they were from the Afghan army. Our driver interrupted us. During the day, he said, most of the Russians stay out of the city, but they come in at night to enforce the curfew. His was an old-fashioned, more formal English with its colonial-period idioms. Previously he had been the driver for an English businessman who had treated him well and had looked after his family. We told him we worked for the BBC. 'Ah, BBC World Service,' he said with a smile. Almost everywhere, however remote the location, I have found people who got their news from BBC radio and our driver was one of them. By the time we reached the hotel Mr Samadali had agreed to drive for us. From that moment on he was our guide, our driver and our translator. I asked him what his first name was and he smiled. He liked the sound of 'Mr Samadali' and it stayed that way.

The Intercontinental Hotel was on a hill and dominated the skyline. It was a six-storey building that reminded me of a Soviet-style housing complex. The hotel brochure invited guests to 'Come with us to a land where caravans plod their way slowly through the streets. Step back into history . . . where Aladdin's lamp lies hidden beneath untold mysteries and every hour unfolds like a precious treasure. The land is Afghanistan.' This mythic land, however, did not extend to the hotel which was plain and functional and felt as if it had been stripped of anything that might remind the guests of where they were.

We had imagined we were one of the first television crews to reach Kabul, but shortly after our arrival at the hotel we ran into Martyn Lewis of ITN. He had arrived the day before, but had been detained for filming Soviet troops. That, apparently, was not permitted. The Red Army was intended to be a ghost army that only surfaced at night. Moscow had calculated that the fewer the images of Soviet troops in Afghanistan, the smaller the international outcry. Therefore getting pictures of them was all the more important.

The next day Mr Samadali picked us up and we went looking for Russians. Inside his taxi, beads and fairy lights hung from the front window, which made it difficult to see the passengers, particularly those in the back seat. So I sat in the front and Mike sat in the back with his camera. When we saw Soviet troops Mike would put the camera on his shoulder and film, while I watched the soldiers' faces to see if we had been spotted. If I thought they were becoming interested in us I would shout to Mike to put down the camera.

Early on we came across a huge Soviet convoy that stretched for over a mile. There were tanks, armoured personnel carriers, artillery, fuel tankers and supply trucks. It was heading towards us and Mike filmed through the front windscreen from the back seat. It was an adequate but shaky shot. Once the convoy had passed we turned around and overtook it, with Mike shooting out of the side window. It became the enduring piece of footage of the Soviet invasion. There were risks if the Russians caught you filming. Some television crews, particularly those that had just arrived in the city, drove out to one of the Soviet encampments and started filming from the road. Not only did they lose their footage but the Russians punished them. They forced them to kneel in the snow for hours, often without jackets, while being threatened that they would be dealt with as spies. It meant, therefore, that most of the early pictures of the Soviet forces in Afghanistan were shot from moving cars.

Gradually, other reporters arrived in Kabul although the numbers remained small. Among them was Robert Fisk, who then wrote for *The Times*. He asked to travel with us. We knew Robert and got on well with him. In strange and dangerous countries I never envied print journalists. I always had the company of a crew with me. The print men travelled alone. Some teamed up with other writers, but Robert liked to hitch a ride with a television crew.

The new Soviet-installed government was scarcely functioning. There were few official events to be covered and no one was giving interviews. It meant we had to go out and find the story. It was the journalism I liked best. In the evening we would study a map and decide where to go. Our journey became the story of the day.

One evening we decided to go to Ghazni, a city 130 miles south-west of Kabul and on the road to Kandahar. There was no good reason to go there. We just thought it was virgin territory, unexplored by other reporters. Our spirits were high as we left the hotel. We were a hunting party. It did not matter that the prey was Russians. We were in the hunt for images. A car full of buddy talk and bizarre humour. Robert had spotted a Soviet-built grain silo on the edge of Kabul. Each day we would pass it and marvel at its concrete stacks, eulogize its greyness. The rusting metal bracing, surely, was a fine example of stark Soviet realism. And then, having delivered our morning grain-silo critique, we were on the open road.

At Saydabad, 70 miles from the capital, there were Russian tanks dug in beside the road. They had got this far. A line for *The Times* but not much for television. Mike could not capture even a fleeting image from the back seat. As we travelled further the road emptied, just an Afghan taxi alone in a landscape of ice and drifting snow.

Then Ghazni rose out of the snow, plain, dark and medieval. The huge battlements of an ancient fort surrounded by vastness and a ridge of receding hills. One of the others had picked up a fragment of history. Almost a thousand years before, Mahmud of Ghazni had established an Islamic empire that reached to India and beyond.

We drove through slushy streets and parked, while Mr Samadali went looking for motor oil. We seemed to be in the midst of workshops and tea-houses. We all got out and stood there, occasionally trying out a smile. A man walked past with a severed horse's head under his arm. I wanted to film but, beyond curiosity, it told us nothing. As soon as people saw us they just stopped and stared and in that way a crowd grew, a crowd of silent eyes. Eventually an older man came across to the car and asked in poor English, 'Are you Russians?' We said we were English and he smiled. More men came and they did not return our smiles. A word, like a spitting sound, passed through the crowd. It was *khal*, the word for 'donkey', but when used about foreigners it was a word of hatred. We looked at each other, confused. Mr Samadali returned and opened the bonnet of the car. The crowd closed in. I asked him what was happening and, for once, he struggled with his English, but gradually we understood him. The Russian army had not reached Ghazni. We had gone beyond the frontline of the invasion and the men around us did not know what the invaders looked like. There was fear in his face as he dropped the bonnet. 'They do not want foreigners here. We must go.'

I hesitated before leaving. We had nothing. I thought about a piece to camera. At least I could tell the story of the city the Russians had not reached. I could see the crowd of Pathans was growing but could not read their mood. They did not have guns although some of the men had long knives in their belts. I tried Mr Samadali again. 'Have you explained we are not Russians?' 'I have,' he said, 'but they don't believe me.' And so it dawned on me that in this isolated place these people had no way of knowing the difference between the British and the Russians.

Another man approached and, with the help of Mr Samadali, said, 'Leave here now. Do not stop for anyone. If you are stopped by people on the road, drive through them. You are foreigners and they will think you are Russians and kill you.' There was no way of persuading them. All of us had heard the story of the group of Russian civilians who had gone to the city of Herat and had been seized by the local people and then skinned alive. Later their skins were said to be on sale in the market place.

So we left quickly. Back on the open road Mr Samadali told us the men had been debating whether to kill us and, for a period, we fell silent. In that market we had learned something: the implacable hostility towards the Russians, towards outsiders who wanted to tame this land. On the way back to the capital we saw the metal turrets of Soviet guns above the highway. Again a line for an article but there was no way we could film it. Robert had a headline – 'Being Russian is risky in Ghazni' – but, without pictures, I did not have much of a story.

Shortly afterwards, and very unusually, an official from the new shadowy government came to the hotel and told us that some political prisoners were about to be released. We were invited to witness this good-news story and travelled fifteen miles out of the city to Polechowkri prison. As we got close we saw in the distance the dark lines of hundreds of people struggling across barren brown ground, a vast treeless plain broken up only by the frozen remains of recent snow. The people walked with their heads down, purpose-fully, with appointments to keep.

The prison was a forbidding place that looked as if it had been modelled on an ancient fort. We could not get to the gates. Thousands of Afghans had got there before us. Some had garlands ready to place around the necks of their relatives. There were men in suits, men in ties. There were turbans, white crocheted skull caps, astrakhan furs. All surging back and forth, waiting for the gates of the prison to open. A Soviet Mi-24 gunship flew overhead and Mike swung the camera round. It was so low I could see the pilots and the loaded rocket pods. Some of the crowd raised their hands and clapped, but they were the few.

Then a small door opened in the metal-grilled gate and a line of men walked out. They were weighed down with metal boxes, blankets, bedrolls and cooking pans. They looked more like refugees than prisoners. Some of the crowd clapped them, but the men rarely responded. Their eyes were on a distant horizon, anywhere as long as it was far away from this prison. It gradually dawned on the crowd that only 118 prisoners had been freed. A murmur rose. News was being passed back. The people became agitated, kicking up the dust in the soft early morning light. They had not walked fifteen miles for this. They surged forward, calling out, encouraging each other. At the gates was a line of Afghan soldiers, uneasy and unsteady, unsure of how to respond. Some among the crowd began pelting them with stones and they fell back. A loudspeaker called for patience but the crowd pushed on. Some climbed up the gates trying to bend them off their hinges. Soon, under the massed weight, the gates buckled and the crowd poured into the compound, colliding with and knocking to the ground some of those who had been released. They were shouting by now, 'Allah Akhbar,' God is Great. The cry was taken up and there was a new intensity about the crowd. They picked up rocks, smashed the windows of the cell blocks and prised open the doors. Three dazed, blinking, middle-aged men were led out into the sunlight. I could see other prisoners pleading to be freed.

There were Soviet soldiers inside the prison, but only a few, and they did not know how to react to this prison break-out. The helicopter circled, awaiting orders. The crowd moved on from cell block to cell block, irritation growing as they failed to find their relatives. As they tore down the doors they broke into Islamic chants. Some called for an Islamic Revolution. These cries seemed to unite the crowd and they worked together. This was more than a hunt for lost relatives. It was a protest against the foreign invader. I watched a Soviet soldier on the prison roof, uncertain and uncomprehending, a young man who had travelled south to defend Socialism and had met only hostility. I thought there might be shooting and we hung back, but we were probably the crowd's best defence. It would have been disastrous for the Soviets to have killed hundreds of Afghans in front of our cameras. The government's propaganda exercise had badly backfired. Kabul itself was calm, deceptively calm, but beneath the surface there was deep resentment towards the Russians and I began to feel there would be no easy victories in Afghanistan.

After filming there was always the problem of how to get the film out. It was not possible to send material by satellite from Kabul's TV station which, in any case, was occupied by the Russians. I could not view the pictures so during the day I kept a note of what we had shot and then wrote a script and we recorded it. The track and pictures would be edited together outside the country.

We took the film to the airport. Some commercial flights were still flying to Kabul – particularly Air India. Sometimes we had someone on the flight who would collect the film from us. More often we would give a package to a member of the crew or a passenger and tell them they would be met at Delhi airport by someone with a large BBC sign.

There were no phones working in the hotel, so there was the added problem of telling London what flight the footage was on. We were helped by the German manager of the Intercontinental Hotel. He agreed to send personal telex messages to a BBC editor in London. The telexes said the Intercontinental Hotel in Kabul was trying to book a hotel in, say, Delhi. The passenger arrived at a given time and should be met. London soon understood that was code for meeting a flight.

From early morning until dusk we would drive, following our instincts. One afternoon we went to the presidential palace. It had been here, a few weeks before, that Soviet troops had overthrown the Afghan leader and prepared the way for the invasion. A shell had gone through the roof and part of the building had been destroyed by fire. Suddenly Steve, the sound-recordist, asked us to stop. He had spotted two old narrow-gauge steam engines parked in the snow. It turned out that he was a railway enthusiast and wanted to take two or three stills for the *Railway Gazette*. He thought the pictures might make the front cover. The engines were in pristine condition, although how they had got there was something of a mystery in a country without a railway. I leaned against the car, relaxed, as Steve snapped away. Then around the corner came some Soviet soldiers. They were angry and demanded the film. Steve was very reluctant to hand it over. 'What possible harm could there be in pictures of a steam engine?' he asked, but the soldiers were insistent. Steve tried to explain that they were pictures for a railway magazine but they couldn't grasp it. One of them thought we were spying. I had never imagined being accused of spying for the *Railway Gazette* but it was happening, like an unfolding nightmare. We could be detained, our equipment confiscated and that day's pictures seized for a moment of train spotting. In the end I persuaded Steve he had to give way and the film was torn out of the camera.

A government official had told us that no journalists must go outside the capital. It was, of course, for our own safety. It was also, of course, the best way we had of seeing Soviet troops. Mr Samadali knew the back-routes which were empty of roadblocks and we continued to travel. One day we were unlucky and were stopped by Russian soldiers. They told Mr Samadali to get out of the car. He was submissive as they shouted at him. Then, with us watching, they hit him in the chest with a rifle butt and his knees buckled. I was angry and frightened as I sat with my hand on the door. This man was being hurt for us and yet I knew if I intervened we would be arrested. Then the soldiers walked away and Mr Samadali returned to the car, his head bowed. He was humiliated and ashamed that his legs had given way. We asked him whether he wished to continue driving for us. 'Yes,' he replied, 'very much. Very much.' With their casual violence the Russians had made an enemy, and for Mr Samadali driving us became his way of striking back. Soon afterwards he took us to a street with neat, small brick houses. He hooted and his family came out and waved.

Once or twice we stopped at the stores on Chicken Street or went to the bazaar. Mr Samadali had advised us to speak our English loudly. In the capital people would know we were not Russians. Several times they would come up and say, 'Welcome,' or 'Americans and Muslims are friends.' Away from the bazaar and closer to the government buildings we would see young girls in their mini-skirts and bright lipstick. With my Cold War eyes I saw

them as Russia's allies, party workers who had been educated in
Moscow or East Berlin. Our sympathies were much closer to the
men in the mountains with their ammunition belts and old Lee
Enfield rifles. They were called 'mujahedin'. I had never heard the
word before but it had a romance about it. It meant 'holy warrior',
and in the looking-glass world the 'holy warrior' became the freedom fighter, on our side, and the modern girls were with Moscow.

On 12 January we decided to travel north along the main supply
route used by the Russians. We had heard rumours that for several
days the road had been blocked by the mujahedin. Eighty miles
north of Kabul was the Salang Pass with a three-mile-long tunnel
that went under the mountains. This was the only paved road from
the north and keeping it open was vital to the Soviet army.

The roadside villages close to the capital seemed undisturbed by
the invasion. Men sat at stalls drinking tea. Bales of straw were
loaded onto reluctant camels. Freshly butchered meat hung from
skewers. As the road climbed towards 12,000 feet and the Salang
Pass we tagged onto the back of a Soviet supply column that was
returning home. Steep cliffs rose on each side of the road. A few
rocks landed beside us, splintering into pieces and rolling away. At
first we thought an animal had disturbed the rock face, then the
falling pieces became bigger and large rocks and boulders crashed
beside us and the trucks in front. Here in the mountains they were
resisting the Soviet invasion with whatever they had.

Then we rounded a corner and there were soldiers guarding the
entrance to the tunnel. In front of us was a line of trucks. I did not
want to be caught outside Kabul and decided that it was better to
go back. Mr Samadali began turning the car but the wheels spun
on the ice, drawing the attention of the Russians. One of them took
his rifle off his shoulder, pointed it at the car and ran towards us.
We all screamed at Mr Samadali to stop as the Russian soldier took
aim. I leaped out of the car with my hands in the air. The soldier
was surprised to see a European and slowly lowered his gun.

We explained that we were journalists from Kabul. Then a
paratrooper walked over, a hammer-and-sickle brace buckle on his
belt. He was an officer from the Soviet 105th Parachute Division.
He had been wounded in the hand by a sniper. There was still
blood coming through the dressing. We were all sympathetic and

asked him how it had happened. 'They're shooting Russians from the hills,' he said with a note of incredulity, as if they had not been briefed that many Afghan people would oppose them. The mood between us eased as if we had a common cause in this wild country. I could scarcely believe I was commiserating with an injured Russian officer. He asked who we worked for. Robert Fisk said *The Times*. 'Ah,' said the officer, 'the *New York Times*.' Robert found this amusing and said, 'No, the London *Times*. It's older and more important.' The officer turned to me and asked, 'What about you?' 'The BBC,' I said. 'Oh, the enemy,' he replied and I laughed nervously.

Beside the road was a Soviet truck, its rear section blown apart in an ambush. I asked the officer whether we could film and almost persuaded him but, in the end, he refused. It was a good story. Here was first-hand evidence that the Russians were meeting resistance. Again it was easier in print. 'Soviet convoy ambushed in icy Salang Pass', ran *The Times* headline. We could not take any pictures at the tunnel but just down the road I recorded a piece to camera next to a Soviet supply truck that was on its side. And on the way to the pass Mike had snatched pictures of tanks guarding bridges. The camera was never steady; it swung wildly; but at least it gave the sense of being there, of Soviet forces on the defensive in the mountains.

Shortly afterwards we were summoned to the Palace of Forty Pillars, which had once been the residence of an Afghan king. The new president, recently installed by the Soviets, was going to give a news conference. Babrak Karmal was fifty; a sharp-faced, good-looking man with aquiline features. He came into the room and sat down in a wide-backed red-and-white-striped chair. His advisers, in their ill-fitting grey suits, stood behind him. Karmal was a puppet who had been flown from Czechoslovakia to run Afghanistan and was a bombastic man who disliked interruption. The Soviet troops, he insisted, had been invited to the country. They would leave when American imperialist aggression ended. The first questions from local and Soviet reporters were deferential and irritated me. I then turned to Mike Viney and whispered to him to stand by. I was wearing a burgundy sweater over a white shirt, which at that moment I regretted wearing but I hadn't travelled with a jacket.

I stood up and asked President Karmal what percentage of the population supported him. I added that I had the impression, after talking to Afghans, that there were not too many. Karmal interrupted me, with a mocking sneer on his face. 'Mr Correspondent of the BBC,' he said, pointing at me, 'the most famous propaganda liar in the world.' His aides and some of the Soviet correspondents broke into applause.

It was a dramatic confrontation and became the story of the day. In Germany, *Bild* magazine devoted a whole feature to the incident under the headline 'One reporter takes on a dictator'. As we left the news conference a man warned me in heavily accented English 'to be careful'. There was real hostility there. I was a little scared, as we drove away, that I had drawn too much attention to myself and the BBC.

It was getting harder to travel but we had heard reports of fighting near Jalalabad, a town that lay at the end of the Kabul Gorge on the main road to Pakistan. Mr Samadali knew a way that would take us to the top of the gorge and avoid the roadblocks. It was little more than a track and the car, weighed down with five of us, scraped the rim of the pot holes. Kabul was a mile-high city, nearly six thousand feet above sea level. The road to Jalalabad was a long descent with precipitous cliffs on both sides. Running beside the road was the Kabul river, fast-charging and foaming with the melted snow. Sometimes the road gave way to a sheer drop and at the bottom lay the twisted wrecks of buses and trucks.

We had not descended far when a car drove towards us, its lights flashing, and braked beside us. The driver was agitated and said there was trouble on the road ahead but couldn't tell Mr Samadali what it was. The man drove off at speed. We debated whether to return to Kabul. The gorge, with its high cliffs and deep crags, was ideal for an ambush in which we could easily be mistaken for Russians, but if there was fighting we wanted to see it. It was a familiar dilemma. Most people would turn their back on danger, but that is the reason we were in the gorge – to witness it – and so we were drawn forward. We drove cautiously with all of us peering up at the rock face.

After a few miles we came to Sorobi, a small run-down village that had grown out of a bus stop. There was little reason to live here beyond serving the travellers using the gorge. There were a few abandoned buses, an old taxi propped up on a pile of rocks, some tea-houses and a barber's shop. It was a slow day for business. We found an Afghan policeman who said the road was blocked, but he had no other details. As we stood beside the road drinking black tea we heard the rattle of tank tracks and round the corner, heading down the gorge, came two Russian tanks followed by two open trucks with Afghan soldiers. As they passed they gave a rousing cheer, but were met only with silence.

Again we debated but decided to follow the tanks from a distance. Near to the mouth of the gorge every tree for a quarter of a mile had been cut down. This was the scene of the ambush and the Soviet tanks had stopped. Rebels or bandits had attacked a civilian car and we were told that several people had died, but there was no sign of their bodies. We waited while the tanks pushed the trees to the edge of the road and then descended further onto a plain where the sun was warm and there were orange groves beside the road. Jalalabad was peaceful, slow-moving, tree-lined and elegant with more horse-drawn carriages than cars. The Russians were there, we were told, but in barracks outside town. It was at night that the shooting started, when the rebels came down from the hills.

We stayed until mid-afternoon when Mr Samadali became anxious. He wanted to return to Kabul as quickly as possible. The gorge was a dangerous place to be after dark. As we left Jalalabad we all saw it together. Beside the road on the right-hand side a young man was standing having sex with a donkey. It was so unexpected that we all shouted together. One of us said, 'Stop,' and the car slowed. Mr Samadali seemed confused as to why we wanted to stop and none of us could explain. Maybe it was just to confirm it, to separate it from myth. Mr Samadali, in any event, was impatient to reach the gorge. We looked back and the young man eyed us warily. He was not disturbed or in any way inhibited by us. Just curious at the faces peering from Afghan Taxi No. 7.

Two days later I had a birthday and, during the curfew, the other journalists threw a party for me. Someone had found some bottles of rough Afghan red wine. Inevitably my presents were an assortment of wooden donkeys and camels.

As the days passed it became harder to work. Mr Samadali was visited by the secret police. They threatened to take away his children if he continued working for us. He looked at the ground when he told me. He was very sorry, he said, and hoped we would understand. I shook his hand and thanked him. A man's family could never be worth two minutes of television. I was not able to tell him that our reports were shown in over a hundred countries and made possible by the courage of a man whose first name I never knew. He had found us another driver, but he was much more cautious than Mr Samadali and our journeys outside Kabul ended.

Even if Mr Samadali had continued driving for us, I was unable to leave the hotel because of sickness and diarrhoea. I was too worn down, too exhausted to recover and the three of us decided to leave the country. The Afghan airline Ariana had a flight leaving for Amsterdam via Istanbul. I was still unwell when I boarded the plane and immediately went to sleep in seat 3F, but was woken by a man leaping over the seats. Another passenger had seen a mouse. The man was quick and agile and cornered the mouse close to me. He picked it up with a flickered smile of triumph and then in one movement killed it with a twist of his hand. It was just one minor incident, but I recoiled and buried my face in a blanket. I knew then that I could take no more, that the tension of working under-cover had left me frayed. The man, it turned out, had been a prisoner at Polechowkri prison where mice were fought over and eaten.

The plane was a DC10 which Ariana had only recently acquired. There was a McDonnell-Douglas instructor on the flight deck and as we landed at Istanbul airport it was snowing. The plane veered sideways and we bumped across the uneven ground between the runways. Just another moment of fear. As we refuelled I said to the McDonnell-Douglas instructor that I did not want to continue on what was obviously a training flight and I got his assurance that he would land the plane at Amsterdam.

For me, too, there was always a come-down, a withdrawal, a weaning off adrenaline. One moment I was sneaking pictures of a Soviet invasion, the next I was pushing a trolley in a supermarket aisle, and I struggled to connect with the mundane world of ordinary life. Slowly the major stories were becoming my life and what happened in between was just waiting for the next assignment. And as the adrenaline subsided and I relaxed, invariably I became sick – coughs and colds and all the minor stuff. It was as if, without adrenaline, my immune system shut down. So I recovered, only to travel again, and I was a hard person to live with.

Afghanistan was the beginning of so much I came to report. Eighty years before, Lord Curzon, Britain's Viceroy of India, had called Afghanistan the 'chessboard on which the game for the domination of the world will be played'. In another time, another century, it was seen as the land where the major powers played out their 'great game' of rivalry. This had all smacked to me of colonial history and I dismissed it, but Afghanistan, in a way I could never have imagined, has been woven into the fabric of my own time. The Red Army lost in the country's rugged vastness and its defeat contributed to the fall of the Soviet Union. The mujahedin were supported and supplied by the United States because of the Cold War. Fighters came from across the Muslim world for Jihad. Among them was Osama bin Laden. The more fundamentalist groups got a larger share of the weapons because they were regarded as the more fanatical fighters. We played the great game but it would return to haunt us. Some time later I would return to the country with the mujahedin, dressed as an Afghan, but that is a another story.

6

You Might Find This Distressing

Fares was unusual for a Kuwaiti. He was an alcoholic in a dry country, although I did not know it at the time. He had approached us in the lobby of the Sheraton Hotel in Kuwait City. A young man in his early twenties with a loud laugh. His loose-flowing djellaba, freshly pressed and brilliant white, could not disguise the fact that he was overweight. Curled around his hand was a red-and-white keffiyeh that he held close to him like a comfort blanket. Fares spoke excellent American English, which had clearly been learned in school rather than in the States. He was, he said, at our service – an old-fashioned phrase that I mistrusted. My first instinct was to turn him down as another hotel-lobby hustler who had seen the stack of camera boxes and sniffed out a buck, but there was something about Fares, beyond his persistence. He said he had connections and did not want paying. After talking with him I judged that, in this oil-rich state, his family probably had money and that he was adrift, eager to attach himself to something or someone. So I took a chance on him. We needed, urgently, a local man with connections.

Though 1980 was not yet over, I was going to war. Already that year I had lived through the Soviet invasion of Afghanistan and had been detained in Iran but now I was heading for a desert frontline. I had seen unrest before on the streets of Belfast and I had witnessed military operations by the Soviets and the Israelis, but this was different. This was war as it used to be fought in the world wars: two large lumbering armies slugging it out, grinding each other down over a swathe of parched sand.

I did not pause to think what war would be like; to be in conflict, to be part of it, to smell it, to know its terror. I just wanted to get there, to get to the action, and that consumed all my imagination, as it would again twenty-three years later. So I never questioned whether I would be afraid or how I would deal with my fear.

War had broken out between two giants of the Middle East: Iran and Iraq. The reasons for the fighting were obscure. Iraq had invaded Iran to seize control of the Shatt al-Arab, a disputed waterway in the south of the country. It also laid claim to part of Iran's oil-rich province of Khuzistan, but these were ancient grievances dusted down to justify war. This was a battle to be the dominant power in the region. Saddam Hussein had scented Iran's weakness, after the fall of the Shah, and saw his chance.

With me were Mike Viney and Steve Morris; the same team as in Afghanistan. We had flown to Kuwait with a view to crossing into southern Iraq where most of the fighting was. We went to the Iraqi embassy to get a visa but it was closed for a few days. I was too impatient to kick my heels in Kuwait, while fighting raged a hundred miles up the road, so I decided to try our luck, to see if we could cross into Iraq without a visa. Fares, it turned out, had papers allowing him to drive in Iraq so we set out for the border just over an hour away. The Kuwaiti police insisted that we sign a disclaimer, that we would not hold them responsible if the Iraqis expelled us. A few hundred yards on, across the desert scrub, was the Iraqi border post. The guard agreed to let us in on condition we went straight to the Ministry of Information in Basra.

Fares had been bubbling since we left Kuwait City. He drove fast and was brimming with braggadocio. He was for the Iraqis in this war and only wished he could join the fighting. At the border he felt he had proved himself with his translating and that only improved his mood. A strange euphoria gripped us. We sat back in Fares's low-slung Buick as if this was a day out. He put on a tape of Boney M and wound up the sound. And that is how we went to war: in an American Buick with pounding music. Then I saw a fighter jet flying fast and low and I thought I heard some explosions. I shouted at Fares to turn down the music. He ejected the cassette and tossed it out of the window as if to say that he, Fares, could get serious too.

In Basra I was torn between taking pictures and going to the Ministry of Information. There had just been an Iranian air raid and a column of smoke rose at the edge of the city. No other journalist had yet reported from Basra and I was tempted to start filming, but I thought it unwise to use the camera without a press pass. The man at the ministry was hostile and bureaucratic. We could not stay in Basra without a visa. We must return to Kuwait at once. I pleaded with him, but he was implacable. I asked him whether we could take some pictures on the way back. No, that was not possible. He was emphatic; if we were stopped by the security police we would be treated as spies. Even so, on our return to the border, we snatched some shots from the car and recorded a piece to camera.

The following day we were back in Basra with the right stamp in our passports. We checked into the Hamdan Hotel, a nondescript five-storey building. I asked Fares to stay with us and drive us to the front, but his enthusiasm had evaporated with the first sighting of an Iranian plane. And then it occurred to me: Fares, with his ability to cross the border, could be our ace in the hole. Each day, late in the afternoon, we could give him our film and he could take it to Kuwait to be edited or put on the overnight flight to London. It would put us at an immense advantage. Most of the journalists were still in Baghdad but even when they arrived they would have to ship their pictures back through the Iraqi capital. We would have at least a day's lead on them. Fares leaped at the idea. As he saw it, he was still in on the adventure.

In the evening there was a blackout and sometimes there were also power cuts. We could not read or watch local television so we sat outside in the mugginess, in a city that looked like an abandoned film set, with the streets empty and the shadows deep and the occasional building caught in a shaft of the moon's silvery light. Each night the air-raid sirens would wail but there were no shelters or basements to run to. We just lay in the darkness, vulnerable, riding our luck. You struggle not to think, you close your imagination down, you push away the thought of a bomb falling on the hotel. When the sirens sounded we would lie in the corridors, as far from the windows as we could get, and listen for the Iraqi anti-aircraft guns. If they were in the distance we would relax a little as it meant the planes were over another part of the city. One night the guns opened up right across the street. I had not even known there was a battery there. The explosion came moments later and the windows shook, the air filled with dust and pieces of plaster fell off the walls.

We had been told that we could not leave the hotel without a minder from the Ministry of Information and ministry officials moved into the hotel. In the early days we just ignored them. Local taxi drivers were only too willing to take a fare to war for a hundred dollars. One of them spoke a few words of English and we made him our regular driver. When he was told to stop driving us we used to sneak out of the hotel at dawn, before the officials were up, and meet him a few streets away from the hotel.

To get to the front we had to pass through army roadblocks. For a day we wore keffiyehs and pretended we were Iraqis, but we quickly abandoned this; it made us look like spies. The key to getting past a roadblock, we discovered, was psychology. Above all, it was necessary to appear relaxed, as if we were totally confident that our press passes gave us permission to go where we wanted. Somehow we worked out that a man eating bread can never look tense. So each morning we would buy freshly baked baguettes before leaving for the front, and when we saw a roadblock we would bury our faces in the bread. Sometimes we would hand them to the soldiers. Often they just waved us through. If they hesitated I would leap out of the car with a large smile, shake every hand and say, 'Taxi – Teheran,' pointing eastwards. They always thought it a joke and let us pass. Often they insisted on sharing tea with us. Most of them, I suspect, had never been given any orders about journalists because Iraq was a country where reporters rarely ever travelled without officials. It simply was not expected that television teams would be driving around in taxis.

It was a frustrating war to cover. There were plenty of Iraqi tanks and guns on the move, but the fighting was elusive. The sounds of battle were always in the distance. For days the only evidence of war was artillery being fired or Iranian air raids. Gradually a handful of journalists arrived in Basra, although the majority of them remained in Baghdad. Among those to reach this southern port city was Robert Fisk of *The Times*, with whom we had travelled in Afghanistan.

One day an official said that he would take a few of us close to the Iranian city of Abadan, which, he told us, had been seized by the Iraqis. Abadan had one of the largest oil refineries in the world. The official provided three land cruisers and the three of us and Robert Fisk climbed into one. We drove along the banks of the Shatt al-Arab waterway where, moored in the middle, were large tankers and cargo ships stranded by the war.

Ahead was a storm-sky, louring and menacing, but, as we got closer, we could see these were oil clouds. Plumes of dense black smoke rose from burning refineries. Beside the road Iraqi gunners continued to pour artillery onto the Iranian positions. We stopped close to Seiba, a village that ran along the water's edge. From there, we were told, we would see Abadan burning. Our Iraqi minders, believing their own propaganda, said it was safe to go into Seiba although none of them wanted to. So one of the drivers took the four of us to the outskirts of the village. In those days we wore no flak jackets, no body armour, no helmets. All of that would come later.

It was a dusty place of mud-walled houses and sand-coloured brick buildings set amidst the date palms. It was deserted and the shutters were down. We walked through the alleyways until we found the waterway. Edging into the open I saw, to my right, Abadan burning – a sea of fire engulfing pipelines and refineries. Some of the storage tanks had melted in the intense heat. In order to film this, however, Mike would be exposed to the opposite bank – the Iranian side – but we decided to risk it. The pictures would be exclusive and were the most dramatic of the war so far.

Almost as soon as Mike began filming there was a crackle of automatic fire. The shots were loud and I could hear the bullets kicking off the walls beside us. The Iranians had opened fire from across the water. Then an explosion, deafening and concussive; it was so close I was certain I had been hit. The walls around us seemed to explode, showering us with dust and fragments of brick. A mortar. Then another, falling beside us and throwing us to the ground. One I heard before it exploded. For several minutes we lay in the mud beside a school house as the trees were shredded and a hole was punched in the roof. In your head, you're pleading. Pleading with anyone, pleading to live. And then our voices. All of them. All of them together. Shouting, swearing. 'Let's go, let's go.' Mike continued filming, filming as we lay there, filming as we ran.

But where to run to? Everyone had a different idea. We ran through alleyways, past waterlogged embankments, and across a square, possibly the main square. I saw Robert crouching, running, white shirt open, talking into his tape recorder. Then we were in a wide alleyway, which was partly exposed to the Iranian gunners. Each of us had to run the space. I got into a starting position with the camera behind me. Steve shouted, 'Go!' but I wasn't ready. Then I was running, low to the ground, my arms pumping as the bullets pitted the building beside me. And each of us, in turn, chose his own time to make the run, judging the moment that seemed lucky, knowing the Iranians were waiting, poised to start firing. We came out at the back of the village in a grove of palm trees, where the mortar fragments ripped through the palms, showering us with dates. Then, ahead, was the Land Cruiser with the driver cowering nearby. All of us together were shouting 'go' and 'drive' as we threw ourselves inside the vehicle.

We returned to the crossroads where the other reporters and minders had waited. I leaped out and did a piece to camera. I was tense and slightly fluffed it, but I let it stand. I had a strong, overpowering sense that we should not stay on this corner. I feared the Iranians would guess we had withdrawn here and would either shell the road or order an air strike. What better way to show the world they were still defending Abadan than to kill some journalists taken there by the Iraqis? I shouted at the driver to get going but he would not move without the word of a ministry official. I became more and more insistent. Even my colleagues looked at me as if I had been panicked by our fear in the village. Finally we were moving and the other vehicles came behind. We were still in sight of the crossroads when we saw two Iranian jets circling over where we had just been.

And afterwards, after the rush of extreme fear, the sheer exhilaration of survival, the arousal, the sensuality of terror. Everyone talking over each other, retelling it – and its danger diluted by laughter until it has been reduced and becomes just another tale of the road. And I came to love those moments after, when the adrenaline was still flowing – the bonding, the camaraderie, the post-game crack.

The day was not over. The Iraqis took us to three hospitals in

Basra. Despite having Red Crescent markings on the roof they claimed they had been attacked, although I couldn't see any damage. They took us inside a dimly lit ward to show us the injured. Many of them were children who had run to the rooftops to watch the planes, only to be hit by shrapnel. The ministry officials strode between the beds, pulling back sheets and covers to show off the injuries. The doctors in their white coats stood aside, their arms folded in disapproval, but there was nothing they could say to officials who were all members of the ruling Baath Party. They would call out the child's name as 'This is Azim, aged five,' and then go looking for the most graphic wounds. One child moaned as she was asked to sit up so we could see where the fragments of metal had entered. Another child cried out in pain as an official removed a light dressing so that we could see the injury better. Eventually I, and others, protested. We even called out, 'Leave them alone,' but the officials would not listen and Mike, Steve and I walked out of the ward and waited outside.

We returned to the hotel and I wrote a voice track to go with the Abadan pictures, and we handed them to Fares who was waiting to make his daily run. There were still a few hours before sunset and I was restless and decided that we should go out onto the Shatt-al-Arab waterway. I did not have much in mind beyond curiosity, the possibility of more pictures, that endless quest for images. We asked a taxi driver to take us to where some small boats were moored. After a brief conversation and the offer of a few dollars to a boatman we were out in the waterway, the ostensible cause for this conflict. Then we saw Iraqi gun positions, anti-aircraft batteries and artillery, and, in the middle of the river, Iraqi gunboats. I had not seen them before and we began filming. Then I heard a shout and saw sailors at the stern of the gunboat pointing at us. Some even raised their guns and Mike put down his camera. The Iraqis untied a dinghy, came alongside, and ordered us and the boatman to go with them.

On deck an officer who spoke English was waiting. We showed him our press cards and explained that we were taking pictures of the river. 'But you were filming this boat,' he insisted correctly. 'Yes,' I said, 'much as we have filmed tanks and artillery. You are at war.' 'It is not allowed,' he replied, 'these pictures will help the enemy.' I realized how it must look to these men; foreigners on the river taking pictures of their positions. For all of that he was uncertain what to do with us and we were left on the deck while he tried to reach more senior officials. I feared we would be locked up or even charged as spies.

While we waited I heard raised voices and I saw the sailors threatening the boatman, pushing him in the chest. He looked terrified. I feared for him and asked to speak to the officer. I explained that the boatman believed we had permission to be on the river. My arguments were dismissed. 'He is an Iraqi and should know.' The matter was left hanging and later we saw the boatman taken away in a military dinghy. Then a siren sounded and the men on the boat ran for their guns. We were now in the middle of the Shatt al-Arab in an air raid on a boat that was likely to be a target and, once again that day, I was afraid. It is always better to be active when frightened and I asked the officer whether we could film. 'No,' he snapped and I could see his fear too. The men around us started firing into the sky, into empty sky. I kept looking for Iranian planes but there were none as far as I could see. As the firing started other batteries nearby joined in, believing there must be something up there. So men on the boats, anti-aircraft guns on the top of buildings all began firing. It was as if we were in the midst of a battle yet unsure whether the enemy had shown up and, after a period, the firing subsided as each group of men, in turn, became convinced there was nothing out there.

Later, when it was almost dark, the officer said we could go back to the hotel. He confiscated our footage and said our names would be passed to the special police. When we returned to the hotel we were worried that one of us might be taken away during the night by security officials so we all slept in one room.

We had not been back at the hotel long when Fares walked into the lobby smiling broadly but carrying our film. We were not pleased to see him. There had, he said, been a problem at the border and he would return there in the morning; so our film, our minutes under fire, had to wait, and every day of delay weakened its impact. Our mood crashed. The adrenaline drained away and, without it, we were bone-weary. In the final moments before sleep that night I wondered why we all did this, risking so much for television's fleeting images. There were no answers; it was just a mood and by morning it had lifted and another day's chase began.

The film ran on the main news the following day, the first action report of the Iran–Iraq war. Someone, a friend, I recall, phoned my wife, Sally, and said, 'You may find the report distressing,' as if she was a viewer who might choose to turn away or switch channels. This was the other side, to be married to someone and to see them running under fire, to hear the same explosions, to see someone risk not just their lives, but your life together. And not to be asked. And to question alone why anyone would want to take those risks. My daughter, Becky, used to turn her back on the television when I appeared. She didn't want to see me. Television took her father away. So I found that others, unwittingly, became entangled with our adventures: a wife, a child, a boatman who was taken away, our taxi driver, who defied the authorities by driving us but who, one day, never turned up and simply disappeared, yet his car was still there, like some accusing finger pointing at us, with a new driver.

More journalists had made it to Basra and in the long dark evenings, when they were not queuing to use the hotel's one phone, we traded accounts of the day. A British reporter told us he had been to the Iranian city of Khurramshahr, which had been seized by Iraqi forces. His paper was running it as an exclusive: the first reporter inside occupied Iran. It hurt me, that we had not got there first, and I immediately changed our plans for the following day. We would, at least, get the first pictures from an occupied Iranian city. Robert Fisk decided to join us.

We left early, crossed the Shatt al-Arab and followed the road to the border. It was choked with Iraqi forces – long columns of trucks pulling artillery and anti-aircraft guns, tanks leaving their dust trails above the desert. Then we saw it, a sign bleached by the desert wind but readable nonetheless. 'Welcome to Iran.' It was written in Persian, Arabic and English and on the left-hand side of the sign was a faded picture of Ayatollah Khomeini. A short distance beyond was a burned-out customs post. The Iraqi soldiers lined up to be filmed, their guns pointing in the air, their fingers forming victory signs in the way that other soldiers before them had been caught on camera. 'Come, come,' said an Iraqi officer and he took us to a building which had on its wall a rough painting of Ayatollah Khomeini. Someone had shot Khomeini's eyes out and the Iraqi officer thought that we from the West would enjoy this. The soldiers pasted black-and-white pictures of Saddam Hussein on the sides of their vehicles. The contrast with Khomeini was deliberate. Saddam, wearing a suit, stared into the distance; a young modern Arab leader with destiny on his mind.

We drove beyond the border and I was back in Iran where only a few months before I had been locked up. Now I was driving along a paved road towards the city of Khurramshahr with an invading army. On either side of the road Iraqis were halted and that surprised us. Tanks, armoured personnel carriers and artillery. All dug in. We questioned this as we drove further and then we saw soldiers staring out of foxholes, hunkered down as if expecting an attack. 'What are they doing there?' we asked each other. Then there was nothing. Just empty desert and the bare outlines of a city ahead of us. We fell silent. Our bright red-and-white taxi was the only car on a stretch of road that led right to the heart of Khurram-shahr. One of us then said, 'I don't like this,' and the doubt spread like a contagion. Something was wrong. Where were the Iraqis? We stopped the car and debated whether to continue. Khurramshahr was so close it was almost calling to us, but the longer we stayed there the lonelier the road became so we turned back to where the troops were. They told us we had driven beyond the frontline. Khurramshahr had not been taken. A small number of Iranian revolutionary guards were holding out.

In my fear at what might have been I became angry. We had driven beyond the frontline on the word of a journalist who had reported the fall of a city. We could so easily have become the casualty of someone else's reporting. That evening I confronted the journalist back at the hotel. Had he actually been into the city? 'No,' he conceded; he had been on the outskirts. We debated words and language and what they meant. Certainly it was true that the Iraqis claimed a city was captured when they had just encircled it, but I was left uneasy.

I recalled Graham Greene's Saigon correspondent in *The Quiet American*, who concluded that 'perhaps truth and humility go together; so many lies come from our pride – in my profession a

reporter's pride, the desire to file a better story than the next man'.
Out here, at the war's edge, guile and chance-taking were rewarded
and beside them humility wilted. Driving most of us, as much as
the story, was competition – to be first with the pictures, to get
where no one else had been – and sometimes, just sometimes, that
came at the price of truth.

The Ministry of Information occasionally arranged tours of the
front. We largely avoided them; they had a reputation for hard
driving and little action but I was tempted by the offer to take us
close to the Iranian city of Ahwaz. We had not been to that sector
of the front and we agreed to go. It was chaotically organized. There
were many officials and few decisions. We were put in one vehicle
only to be ordered out and transferred to another. We waited and
watched as the officials argued with each other and the searing sun
rose in the sky. Eventually we left in a Soviet-built jeep. We raced
through dense reeds that were higher than our radiator. Some of
the time we drove blind with just the sound of the vehicle slapping
against the reeds. We knew there were other jeeps hurtling through
the undergrowth and asked the Iraqi driver to slow down, but he
was a military man with pride and he ignored us. Then we hit a
small gully where water had drained away. We were all thrown up
into the soft-skinned roof. Mike was holding his camera, a heavy
Arriflex BL, which flew into his face. The eyepiece struck his nose,
which began bleeding heavily, but still the driver would not slow
down.

We emerged onto a dusty plain, flat and shimmering in the
midday heat. Out in the desert the temperature rose to 40 degrees.
Somehow we met up with the other vehicles and this journalistic
convoy continued driving for an hour or more. We found the Iraqi
army spread out in the vastness; one gun then another, a hundred
yards apart, all arranged according to the military manual. Every so
often we stopped and the arguments began, not with the officials
but between the journalists. The issue was water. We had put cases
of bottled water in the back of our jeep but some reporters had
not thought about surviving the desert heat and now in the middle
of the day they were suffering. Some of them ripped open other
people's cases and just took the water. A photographer demanded
that we share what we had. I refused, saying I had packed just

enough water for my crew, but they were desperate. A few of them formed a group and threatened to seize the water. This was about survival, and men and women were changing in front of us. We handed over some bottles, but the atmosphere was tense, even dangerous.

We were taken to various gun positions and allowed to interview the soldiers, while the ministry officials listened. Then two Iranian fighter jets streaked across the desert and wheeled into the sky before choosing their target. We stood there looking upwards, helpless, waiting for them to decide which position would be destroyed. We saw them fire and moments later an Iraqi truck exploded and, with it, ammunition and fuel; a column of black smoke rose into the crystal-blue sky. And that seemed to be how war was. Random. A shape in the sky deciding who would live and who would die, and I couldn't wait to leave. As we drove back there were more jets and we pulled off the one paved road and found our piece of empty sand, and waited for the wheel to settle on someone's chosen number.

Later we drove back to Basra, another gruelling, charging drive through ribbed sand and tall reeds. By the time we reached the hotel something had changed. I could tell by the silence. The day had broken something in us – perhaps it was our will to continue, perhaps it was our courage. Courage is not inexhaustible. It has a limited supply. It can be refilled over time, but when it is used up that is the moment to leave. Perhaps it was the reality of the war, the unforgiving desert heat, the Iranian jets circling, the futility of it, the sense that a life could so easily be lost out there. Mike finally said what we were all thinking. He did not want to go back to the front and I have always believed that once one person in a team has reached that point then we should all leave together. The war, for us, was over.

So, the following day, we headed for the Kuwaiti border where Fares had arranged to meet us. It was already getting dark when we were stopped by a group of Iraqi soldiers on a remote section of road. They spoke no English but pointed their guns at us. They ordered Mike out of the car and signalled that he should bring the camera. We argued with them, but the men had guns and Mike was taken off into the darkness; we imagined the worst. He was led to a trench where there were other soldiers. All they wanted was to be filmed, just a group of men a long way from the front who wanted their time together to be recorded somewhere.

By the time we reached the Kuwaiti border post, the guard was preparing to leave for the night. We did not have a visa to get back into the country and the man would not wait to discuss it. He shrugged his shoulders, climbed into his air-conditioned car and drove to Kuwait City, leaving us in the scrub of no-man's-land. We met Fares and we asked him to tell a diplomat at the British embassy where we were. Much later that evening, the wife of the diplomat arrived at the border with some food and water, a gesture I have never forgotten. We also found, moving through the desert, a rug-seller and we bought three garish rugs with tiger heads on them and wrapped ourselves against the chill. The desert was a place of extremes. During the day a burning heat, but at night it could be bitterly cold.

The following day we arrived in Kuwait City and Fares wanted to talk. He did not want payment, but he needed my help. He was desperate to leave Kuwait and to settle in the United States. That had been on his mind all the time. I told him it was not in my gift. I was not even an American citizen, but I promised to have a conversation on his behalf. Whether he made it or not I never found out.

It is always a sweet moment, when danger lies behind you, and the trip is over. You linger over the mundane – like a coffee in the Sheraton – savouring its normality. All of us felt good; no one had been able to match our coverage from the frontline. Even as I was relaxing I heard news of an act of initiative which was so bold that, for a day, it left our reports in the shade. Stranded in the middle of the Shatt-al-Arab waterway were a number of international vessels and their crews, prisoners of the war that waged around them. On one of the ships were several British women; one of them, bizarrely, was on her honeymoon. She was the wife of one of the engineers.

The ship's owners had contacted Jon Snow, the ITN correspondent, and together they discussed how these women could be rescued. Jon came up with a plan and one night, wearing a diving suit and his face blackened with mud, he waded and swam towards the ship. Without alerting the Iranians on the other bank, they got

Arrivals ←

Check in ←

Pick - up point

1 » A young correspondent as portrayed by the *Radio Times*

2 » President Bush before his gaffe in Sudan

3 » Early years as a correspondent

4 » Filing a track in an Iraqi bathroom during an air raid in 1980

5 » A stop in the desert that outraged our Iraqi escorts

6 » Ayatollah Khomeini arrives to vote in Qom

7 » The mob breaks through the prison gates in Kabul

8 » Reporting from the front in the Iran–Iraq war

9 » Running under fire outside Abadan in the Iran–Iraq war

10 » The Reagan campaign in 1980

11 » Visting Korczak Ziolkowski in the Black Hills in 1980

12 » The end of our rescue mission in Sudan

13 » Imelda Marcos preparing to sing to God

14 » Going undercover with the Mujahedin into Afghanistan

15 » The Mujahedin with captured Russian tank

16 » Preparing to interview Oliver North after the Iran–Contra scandal

the women off the tanker. It was a brilliant coup and rightly received lots of attention. Many jobs require daring and risk-taking, but it seemed with television news that the hurdle was set high and, over the years, it was to go higher, as the audience expected to be taken to the heart of the most dangerous events.

Television had provided a snapshot, an impression of the war. Our pictures revealed the destruction of Abadan, the dogged resistance of the Iranians, and the Iraqi failure to capture Iranian cities. So much, however, was not told. Ordinary people, with all their fears and losses, were often extras, consigned to a minor role compared to the machines of war. International attention soon moved elsewhere and, over the years, these two countries fought themselves to a standstill; a World War One-like quagmire, where chemical weapons were used and 800,000 died.

In 1984 I returned to Iraq and the utter waste of war. I used to stare from my hotel window in Baghdad and watch the taxis carrying the wooden coffins on their roof racks. So many of them. Always a sign of another bad day at the front. The war assumed its terrible grinding routine. So little territory changed hands that in southern Iraq they had even built a barber's shop under the front line. The mark of the Iraqi officer class was the paunch. The officers sat and ate and ordered waves of soldiers over the trenches to be cut down by the guns of the Iranian Revolutionary Guards.

During our visit we were driven by Iraqi officials from Baghdad to Basra. On the way we stopped beside the road for a piss. The desert was flat, featureless, the colour of wet cement. Alister Bell, the sound-recordist, had been asleep in the car. He got out and looked around at the drab landscape and in his half-sleep came up with his flash of insight. 'Look,' he said to the Iraqis, 'why don't you just invite a few Iranians over? They could see it's a load of shit. You could all have a drink and fuck off home.' The joke backfired badly with the Iraqis and I was embarrassed by it, but underlying it was the burning question: for what were so many dying? This was an honour-fight in the desert. 'To find quarrel in a straw / when honour's at the stake.'

Later the Iraqis took us to the northern front. We went to Kirkuk and then were flown by helicopter to the fighting. Alister had mentioned to the Iraqis that it was his birthday. When we arrived

at the Iraqi artillery positions the colonel in charge offered Alister
the chance to fire one of the guns. In a moment of generosity he
went further. Thirty-three shells would be fired; one round for each
of his years. The troops were all laughing and it would have been
so easy to have pulled the string and walked away, the consequences unknown. I wanted no part of it. The Iraqis insisted, as
though, by denying them, we were rejecting their friendship, but
we turned them down. The obscenity of it, possibly wiping out a
school or a family in a birthday salute, was too much. The Iraqis
couldn't make us out; there had been so many casualties in this
war that they had grown careless of a life.

What was not reported was that Saddam was our man, the
West's man. We supplied him, we fell over ourselves to sign contracts with his regime. Khomeini, with his brand of radical Islam,
was feared more than the dictator in Baghdad, so we fell in behind
Saddam. At the time, I interviewed Tariq Aziz, then the Iraqi foreign
minister and one of Saddam's faithful servants. He was a bright
man who sat there in his military green fatigues, an ivory-handled
pistol at his hip, twisting a Cuban cigar in his mouth. I adopted a
high moral tone about the war. How he must have laughed at me
knowing, as he did, that there was a queue of Western contractors
waiting to supply the Iraqi military machine.

7

Fields of Dreams

All of us are waiting, waiting for the lines. We are penned in, confined to a raised platform on one side of an arena somewhere in Cincinnati, Ohio. We are smiling at each other – seasoned correspondents, frazzled producers and world-weary cameramen. Smiling because we know it's coming. The red-white-and-blue-sequinned drum majorettes have finished and the crowd is looking to the man, the man who would be president. My cameraman and I have found a corner in the pen. The American networks have a place reserved at each campaign stop; we have to jostle and compete for our space with a view of the stage.

These are the last days of the 1980 presidential campaign and I am covering Ronald Reagan as he glides through each event, ruddy-cheeked, grinning his aw-shucks grin and selling optimism. We have been on the road with him for some weeks and know the old actor's routine and wait for it. There are a few introductions, a couple of one-liners and then Reagan says, 'I just can't resist telling you this,' as if the idea had just come to him and the audience was about to be let in on something. And that is also our cue. Like some chorus line we mouth the words and hold the pauses in perfect time to Reagan's story as it unfolds. 'Nancy and I were campaigning earlier in the primary, doing some door-to-door work, and I knocked on a door and said that I was running for president and this was my wife. The man said, "I don't know who you are." I said, "We're from California," but it meant nothing.'

We are hitting every one of Reagan's words and fighting back the laughter. The audience are looking at us with intense dislike, with that 'why doesn't someone throw the bums out' look. Reagan continues, recounting what he told the man on the doorstep. ' "We used to be in pictures." Still a blank. "My initials are RR," and with that the man's jaw dropped, his eyes popped open and he turned around and yelled into the house: "Maw, come out here, it's Roy Rogers and Dale Evans."' Roy Rogers, an old screen-cowboy, just happens to be on stage, feigns surprise, and then roars with laughter, and the crowd joins in. We laugh, too, but at ourselves mimicking the candidate. The story never changed, be it at the Tranquility Park in Houston or the airport in Fort Worth. Reagan had it off, word perfect.

I travelled on with Ronald Reagan to Los Angeles to await the result, while my colleague Martin Bell followed Jimmy Carter's campaign. In Hollywood there was a lot of talk about a Loony Tunes presidency if Reagan won. Back in Britain, too, my friends were appalled at the idea of a Reagan Presidency. To them he was defined by a single quote, by a comment about conservation and California's Redwood trees. Reagan had said, 'When you've seen one Redwood tree, you've seen them all,' and many people never got beyond that. He was an easy man to mock but, up close, a much harder man to dislike.

On election night I was in the ballroom at the Century Plaza Hotel with Reagan's closest supporters. The candidate was upstairs in his suite taking calls and watching the results. When he came down he knew he was not just the next president, but had won a landslide. Even liberal Massachusetts had bowed to him. I was standing close to the stage when he came in. He recognized a friend close to me and bent down to shake his hand and, as I looked into his face, I was certain he had been crying. There was a tearstain under one eye. It was as if this sixty-nine-year-old could not quite believe it himself that he had landed the main part. He gripped the podium and said, 'There's never been a more humbling moment in my life.'

Reagan had a way of speaking, a directness, a simplicity, and people wanted to believe him. He reconnected them to their myths. President Carter had spoken of an 'era of limitations' but the American public was not ready for that. They wanted to hang on to the dream of unlimited horizons and a better tomorrow, and that is what Reagan offered them. Morning in America. As I looked around me I saw one yellow banner raised with the simple slogan 'We're

No. 1'. That is what swung the voters, an effervescence, a feeling that the best days lay ahead. Reagan was not a detail man; he trusted his instincts, bedrock American values honed out west. His view of the world was Manichaean – black and white, good guys and bad guys. Communism was the evil empire and he was destined to fight the last battles of the Cold War; they would be shadowy, dirty, and fought in isolated hamlets, and I would get caught up in them.

Reagan retreated to his ranch at Santa Barbara and I went to the beach at Santa Monica. The campaign was over and I had time, empty time, but I couldn't enjoy it. I was restless, unsettled, disconnected from my family back home. The year's chasing was done – Afghanistan, Iran, Iraq, America – but I was finding it hard to come down and I had my first serious doubts about this job that I had wanted so much.

While criss-crossing America I had heard about a man in South Dakota who was carving a mountain in the shape of Crazy Horse, the Sioux Indian chief. Something about it – the impossibility of the man's dream, the sheer cussed bloody-mindedness of it – caught my attention. Perhaps, too, it was the remoteness of the location; the Black Hills seemed a long way from anywhere, and that is what I wanted – to lose myself for a while. Somehow I persuaded the BBC there was a story there.

The mountain carver was Korczak Ziolkowski, a man hewn out of the old frontier. When I first saw him I thought of figures I had seen in faded sepia photos or daguerreotypes from the previous century. He made no concessions to the modern. He had a salt-and-pepper straggly beard, a tattered cowboy hat and a skin jacket with tassels. Everything about him said he was his own man and not to be messed with. He liked to keep you a little on edge as if a word out of place could get you run off his property.

We stood together in the cool November air and looked out at a granite mountain where you could just see emerging the first outline of Crazy Horse and the head of the horse he was riding. Korczak had been at this since 1948 and that shocked me. Over thirty years and barely an outline. Back then he had been dis-charged from the army with just $174 in his pocket. The scale of his dream was enormous. The sculpture, when completed, would be the largest in the world, bigger than Mount Rushmore; it would be even bigger than the Pyramids of Giza. It would stand nearly six hundred feet high. The horse's head alone would be the height of a twenty-two storey building. Crazy Horse's outstretched arm would be able to hold four thousand people.

We talked on until the sun fell behind the mountains. He asked me if I wanted a drink and I said I'd like a glass of wine. 'I asked you whether you wanted a drink,' he replied, with the emphasis on the last word. I feared I had offended him. 'Whiskey,' he said, 'that's a drink.' And so we sat in his studio and drank whiskey together.

Most of the carving was done with sticks of dynamite. He and his sons would place the charges and withdraw. Seven million tons, he reckoned, had been blasted off the mountain so far. The more precise chipping was done clinging to a rope harness using drills and jackhammers. It was dangerous work and he thought he must have broken every bone in his body over the years. He was proud of that, as if it confirmed the immensity of his dream.

He was asked to carve the mountain by the Sioux chiefs Standing Bear, Man Afraid and High Eagle. He showed me what Chief Henry Standing Bear had written: 'My fellow chiefs and I would like the White Man to know the Red Man had great heroes too.' So Korczak pitched his tent amidst the pines and the rocks, felled some trees, and built a home. There were no roads, no water, no electricity. Over time he constructed a sawmill, and that funded his carving, and then an Indian museum, and that brought him paying visitors.

We talked on, and that evening I had dinner with him, his wife Ruth and their ten children. They were all caught up in this dream. There was a selfishness about it; the children were often mocked at school and many in the local community thought he was nuts but Korczak didn't give a damn. He almost liked it that way.

After dinner we drank on. A thought had nagged away at me all evening. This man was over sixty and his life's project was years from being finished. I tiptoed around the subject, but he came straight out with it: he would not live to see it completed. All those hard-scrabble years of dynamiting, hanging from ropes, bulldozing rock and never to see it seemed not to trouble him. He had left books with precise instructions. Either his family would finish it or someone else would. I wondered whether he had ever had doubts about carving the mountain. 'Yes, early on,' he admitted, but then, over time, too much of his life had been invested to pull back. The dream had become part of who he was; he could not be separated from it. I understood that – how something becomes part of your bloodstream. You think you have choices, but they are narrower than you imagine; by the time I left the Black Hills I had concluded that I could not turn away from the life I had chosen.

A few months later I got a call from Mark Starowicz, an editor with CBC, the Canadian Broadcasting Corporation. He was staying at the Churchill Hotel in London and asked me to join him for a coffee. With him was Bernie Zuckerman, a senior producer. They were, they told me, about to launch a new programme called *The Journal*. It would go out five nights a week and would contain news, interviews and in-depth reports. They had seen my work and wanted to know whether I would join the show. I would get to make ten-minute reports instead of the usual two to three minutes. I promised to consider it. There were two other things, Starowicz said: it would mean living in Toronto in Canada, and I would have to become an immigrant.

I had never been to Canada before and knew little about it and yet, before I had left the hotel, I knew I was going. The adventure of it. Starting out again in a vast unknown country. A dream of sorts. The chance of reinvention. I surprised myself at the ease with which I could shed a skin and become something else. A Canadian. It may have been that since boyhood I'd never had a sense of belonging, or maybe I had travelled so much that place had lost its meaning.

My family was less certain. Ties would be broken, friendships put on hold, the warmth of a wider family left behind. There were unanswered questions. What was this for? Were we emigrating? Would we ever return? But they, too, were hooked up to my whim and we packed for an uncertain future. The last story I covered for the BBC was the assassination of Anwar Sadat, and then I told them I was off, like a sudden divorce. There were no letters of thanks, no leaving parties. I shook the hand of the editor of television news who held open the possibility of a return but 'only if I crawled across his carpet'. So what I had striven so hard for – to be a BBC correspondent – I casually walked away from and boarded an Air Canada flight.

The plane stopped at Montreal airport and this was my diary entry for 3 November: 'Although it was early November the trees were bare. The sunlight was weak, without warmth. On such a day in England it would have been January. Beside the runway was the guard of honour; a dozen snowploughs and tracked vehicles. All waiting, knowing what lay ahead. In the distance were hills; their outline blurred by a blue-cold haze. Beyond, a vast expanse of remote, forbidding territory. It was a strange place to choose.'

I was now an immigrant and just a little guilty about it. I felt I must have taken someone else's place. The thought haunted me during the written part of the driving test. It was humbling to look around and to see faces from every corner of the planet all eager to absorb every detail of their new country. For many of them this was their best chance of a good life and they were determined to seize it. When it came to the practical test I was casual about it; I had been driving for years. I jumped into the car only to be stopped moments later by the examiner who said, 'You are aware, sir, you are driving the wrong way down a one-way street?' Outside the car, I saw mainly Asian faces staring at me with disbelief that a man could be so careless.

We were new arrivals, Canadian-landed immigrants, but it was very different from emigrating to America. Canada is a country without myths. There is no Canadian dream, no manifest destiny, no last great hope, no burden of expectation, no exceptionalism. North of the border the pride is different. It is quieter, less obvious. For most people, Canada is about quality of life and civic values, street safety, health care, tolerance. There were no founding fathers, no stirring words about liberty and the pursuit of happiness. We all learned 'O Canada' and that was about it; we were not expected to fly the maple leaf from the front porch.

Mark Starowicz, *The Journal*'s editor, believed passionately in first-person, authored journalism. He wanted authentic voices, authentic sounds, and he encouraged us to experiment. Another new arrival on the show was Neville Bolt, a producer who loved music and pictures. I always thought he would have shot brilliant commercials. He and I teamed up together.

For Canada there was one major foreign story at the time and it was Central America – countries like El Salvador and Guatemala, places with vicious civil wars between leftist guerrillas and government forces. What made these conflicts newsworthy was the attitude of the United States. The Reagan administration believed Communists were sowing subversion in their backyard. Who was behind this? Cuba. It was all a throw-back, history running on a loop, Cold War drums beating again. The same official who had pointed at grainy spy-photos during the Cuban missile crisis was back on stage, his pointer-stick finding Soviet-style barracks in Central America.

The country in the Reagan administration's sight was Nicaragua. It had had a revolution in 1979. The dictator, President Anastasio Somoza, had been overthrown by a guerrilla army called the Sandinistas. It was a popular revolt and many of the fighters were liberals from the middle-class, but among its leaders were Marxists and they were gaining in influence. Washington suspected that Nicaragua was becoming a base for subversion; that it was hosting Cuban advisers and that they were actively helping guerrillas in neighbouring countries like El Salvador and Guatemala. There was fevered talk of a domino effect; that all these countries could collapse into mini Cubas. For Ronald Reagan and his closest advisers this was not about policy, it was visceral, neural; anti-Communism reached to the core of who they were and Central America was not going to be 'lost' on their watch.

We arrived in Nicaragua in March 1982 just as America was turning up the accusations against its leaders. Managua, the capital, was a run-down, damaged place with drab, low-rise buildings. I noticed first the empty spaces, a house missing in a street, a downtown corner empty and overgrown. The city was still scarred from an earthquake ten years before. We wanted to meet the Sandinista leaders, these new Castros, but the commandantes were hard to reach. Our calls were met with a brush-off. They suggested, instead, that we join a bus tour of convicted killers. The Sandinistas, they told us, were about re-education rather than revenge. So early one morning we went to a prison and watched as men in light-blue prison uniforms were led onto a white school bus. These men had all been the thugs and enforcers for Somoza's National Guard. The idea was that a tour around their old city might encourage them to see they had a future in the new Nicaragua. The men gazed out of the bus windows without expressions. They had blank, closed-in faces. Their eyes were dead, unable to connect in a way I had seen before in people who had killed. We stopped at a fast-food restaurant, where the prisoners were serenaded by some scruffy street-kids unaware of who their audience was. Maybe they hoped for some money, or maybe they just felt like singing, but I saw the eyes of one of the men moisten, as if touched by a memory, something lost way back.

The absence of revenge was impressive, and rare, but it was a veneer and I was struggling to get beneath the surface. A few days later we went to a rock concert beside Managua's deep lagoon. Sitting amongst the crowd was Tomas Borge, interior minister, Marxist and one of the commandantes. He wore fatigues, a Cuban-style military cap, dark glasses and in his hand was a cigar. When he saw our camera he smiled, raised his hand and then clenched his fist. And beside him were women, beautiful women. One of them wore a Che Guevara black beret over her long black hair, but she had found space for silver earrings. This was revolutionary chic and they flaunted it, enjoying the tremors it was causing in Washington.

More than any story I had covered I felt an outsider, peering over a fence. Were these smiling commandantes exporting revolution, subverting other countries, wanting to turn Central America into little Cubas – or was it American paranoia? I wanted to answer these questions but all I had were fragments. We found a video of a military parade organized by the Sandinistas. The soldiers goose-stepped like the East German army, there were new Soviet armoured personnel carriers and laid over these images was stirring music that reminded me of Russian *agitprop* films: the breathless commentary, the patriotic soundtrack of May Day in Moscow. We were told the city was full of Cuban advisers, but I couldn't tell a Cuban from a Nicaraguan. Then, while we were there, all constitutional rights were suspended and censorship was imposed. The country, according to the government, was under attack from counter-revolutionaries. A few days earlier, we had filmed a bridge near the Honduran border that had been blown up. The commandantes were convinced the CIA was behind this. Cuban-style bloc committees were formed. Vacant lots in the capital were now taken over by militias preparing to defend the country. All of this we filmed and our store of images grew, but what story these pictures told was harder to know.

Then, finally, I was told I could meet Sergio Ramirez, a member of the ruling junta. When I arrived at his office Bianca Jagger was sitting there wearing a black linen suit with a maroon scarf tied at the neck. She had natural authority – it was not her connections or the name Jagger, although they undoubtedly helped. It was her bearing, her high cheekbones, her stern gaze that warned you off viewing her as a former model and Studio 54 party girl. She was Nicaraguan, the daughter of a Managuan businessman, and clearly knew Ramirez, and I could see he was flattered to have her there. He was an intellectual and he was used by the regime as a frontman, as the acceptable face of the revolution. I peppered him with questions which, in their directness, had an edge of hostility about them; how many Cubans were in the country, how many Soviet advisers were there, why was the press censored? I was relentless and demanded answers. Bianca turned on me and called me a 'colonial bastard' and her eyes blazed with contempt. I was angry, stung by her attack, and it still rankled with me when I returned to the Intercontinental Hotel, where Bianca was also staying.

I mentioned the incident to a young, well-connected Nicaraguan who had helped us set up some interviews. He knew Bianca and was keen that we made up; he invited both of us to a barbecue at a middle-class villa in Managua. She was less harsh and half apologized for what she had said, but explained that a few months before she had been visiting a camp in Honduras with refugees from El Salvador. While there she had seen men, paramilitaries in civilian clothes, trying to abduct and kill refugees. These were the death squads and, in her view, Washington was backing them. She was easy to talk to, even funny, but she had found her cause, and in her certainty challenged me to travel further into the hills and hamlets of Central America. Shortly after that we left Nicaragua but we were back in the region within months.

We returned not to Nicaragua, but to Guatemala – a land of mystical, damaged beauty. Cool highlands and humid rain forests and volcanic lakes. Sugar cane and cotton and high mountain coffee. A military government, plantation owners, campesinos, Quiche Indians and, in the hills, left-wing guerrillas. It was richer, more diverse than its neighbours, but it had the same curse. Another sad, poor, divided society with rich landowners and peasants and not much in between. The losers, as always, were ordinary people. The guerrillas demanded that the villagers feed and support them, but, if they did so, either the army would destroy their hamlets or, worse, they would be visited by the right-wing death squads. In this almost classic struggle between left and right, thousands were dying. Our problem was in showing it. The roads were dangerous and many of the villages inaccessible.

Late one afternoon we heard word of a massacre. Over fifty men, women and children killed. We found the area on the map and debated whether or not to go. The drive would be gruelling, mainly on tracks where maps would not help, and potentially dangerous. Neville was for it and so was I. It was a chance to get beneath the skin of the story. Our sound-recordist George, however, was withdrawn. Later that evening we found him in his room; he had written a farewell note to his girlfriend. We told him he didn't need to come with us, but he felt there was shame in staying behind; so next morning he woke up to a day he did not expect to survive.

We left before dawn in a Volkswagen minibus and drove through flatlands with cattle ranches and tall fields of sugar cane. We then climbed into the hills past wooden huts and corn stalks. As we approached the hamlets, we caught sight of people running; they were so terrified that the sound of a vehicle had them scampering for the undergrowth. It was hard to find anyone to give us directions. We drove on endlessly, up mountain paths and across river beds until ten hours later we found a man who knew the village and directed us to it.

We smelt it first. Burning wood. Then, between clumps of corn, we saw the charred, smouldering frames of the huts. That is all that remained standing. On the ground lay the corrugated-iron roofs and the smashed cooking pots. What unnerved us, however, was the silence. There were no birds, no chickens, no dogs. Nothing. Just a chilling silence. It was as if the animals knew there was death here. Evil clung to the place and none of us wanted to stay. We decided we could film for only thirty minutes if we were to get out of the mountains by dark. We saw where the people had been buried; we found fresh mounds of earth and twigs that had been bent into lopsided crosses. Someone had returned to the village to bury the dead, but they had gone. There were no eye-witnesses, no one to talk to.

We finished our work and started to drive back. We had not gone far when we were surrounded by men with guns. They weren't in uniform and some had scarves pulled up over their noses. None of them smiled. They just stared through the windows of the vehicle, as if sizing us up. Travelling with us was our translator, Eduardo Canel. He was studying politics in Toronto, but was Uruguayan and had known some of the Tupamaros guerrillas. He was very calm with them; all of us were scared and George was in tears. Eduardo had to decide whether these men were a death squad or guerrillas and on his choice our lives could depend. The conversation was slow, with pauses. Eduardo decided they were a death squad and told them the government had sent us to see a massacre carried out by guerrillas. It was a good call. Afterwards he told us how he had listened for words or phrases that might reveal who the men were. The left and the right used different idioms. I had looked into the faces of a couple of the men; I wanted to know what it was like to kill women and children, to live with yourself afterwards. But killing is not a difficult thing once the language has sorted its victims into Commies and Gooks and all the other names we give our enemies.

Back in the capital we wanted to try and find the men behind the death squads. Some were linked to the military but others were powerful landowners and politicians. Fingers pointed at Mario Sandoval, who owned a sugar plantation and was founder of the far-right National Liberation Movement – the MLN. He was a warrior against Communism with a private army of five thousand men. He had promised that, if elected, he would kill a thousand

Communists a week. The country was 'infested' with Cuban-trained guerrillas and they must be 'exterminated'.

We met his daughter and her friends first. They hung out at the bar of the Camino Real Hotel. They had the confidence of money and divided their time between Guatemala City and Miami, where the sons and daughters of other landowners went to play. They were carefree and untroubled by the war that waged around them. Communists were evil people and deserved to die, his daughter said. And once you accepted that the rest was easy. I mentioned that women and children were being massacred. That was the work of the Communists. There was no way through. Her father was a great patriot who loved his country.

We first saw Sandoval himself on the campaign trail. He and his cavalcade would turn up in some dusty square with its bleached, whitewashed church. Other owners had promised to deliver the plantation vote and the workers arrived in high-sided trucks, packed in the back, so that all you could see were wide-brimmed straw hats turned up at the sides. They lowered the side of the truck and the workers climbed down, watched over by men with pump-action shotguns and pistols stuck in their waistbands. A band played, but it was a political fiesta without joy.

Mario Sandoval agreed to an interview at his house in Guatemala City. I knew it would be difficult asking a man whether he was head of the death squads. We sat in the courtyard at the back of the building. Sandoval had had cancer in the throat and spoke through a voice box, and his speech was difficult to follow. His friends called him 'the godfather'. In a tree beside us was a tethered monkey, who would occasionally hurl himself against his chain. Sandoval sat there in a blue short-sleeved shirt, holding a white handkerchief which he used to wipe his brow. I began gently, but eventually asked him, 'Why do people say you are the leader of the death squads?' It was easy for him. 'People say lots of things,' he shrugged. I persisted, 'Are you the leader of the death squads?' It was ridiculous, he said. And I was stuck there without any evidence, only rumours. I waded on, trying to get something out of this man with his monkey beside him. All I got was the certainty of his belief, that the only good Communist was a dead one.

After the interview he was cool towards us. A few days later, as

I was leaving the Camino Real Hotel in Guatemala City, I walked past a large four-wheel-drive pick-up truck. As I passed, the windows came down and a man drew his finger across his throat. So simple. Message delivered.

As Guatemala suffered, the preachers flew in with floppy Bibles and eyes that burned bright with commitment. They were mainly evangelical preachers from the United States. Even the church ended up taking sides. The Catholic priests, with their liberation theology, were seen as Communist sympathizers. The Evangelicals were on the side of the government and the military. Some were just in the preaching business.

We met one at the Camino Real Hotel. She was in her late thirties, her dark hair piled high, her lips full and red; she wore a dark-blue pencil skirt and high heels. She preached in Spanish and with passion. One moment her face was distorted with righteous anger, the next she was soothing and seductive. Her audience, mainly of women, rode the waves with her. Some stood, their eyes closed as in a trance, their hands waving in the air. People were encouraged to come forward, to stand in front of her, and as they stood there she demanded the spirit seize them. With the palm of her hand shaking she struck their foreheads and they passed out, falling backwards into the arms of the catchers behind. And the more who had this religious moment, the more there were who wanted it, to feel the same, to let it wash over them.

Guatemala had just got a new president – a general, and an evangelical. Suddenly, preachers mattered and we asked this woman if we could film her preaching. A few days later she invited us to a large house in Guatemala City where she was preaching to a crowd on the second floor. We started to film and, with the cameras running, she called out my name and invited me to the front. She introduced me to the audience and, taking my hand, asked me whether I loved Jesus. I nodded and she invited me to sing with her. And there we stood, holding hands, as she sang into a microphone and I mouthed anything that came into my head, wishing I was anywhere but there, and casting dangerous looks at the cameraman that demanded he stop filming.

Later the preacher came back to the hotel with us for an interview and she was joined by her sixteen-year-old daughter. The interview was to be done in one of our rooms and, at the lifts, they laughed together as if they were on a date. The daughter said to her mother, 'Don't think I'm going to let you go up there alone.' And in the room the daughter lay on the bed and said how comfortable it was and the preacher flirted with us.

Their man now ran the country. General Rios Mont – a born-again Christian and one-time Sunday school teacher – had come to power in a military coup. He was a small man with hard, beady eyes, jet-black hair and a walrus-like moustache. He belonged to the California-based Gospel Outreach church. The military chose him because he wasn't corrupt and they thought he might attract American support. What the junior officers wanted was a fresh approach to fighting the left-wing guerrillas. One of the guerrilla strongholds was the Quiche region where the Mayan Indians lived, a people with their own languages and traditions.

Rios Mont launched a fierce counter-insurgency offensive against the guerrillas using tactics borrowed from the Vietnam war. The villages were emptied so as to cut the guerrillas off from the Indian population. Once the area was cleared it became a free-fire zone for the military; anything moving there they could shoot. People were moved into secure hamlets where they were given food and, if trusted, weapons to defend themselves. The policy was called 'beans and bullets' and was how Communism would be defeated.

We took a helicopter into the remote Quiche region. Beneath us was an eerie, empty landscape of untended fields, of charred Indian huts – some still smoking, and horses running wild. We flew over bear-pits with sharpened stakes: Vietnamese-style traps set by the guerrillas.

When we landed an entire village turned out to meet us. More women than men; barefoot Indian girls in bright hand-woven skirts and deep vibrant red shirts. They did not smile or speak, but just stared at us. David Donnelly, our cameraman, got out of the helicopter and walked towards them hand-holding the camera. They did not know what it was. Most of them just stood there, rooted to the ground, uncertain what to do. Others backed off as if frightened of what this machine might do. We could not communicate with them and so, along with the preachers and the soldiers, we were just another group of outsiders. Fear had left them passive;

they had been herded into these fortified villages and that is where they stayed, frightened of both the army and the guerrillas.

We flew on to Nebaj, another Indian town. Music was playing, slow and haunting. There were people in masks – a deer's head with antlers, a primitive cubist face. They danced a slow, sad shuffle to a single drum beat and a pipe. It was a feast or a saint's day but no one smiled. As the corn beer took hold they clung to each other. To one side was a shrine, lit by candles, and laid before it were Coca-Cola bottles, corn husks and dolls. Catholicism and animism thrown together. So many outsiders had come here, to change them – the Spanish, the preachers, the military, the Marxists – until they did not know who they were. The music played on while, one after the other, the villagers collapsed.

Although we had flown over the free-fire zone I wanted to go there, to see this land drained of its people. We drove to Chimalte-nango where, just north of the town, there was a free-fire zone extending twenty miles by forty miles. We took the precaution of visiting the local army commander and telling him where we were going. We did not want the army mistaking us for guerrillas. The commander was relaxed and shouted after us as we left, 'If you see the guerrillas tell them to come in and surrender.'

We drove for half an hour. There was no sign to indicate we were entering a free-fire zone. Gradually we noticed the absence of people and then we came to a few abandoned huts. They had not been damaged; they were just empty. We drove further into a valley along an uneven track until we came to a hamlet. The grass was overgrown, waist high. Last year's dead corn stalks had not been cleared. In the porch of one of the huts was a painting hanging crooked. In the grass lay a decomposed body half inside a pair of blue jeans. And we noticed it again: the silence. No barking dogs, no birds. Just a lifeless valley. It was like visiting a land after a terrible disaster where nothing had survived.

I was driving the VW minibus slowly but I did not see the shallow trench that stretched across the track until it was too late and the front of the vehicle had tipped into it. We all got out and tried to lift the front of the minibus, but it was too heavy for the five of us. We removed all the camera equipment from inside but still we couldn't move it. We were now stranded inside a free-fire zone with no possibility of being helped. We decided to split up. Neville, Eduardo, the translator, and I would walk back to Chimaltenango, while the cameraman and sound-recordist would stay with the equipment and the vehicle. None of us liked it. The two staying behind would be alone inside a free-fire zone without a word of Spanish.

We began walking back to the town. We had not gone far when I saw movement on the track ahead, about a quarter of a mile away. It had been fleeting but I had seen it – men leaping into the undergrowth and taking cover. They had disappeared, but we knew they were there, either guerrillas or the army. I was wearing a white short-sleeved shirt with epaulettes. I whipped it off and began waving it. The three of us stood in the middle of the track, where we could be observed, our hands half-raised so that the men out there could see we were not carrying weapons. We waited like that for several minutes, knowing that we were being watched and assessed. Gradually a line of men in uniform emerged and walked down the track towards us. As they got closer we could see they were soldiers.

They were unfriendly and suspicious and pointed their guns at us. 'What are you doing here?' they demanded to know. 'It's only the guerrillas here,' they said. Eduardo talked a lot but I could see he was anxious. He told them we were reporters and that our vehicle had broken down. The soldiers moved a few steps away and talked together. The sergeant then asked to see the vehicle and Eduardo said he would go with them. Half the unit would stay behind with Neville and me. Before he left Eduardo said to me that they suspected us of smuggling weapons to the guerrillas. He also pointed out one of the soldiers and told me to be careful of him. 'He can kill easily,' he said.

The soldier was young, barely eighteen years old. He smiled a lot but it did not seem to relate to anything. It was the vacant, chilling smile of a disturbed man. I didn't want him to see me looking at him, but I noticed his eyes, again the dead eyes of a man who had killed before and who could kill again with little more than a shrug. We sat on the track while the soldiers fiddled with their guns, removing the magazines, replacing them, pressing the trigger. Killing us would be a matter of little consequence. We were in a free-fire zone and it would be blamed on the guerrillas. Beside the track the ground fell away and below us was dense undergrowth. I promised myself that I would run and take my chances rather than just sit there and be shot.

Eduardo, the crew and the other soldiers returned. They had not been able to shift the vehicle and had brought with them as much of the camera equipment as they could carry. We all walked back along the track in the direction of town. Eduardo was still very uneasy – the soldiers had not decided what to do with us. Some of them still believed we were trying to contact the guerrillas. We told the soldiers that that morning we had met the commander in the town and that we should go to the barracks. After walking for half an hour we found their truck and they told us to get in the back.

We drove a short distance and then we stopped in a clearing and the soldiers got out. 'Why have we stopped?' I asked Eduardo anxiously. I could see fear in his face. He talked fast, talking for our lives, using every argument that might make them hesitate before killing us. I remembered that a few days earlier we had met the top general in the Guatemalan military and I had his calling card with me. I handed it to Eduardo and told him to tell the soldiers that we knew the general. They passed the card between them, turning it over in their hands, examining it. Eduardo continued talking. We had an appointment to interview the president, which was true, and they could phone his office. Then we were ordered back into the truck and driven to their barracks.

We learned more. Apparently the soldiers had come looking for us. Someone had reported our vehicle, saying there was a machine gun in the back. They had probably mistaken our tripod for a gun. And then it dawned on us, the vehicle getting stuck had probably saved our lives. If we had driven back up the track the soldiers would most likely have just opened fire. Here, in the hills of Central America, the last conflict of the Cold War was brutal and dirty, with the only certainty that the losers were ordinary people, the peasants and Indians.

I came back to Central America once more, to Honduras, the northern neighbour of Nicaragua. The Reagan administration was keeping up the pressure on Nicaragua, accusing it of being the quartermaster for the region's guerrilla groups. There were, however, persistent reports that Washington was doing more than exercising its diplomatic muscle, that the CIA was secretly funding Nicaraguan rebels called the Contras. There were many rumours but no one had filmed this CIA-backed force that was said to be in Honduras.

We flew to the capital, Tegucigalpa, which had the feel of a small slow-paced, humid southern town. Our plan was to talk to Nicaraguan exiles, hoping they might lead us to the Contras. We had met an American in a bar who was young, hazy about what he was doing in Central America, but well informed. He said the man we should talk to was John Negroponte, the American ambassador in Honduras, and he promised to make a call on our behalf.

Shortly afterwards we were in John Negroponte's office. He was articulate and sharp, too sharp for this sweltering banana republic. He had cut his teeth as a foreign service officer in Vietnam. After we had interviewed him, he gave us a file with names and addresses of Nicaraguan exile groups. The locations were obscure and difficult to find and we began to wonder whether this photocopied file was intended to mislead us. We drove to one of the addresses which was close to the border with Nicaragua. In one village we heard about a trade union leader who had been killed because he had seen too much, and we went to his house. The man's mother was there, his widow and his teenage son. The man had been found in a dried-up river bed close to the border. They believed he had been killed by Honduras's murky secret police who discouraged people from rooting around the border areas.

While we were at the house, two men turned up and just stood there. They were menacing in their silence. The son had an epileptic fit and the widow believed our presence had brought the men there. She screamed at us, 'Get out, get out.' We went at once but, as we left, she gave us the name of the border town near where her husband had been found. We went there but no one wanted to talk to us. One old man said he was too terrified to speak and would not answer any direct questions, so we asked him what he heard at night when he was lying in his bed. 'I hear a lot of steps,' he told us. 'Many boots.' We found his house and it was close to a school. The teacher, Rosita, was friendly, and said she knew there were people in the hills. We asked her how to get there and she sent two kids to show us the track.

It was freshly carved out of the hills, the soil was soft and orange-brown. In our four-wheel drive we followed the track as it wound through clumps of pine trees. In my mind I knew we had found something – this was much more than a farmer's track. We came around a corner and there was a wooden barrier across the road and men in military uniforms. They pointed their M16s at us and told us to get out of the car. They were wary, suspicious, uncertain what to do with us. They led us into their camp, told us to sit down, and gave us mangoes to eat. They got on a short-wave radio and called their commander.

While we waited, I said to the others that we had found the Contras. There was no doubting it. This was not a rag-bag group of rebels, this was a well-equipped force. I told the others to memorize every detail in case we weren't allowed to film. Everything about the men said money, their new boots, the freshly pressed fatigues, the modern tents and the heavy machine guns that had probably never been fired.

The commander was a middle-aged man who, after shaking our hands, said, 'You shouldn't be here.' He wanted to know who sent us. Once again I pulled out a calling card. This time it was that of the American ambassador, John Negroponte. The ambassador, I told the man, knew what we were doing. He examined the card then went away and used the radio. When he returned he told us to leave. I asked if we could film. 'Not now,' was the answer, but he promised to come to our hotel in the capital the next day. He was a commander taking orders and we had no doubt they came from the American embassy.

When we left the camp we wrote down every detail, every tent, every badge, every gun. The following day, as we expected, the commander said that we could not film the camp; but he was clear about his mission – the overthrow of the Nicaraguan government. We returned to Canada and brought in a sketch artist to illustrate what we had seen. We were the first journalists to find the Contras and to see how the CIA was backing them. Our report was later entered into the Congressional record in Washington.

This was Reagan's secret war and one of the last conflicts of the Cold War. It was shadowy, clandestine, but in the end these anti-Communist warriors won. The evil empire, the Soviet Union, collapsed and I would be there at the moment when Communism ended. John Negroponte, that veteran of Vietnam and Central America, became US ambassador to Iraq in 2004. Central America, after the end of the Cold War, sank back into obscurity, ignored by governments and news networks.

Korczak Ziolkowski died the year after I met him, his mountain unfinished. 'When the dreams end,' he had written, 'there is no more greatness.' Most achievers had their fields of dreams. Governments too. Great causes embraced. Sometimes they were battles between good and evil, but often it was not that simple. Invasions and secret wars, in defence of great principles, were gambles that sometimes paid off, but they could be a violation that churned a country and left chaos behind.

8

A Night With Junior Jesus

I had woken with thirty-four mosquito bites. That surpassed the previous night but not by much. Counting had been difficult. There was no mirror in the hotel room and I had propped a make-up mirror against the wall to get an accurate count for my back. Some of the bites were in large clusters as if a gang of mosquitoes had arrived and feasted together.

For two days I had been running a fever. During the nights the heat never receded. It hung there. Even if I lay completely still the sweat continued to run from my body. The sheet was always damp. The ceiling fan had stopped again. There was no electricity. Large green-and-red geckos ran up the walls, but I'd long since ceased caring whether they were dangerous.

This was Accra on the west coast of Africa. The statistics didn't tell the half of it. The humidity was 66–95 per cent and the temperature never fell below 76 degrees. It sucked the energy out of you. We were stranded in a broken-down hotel with little to do but regret we had ever accepted this assignment.

The fact is we were waiting, waiting for an interview with the revolutionary leader. Some still called him J-J or even 'Junior Jesus'. The world knew him as Flight Lieutenant Jerry Rawlings, the leader of Ghana. The year was 1982.

The reason for the assignment was never very clear but Jeremiah Jerry Rawlings was catching the attention of Washington. The two men he admired were Fidel Castro and Mu'ammer Qaddafi. That scared some people. Rawlings had spent time in Tripoli and was setting up councils modelled on Libya's People's Committees. That scared people some more. This was a time of paranoia when small nations were in either the Soviet or the Western camp. What

Rawlings really believed no one knew and, I suppose, that was the problem.

We had imagined that getting an interview with him was just a matter of asking, but Ghana didn't work that way. The leader had dispensed with appointments; he even spurned using government offices. The country ran on spontaneity, revolutionary rhetoric and the whims of its mercurial leader.

Without Rawlings there would be no story. There was no market for pieces on Ghana, but there was one for items about a maverick leader cosying up to Qaddafi. That was the way the news business worked. The Third World did not sell. 'The new Qaddafi' did. We had, therefore, to see and talk to the main man, otherwise the trip would be an expensive waste of money and, rather foolishly, I had given my office the impression that I could 'deliver' Rawlings.

So we waited, the only guests in a hotel that was no longer certain it was open. Most days the hotel was without food. Once, we were told the kitchen had found two eggs and we sat down at a table, but by the time the eggs arrived the yolks were missing; they had apparently been stolen. At the official exchange rate eggs cost $75 each. Most mornings we had to drive to the market to haggle for bananas and yams.

Jerry Rawlings was something of an enigma. He was the son of a Scottish father and a Ghanaian mother. He was thirty-four years old and a talented pilot who had first come to power in an army coup in 1979. He had his own brand of revolutionary chic – dark glasses and a multi-zippered flight suit. His first act was to declare a 'holy war' against corruption. Traders were asked to reduce their prices, and when they refused the market was razed to the ground. The 'market queens', who were accused of profiteering, were flogged publicly. Three of the country's former leaders were lined up at an army firing range beside the sea and shot. The people had approved.

After 112 days, the whirlwind passed. Jerry Rawlings handed back power to an elected government, just as he had promised. Africa took notice. It was an exceptional act on a continent grown weary of coups carried out in the name of future democracy, but it did not last. Rawlings reclaimed power in a second coup in December 1981. This time it was to save Ghana from 'economic vampires'. The country was in free-fall. Money had all but lost its meaning. Food was being hoarded. The factories, which had no spare parts or raw materials, were scarcely running.

Our first problem was how to get a message to him to say we wanted an interview. He didn't seem to have an office. He had made enemies and he knew they were plotting against him. So he kept on the move. Telephones rarely worked.

In desperation, we decided to go to the Burma Camp, the army headquarters on the outskirts of Accra. I have seen such places all over the world: bungalow-style barracks, a parade ground, barbed wire, sandbags and soldiers edgy and suspicious. This was a time of coups and attempted counter-coups. Barracks were often the place where the struggles for power were settled. Burma Camp also had a reputation for interrogation and torture.

I approached a young soldier behind a wall of sandbags and asked how I could get a message to Jerry Rawlings. I explained that we were a television team hoping to interview the leader. Almost immediately it seemed a dangerously naive plan. The soldier said nothing, but stared at me. I explained again, but I could see I was getting nowhere. So I said, 'Thank you,' turned around and headed back to the car. There was a shout: 'Stop!' and I saw the soldier had raised his rifle. I edged back towards him. He now wanted to detain me. I reeked of suspicion and he did not want to take the risk of letting me go. I asked to see the senior officer at the base. After I spent twenty minutes sitting on a wooden bench in the guardroom a captain came over. I explained again that I wanted to get a message to Jerry Rawlings. He took all our details and where we were staying then I was free to leave, but he had promised nothing.

So for over a week we visited embassies, businessmen, well-known Ghanaians, government officials and left the same message and the same letter in the hope that someone somewhere would pass it to Rawlings.

While we waited we travelled inland to Kumasi, the capital city of the Ashanti. Why we went there I don't know but it passed the time and the name Ashanti drew us. Ashanti was the kingdom of gold, of gold mines. It was why the Portuguese called that part of Africa the Gold Coast. The British had invaded in 1874 and carted off the golden king's regalia. What had remained was a rich tradition: sumptuous ceremonies with vibrant colours and swirling silk umbrellas.

We decided that the king, the Asantahene, who had a degree of independence, might be a useful interview in our Rawlings film, if we ever got to make it. Soon after we arrived in Kumasi, I met one of the king's aides. It was possible, I was told, that the king would meet us, but there was an important protocol to a meeting. We had to bring the king a gift, but it must not be presented directly to him. It must be placed on the floor beside where I was sitting and a servant would remove it. The king would notice a gift had been made. 'What kind of gift would be appropriate?' I asked, knowing that the markets were almost bare. 'A bottle of whiskey would do fine,' said the aide. Secondly, he said, it was polite to approach the king from his left side.

Word soon reached us that King Otumfo Polu Ware II would meet me. We got a taxi to Mahhiya Palace, which was on a hilltop surrounded by trees. The palace was a two-storey, unassuming building. There was a short drive, a gaggle of noisy peacocks, which had been a gift from the Shah of Iran, and an old Rolls-Royce. I walked down the drive clutching a whiskey bottle in a brown paper bag. The door opened and there was the Asantahene, a tall, distinguished man wearing a robe of deep-blue brocade. Unfortunately his right-hand side was facing me so I tacked to my left but as I moved he turned with me. I kept going, hoping somehow that I could reach his left side, but I collided with the wall. Then in a deep, educated English voice he said, 'You are very welcome,' and shook my hand. There was a slight smile on his face, no doubt brought on by my walking into a wall.

We went into a sparsely decorated room and the king sat on a carved stool. I had been told about the stools. The throne was known as the Golden Stool. Stools were very personal and used only by their owners. When vacant they were tipped to one side so alien spirits could not sit on them and thereby enter the soul of the owner. I sat on a chair and placed the whiskey bottle on the floor. Within seconds it had been collected by a servant who carried it away. The king gave an imperceptible nod. Around his wrists were several bands of gold and on his fingers heavy rings. He was an interesting and intelligent man who knew the limits of the Ashanti independence. If he pushed too far he risked losing what freedom they had and their vibrant cultural heritage. Our visit did not coincide with one of their ceremonies, but we managed to film some Ashanti in traditional costume. However, this was only an interlude and soon we were back in Accra and waiting for Junior Jesus.

One diplomat told me that the Ghanaian leader used a seventeenth-century castle beside the Atlantic, but that I would never reach it because there were troops and roadblocks. He also told me there was a mysterious Englishman working for him.

It seemed a better lead than anything else, so we set out for the castle. We had only just glimpsed a whitewashed building when we were stopped. I explained again who I was and was told to wait. Ten minutes later a very English voice called to me from behind a gate. 'Gavin, come on in,' said a man in his thirties who wore a white, sweat-stained shirt and had a pronounced limp. There was something unexplained about him. He had manners, but they came with menace.

There was no explanation as to what he was doing in Ghana or how he had ended up an aide to Jerry Rawlings. Inside his spartan office the man said there was a problem. Yes, they knew we were in the country and were wanting an interview. One of our messages had got through. They had done some checking up on me and someone in London had told them I had done a highly critical film about Robert Mugabe, then prime minister of Zimbabwe. I tried to defend it but he waved my arguments aside. Rawlings was insisting that a copy of the film be flown in so that a 'fair' verdict could be reached. There would be a 'revolutionary' viewing which Rawlings would attend to decide whether I was a 'neo-colonialist'.

I felt the project draining away, dying amidst the heat and chaos. It would take days to get the film to Ghana and there was no guarantee Rawlings would see it immediately. I was also not very comfortable with the idea of showing my film to a group of coup leaders. I began explaining the difficulties, but he didn't want to hear. Accept the deal or leave the country. I said I had no way of contacting my office. The phones didn't work. 'This one does,' he said with a half-smile, pointing to a phone on the desk. So, standing in front of him, I phoned Toronto and explained I was in what passed for the president's outer office and needed a film sent to me overnight or we were coming home. 'We'll get on to that,' said the editor and I knew we were staying. Two days later the Zimbabwe film arrived in Ghana.

So we returned to the mosquitoes, the geckos and the long nights when the air never moved and the only distraction was a case of Star beer. Late one afternoon the manager of the hotel found me and told me we would be going to the castle later that evening. An escort would come to the hotel. Even with an official travelling in our car we were stopped a hundred yards from the gates. We were then ordered to walk in a single file with our hands raised above our heads. Everywhere there were men in dark glasses with guns. Rawlings trusted no one, including the army that brought him to power.

His office fortress had a makeshift air about it, as if he did not expect to be in power very long. There were a few files, a flying helmet and, inexplicably, a set of drums. In an adjoining room were two inflatable liferafts, carefully packed. This was the means by which Rawlings and his friends would escape if the castle was attacked. They would lower the rafts into the Atlantic below and disappear.

For long periods we were left on our own. We had no idea whether we were going to see Rawlings, show our film or get an interview. There was no sign of the Englishman and our escort said little.

At about 11 p.m. we were told we were leaving for a drive. That was all. No more information. Alister Bell, the sound-recordist, became very uneasy about what was planned for us. We all shared his concern. We were taken down the castle stairs and put in a jeep with an escort of soldiers. Our car pulled in behind.

Alister's agitation grew. 'Do you think Rawlings has a sense of humour?' he asked me. I had no idea. Alister then confessed to a problem which, even at the time, struck me as surreal. He had in his pocket an audio tape. It might have been a Peter Cook and Dudley Moore sketch or a moment from *Monty Python*, but the scene revolves around a schoolboy called Rawlings who is about to be beaten. The master says, 'Come into my study, Rawlings. This is going to hurt me more than it hurts you.' Rawlings replies, 'I'm twice your size.' 'In that case, Rawlings,' said the master, 'everything will be fine,' and canes him. It had greatly amused Alister up until now.

As we left the castle gates we noticed a Japanese jeep had joined our convoy. As it came alongside we realized it was being driven by Jerry Rawlings. The vehicles drove through Accra's deserted streets. It was five minutes to midnight and five minutes to curfew.

We arrived at one of Accra's few modern housing complexes and the home of one of Rawlings's trusted friends. The main room was small with a couple of sofas and a TV set. I had the Zimbabwe film with me and suspected that it was here that I would be judged. At first Rawlings scarcely acknowledged us. He was a tall man, over six foot, wiry and athletic. He crackled with nervous tension. He paced the room and the corridor, listening to the static and voices from his two-way radio. Survival was a preoccupation. Outside the house I had noticed how few soldiers there were. Each night only a small number of loyal troops were told where he would be staying. Even the army command could not be trusted with that information.

It was not clear who was who, but one of the men announced that we were going to watch a film on his VHS machine. I thought it would be my Zimbabwe documentary, but he inserted his own tape. It began as a natural history film with scenes of animals attacking each other. Then sequences followed of humans attacking animals and an elephant having its head blown away. It was extraordinary and chilling. While Rawlings sat or paced in an adjoining room, we had to watch, without explanation, scenes of appalling cruelty, of humans attacking humans. There was footage from South America of white mercenaries attacking peasants. Men were castrated and their genitals stuffed in their mouths. Then the film showed a tourist in an African game park, who got out of his car to film a lion. The man was jumped on by another lion and dragged off while his wife and children screamed in the background. He was then eaten by the rest of the pride. There was a look of horror on the faces of my colleagues as one grisly scene followed another. Our host said little. He too gazed at these pictures with fascination. When the tape ended I pretended to be unperturbed and asked who had made the film and where the clips had come from. No one was fooled. We were all scared.

All the man would say was, 'Interesting, don't you think?' We all nodded nervously as he fiddled with the tape machine and said, 'I have something else for you.' This time it was a home movie of Rawlings with his troops. It began with what, in different circumstances, would have been a comic incident. When Rawlings arrived the sergeant shouted, 'Atten*tion*.' As he emphasized the 'tion' his teeth flew out. We all saw it but none of us laughed. None of us had any confidence as to how the night would turn out.

In the movie Rawlings strode up and down, tripping over the ideas tumbling from his mouth. He told his troops that imperialist mercenaries were coming. He knew the date, but he was not letting on. Last time he had warned of an invasion his enemies had not turned up and this, he said, had led to a 'certain apathy'. Next time, he told the bemused soldiers, he would allow the mercenaries to come and some of them would be killed. Then they would understand.

While we had been watching this an attractive woman had come into the room and sat on the sofa to my left. She introduced herself as Rawlings's wife. She was articulate and began complaining about films made about Africa. A couple of younger men came into the room and it was soon apparent that this group would be the jury on the Zimbabwe film.

I was not looking forward to the showing. The film had revealed for the first time the presence of North Korean soldiers in Zimbabwe. It had also captured something of the brutality of Mugabe's Fifth Brigade as it had stormed into the townships of Bulawayo. All of this I could defend, but the opening of the film – even at the time – had left me a little uneasy. While in Zimbabwe we had come across a witch doctor who had thrown his shells on the floor and announced there would be war. We had filmed his act and somehow in the edit suite the sequence had made it into the final cut.

Our documentary began playing and Rawlings wandered off into the house. During the 'witch doctor scene' I tried to divert their attention with some scrap of information about Zimbabwe. Rawlings's wife, the house owner and a couple of young aides watched intently. They sometimes shook their heads and interrupted.

Towards the end of the film Rawlings joined his wife on the sofa. For a moment she was distracted. She stroked his thigh and tried to get his interest, but he was on the edge of exhaustion. He lay back, closed his eyes and crossed his legs to reveal an ankle holster with a miniature pistol. One aide later told us, with admiration, that Rawlings rarely slept for more than an hour at a time and even then it was rarely in a bed and never in the same house.

When the film was over the room exploded with criticism. Rawlings's wife wanted to know why we were so critical of Mugabe. Another man said it was an anti-African film. So we argued into the night, like college students, while the revolutionary leader slept beside us. For ten minutes his head rested on my shoulder.

At about 4.30 a.m. Rawlings woke, full of rage. He launched into a bitter denunciation of the West. 'Look at what you're doing,' he said, pacing the floor. 'You build houses for Africans that are like ovens and lay carpets on the floors. Then you come around trying to sell us air-conditioning.' We tried to protest but he was in irascible mood. 'You are like the tourist,' he said to no one in particular. 'The only difference is that you haven't been eaten yet.' For a moment there was silence, then Alister Bell said, 'Actually, we have to be going.' Even at the time, despite my apprehension, this struck me as absurdly funny but I could see from Alister's strained face that it had been unintentional.

Then at 5 a.m., as the curfew lifted, Rawlings was done with us. No, he did not want to talk further. No, he did not want to give an interview. We walked out of the house and into our car. None of us said much for a while but before we got back to the hotel we had all agreed that we would leave Ghana later that day.

I was still asleep when there was a knock on the door and the hotel manager told us we had to go to the port of Tema. This had come from Rawlings. I woke the others. The night with its violent images and erratic behaviour had unnerved us. None of us wanted to go to Tema, but we felt we could not board that evening flight without one last try to salvage something from this trip.

For a man who had had no more than two hours' sleep Rawlings was high on adrenaline. Ghana was on the edge of starvation and he had come to the port to exhort the workers to load sacks of fertilizer more quickly. He did not acknowledge us as we began filming. He strode through the piled sacks berating the workers for their idleness. Turning suddenly towards one worker he pointed accusingly, 'Because you're malingering, Africans will starve.'

He then leaped aboard a truck and began frantically loading fertilizer. Sweating profusely he ordered the workers to form a line. Still he was not satisfied. 'We have too many spectators,' he shouted and ordered every man to carry two sacks. Then he was off again, tearing through the port, urging the crane drivers to work faster, leaping onto another truck and working until his clothes ran with sweat.

He burned with the belief that the West was not needed and that through hard work Ghanaians could save themselves. Amidst the cranes and sacks, he seemed a hopeless figure raging against the inertia that had settled on his country. Even as he moved through the port, the work effort dissipated in his wake.

After two hours Rawlings sat back, exhausted; he was a man conducting a revolution against insuperable odds. I seized the moment. With the camera running I began an interview. I asked him about his admiration for Castro. Had I been to Cuba, he demanded to know. No, I had not. 'I want you to go, you and I,' he said, slapping me on the shoulder.

With a crowd gathered around us I mentioned to him that he had offered to face a firing squad if what he was doing for the second time did not meet with the people's approval. Hesitating for a moment he said, 'Friend, I have given up my life already. I am not prepared to spill a drop of blood for a thousand fools, but I will willingly give up my life for one wise man.'

So we left for the airport with a film of sorts. It had been a wild, unsettling encounter and we were pleased to leave. At the time I did not know what to make of Rawlings. In the film he came across as one of Africa's young zealots, extreme and possibly dangerous. It was too harsh a judgement. He was to stay in power for more than twenty years, giving Ghana a stability his neighbours could only envy. He turned out a pragmatist. Rawlings the revolutionary had said that 'aid enslaves' but that didn't prevent him negotiating with the IMF and the World Bank. Later, I wondered whether television and I had failed Africa again. Rawlings had more than fitted a stereotype and I had gone along with that. I would return to that continent again, where the truth was always elusive.

9

Craziness

The cameraman turned to me and without in any way lowering or disguising his voice announced, 'These guys don't half soak up the light.' I cringed with embarrassment and thought about an apology. 'These guys' referred to Africans. Sitting in front of us was the Reverend Ndabaningi Sithole, a Zimbabwean politician, whom we were about to interview. The cameraman had been having trouble with the lighting and had just held a light meter to Sithole's face when he made his observation. He had discovered what most cameramen know – that black people need to be lit differently – but he was from the Canadian plains, from Saskatchewan, where the faces were white, and he was an innocent abroad.

When the CBC programme *The Journal* started it needed to hire cameramen and soundmen and some of them had never travelled outside Canada. Kevin, one of the recordists, was a biker who, even on a shoot, wore his leathers. It was only when he got to Israel and removed his jacket in the heat that it was discovered he had a swastika tattooed on his arm. It hadn't occurred to him this might cause deep offence. His arm had to be bandaged with camera tape for the duration of the trip. He was suspicious of eating in foreign lands and had filled a camera case with cans of food, which he would heat under the hot tap in his room. Abroad was alien and lonely and, in the Middle East, he became homesick. He ended up phoning his bikers' club and asking his mates to bring his bike to the phone so he could listen to the reassuring growl of its engine. He stayed on the line long enough to rack up several hundred dollars in phone charges and that is how we came to know of his pining, his longing to hear from his bike. Canada and America are so vast that many of the people I worked with had not left the continent. Some were open to foreign cultures, others were not and they sought safety in fast food, in brands and hotel chains whose names they knew.

Most of the cameramen, however, produced excellent pictures even if they had not travelled much outside the vastness of Canada. A television reporter is hugely dependent on his cameraman. The reporter might be a sharp operator, an imaginative story-teller, but without the pictures he fails. The cameraman has to understand the story almost as well as the reporter to know the action, the close-up, the cut-away that captures the essence of it. Often they get one chance at it, there are no retakes. The moment happens, the car arrives, the crowd runs, a shot is fired and it's over. A news cameraman has to be courageous, often more courageous than the man or woman who appears on screen. While the reporter can stay low, or hide behind a building, sooner or later the cameraman has to break cover and take the extra risk or the story goes untold. I have always tried to go with the cameramen into the dangerous places; if there is a risk it seems only right that we should take it together. But in the early 1980s reporters were becoming more dependent on the pictures of freelancers, on the agencies, and I noticed it first in the Middle East.

In June 1982 Israel invaded Lebanon. Sixty thousand Israeli troops, led by more than five hundred tanks, swept across its northern border towards Beirut. The aim was to crush the Palestine Liberation Organization. There was also a hope that the invasion might bring some order to a land scarred by civil war. As the Israelis pushed towards the Lebanese capital they clashed with Syrian forces and there was a fear of a wider Middle East conflict.

We immediately flew from Toronto to Israel. I had not worked with the cameraman or soundman before and neither of them had covered a war. When we arrived in Jerusalem we were required to register with the IDF, the Israeli Defence Forces. Registration gave us a press card and permitted us to travel to the fighting, but the Israelis did not want television crews roaming over the battlefront. They had a system of escort officers, usually lieutenants or captains, who would travel in the car with you. They were minders whose main concern was that a picture might reveal the identity of an

Israeli unit and its location. They also exercised a measure of control. Usually it was subtle, but sometimes they simply wanted to prevent filming of an embarrassing incident – the building bombed by mistake or a shell that had gone astray.

The invasion brought scores of television crews to Israel. Most of them, particularly from North America, preferred covering Middle East conflicts from the Israeli side. They expected Israel to win and so filming alongside Israeli forces was considered the safer option. It was also cultural. The Israelis seemed more like themselves and therefore understandable; the Palestinians seemed more foreign. So many reporters arrived in Jerusalem that there were not enough escort officers, and the Israelis worked a rota system. Some days you would get an individual officer who would go with you into Lebanon. On other days you could join a bus tour, but that was restrictive and you had no control over where you were going or how long you stayed there. One thing was clear: the Israelis did not want reporters crossing into Lebanon unaccompanied.

It was a difficult system for us because we needed to send back daily reports. We developed a gruelling routine. Each day, at around 4 a.m., we would leave Jerusalem and drive to the Lebanese border. At 7 a.m. the reporters and cameramen would gather around the IDF press officers and learn who was getting into Lebanon. We would work until late afternoon and then drive back to Jerusalem and edit the story. We would send it to Canada at around 1 a.m. the next day and then snatch a couple of hours' sleep.

Getting into Lebanon was critical. That was where the story was. Otherwise we were left to record the sound of artillery in the distance or we had to rely on other people's pictures. Some TV correspondents settled for that. They recorded a piece to camera in front of some Israeli armour, used agency pictures, and gave the impression they had been in the heart of the action. The problem with other people's footage was that it was hard to interpret, to assess, because you rarely knew the context in which the pictures were taken.

In the first few days it was difficult to know the scope of Israel's ambition; most of us thought the operation was intended to destroy the PLO's positions and artillery in southern Lebanon. But each morning, as we drove through Galilee, we noticed the convoys of armour moving through Israel and it had the feel of a much larger operation.

Four days after the invasion began, the Israelis agreed to escort a line of press cars to the town of Nabatiya; there had been fierce fighting with the Palestinians, but it was now in Israeli hands. An Israeli officer rode in one of the cars and we all followed behind. I was soon frustrated; the town was largely empty. A few families remained. Old women did their daily chores, denying the violence around them. There were some damaged buildings but the war had moved on.

I then saw an opportunity. On the outskirts of town was a huge column of Israeli armour; Nabatiya had clearly been a holding point. The lead tanks were already moving east towards the Bekaa Valley. I realized that we could slip into this column and I knew enough about convoys to be certain that once we were in it we would be sandwiched between tracked vehicles which would not bother with us. It required a split-second decision. It meant breaking away from our escort; it also meant we were, potentially, travelling into battle. The decision involved two other individuals as well, the cameraman and soundman, but there was no time to fully discuss it. As soon as the car with the escort officer was out of sight I drove our vehicle into the moving column. I could see in the faces of my colleagues that they were troubled and uneasy; they had not agreed to this. It was their lives and they should have had a say, but the car was now in a convoy and there was no turning back.

We drove along narrow tracks bordered by groves of trees and rocks. The sky was a bright crystalline blue. To look away from the road was to imagine a Mediterranean holiday but we were in the midst of a major operation. Giant helicopters flew overhead carrying shells in netting slung beneath them. Smaller Cobra helicopter gunships flew alongside the column. In fields beside the track large 175 mm artillery guns fired over our heads. There were spotters for the artillery who overtook us; soldiers in jeeps with their coloured poles. I had not seen an advance like this before – the speed, the organization. And all the time the running soundtrack – the beat of rotor blades, the thump of heavy guns and the whine of the tank tracks. Then a moment of farce. The column stopped and soldiers climbed off their tanks and personnel carriers. Ahead of us a missile on top of a tracked vehicle had caught in a tree. We all stood around as if discussing a road accident. An officer appeared and shouted in Hebrew, the branch was cut down and we moved deeper into the Bekaa Valley.

Then a new sound. Planes. Fighter planes. Some of them we thought were MiGs and therefore Syrian, and we were an inviting target – an Israeli convoy on a narrow track. And I could see the anxiety in the faces of those with me. Then more planes, some cart-wheeling, some being pursued by missiles. There was an explosion and we saw a plane spiralling down, and in the distance black smoke rose from where it had crashed. I kept asking the camera-man, 'Did you get it?' The cameraman tried a few pans from inside the vehicle but it was no use. We needed to be standing on a hill and filming instead of sitting in an armoured column. Our small white Japanese car was tucked between two armoured personnel carriers and partially sighted. This day, as it turned out, saw the largest dogfight since World War Two. And we were in the midst of it. Nearly a hundred planes were in the sky. Israel and Syria went head to head and technology triumphed. The Israelis were using a plane – like an AWACS – which could see the Syrian fighters as they took off. Nearly thirty Syrian planes were brought down. It was an important day in the Middle East and we were there, but we couldn't capture it.

For the cameraman the pressure was intense. He was taken to a place he did not want to go. Then I, the correspondent, badgered him, my questions laced with a note of accusation. And my frus-tration didn't subside. I kept on about this being one of history's days and we were missing it. And in the cameraman's face I saw the question, 'Why am I doing this?' Later that day we returned to Israel. The escort officers were furious and banned us from entering Lebanon for a period.

Gradually the scale of Israel's ambition was realized. Its forces reached the edge of Beirut and its plan was to force Palestinian fighters out of the city and out of the country. Only under inter-national pressure did it stop its operation. When the Israeli advance halted we finally paused. For seven days I had slept for no more than two to three hours a night. I closed my door at the Jerusalem Hilton and woke up twenty-four hours later. I had missed an entire day.

A few days later we returned to Canada. I had a sense of unfinished business. So often television news skims the surface with its powerful instant images, and then its promiscuous eye moves on. The best reporting was more patient and less hurried. Israel's military operation proved the easy part, as I would find with other wars. The Israelis had hoped that with the Palestinian fighters gone a new, more stable Lebanon would emerge, but they could not fashion a new Lebanon with their guns. Resistance grew and with the ambushes came Israeli retaliation. And, later, I would meet Israeli soldiers who did not like what they were doing, who felt their own values were compromised and corrupted by the operation. That was also a story.

What followed in Lebanon was chaos, violence and craziness. Israel, with its casualties mounting, wanted out. The United States had sent in the marines to oversee the withdrawal of Palestinian fighters from Beirut. But in October 1983 their barracks were bombed and over 200 marines killed. The Americans began pulling back to ships off the coast. A dangerous vacuum was left behind and it was filled by warring militias.

That was the Beirut I returned to in February 1984. From a distance it seemed like a city beyond redemption, that had imploded on itself. The public had tuned out, unable to follow the militias and their shifting alliances. There was a case for reporting the disintegration and I suppose that is why we went, but we sensed the viewers had lost interest and that made the assignment harder.

I was with cameraman Michael Sweeney, his soundman Alister Bell, and John Scully, a producer. Michael was an excellent, thoughtful cameraman. Alister loved the adventure of unstable places that allowed him to play out his own sense of the absurd. All of us were apprehensive.

The only way into Beirut was by ferry. The airport was closed. The ferry ran from Larnaca in Cyprus to the port of Jounieh, which was north of Beirut and on the Christian side of the divide. The crossing took about six hours and for many Lebanese this was the only way of getting in and out of their country.

We boarded the ferry late in the evening and even in port we could feel the swell. The ferry looked like another line's cast-off. The paint had been worn away by the sea spray. It was a stripped-down service as if someone had decided the Lebanese route was not worth spending money on. It was gone midnight when the ferry left port. We decided to eat before finding a chair to sleep on. The restaurant was like a factory canteen. A few stained tables and chairs on an old wooden floor. On offer were kebabs, burgers and chips, but before you go into a dangerous place you cease minding about food. What matters is survival. So we filled our plates and sat at the tables with the other travellers.

The swell increased and the ferry lurched; it leaned over until it was caught by another wave which tipped it back in the other direction. As the ferry dipped we all slid across the floor – tables, chairs and passengers. All moving together. Ending up against the cabin wall. Then just as we began to untangle our plates and chairs we were sliding back the other way until we collided with the wall opposite. Then back again. None of us could stand or escape. It was like being on a theme-park ride. We could only cling to the tables and chairs as they raced from side to side. Plates fell from the tables, smashing on the floor and discarding ketchup, chips, peas and burgers. And the spilled food travelled with us from side to side. One man, an older Lebanese man, tried to leave, but mis-judged a lurch and he was sliding with the food and the coffee and the smashed plates. I tried to help; it was like offering a hand to a man in the water, but I lost hold of my plate and it fell to the floor. And Alister was laughing; the sheer absurdity of it. All these human beings clinging to tables and smeared with food.

We all chose our moment to make our escape, leaving the restaurant littered with food as if there had been a fight. By dawn it was calmer and the Lebanese coast was in sight. I saw the dinghies, two of them racing towards the boat, but did not pay them any attention. I thought they might guide us into port but, shortly afterwards, the ferry slowed and the engines stopped. I noticed the passengers first; some of them were talking to each other in low, confidential voices. Their faces were troubled. Strangers had con-versations. I sensed something was happening and began asking questions. No one had any details but one man said there was 'trouble' on board. Then a woman appeared from the lower deck and announced that the ferry had been hijacked. The passengers crowded around her wanting to know who the hijackers were, what faction they belonged to. She knew little beyond the fact that gunmen had seized the boat. Another passenger said the gunmen were after one passenger.

We hung back and waited. I wanted to remain out of sight until it was clearer what these men were after. After an hour the engines restarted and we began moving along the coast slowly. Two of the hijackers appeared in the galley. They were young men, late twenties or early thirties, with guns, but they were not aggressive. People wanted to know what was happening but the men stood around awkwardly, saying little. Alister, somehow, saw humour in the situation and asked the men whether they could recommend any good beaches. He spoke to them as if he had run into mates in a bar. They stared back in disbelief. Alister continued discussing possible locations as if the entire Mediterranean was now open to us. One of the men finally snapped, 'It's not funny,' as if frustrated that this hijack was not being taken seriously enough. I eased Alister away.

The confusion continued. The ferry moved slowly and then stopped again. A boat came alongside. It was possible that a passenger was taken off, but none of the crew told us what was happening. Most of the passengers sat quietly, resigned to waiting. They were more frustrated than afraid. Then we were told that we were putting in at the Port of Beirut rather than Jounieh. The gunmen, it seemed, had left the boat. Jounieh, for some reason, was closed, and the Port of Beirut was where we were heading. Everyone found their voice. The passengers were furious. The Port of Beirut was on the so-called Green Line that separated Muslim west Beirut from the Christian east. It was frequently shelled and was one of the most dangerous parts of the city.

The crew finally came around and told everyone to get ready. The ferry would dock for no longer than three minutes before putting back to sea. Anyone not off the boat would be taken back to Cyprus. We explained that we had eighteen camera boxes and doubted whether we could carry them to the dockside in three minutes. The crew were scared and unhelpful. 'Three minutes,' and they held up their fingers as if we had not understood them. As we came into the port the passengers crowded by the exit at the stern. The crew did not tie the ferry up. They lowered a ramp – more like a wide plank without safety rails – and began shouting at everyone to get off the boat. The passengers surged forward, pushing each other and running. We were last off and formed a chain, passing boxes to each other and piling them up on the quayside. We were taking too much time for the crew and they began throwing our boxes off the boat. One of them fell into the water and sank out of sight. They didn't care; they wanted to get back to sea. Within three minutes the ferry had left. We were on the quayside and alone. There were no cars or passengers; they knew this place and had all fled. Around us were wrecked warehouses and, in the distance, taller buildings pockmarked by war.

We were stranded with seventeen cases in a place that was shelled daily. We were so anxious to get to safety that we considered leaving our boxes behind, but, even in the midst of fighting, we suspected they would be gone by morning. It was raining and we hoped that the weather might deter the militias from firing at each other. Two of us walked towards the exit and managed to call the hotel where we were staying. The manager sent a car for us and an hour later we were in the relative safety of the Alexandre Hotel.

When journalists were in the east of the city this was where they stayed. Most reporters like to stay together; they feed off one another's stories and keep a watchful eye on each other. On this occasion the hotel was almost empty. It was close to the Green Line. Frequently, shells landed around the hotel and when the shooting started the guests were ushered into the basement. That night we went onto the roof and looked across the city. By Beirut standards it was quiet, just the occasional burst of gunfire. We stood and watched phosphorus-tipped tracer bullets arc across the sky. There seemed little point to the firing. It had been going on for so long that it had become a way of life. Men just loosed a few off, out of boredom and to mark their territory. Nothing was gained by it. No buildings were taken or land seized. Only the odd life was lost in war's random way.

Standing there, overlooking the city, I wondered what we were doing there. How could we explain this mosaic of militias? Was anyone interested? There was a Lebanese government under a

Christian president, but it controlled a few enclaves and not much more. There was a Lebanese army but it was disintegrating along religious lines. There were militias. On the Christian side there was more than one. Sometimes they fought each other. On the Muslim side of the divide there were Amal and Hezbollah. And then there were the Druze who were siding with the Muslims.

It was baffling in its complexity and we did not try to explain it. We decided instead to tell the human story, how lives were lived in a city which, in parts, looked like Berlin after World War Two. We focused on the Green Line. Each day fire was traded across the line, but living on both sides were ordinary people, hunkered down, huddled in basements, just waiting out the madness. And that caught my imagination.

There were a few crossing points over the line. They had to be assessed each day. There was always a risk. The Museum crossing opened at 7 a.m. unless there was shelling. It was often a chicken run, a wild dash at speed – a hundred dangerous metres between religions. Journalists and diplomats had lost their lives running the divide. On the first morning we got down there, the smoke from the night's shelling still hung in the air. There were red-dirt barricades and, beyond, blackened buildings with gaping holes gouged out by rockets. Every wall was pitted. In some you could see where a tank shell had gone through the concrete. And amidst the rubble and the dereliction were gunmen from both sides. As we filmed, the fighting resumed. There was no trigger for it, no reason. It just resumed. The crash of a mortar. Then shells, tearing off more pieces of building. There was nowhere to run. Just a ditch. As we pressed ourselves into the red dirt, the producer, John Scully, mentioned that his wife was in New York City in a ballroom-dancing contest. And we all agreed the injustice of it all. That she was dancing and he was being shelled.

Then the firing stopped and the crossing reopened. No one questioned it or tried to understand it. It was the way it had become. We drove along the Green Line to the positions held by the Christian gunmen. We climbed through empty buildings, up crumbling stairwells, through holes in walls, until we found the men on the frontline. They wore fatigues and were dirty and unshaven. Some wore bandannas. Around them were cigarette butts, empty cans of Coke and expended ammunition. The Muslims were just metres away. The men knew the other side's sniping positions. When the muezzin started the call to prayer the Christians fired a few rounds. It was done casually. They could not see the mosque. They just wanted to get under the other side's skin, to insult them. The men were unemotional. It was about killing Muslims. There was something primal about it. 'We survive by killing,' said a young gaunt-faced man, using a phrase I had heard before. The Muslims wanted to destroy their way of life and drive them out of the Middle East. That was how they saw it. A fight for survival, for belonging, for identity. And when a Muslim moved you shot him. You waited patiently. A good shift was when you got one. Elsewhere in the city Muslims and Christians talked. They had lived together, and many were friends, but those webs of friendship were being snapped and here, on the Green Line, it had gone way beyond that.

The Muslims returned fire and the building shuddered, splinters and concrete fragments flew through the air. The fighters didn't even flinch; they flicked the dust off their clothes. It was nothing, they told me. Just normal. One of them, a middle-aged man, wandered off to visit the grocery store, which was two floors underground. Another leaned his gun against the wall. On the butt was the picture of a Christian saint, an icon. The image was a mascot, a charm, a layer of protection. A saint in their corner. God on their side in a shooting gallery. We stayed for a while amidst the cursing, cursing the shit world, cursing the Muslims. And the men held their crucifixes. And the wind blew through the vacant windows, stirring up the smell of garbage. One of the men had a beer and we shared it and spoke of women. Christian women fucked and Muslim men fucked them, but it was difficult to take a Muslim woman. And in this dirty foxhole that is what it came down to. Another injustice, the injustice of a fuck.

We crossed the Green Line and found the area that we had seen from the Christian side. The mosque was in a cellar beneath the rubble. There was sniping and the militiaman beckoned to us to follow him as he weaved between buildings, out of sight of the men we had just spent a few days with. Families were still in the neighbourhood, living in the basements. In one there were sixty women

and children. Refugees in their own city. When there was a lull in
the fighting someone was sent out for food. Sometimes they all came
out to breathe the air, but they never strayed far from their shelters.
The Muslim fighters, too, believed they had justice on their side and
that the Christians had too much power. They had their own icons;
pictures of Ayatollah Khomeini were plastered on their AK47s. And
they fired at the Christians, at the infidel and shouted, 'God is Great.'
This was an Islamic Holy War, they told us, which would end with
the liberation of Jerusalem.

We did not stay there during the night; we went to the Commodore Hotel. When we left the line we took our chance. You fear the
random round. We drove fast and watched the tracers flying alongside us. The hotel was also a kind of basement. Everyone here, too,
was riding out the fighting. The Commodore was the journalists'
watering hole on the western side of the city. When you walked
through the door, the bar was directly ahead and all evening we
swapped stories of escape, of survival and of fear. This was not
drinking for taste or for relaxation. It was drinking to forget. As I
stood there I noticed the speed with which the first drink was taken.
It was downed quickly, to move on to the second and third in
search of that moment when the pain, the stress, or whatever it
was, eased.

In the background was a grey parrot, Coco – a mascot to survival
and to craziness. Coco had learned to make the sound of an
incoming shell. So we drank to the whine of shells. Someone had
made a rock video of it all. He had edited shots of shells landing,
planes strafing and rockets exploding to the Meat Loaf hit 'Bat out
of Hell'. Craziness. That is what I thought. The whole thing. And
some reporters were into it. The day's risk was the day's high. For
some this was less about reporting and more about losing themselves. The drink, the drugs. Everything. The hashish, the cocaine,
the amphetamines. All to forget. Even the fucks were about forgetting. Out to sea, the American battleship the USS *New Jersey* hurled
shells as big as Volkswagens into the mountains and with each shell
the city shuddered.

Beirut was falling apart. The management hid the bottles from
the Muslim militias and operated the 'laundry room' where hotel
bills were altered in our favour. It seemed like the last days of

something. Reporters spoke about getting out. They stood at the bar in white T-shirts with red lettering in Arabic, French and English: 'Sahafi! Ne Tirez Pas! Journalist! Don't shoot!', but lives were being lost anyway. Each night, or so it seemed, someone did not come back. One evening we bumped into John Axelson, a Canadian I had worked with before and who had taken me out on his boat on Lake Ontario. One night he arrived in the bar and he saw us but he was somewhere else. We had to pull the story out of him. He was on assignment, working as a freelance for an American network. He had landed after dark in a Christian enclave. Somewhere up the coast. Or maybe it was down the coast. He didn't even know where it was. His leg was peppered with shrapnel. Small shards of lead. He was wired and scared beyond belief. We told him it was time to go home, but he intended to stay, to make the money that would put him over the top. He had no idea any longer what it was all about. He had found some antibiotics for his injuries and Scotch for the rest. This moonscape of a once-civilized city was descending into self-destruction. At the bar someone told a story about a mental hospital on the eastern side that had been shelled. It had frightened the staff, but not the inmates. As someone said, 'The patients became sane and the doctors went crazy.' It was easy here to become damaged and not know it.

The Lebanese loved that word 'crazy'. Even they could not believe the madness, the shelling of neighbourhoods, the destruction. I couldn't see where to take my reporting. The images had lost their impact. The human stories had been heard before. There was a helplessness about the city during those days. So we decided to leave. We found a hydrofoil that would take us back to Cyprus. It was full of people and I sat outside on the deck above the cabin. On my Walkman I had Beethoven's Sixth Symphony, the 'Pastoral'. Just a few bars and it removed me, took me away, as if I was no longer in the city but viewing it through a screen. Beirut receded and the music soothed. An Israeli jet swooped out of the sun and flew low across the boat. A few of the passengers screamed but, lost in the music, I marvelled at its balletic looping. All I knew was that I craved normality.

There was a Lebanese postscript. Shortly after I left Beirut Westerners began being taken hostage. Most of them were American but there were some British too. The fate of the hostages became a political issue for the Reagan administration. Hostages, yellow ribbons, were symbols of American impotence, and impotence had done for President Carter. Bringing the hostages home became a political necessity for President Reagan. Some hostages were freed although others were taken. In November 1986 the world learned just how those hostages had been released. They had been bought with weapons. It was a scandal and for a brief period it appeared that it might destroy the Reagan presidency. America had sold arms to Iran in exchange for the hostages and used some of the money to support the Contras in Nicaragua. It was an illegal operation run out of the White House.

The man at the centre of this was Oliver North, a lieutenant colonel on the National Security Council. The plan had been authorized by his superiors, but he was the energy, the dealer, the operator. North was a believer, an evangelical, a man who shared Reagan's dream; as he saw it, he was a servant in the cause of freedom. He became the fall guy for the scandal and one of the most famous faces in America.

The scandal did not stop the hostage-taking. Once it was established that the West would trade, more people were taken. Among them was Terry Waite, the envoy of the Archbishop of Canterbury. He had been negotiating with the hostage-takers and it had been presumed that he had helped negotiate the release of some of those freed. Now it seemed it had not been so simple, and he had been tarnished by the news of arms dealing. In January 1987 Waite returned to Beirut to salvage his reputation but was snatched off the streets and disappeared into silence and the occasional rumour.

Over a year later Mark Thompson, the editor of *Panorama*, asked me to see if we could find out what had happened to Waite and why he was being held. It was a sensitive assignment from the start because we could never broadcast anything that might endanger him. I flew to Washington and found that Waite was the unmentionable subject. No one would talk about him on or off the record. I took General Richard Secord, one of the men closely involved in Oliver North's operations, to Blackie's House of Beef. As we talked I filtered Waite into the conversation. Secord interrupted, 'If this is all about Waite you can forget it.' The doors were being slammed, but a little too firmly and that intrigued me.

Just when I was running out of calls to make and people to see I called Robert Oakley, who was Director of the Office for Counter-terrorism and had worked with Oliver North. I had tried him a number of times and when he came on the line he said, 'I can give you a minute and a half.' So I made my pitch: 'I'm a senior BBC correspondent. We are preparing a programme about Terry Waite but it will not be broadcast until after he is freed and I can guarantee that, but I would like to talk to you on background.' There was a pause and then he said, 'Come round.'

Oakley was a career diplomat who wore his ideology lightly, unlike others in the administration. As we talked he said, almost casually, 'Terry was the frontman. Ask Ollie.' In a few phrases, I had an extraordinary story. Officials in the White House had, without his knowing, used the Archbishop of Canterbury's envoy as a frontman, a cover for their illegal trading of weapons, and that man was now paying a terrible price in a Beirut cellar.

Over a couple of years, producer Peter Molloy and I met senior American officials and those closest to Waite. Many of them opened up to us. They showed us diaries, notes, transcripts, and played us tape recordings. Waite and North had met numerous times. Officials told us that North considered fitting Waite with a tracking device when he met the captors.

I was intrigued by North. He stood straight-backed before a Congressional committee, raised his right hand, promised to tell the truth and then lied. It was a soldier's lie in defence of the greater good but a lie all the same. Later, North and I met at the Jefferson Hotel in Washington and he gave me the first British television interview. He was earnest and polite. The marine haircut had gone but his hair was still short, the parting pure, his shirt pressed white, his tie sombre apart from two red vertical stripes. His voice was full of conviction. I asked him about the lies, lies to Congress, lies to the Iranians. He had told his Iranian contact, 'President Reagan told me that he thinks Saddam Hussein is a shit.' He just made it up to imply that America was tilting towards Iran. He cheated the Iranians, overcharged them for missiles, and diverted the money to his favourite cause, the Contras. How, I asked him, did that square with his Christianity. 'Gavin,' he said, 'I am a frayed, flawed mortal like the rest of us . . . I believed that the goals were noble.'

Then, looking me in the eye, he added, 'Gavin, I open my heart to God every day.'

I asked him whether he prayed for Terry Waite.

'I do,' he replied.

'What do you pray about?'

'I pray that the good Lord will soften the hearts of those that hold Terry. He was brave beyond my ability to describe it, Gavin.' And his eyes moistened.

'Did you use him as a cover?'

North would not answer.

'Do you feel any guilt in regard to how you dealt with him?'

'Guilt,' he replied. 'I have a hard time with the use of the word.'

Nothing had shaken him, his utter certainty that God was on his side. He had told lies but they were justifiable lies, wartime lies, untruths that soldiers understood. Lies in defence of freedom. Lies for the struggle against Communism in Central America. They were freedom's battles but, up close, amidst the hamlets and the death squads it was hard to be so sure.

One of those freed by North's weapons dealing was Father Lawrence Jenco, a Catholic priest. I went to Illinois to see him after his release. 'Here I am, a single person,' he said. 'I have no wife, I have no children, and you're exchanging me for arms that are going to kill men, women, children, by the thousands for one man. What tremendous foolishness.' Or craziness.

Lebanon was a place of failure. Israel invaded and withdrew, leaving behind a country with deeper scars; America retreated under fire; the militias grew careless of human life and television struggled to tell the story. We had the images, a whole video library of men firing and shells landing, but these were often people without names and buildings without families – just a Middle Eastern arcade game. The audience turned away. I felt then, and many times since, that even in news's fleeting minutes the image is not enough, that it has to be connected to people and their lives.

Beirut as a city bounced back. The strong hand of Syria helped, and so did a resilient people who had grown weary of street fighting. In 1984 I would never have guessed it, but on-the-day verdicts are often shamed by events.

10

Rocking for Africa

They could not contain themselves. They had pulled it off beyond their wildest dreams. They were still bubbling, horsing around. These were the Band Aid trustees in the heady days after the Live Aid concert. They had rocked for Africa, sixteen hours of music, and had made giving cool. Freddie Mercury had belted out the performance of a lifetime and all of this for a cause: Africa's starving.

It had been Bob Geldof's idea and he had yet to come down. He sat there in a crumpled blue shirt, unkempt, red-eyed and fashionably wasted. He managed to give the impression of having enjoyed a heavy night, even if he had stayed home. Around him was the team he had assembled and they were talking numbers, large numbers. The money was still coming in. Geldof wrote a few figures on a notepad and said, 'We could end up with as much again as we made in the concert.' Phil Rusted, the accountant, nodded. He reckoned £65 million might be the figure. Harvey Goldsmith, the concert impresario, shook his head. He thought it might be more.

Another of the trustees burst into the American national anthem, not the words, but the music, which he bugled out to the others before reading, in an American accent, a letter from Congress that designated 'July 13, 1985. Live Aid Day'. The politicians had trailed behind on Africa; they had all but given up on it but now they wanted to be seen with Geldof, to steal a little of his shine. Doors, those heavy establishment doors, had flown open. It was both serious and a laugh. Geldof had been invited to the White House in Washington. 'We stole the memo pads from the office of the vice-president,' he told his colleagues. They couldn't resist a few presidential souvenirs. Geldof had been into the offices once used by Bob Haldeman and John Erlichman, men disgraced by the Watergate scandal, and he was still full of it.

I was there, sitting at the room's edge, in this north London warehouse. We were making a film for BBC *Panorama* about how Band Aid intended to use its money, and they had agreed that we could follow them for six to eight weeks. They were open, unguarded, but the hard part lay ahead. They had money and everyone wanted it. The aid agencies had already been around. Many had not even bothered to outline the project they wanted financing. 'They're only here for the cheque,' said Geldof with disgust. He made a speech and told them to 'fuck off '.

This was not just money; it came wrapped in the hope and idealism of a new generation. They had entrusted it to Geldof. They liked his 'punk diplomacy', f-wording his way past the bureaucrats and governments who only told him why the starving could not be helped. During the Live Aid concert he had gone on television and thumped the table and told the audience, 'You gotta get on the phone and take the money out of your pockets. Don't go to the pub tonight. Please stay in and give us the money. There are people dying now. So give us your money.' And they did. They could not resist him, this dishevelled Irish rock star.

Now he had his chance and all eyes were on him. The questions were complicated. How much money should go on short-term relief and how much on long-term projects? One country was facing an immediate crisis, and that was Sudan. Food aid had arrived but they had not been able to move it out west, to where the people were starving. In a few weeks the rains would come and the desert tracks would be impassable, and tens of thousands of people would be cut off without food. Geldof decided this was where the first money would be spent and in a matter of days we were heading for Africa's largest country.

I had returned from Canada and was living back in London. It had been a difficult decision to leave Toronto and for months afterwards I regretted it. I missed the space, the vastness, the edge of wilderness, the places unexplored. I missed, too, the people. They were careful, attentive to friendship. They worked at their neigh-bourhoods. Somewhere along the line a little of the country had seeped into my bloodstream. I had even acquired its accent. Not fully, but a trace. CBC had encouraged me to change my phrasing and in a London bar a woman had asked me where was I from. I was torn between two places and unhappy. To return is to go back, to pick up old ways, old acquaintances, and can feel like a retreat. Some friends had advised me, 'Never go back. Only go on,' but the pull was the same as it had always been, to be at the heart of events and I felt the BBC – the world's largest news organization – would take me there.

It is not possible to treat famine as another story. It points its finger accusingly. You film but you feel a sense of shame – to stand there, having eaten a full breakfast, and to watch desperate people scrabbling for food, foraging in the dirt for a single grain; and to know that back at the hotel there is a menu with choices, leftovers that will be binned. You wonder what it is that keeps these two worlds apart.

Soon after we arrived in Sudan we flew to Nyala, a dust-blown town at the end of the railway line. While we were there the first food train in two months pulled in. As it slowed dozens of women rushed across the tracks – a swirl of fabric, saris hitched up, head-scarves unravelling. They clutched sharp sticks, which they jabbed through the cracks in the wagons, piercing the bags of grain. Then they ran alongside the train holding out chipped enamel bowls or baskets, collecting the grain as it seeped out. A woman stumbled under the wheels. I heard the cry and began to run to her but a hand grabbed her and pulled her off the tracks. The women worked in packs because the train was guarded by police with wooden canes; as they lashed out at one group of women, another made it to the train and took their chance. There was a madness about it, to be beating starving women because they were the wrong starving. The train disappeared inside a locked siding and the women picked over the ground. Children – some as young as three or four years old – joined in sifting the dirt for a single grain. Afterwards there was chatter, even some laughter. There had been small triumphs. Some bowls were half full and there was excitement in that. Then they retreated to the shadow of a rail-yard building to wait on another chance.

There was a scandal about what we were seeing. It should not have happened. The food was in Sudan, most of it donated by US

AID. They had given the job of distributing it to a private American–Sudanese logistics company, Arkel-Taleb. They had come up with a plan. The grain would be trucked six hundred miles from Port Sudan to the town of Kosti. From there it would be taken by train a thousand miles to Darfur in western Sudan and distributed locally. The trains needed to move a thousand tons a day to the west before the rains came and cut off the region. The operation's success depended on the rail link. As a relief worker was to remark later, 'It was about as wise as investing in a scrapyard.' There was only a single track; sometimes it buckled in the heat; sometimes the ground beneath the track gave way. Often the rusting train broke down. As early as February the relief agencies were warning that the railway was failing to deliver but in February Arkel-Taleb signed another contract which was just as dependent on the trains working.

By May, US AID realized they were losing the race to get the food to the west. The Americans, fearing a disaster, ordered Arkel-Taleb to start using trucks in place of the railway. But when the company entered the market to hire extra trucks, the local truckers realized they had the Americans by the throat. Trucking prices trebled. Arkel, alarmed at the higher prices, demanded a new contract from the government. So the weeks passed. Too many people were numb to the suffering out west. In the event the rains came early and only 20 per cent of the food was in place.

And again the madness, the madness of bureaucracy. While companies and truckers and agencies argued the food piled up in Kosti. There was so much it could not be properly stored. Some lay in the open and was damaged by rain. Other bags had split and the food grain lay on the ground. Within sight of the depot were thousands of people who had left their homes in search of food. They were pleading, 'Why can we not eat when there is so much food?' The private contractor got paid only if he delivered it further west. I had rarely seen a UN official so angry as Winston Pratley. He told me it was a 'calamity of mismanagement and bureaucracy'.

In August 1985 we flew out west to Geneina, to the region with the worst famine. There was some food in the town but the news from the surrounding villages was bad. The rains had started. Desert tracks had disappeared in flash floods and the wadis had filled with water. A single journey could take weeks. We followed a blue Bedford truck out of town. On the back, behind a high-sided metal cage, were sacks of grain. The truck was old, its bodywork pummelled by age, its engine groaning through the gears. Sitting on the sacks were guards, back-up drivers, and volunteers. At the first wadi the truck stopped and everyone got out. A man waded into the water, tested the ground and probed the depth. Then the driver revved up the engine and drove into the water. The front of the truck sank into a hidden hole, disappearing under the mud. The grille was submerged. Then it rose again only to crash back under the water. There was a wrenching sound as if the chassis would be torn from the body. After all the grand plans to move the food grain, this is what it had come down to: single trucks slithering through the mud. What made this famine worse was that the people had been told to stay in their villages because the food was coming.

Not far from the town we came across the starving. They were too weak to move. They were even beyond curiosity when foreigners with cameras entered their village. They sat there listlessly, with a faraway gaze. There was an older woman with braided hair. Her whole body was shrunken. The skin was loose on her; there were folds under her eyes. Her rib cage reminded me of the skeletons of dead animals that lay out in the desert. Flies buzzed around her mouth and she was too weak to wave them away. Nearby there was a child, aged three or four, with a distended stomach and an old face. We filmed them, which in its own way was a kind of obscenity. The village had been reached, not with food but with cameras. We gave them biscuits, everything we had, but it was more for us than for them. A handout to ease the conscience, but we knew it only delayed the moment. Having got our pictures we climbed back into our Land Rover and left them. There was always the comfort that our images might save others by seizing the world's attention. Sometimes that happens, but often the starving become just another backdrop for a piece to camera.

The European Economic Community – the EEC – began flying C130s to Geneina. It was all a sign of failure. 'When you see C130s flying,' someone told me at the time, 'you know someone has goofed badly.' Bob Geldof was dismissive. The flights were the worst of gesture politics. 'It was silly,' he told me. 'Just a waste of time and effort.' Each flight cost $15,000, which worked out at about $1,000 a ton of grain, and the flights could deliver only a fraction of what was needed. But Band Aid could not stand on the sidelines and Geldof and the trustees took their first major decision: they bought a fleet of trucks to help move the food grain. Phil Rusted, their accountant, said he would fly out to take possession of them and we agreed to go with him.

Most days one or two C130s flew to Geneina. Even this was a grindingly slow operation. After each take-off and landing local soldiers had to walk the landing strip picking up and removing the larger stones that had been shaken loose by the previous flight. The planes were flown by several European airforces including those of Belgium, Denmark and Germany. And it became party-time. Sudan was a large, broken down country unable to police its own territory. The food was delivered out west and on the way back the crews looked for fun. We were all staying at the Hilton Hotel in Khartoum. The C130s would buzz the hotel, flying beneath the windows, dipping their wings at the girls by the pool. The flights became parties. In a dry country, there was beer on board and they would invite along flight attendants who were on a stopover in the Sudanese capital. They would dress the young women in jumpsuits and they would come out west to the famine, for the ride. Once, on the way back, they buzzed a line of Sudanese soldiers who scattered and fell to the ground. And everyone laughed. It was a way of saying to Sudan, you need the food so we'll do what we like in your country. This was famine relief as fool around time, when an aching land became a playground where you could land your plane where you liked, drink beer, have some women for company, and just beyond the desert runway they were dying.

Band Aid spent its first $5 million. They bought forty trucks that were already in Sudan and another ninety-four in Kuwait. Phil Rusted arrived in Khartoum and we went with him to a depot on the outskirts of the capital to see the trucks. We drove through the gates and fell silent. All of us. It looked like the waiting room for the breaker's yard. The Magirus and Mack trucks had not been used for two years. There was a thick layer of sand inside the cabs. There were parts missing. Some looked as if they had been dumped after an accident. Rusted, a decent man who cared about Africa, tried to make the best of it. He still thought it was a better use of Band Aid's funds to repair these trucks than buy new ones and he arranged for a team of mechanics to fly out.

I worried about how I would report this. The trucks looked a bad buy and time was against them. The rains promised that later in the year there would be a bumper crop. If the people could survive a few months then the short-term crisis would be over. If Band Aid was to make a difference it had to get its fleet moving within weeks and that looked doubtful. I was torn. It would be so easy to knock Band Aid, to sneer that the money was being wasted and make an early, harsh judgement.

We needed some more material before returning to London so we flew back to Geneina. While filming in the town we met two men who had walked for miles in search for food. They said the people in their village were exhausted and close to death. They had been living off ants' nests but the rains had washed those away and they now had nothing. Maybe I was just worn down by the impossibility of it all, or maybe I was frustrated by standing on the sidelines, but I decided we would launch our own aid delivery to these men's village.

We were all for it: Tom Roberts the producer, Alex Tudhope the cameraman and Freddie Downton the sound-recordist. In the town there was a fleet of German army trucks but none of them worked. All of them had been cannibalized for spares. By chance we met Tim Farr, a young British engineer who worked for Land Rover but had volunteered to help the Sudanese army draw up a list of spares. He agreed to help us.

We approached the local colonel and asked him whether we could take one of his army trucks to a village if we could repair it. He bristled a little at the suggestion that a group of foreigners would take one of his trucks. There would be a loss of pride. Local people would see it as a mark of his weakness, but, even so, he agreed.

So we set about rebuilding a six-wheel-drive army truck. There was a new energy about us. We now had a cause, a mission, and we raced around the town, defying the heat. Someone located fuel and soon others got caught up in this operation. Local soldiers scoured the town for tyres and then found some in a warehouse. A small crowd gathered. The word had gone around that something was happening out at the army base. They sat there silent and curious. I had batteries flown in from Khartoum. The engineer worked on the dynamo. The more the colonel saw the less he liked it. Soldiers were now taking orders from us, but after three days we had the truck working.

We went to a depot and loaded up a hundred sacks of food grain. As we drove back through the town we were surrounded by the hungry. They ran at the truck, defying us not to stop. When we slowed they tore at the bags, slitting them open and gathering the grain as it spilled to the ground. They were pushing, jostling and giving out an occasional scream. They had desperate, intense faces. I shouted at them, waving my arms, as if they were some herd of animals that needed shooing away. I was now telling hungry people they could not eat and all because I now had my truck and our little mission that we wanted to film.

Before we left the town we collected an escort of soldiers. The colonel thought there was a risk the truck could be attacked by bandits. We also needed the men to guide us to their village. The soldiers with rifles sat on the bags of grain in the back of the army truck and we came behind in our borrowed Land Rover. There was only one bridge out of the town and I noticed that underneath it the river was swirling and bloated. At the first wadi the heavy truck sank in the mud. The right rear axle disappeared. The driver gunned the engine and the dark brown water was churned into the air and the wheel sank deeper. The men from the village jumped into the water with stones, hoping they could give the truck some grip. In those minutes they fought for their village; they held their breath and dived under the water trying to build a rock base, but the six-wheel drive had failed. We unloaded the sacks and carried them to a dry bank and then attached a tow line but it snapped. Our mission had failed at the first wadi.

The sky darkened, rain threatened and we had a hundred sacks of food grain lying in the open. Not only had we failed the village but we now risked spoiling these people's precious food. We got in the Land Rover and drove back into town and asked the colonel to help us return the food to the depot. He was furious. Who did we think we were, he asked. And it was not an easy question to answer. The following day we hitched a ride back to Khartoum in a C130.

Band Aid was already working on its fleet but only six trucks were running. Others were beyond repair and had to be written off. Back in London they held a crisis meeting and considered pulling out of the trucking deal. I was still undecided about the line I would take with the story. I went for a coffee with Bob Geldof and we talked frankly about the trucks. He was not the least bit defensive. 'We've been under criticism since we started,' he said, 'so I'm used to that.' I told him he risked getting his fingers burned. 'I don't know any people who've been into Africa who haven't had their fingers burned one way or the other,' he said. Then he added, with a flash of defiance, 'And the people who've had their fingers most burned are those who are dying.'

The trucks were a setback; rocking and raising money was easier than getting food to the starving. Over time Band Aid bought a fleet of new trucks. Most of its money was spent on water wells, storage tanks, tools and fertilizers, which gave some hope that famine might be avoided in the future. When I reported I softened my criticism because in Africa's harsh interior everyone messed up, including us.

11

Imelda Talks to God

It was the end of 1987 and I was sitting on the stone steps of a cockpit waiting for the next bout. The owners paraded their roosters and the men around me placed their bets. We were hemmed in behind a white jailhouse grille encircling a small ring covered in sand. Some of the men were standing with their arms outstretched, others pressed their faces between the bars, trying to catch the attention of the bookies below. In the stifling heat they shouted numbers. We were all tight in together. Just men and the smell of last night's sweat left over from the bars and the girls.

Then the cocks, still held by their owners, were shown to each other. They pecked the air aggressively, eager to settle the fight. Each of them had a three-inch razor-sharp blade attached to a leg that glinted in the yellow light of the pit. These were fighting cocks trained to strike with their spurs. One of them was almost white, helpful colouring for the men in the tiers who craned forward, eager to follow the contest.

As soon as the birds were released they flew at each other. They lashed and flailed and fought close in, a bundle of writhing feathers. Then the white cockerel half flew into the air and lanced the other bird. In less than a minute it was over. The winner tottered about, streaked in blood, before being picked up by a smiling owner. The feathers and the dead rooster were swept away and the ring cleaned for the next fight.

I asked my guide, a student, how the men spotted a winner. 'They can't,' he said, 'but they think they can. They believe in instinct, in luck, in chance, in miracles.' This was the Philippines and we were filming at a pit on the outskirts of Manila. It was a

Sunday and this is where the men came after church, to gamble, to lose themselves.

I wanted to talk to the men because, increasingly, it seemed we were telling the story of two women. One was a front-cover face of the year – a leader who had launched a peaceful revolution and driven out a dictator. The other was not the dictator but his wife. She was famous for her excess, for her shopping, for her shoes. The world sneered, whilst wanting more of her.

The two women were Cory Aquino and Imelda Marcos. Cory was demure, Imelda vulgar. Cory was understated, Imelda nightclub flash. Cory wore $40 dresses, Imelda loved shoes, three thousand pairs of them. And that one fact defined her. The woman with three thousand pairs of shoes. At the pit someone had suggested a hen fight. Cory versus Imelda. It made the men laugh. Some of them wanted flash. It was what they expected in a leader. Others wanted a miracle and saw Cory as a kind of Blessed Mother. In the local stores they were selling Cory dolls.

No one had bothered much to report the Philippines. It was one of those places that television news ignores. It requires a moment, a drama, a person to draw in the cameras. That had happened in 1986. For twenty years the country had been run by President Ferdinand Marcos and his wife, Imelda. Marcos was fiercely anti-Communist and a friend of America, but he had trampled on human rights and he and his wife had looted and plundered and grown rich.

It had started to unravel in 1983 when Benigno Aquino, an opposition leader, had returned from exile. He did not even make it beyond the tarmac before he was shot dead. Marcos denied everything, but at that moment his power began to ebb away. The people forgot their fear and took to the streets where they found others who shared their anger and shame.

In 1986 Marcos had called a snap election, calculating he could win it or steal it. But the assassinated politician's widow, Cory, decided to stand against him. She did not really have a programme, but that didn't matter. It was what she stood for that counted. Decency. She was a slight woman, a bespectacled mother of five who wore yellow dresses during the campaign and ended up launching a yellow revolution.

When the election was over the goons tried to rig the result, but the nuns linked arms around the ballot boxes. When the tanks came onto the streets the nuns and the people stood defiant. The soldiers hesitated and, as with other dictatorships, in that moment of doubt the certainty of their power was lost. And the people sensed it. Within days the military leadership had abandoned Marcos, and he and his wife were whisked away to Hawaii and exile. Cory Aquino became president.

It had been a heady time. People power. The yellow revolution. The world had sat up and taken notice. That had been twelve months before. We had returned to report on what had happened to Cory Aquino, the heroine of the streets. There were four of us: myself, Peter Bell, Richard Adam the cameraman and his recordist, Mervyn Broadway. We knew that to make the film work we had to deliver Cory Aquino, and the Marcoses in exile. We argued over the former president and his wife. After all they were the past, but Imelda was still a draw and she and her husband were plotting their return.

In Manila their cronies worked to keep the flame alive. One of them had the idea of a mass baptism to celebrate Ferdinand Marcos's seventieth birthday. A crowd of a couple of thousand gathered in front of the Manila post office and were given red, white and blue balloons with the face of a much younger Marcos stencilled on them. Others had colour photos of him. Then a line formed with about three hundred infants and their parents. The babies were not only to be blessed but renamed after the former dictator. A tame priest was there with a glass bottle of holy water. He held his thumb over the lip, lifting it when he wanted to splash the infants' foreheads. So that day there were many baby Ferdinands and Imeldas but that was not enough for some of the crowd. They wanted to remember both Marcos and his wife so they blended the names together and the priest blessed little Ferimarc and little Fermelda.

Many worked on the large haciendas, owned by Marcos's supporters, and had been bussed in. But not all. Some were nostalgic for the dictator and his wife. 'Then we had been safe,' said a man in his early thirties, 'but now . . .' His voice trailed off as if it was too obvious to finish the sentence. 'And, of course, there was

Imelda,' added the woman beside him. 'She had been so beautiful.' 'She gave her name to a hospital,' another woman said. That was one of the tricks of power and Imelda understood it. Some of the people never expected a better life but settled for spectacle and glamour like at the movies. And Imelda, the former beauty queen in her lamé and sequins, provided that.

We kept phoning the Marcoses' house in Hawaii but they had yet to decide whether or not to see us. It was the same in Manila with Cory Aquino. A year after the revolution she was less accessible. Her office told us an interview would not be possible. By chance she came to the Manila hotel where we were staying, to deliver a speech, and we took along a camera. The easy smile, the spontaneity, had gone. She was guarded, uncertain of those around her. 'What sets me apart,' she told the lunchtime audience, 'is that I bring us together.' Just a short while before it had all been so different. She was fêted around the world. Now she was having to justify her power. I introduced myself and asked for an interview. She looked jaded. Her face smiled out of habit, but not her eyes. She was polite but brushed me off, referring me to her office.

The fact was that she had had to change. Her strengths were attacked by the old Marcos crowd as weaknesses. Her enemies mocked her innocence, her goodness made her weak, her lack of politics made her gullible, her inexperience made her soft, particularly on the Communist rebels in the hills. She had negotiated a ceasefire and that made some of the military restless. A few months earlier there had been an attempted coup against her. Whilst soldiers fought each other in the streets a private Boeing 707 was discovered parked on a runway in Hawaii. Marcos had been waiting and hoping for the call that would bring him back to power.

So Cory Aquino was having to answer her accusers. 'Can she hack it? Is she weak?' she asked. 'Well they can forget it. Although I am a woman and physically small I have blocked all paths to power except through elections.' But the price of keeping power was in making deals and compromises and some of her supporters felt betrayed.

We made our pitch again to Malacanang Palace, Cory Aquino's office. Cory had been the face of the revolution, we told them, and British and international audiences would expect to hear from her.

They had listened to a thousand similar pitches in the past year and promised to get back to us, but they were not hopeful. We had a dilemma. We had travelled halfway around the world and could not just return empty-handed. So we had to stay, gambling that we could change the mind of both Cory Aquino and the Marcoses. While we waited we travelled in search of the heart of the country. Sprawling shanty towns; sword cults in jungle villages; a gold rush where people died in underground tunnels; rural settlements caught up in the vicious fighting between the Communists and the army. I had never been to the Philippines before. You read the cuttings on the plane and think you know a place, but you rarely do. That has been my experience, and it was so here too.

So we took off, first to the outskirts of Manila and then to the islands in the south. Our guide in the capital was Sister Mary-John Manazan. With her large-framed glasses she looked like Cory and was one of the nuns who had defied the tanks. She took us to the slums. For her the revolution had been about these people. Now, she sensed, they were no longer the priority.

There was nothing regular about the slums. Everything was tacked on. People arrived, found some wood and assembled a shack and, if they were lucky, scavenged some metal-sheeting for a roof. The gullies between the shacks ran with milky-grey waste-water. Girls sat on their haunches pounding the washing. The slums crackled with energy. Young lean men in stained shirts pushed past; some hauled materials; some shouted; some hammered; some sold pieces of fruit or the odd cigarette. Everyone was caught up in the daily battle of survival.

Slums are difficult places to film. They do not want you there. You are an intruder from another world. They know the camera is pointing at their poverty and they resent it. They are too canny to believe they will benefit from a few moments on foreign television. Fortunately, Sister Mary-John had friends there, mainly women with children and without men. I squatted in a doorway and talked to them. Cory meant little, nor did people power. The slum-dwellers of Tondo had joined the protestors during the revolution. They had swept into Malacanang Palace and seen the designer gowns and the racks of shoes and, for a few days, they believed that with the dictator gone their lives would be different. But revolutions nearly always disappoint. The best is always the struggle itself, when everyone stands shoulder to shoulder, caught up in a great cause. Then, afterwards, people return home, to what was before.

Close by was Smoky Mountain, a vast mound of waste. Each day it was scaled by scavengers combing it for what could be reclaimed and sold. It was like a mine with hundreds of people working the face, turning over the cartons, the tins and the mushy trash. They lived amidst the rotting smell, the leaking chemicals and the hospital waste. On the tip-face they gambled their lives and those of their children who foraged beside them. They had a chance and that made them better off than others. Some had become Smoky Mountain's middlemen, offering a price for scrap and then selling it on.

There was no escaping the smell. You never got used to it, said one man. I wanted to retch but for no one to see me. It would have been a kind of insult, intruding on them and then showing I could not stomach it. I felt helpless, overwhelmed, silenced. All my certainties dropped away. We chose not to tape Smoky Mountain; it had been filmed before and the image had been overworked, but I also had nothing meaningful to say. We did take pictures in the slum and interviewed Sister Mary-John, who was indignant that the revolution had betrayed the poor.

But this was only part of the story. The sister and others had told us that outrage and injustice had persuaded some to leave the slums and join the ranks of the Communist guerrillas in the hills. We should go to the islands in the south and see what was happening.

We flew to Mindanao where the battle with the Communists had been at its most intense. Davao was the murder capital of the Philippines. It was a spread-out city of wooden shanties and lean-tos. They perched precariously alongside streams that smelt of soap and urine. Some of the shacks could be entered only by crossing these streams on wooden planks.

Here, far away from the capital, there was a local strongman. Lieutenant Colonel Frank Calida strode through the shanties surrounded by an assortment of gunmen. He wore sunglasses, a baseball hat with gold scrawl on it, a grey sweatshirt and a tan-coloured holster with a pistol. In his hand he had a two-way radio.

Colonel Calida was a fanatical anti-Communist, a big, beaming confident man who drew his inspiration from American films. Sylvester Stallone was his star. 'No one can be neutral about godless Communism,' he later told me, sitting under a poster of Rambo.

His answer to the Communist rebels was vigilantes – arming local people who then controlled the neighbourhoods. These vigilantes were called Alsa Masa or People Rising. They did not have uniforms, just guns. They swaggered down the narrow streets in shorts, flip-flops and sweatshirts which bore the logos of foreign football teams. They had a collection of guns – automatic rifles which they swung casually across their shoulders, and pistols which they stuck in the belts of their trousers. Some local people feared these vigilantes as much as they feared the Communists.

Colonel Calida, with American advice, had also encouraged born-again revivalist Christian groups. One humid evening we were taken in the darkness to a large wooden hut to meet Kumander Lahi, a self-styled faith healer and leader of the Army of Democracy and Morality in Christ.

Kumander Lahi stood in the middle of the room under a flickering light. He was surrounded by men with headbands and machetes and guns. Lahi was a good-looking man in his mid-thirties with dark hair and a red sweatshirt. He stood behind a makeshift lectern which had a microphone. He played a few chords on an electronic organ and sang, in English, the old hymn 'He Leadeth Me'. The men in the half-light watched him, their faces dazed with the unfamiliar music. These were his bolo brigades, his midnight commanders armed with their bolos or machetes.

Lahi was a preacher showman. He told his men that if they were free from sin they would be immune from injury in battle. And he had a way of proving who was pure and who was not. From behind the lectern he drew a long sword and slashed a nearby table. The blade wedged in the wood, convincing all the men in the hut of its sharpness. Lahi told them that the sword would not draw the blood of a man of God. He lifted his sweatshirt and swiped the sword at his clenched stomach muscles. There was a red line but no blood. There was a murmur among the men.

Lahi asked me whether I would take the sword test. He laughed when he asked me but I could see in the faces of some of the men that they were curious to know whether we were pure or not. I told him, 'Another time,' and headed sharply for the exit.

Kumander Lahi was not alone. As we travelled further into Mindanao we found that sword cults were being revived. In one village about twenty men were lined up, stripped to the waist, in front of a local religious leader. They called him the Dahtu, although no one could spell his name. He had an unbuttoned blue shirt, and a picture of Jesus hanging from a string around his neck. This was an initiation ceremony to test whether the men had God's protection. If they passed they would be the new power in the neighbourhood and, certain of divine help, would fight to keep out the Communists.

The Dahtu held his hand above each man as if he was giving them a blessing. They spread their arms wide, their legs apart. Then the Dahtu picked up a sword and slashed their thighs just beneath the groin. These seemed like practice strokes before he swiped their stomachs. The men tensed as the sword bounced off their stomachs. In such ways the villagers were enlisted to fight the Communists.

Before coming to power Cory Aquino had promised to rein in these vigilantes, but now she gave them her support. It was part of the price of keeping the military on side. 'The answer to terrorism,' she said, 'is not social and economic reform but police and military action.' Some of her closest supporters were disillusioned.

We had been phoning Cory Aquino's office while on the road. We told them that we had filmed with the vigilantes and that some of her allies had told us that Cory had betrayed the revolution. We felt it important that the president answer these questions. She relented and agreed to see us at Malacanang Palace.

When she walked in she reminded me of a small-town lawyer or a mid-ranking manager. She was efficient, her handshake brisk. She wore a pink suit and a white shirt, with soft red lipstick. I felt her instinct was to chat, to relax, to talk about our travels, but she was careful with herself. It was as if she had been had too many times before. I made a remark about the decor of the palace. She turned it aside and sent me a message: if you see me as the smiling housewife, you misjudge me. In power she had grown a second skin. When I said that some felt betrayed by her, she retorted, 'I did not promise instant miracles.' When she emphasized a point she raised her eyebrows. She never dropped her smile but her eyes were steely. Nothing I told her about the vigilantes ruffled her. 'I will look into that,' she said when I mentioned they were abusing their power. She was frustrated, exasperated that people did not understand the pressures on her. All she knew was that life was better than under Marcos. I asked her about Imelda but she would not be drawn; she did not want it to be about two women.

Before we left the Philippines we saw her visit her husband's grave. She stood there, in a dark-blue suit, threading the beads of a rosary through her fingers. A small, defiant, stubborn figure that would not allow herself to be muscled out of power.

We flew direct to Hawaii. The Marcoses were still holding out on us but they were more encouraging when they heard we had spoken to Cory Aquino. We stayed at the Sheraton on Waikiki beach and waited and watched the surf. The former dictator and his wife were in the hills just fifteen minutes away.

Then the call came. They would see us at once. We drove up Makiki Heights Drive until we saw a large white two-storey house surrounded by a high wall. We stopped in front of a chain-link fence as we had been told. Two or three unsmiling guards were watching daytime TV in a garage. They were not in a hurry. They searched our equipment and then we sat in the car and waited for half an hour. We asked them whether the Marcoses had been told we were there. 'Just wait,' they said. It had, apparently, always been this way in the Philippines.

Then the gates opened and we were taken into a living room where the former president was reading a paper. He wore the barong tagalog, the white Filipino national shirt worn outside the trousers. He rose stiffly and was formally polite. 'You are welcome,' he said. His face was puffy as if he had been on medication, possibly steroids.

He wanted to know how we had found the Philippines. He was alert and inquisitive. Every piece of negative news he seized on as some kind of justification. As we spoke I looked around. The room was white but on the sofa were pink cushions. On one of them was a large heart. Another had the embroidered words,

'I love champagne and cash.' Even with Marcos talking to me, I had to suppress a laugh. I didn't know what to make of it. This was the caricature of their regime. I wondered whether they had a sense of irony as yet unseen. It was all in the word 'cash'. Not wealth, but notes that can be displayed, flashed, pulled out in a wad. Champagne and cash. A lottery winner's cry. And then another thought crossed my mind that possibly Imelda had bought it, finding in its words a beautiful thought.

Marcos saw himself as a man misunderstood. People would soon come to their senses. He understood the threat posed by Communism. He felt Ronald Reagan would have stood by him if he had not been misled by his advisers. I then asked him about an interview. He was not sure. Every time he spoke it was used against him, he said.

We were joined by Imelda. She was friendly and almost playfully began urging her husband to give us an interview. He seemed tired and listless as if even a brief conversation drained him. She bubbled with energy. Marcos wanted to rest before deciding on the interview and we went out with Imelda.

She was flirtatious. She wore tight, figure-hugging fake-snake trousers and a white shirt. She smiled attentively, certain of her attraction. She wanted sex to be part of this. She wanted me to consider her as a woman. That was her way. When another reporter had questioned her about an alleged affair with the actor George Hamilton, she had replied, 'At least he's a handsome man.' She liked to mention that after she had visited Colonel Qaddafi there were rumours that she had slept with him. It was laughable, of course, but she liked the stories. All of this I recalled as I followed her around the kitchen while she fixed us a lemonade.

We talked as if we had known each other for years. 'You know,' she dropped into the conversation, 'we have almost no money.' She took me out into the garden with its views of the hills and over-looking Waikiki below. She had, she told me, planted some of the bougainvillea. 'I want to be surrounded by what is beautiful,' she said. And that was her creed and her excuse. She had just wanted to make the world a more beautiful place. She had never had three thousand shoes, she pointed out, just one thousand and sixty. 'They counted them, you know,' she said. And so she sat there, without a trace of shame, bubble-wrapped in fantasy.

She then grabbed my hand and said she was going to sing to God. She took me to a corner of the garden where, under the trees, she had built a little open-air chapel. There were fairy lights in the branches and an altar set back in the shrubbery. A few chairs had been put out, and a microphone.

I asked Imelda if we could film her singing to God, but she refused. I could see Richard Adam, the cameraman, itching to get his camera out. She then stepped in front of the microphone, holding a rosary, and said, 'God, I'm going to sing to you.' It was said in a way that God might feel lucky. She then sang a hymn unaccompanied whilst we stood and watched. There was no humility about her. She sang like a star, her hips swaying slightly. When it was over she threw in a prayer. 'God,' she said, as if talking to a floor manager at Macy's or Harrods, 'you know how much we are suffering.' Here there was a slight note of impatience that God was not moving faster. 'We are,' she said, 'your true friends and we have been driven from our homeland by those who hate you. We ask you for justice.' And it was over. A servant switched off the microphone and we walked back into the house. When I used the bathroom I noticed a line of large Louis Vuitton cases outside their bedroom as if they were on vacation, just waiting for the call home.

The former president had changed into a dark-blue suit, a white shirt and red tie. I thought he had been wearing make-up when we first met him, but now I was certain. His face was fleshy, loose under the chin. His hair improbably jet-black. He was ready to be interviewed. 'I would like to go back to the Philippines because I feel I may be of help,' he said, as if the dictatorship had never happened. He, like Imelda, was bathed in self-pity. He believed he was the victim of a great injustice. 'I was taken out of there against my wishes,' he said, 'but I believe in miracles and that's what I'm praying for.' I asked him whether he'd like to be president again. 'If you were in my place,' he said, 'what would you think?'

By this time it was early evening and Imelda said that she and her husband would attend Mass in the garden. 'Each night,' she said, 'we say a special novena.' We could film them, but only from behind. She changed for Mass into a black dress with huge gold leaves that fell from the shoulders. Ferdinand Marcos took the small timid steps of an ageing man. They sat at the front on white garden chairs in a pool of light. Behind them were half a dozen servants, fellow-exiles and some old friends. As they sat down a priest intoned, 'We are joined by our beloved President Ferdinand Marcos and the first lady.'

The altar, twinkling with candles, carried pictures of St Martin de Porres, the patron saint of the humble. Imelda's voice, carried by the microphone, dominated the Mass. Richard Adam moved around through the trees to get a front view of the former president and first lady of the Philippines in their exile retreat.

Then Imelda gave a slight signal to the guards and we were told to leave. There were no goodbyes. We were just hustled out. Imelda had tired of us. As we headed towards the gate I looked back. I could see Imelda standing tall, still singing, trying to catch God's attention.

It had been the story of our trip. Praying and gambling. Marcos was waiting on a miracle. Imelda clung to her rosary. Cory Aquino too. The families on Smoky Mountain gambled their lives as did the gold-diggers and the swordsmen of Mindanao. The men at the cockpit believed in luck, chance and miracles and, in that, were not alone.

When we returned to London we gave only limited space to our meeting with the Marcoses. We felt that Cory Aquino was the story but, afterwards, I was only ever asked about Imelda. She, in all her vast extravagance, was a celebrity and that is who people wanted to know about.

Cory Aquino served as president for six years and kept democracy alive. Ferdinand Marcos died in exile in 1989. Imelda returned to the Philippines but was later indicted on corruption charges. The Marcos fortune was estimated at between five and ten billion dollars, but nothing like that has been found.

12

Fishing With the Mujahedin

This was down-time. A break from war. Late afternoon entertainment when the worst of the sun's heat was past. The men had cut the head off a goat and the carcass had been flung to the centre circle of the parched ground, and they waited for the game to begin. For the previous twenty-four hours the carcass had been soaked in cold water to make it stronger. Both teams were mujahedin, Islamic fighters who had slipped back from the war in Afghanistan to visit their families in the untamed lands of the North West frontier.

The players were on horseback, about thirty of them. There were two teams, one wearing black quilted jackets and the other turned out in dull yellow. They had numbers on their backs. I never saw the signal that started the game but a rider swooped down, picked up the carcass, held it close against the flank of his horse and rode towards a pole. Another rider headed him off and the other horses closed in. There was a ruck, of animals, of men shouting, whips in the air, rearing horses, their hooves landing on the backs of the other animals. The riders never blinked in the maul, careless of the whips and the flailing hooves. They scrapped together, yanking, hauling, pulling at the goat. A bearded man wrestled the carcass onto the front of his horse and tried to break away, but another rider, leaning far out of his saddle, clung to the dead animal's leg and neither man would give way until once again the other riders circled them. It continued like this – hard riding, brute strength, a struggle in the saddle – until a rider snatched the headless goat free, rounded a pole and carried it back to the centre circle. The crowd, only men, on the sun-bleached white mud walls shouted out their approval.

It was 1988 and I was about to travel with the mujahedin, with men like this, into Afghanistan, to go undercover, to dress like them, to be like them. In the West they were romanticized, fêted for their courage, for their resistance to the Soviets. The CIA was spending millions supporting them but, as I sat on my haunches watching, I realized how little we knew them. It mattered only that they were our enemy's enemy. When the game was over there was the smell of horses, of men, of sweat and days-old sweat, of droppings, all stirred up in the heat and the dust, and the muja-hedin commander praised Allah and the men felt good. This had been the ancient game of Buzkashi.

The day before I was due to cross the border we went to a hospital in Peshawar, in Pakistan. The wards, the corridors and the courtyards were full of men – particularly young boys – without legs and arms. All had been injured by mines, by the millions of butterfly mines that had been floated down into Afghanistan's tracks and passes. To curious children they looked like toys, but under the gentle pressure of a child's foot they exploded. Others were cam-ouflaged as stones and pieces of rock. They were hard to detect, and they took off a leg. At the hospital the boys were learning to walk with artificial limbs. I looked at the younger boys who would never run again or kick a ball. They all seemed strangely contented, at peace with themselves, quiet and uncomplaining. They had been told that they were special, that they had been injured in a holy war and in the next life would be honoured above others.

There were so many boys and wounded for what? For a super-power's ambition. And in pursuit of that, millions of mines had been seeded. I turned away. I had to. The longer I stayed in the hospital the harder it would be to go into Afghanistan and risk the same as these boys. The smell of disinfectant, the bandaged stumps, the metal tread of the prosthetics on a stone floor. It was all closing in on me, unsettling me, demanding an answer as to why I was doing this for one of television's fleeting moments.

That evening we stayed at the Intercontinental Hotel in Pesha-war and I decided I needed a drink, which was a mistake. The country was dry but in certain hotels non-Muslims could drink alcohol in special rooms. I went to reception and said I wanted a drink. I was told to wait and then the assistant manager asked me to follow him. He carried a bunch of keys and we walked down a dark corridor until we came to a door, which he unlocked. Inside, he switched on a light; the room was windowless and smelt of stale air. He asked me what I wanted and I said a beer. The room was small, bare-walled and wood-panelled. The man left me for a few minutes and returned with one bottle, which he opened. It was the most miserable beer in my life, a drink unshared in a cell-like room. It felt like a last drink, a condemned man's drink, and I half expected to hear the shout 'dead man walking' as I scurried down the corridor back to my room.

The next day I flew to Quetta in Baluchistan. I was joined by Rafi Ameer and Peter Jouvenal, the most experienced cameraman covering the war in Afghanistan. He spoke Pashto and was gritty and courageous. At Quetta airport we were met by two men from the National Islamic Front for Afghanistan, one of the mujahedin groups. They did not take us into the city but to a brick house standing on the edge of a field where we had to change into Afghan clothes. I dressed in a loose-fitting light-olive shalwar and a long tunic that came down to my knees. On my head I wore a light-brown pakol, a flat, round woollen hat with a rolled brim. I had grown a few day's stubble but with my blue eyes I doubted whether I would pass as an Afghan fighter. Our escorts were unconcerned. Apparently there was an Afghan tribe with eyes like mine. They told me to stay silent at the roadblocks and to pretend I was sleeping. They would explain I was sick and had lost my voice. All of this was necessary because the Pakistanis did not want foreigners, particularly journalists, travelling into Afghanistan and seeing the extent to which they were supplying and supporting the mujahedin.

We left at once for Afghanistan in a Toyota Land Cruiser and headed for the border town of Chaman. Just outside the town we were stopped at a roadblock by Pakistani police. The light was fading and the policeman shone a torch at me as I lay slumped in the back, my pakol pulled down low. It was a casual check and we were waved through. We drove into the night, a jarring, jolting ride over a rough mountain track. I never knew when we left Pakistan but sometime during the hours of darkness we stopped beside some caves and bunkers. This was Toba, a forward supply base for several mujahedin groups, and in the vehicle lights I glimpsed the scale of the operation supporting the resistance. There were ammunition boxes piled high and racks of rockets and shells, most of them paid for by the United States.

There were men here, fighters swathed in ammunition who embraced each other. They carried 122 mm rockets and stacked them on the floor of the jeep. I looked at Peter and asked, half jokingly, 'We're not going to drive like this, are we?' and he nodded. The men threw in some bags of flour and a few cans of diesel fuel and we drove further into Afghanistan with shells bouncing under my feet. Behind us were two open-backed vehicles with a handful of fighters.

By dawn we were driving through narrow streams and dried-up river beds. I was still worried about the shells on the floor and asked about mines. The men shrugged. If it happened, it was God's will. As we left the cover of the hills our convoy, leaving a long dust trail, stood out in the vast landscape. I kept swivelling my head, looking for Soviet helicopter gunships. It was a waste of energy. We were totally in the hands of these fighters. Their risks were our risks and there was nothing I could do to change them.

As we got closer to Kandahar it became warmer and greener. We stopped in a pomegranate grove and were joined by other fighters. There was an ease about them, a lot of laughter. They liked this way of life. Just men together at war. And when they tired of fighting or wanted a woman they returned to their families in the refugee camps across the border.

They all knew the Soviet troops were heading home, their will to stay in this wild country broken, but the mujahedin did not want them withdrawing with pride and leaving behind a friendly government. They wanted to humiliate them and to taste the victory. One of the men slung a light tripod off his back and set it up on the ground. Another man, who had been walking with a rocket on his shoulder, placed it inside the tripod tube and together they aimed it at the city's airport, which was still controlled by the Soviets. A fighter peered along the line of sight and then ran a cable twenty metres away and fired. The rocket, in a flash of orange and a flurry of dust, headed towards the city. It was imprecise but that did not matter. These attacks were almost daily and were a way of wearing down the enemy.

More pick-ups arrived, overflowing with fighters. One truck had an anti-aircraft gun which was there to protect a guerrilla commander. He was Hamad Gailani, the son of Sayyad Ahmed Gailani, one of the more moderate mujahedin leaders. Before the Soviets invaded he had been a Peugeot dealer in Kabul. His son had been educated in the West and spoke English. He was not a natural guerrilla leader and did not belong in the hills. He had spent too long away, but if he was to have influence in the future he had to fight. Afghanistan's future leaders would grow out of the war.

We were now a convoy of eight or nine trucks with perhaps fifty or sixty fighters. As the light faded we moved into the city. Some tracer rounds flew towards us, but the fighters did not even shift in their seats. The streets were empty and dark and we stopped in the courtyard of a house. There was food waiting for us and we sat together and drank tea. The attack, I was told, would be at dawn. There was a Soviet post a short distance from where we were staying. We had no body armour or helmets and I wanted to know what we were getting into. The fighters did not want to bother with explaining, all we had to do was follow them. It seemed this was a regular, almost daily attack. The mujahedin would pepper the post with automatic fire and rocket-propelled grenades. The Soviet troops would always fire back and one or two fighters would be killed or injured. We talked in the candlelight – half-lit faces, a flickering orange light on one side and shadow on the other, men sitting together on their haunches picking at their beards.

What was the point of the operation, I wanted to know. The commander saw that I was sceptical. His men did not expect to take this small base, he explained. The purpose of the attack was to demoralize the Soviets, to make them feel isolated in a foreign land. This was a slow war of strangulation. The attacks often began as the first call to prayer echoed across the city. For the fighters this was a holy war, a chance for martyrdom, and the men around me were relaxed. There was none of the tension that I had seen elsewhere before men went into action. These fighters were nonchalant, unconcerned; some were already sleeping soundly, slumped on the floor.

As I sat there I decided I did not want to go on this operation. Something had unsettled me. Perhaps it was the ready acceptance of a few casualties, perhaps it was going into battle with men whose view of life and its value was so different from my own. Peter was willing to film it, but for once in my life I said, 'No.' The commander was disappointed. He wanted the video of his men in action to raise more money and recruits. I could see a glance of contempt in the faces of the fighters who were awake. To them I was showing fear and they did not respect that. I lay on the ground but did not sleep, unhappy with my decision but fearful of joining them and their war.

Before it was even light the fighters had crept away. A few remained with us and we withdrew from the city to the outskirts. There were useful shots to be filmed. The roads were littered with rusting, blackened shells that had once been Soviet armour – armoured personnel carriers, tanks, trucks. In the space of a mile there were a hundred destroyed vehicles. The Soviets and the Afghan government now supplied their bases by air. The roads were too dangerous.

Later we were rejoined by the other fighters. The attack had gone well and there had been no casualties. The men were cheerful, buoyed up by the fight, by the bond of having been in something together, of having risked their lives. We drove to a dam not far from Kandahar. The reason for going was unexplained. We climbed and below us was a light turquoise lake set amidst grey barren rocks. At the summit was a concrete building that overlooked the dam and was either a control room or an office. The track that led to it was bordered on each side by high rocks. As our convoy drew up there were shouts and gunmen pointed their weapons at us. They were another group of mujahedin. An argument followed and before I could get out of the Land Cruiser I heard safety catches coming off and men were diving behind rocks and taking up firing positions, ready to fight. We were right in the middle, stuck in a vehicle unable to reach the relative safety of a boulder. I lay on the floor and waited for the shooting to start. Then I heard voices and the talking resumed. A negotiation. I left the vehicle and found a rock in case the talks broke down. The mujahedin at the dam feared we had come to seize it, to take away their prize from them. Our group could stay but they had to line their weapons up against a wall. There were so many different groups: factions, families, tribes, old friendships. Deals were made and deals were broken. Men embraced and men fought. Alliances were sealed and then shifted. And all these groups were armed. There was a common enemy in the Soviets but once they were gone I was certain there would be no peace in this lawless country.

After the stand-off, a chance to relax. The commander announced we were going fishing. When he said it, I laughed. It seemed so incongruous, so out of place. We found some rocks overlooking deep water and I sat in the sun, breathing deeply, easing the strain, waiting for some rods to appear and wondering what the fish would be like. A fighter pulled a grenade from his belt, removed the cap, held it for a couple of seconds and then dropped it in the water. The explosion echoed off the rocks and the other men walked over to see what was caught, what fish floated to the surface. The blast stunned the fish, explained one of the fighters. We all peered down and eventually two white fish lay on the water; there were cries of approval as one of the fighters jumped in and pulled them out. More grenades followed. The fish were grilled on a stick and then broken into pieces and wrapped in chapatis. The men chewed cautiously, occasionally spitting out the tiny fragments of shrapnel. I was not altogether surprised when – after a few more grenades – the fish had disappeared.

So we roamed, a band of fighters, in a harsh desert landscape. Occasionally we passed other groups. Loose affiliations. Rivalries concealed. There seemed little coordination. This was a war of wandering, of random rocket firing, of the impulsive attack, but these men were winning. I needed to get back across the mountains to Pakistan and for the return journey Hamad Gailani and his men handed us over to another group that was part of his organization.

Our escort was also a commander. The fighters embraced his hand and showed him respect with a slight tilt of the head. He was an older man with a long, flowing white beard and a leathered, craggy face. His name was Haji Latif and his nom de guerre was the Lion of Kandahar. He was in his seventies and was a legendary fighter. He had a bandoleer of bullets slung across his chest and wore a captured Soviet pistol in his belt. There were stories about him, how he rode a motorbike into battle.

I never did discover why he escorted us. Maybe he was heading for Pakistan anyway. He sat in the passenger seat of his four-by-four, his fighters clinging to the back. When we stopped for prayers and tea I tried to talk with him. He was slightly amused by my interest and attention. He was proud of having fought the Soviets for nine years and wanted to kill some more, but only because he was defending his land. He was an unbending, fierce man as hard as the terrain, but he was not a fanatic. He was the kind of leader I thought the West was backing but, as I discovered, there were others who got a far larger share of the weapons.

We crossed the border and a few days later I was in Peshawar interviewing another guerrilla leader, Gulbuddin Hekmatyar. I wanted to see him because he was the favoured man – the commander to whom the Pakistanis were channelling the best equipment. Most of it was paid for by the United States. I had heard stories about Hekmatyar. He was the extreme face of the mujahedin. His men were accused of murdering a journalist. He himself was said to have thrown acid in the face of a young unveiled woman at Kabul university.

His headquarters were in a middle-class suburb on the edge of the city. His men were sullen, cold and hostile. We were made to stand, to wait. Eventually we were invited in and Hekmatyar appeared. He scarcely concealed his contempt. I offered my hand but he ignored it. He wore a black turban and underneath it his eyes were wary and hard. I thanked him for talking to us and gave a half-smile, but there was no response. I asked him whether he was grateful to the West, to America, for backing the war against the Soviets. He refused to acknowledge any Western help and said all his weapons had been captured in battle. It was a lie that he delivered comfortably. I asked him about the future of women in Afghanistan. He questioned what it had to do with me, a non-Muslim. I said there were women's groups who were concerned that if he gained power their freedom would be curtailed, but he would not discuss it with me. I then asked him about the incident when he was said to have thrown acid at an unveiled woman. He dismissed it as rumour and decided the interview was over, walking away without even a goodbye. At around the time we were there an all-woman camera crew went to interview him. He refused to shake their hands and said he was 'insulted' that a news organization had sent women to see him.

Afterwards I felt an intense anger. The Americans were so focused on defeating the Soviets in Afghanistan that they were prepared to back the most hard-line Islamic groups with a leader who chanted 'Death to America' at his rallies. We were the infidel and I felt it in Hekmatyar's chilling disdain. There was not a shred of gratitude to the West for helping to free his homeland.

Before I left Pakistan I met another, younger, man from the Afghanistan National Islamic Front. He was welcoming, urbane, with a wry sense of humour. He wore no cap or turban, his head was shaven and he liked to pass his hand over it while he thought. He wore a light-olive, almost white, shalwar. We spoke in a shaded garden. The mujahedin were winning, he said, but he feared for his country. The rifts between the groups were becoming 'larger and more dangerous'. Some of the more hard-line parties, he complained, were receiving the best weapons. 'That would be a disaster for Afghanistan,' he predicted. His name was Hamid Kharzai.

Hekmatyar did not gain power, but the extreme fundamentalists did and the result was the harsh rule of the Taliban. Their most famous guest was another extreme guerrilla leader, Osama bin Laden.

Within a year of my visit the Lion of Kandahar was dead; he had been poisoned, probably by agents of the Soviet-backed Afghan government.

Hamid Kharzai's worst fears came true and it was only after the Taliban were overthrown with American help that he became Afghanistan's new leader.

13

Dancing Bears and Brezhnev's Chair

It was the strangest of train journeys. Just a few passengers and we were all locked inside the carriages. A soldier, a British soldier, threaded a heavy chain through the handles of the door. There were enough rations to survive a three-day siege and each soldier was issued with ten rounds of ammunition. The waiters in the restaurant car wore pressed white dinner jackets and bent stiffly over starched tablecloths and bone-china crockery. The meal cost sixty-two pence and the bottle of wine, eighty-two pence; the prices had gone unchanged for twenty years. It was like travelling on the old Brighton Belle, but we were behind the Iron Curtain and this was the British Military Train.

The year was 1981 and the Cold War simmered. The train ran from Brunswick in West Germany through East Germany to Berlin. It had been operating daily since 1945, along a rail corridor that the West had insisted on and the Soviets had reluctantly agreed to. It was a service with its own frontline rituals of East meeting West.

The only passengers who could use the train were British military personnel and their families. As soon as we crossed into East Germany, past the control towers and wire fences, the train stopped. The West German engine was uncoupled and was replaced by a Soviet-designed diesel. Then three British officers marched down the platform and saluted three Soviet officers. Documents had to be handed over, detailing who was on board, before the Soviets allowed us to pass. I was not on the list and neither was my cameraman. If the Soviets had known about us they might well have created an incident. In earlier times all the window blinds had to be drawn and British soldiers were warned not to look out of the windows. The restrictions had eased a little but even so it was considered too sensitive to film the quaint plat-form ceremony.

Then the train lurched forward and we travelled through East Germany. In the toilet I was shown a spy hole that enabled the soldiers to steal a few pictures of tank parks or soldiers or anything else behind the Curtain. This was the looking-glass war with all its games and customs.

In West Berlin the British military flew me along part of the Berlin Wall, which ran for over a hundred kilometres. The wall itself was plain, as if knocked up in a hurry with an eye to cost; a line of faded white concrete panels about twelve feet high. This was the outer perimeter. A hundred yards in front of the wall was an electrified fence. There were ditches, tank traps, spotlights, auto-matic firing devices, steel-mesh mats with long protruding nails and German shepherd dogs that roamed on long leashes. All of this just to hem a people in. It made East Berlin appear as a vast prison camp patrolled by 15,000 border troops. The wall was twenty years old when I flew along it and was the Cold War's defining architec-ture. It was at once familiar but still shocking. The sheer scale, the immense effort to maintain it, the fear that built it. It was one of the moments when I felt an intense anger, a helpless frustration. Since it had been built in 1961, several thousand had escaped and over fifty had been killed trying to flee. Many more had been caught.

The helicopter landed and the British troops took me to a platform close to an East German control tower, and there we eyeballed each other. East against West. A long stare across the wall. The East Germans pulled out binoculars and we did the same. There was never a wave or a smile, just an icy stare. As we turned to go I noticed a woman at a window of an apartment block on the other side of the wall. She was waving at an older man who stood close to us. He took his hat off and held it across his chest in what seemed like a gesture of respect. Then he drew out from his suit pocket a crisp white handkerchief and waved it. The woman waved back and the man dropped a tear. He did not want to talk to us and walked away with heavy shoulders. Who they were and what their relationship was I never found out, but this was another ritual – two human beings reaching out to each other in a divided city.

In August 1981 I got to cross into East Berlin for a day. The East Germans were celebrating the twentieth anniversary of the building of the wall. There was ritual here too. The speakers on the lamp posts pummelled us with stirring Party and patriotic songs. Red flags, like giant curtains, were paraded before a viewing stand. Ten thousand members of the Workers' Militia goose-stepped down Karl Marx Allee in their grey-green uniforms. I happened to be close to the East German Communist leader as he arrived. Erich Honecker wore a white straw hat with a black band which he took off before he climbed onto the platform. He was a bleak, austere man. A grey apparatchik whose lies were as bold as the wall he had ordered to be built. He never referred to it as 'the wall'; it was always the 'the anti-fascist protection wall'. It had, he told the crowd, saved humanity from World War Three and had prevented an invasion from the West. I wondered then about a whole society living a lie. Were any of the border guards puzzled as to why the tank traps were set to prevent a break-out rather than a break-in, or did they just bury the lie? I looked into the ranks of the militia, the so-called fighting groups. Many were distracted, far away, talking to each other as Honecker's seventeen-minute speech flowed over them. Perhaps that was the answer; they just went along with it. Then everyone sang the 'Internationale' and Young Pioneers ran through the ranks of the militia and presented them with carnations. There was nothing German about the ceremony. It was a copy, a Socialist order of service drawn straight from Moscow's manual. Any hope of change seemed remote.

In 1989 I returned to East Berlin. There had been daily demonstrations, in places like Leipzig, demanding democracy and free elections. The Party had hesitated to use force against its own people, uncertain of Moscow's backing. I arrived in the city on 9 November without a crew. They were flying into West Berlin later that night. The Central Committee of the Communist Party was in special session. I left the Grand Hotel where I was staying and walked down to the building where the Party was meeting. Red drapes still hung from the building and a few old-timers wore Lenin badges in their lapels, but outside there were clusters of people locked in intense argument. Everywhere, there was expectation and rumour. People stopped me to ask what was happening. In those

few encounters I began to sense the Party was finished. Its authority
lay in certainty, in playing the leading role. The crowd knew the
demonstrators had laid down a challenge and the Party had to give
its answer. The longer it paused, the quicker its grip on power
weakened.

It was 6.55 in the evening when a senior Party official gave a
news conference. I was at the back of the hall when Guenther
Schabowski used these words: 'If you want to go, you are free to
leave.' It was difficult to know exactly what he meant. Someone
said the Party had agreed to open the wall but I found it impossible
to believe. I returned to my hotel and switched on the news, but
there was no mention of the announcement. I could not verify the
story and, as the evening wore on, I doubted it. I lay on my bed and
fell asleep. A short time later I was woken by shouts in the street,
which I thought was unusual for East Berlin. As I lay there I picked
out the word *'Freiheit'*, 'freedom', shouted over and over again. I
looked out of the window and there were groups of people walking
and calling *'Freiheit'* to each other. I raced from my room and
headed through the dimly lit streets towards Checkpoint Charlie,
one of the crossing points to West Berlin. As I walked there were
people, couples, groups, tumbling out of apartment buildings and
falling in beside us. Many of them were young, their faces alive,
daring to believe. Suddenly, it seemed, we were no longer individuals but a crowd, drawn close by hope. As we got near to the
checkpoint we slowed together. No one was leading but we all
moved more cautiously. From the West German side we could hear
cheering, the sounds of a party, of celebration. In that moment,
defined by a distant sound, some around me knew their world had
changed and they embraced, their tears running onto their friends'
shoulders. Ahead of us were East German guards but they looked
unsure of their role and stood back in the shadows. Beyond them
on the other side of Checkpoint Charlie was a bear, a dancing bear
up on its legs. Someone placed an East German border guard's cap
on its head and the crowd laughed and drank from bottles. Then a
middle-aged couple walked past me towards the checkpoint and
kept walking. Just two ordinary anonymous people. The crowd fell
silent and watched this slow agonizing walk into history. The guards
did not stop them. They just checked out. On the West German

side there was a roar and the couple were embraced, swallowed up in celebration. A man hugged me. A complete stranger. We never exchanged a word.

Then I had a slice of luck. Beside the dancing bear was Jenny Clayton, my producer, and Lex Tudhope, the cameraman. Somehow we all saw each other and they walked across to the East. Now on one of history's nights – one I had nearly slept through – I was there, living it, and able to capture it on camera. Together we walked towards the Brandenburg Gate, a historic gathering point when the city was undivided.

We were separated from the gate by the wall and a line of East German police. We were cautious about breaching their lines and stopped beside them. The crowds around us were growing. From across the wall we could hear the sounds of cheering, of chanting, of music. A man in a black leather jacket and blue jeans appeared on top of the wall. He stood there, legs apart, his arms outstretched, his fingers spread in a gesture of victory. He became the focus for the crowd, as if this man held the key to the moment. Only a short time before he would have been shot. Some East German guards turned a fire-hose on him but it seemed half-hearted and soon others were on top of the wall, stamping on it, celebrating their defiance.

As we waited, I noticed army trucks arriving and border guards getting out to our left and to our right. They were clearly visible, back-lit by an orange light. We all feared that shooting might start and we looked for cover, for a place to run to, but the guards stood around as if waiting for orders. Then some young men jumped off the wall into East Berlin and walked towards the police lines where we were standing. They were smiling and offered their hands to the police, who did not know whether to shake them or arrest them. And in those gestures of hesitation, of uncertainty, of bewilderment, the authority of the German Democratic Republic, with its feared secret police, the Stasi, crumbled. It is the curse of authoritarian regimes that at the moment they reform themselves and relax their grip they are at their most vulnerable. The crowd around us sensed it and was no longer afraid. A couple with a sparkler walked towards the wall, shrugging off police requests to stay back, but the request had been polite, pleading, and only emboldened others to follow.

They showed no hostility towards the police, they just humiliated them. A West German girl kissed one of them. He did not smile or flinch, he just stood there. Flowers arrived and were placed in the policemen's hands. They did not know whether to hold them or throw them to the ground. There were no orders for this. One of them broke ranks and smiled and the crowd cheered. They were now in charge, orchestrating this event.

The police held their line, but people streamed through it anyway. Backwards and forwards to the wall. Some were pulled up and stood looking down on two halves of a divided city. A man was passed a pickaxe and began chipping pieces off. Surely now, I thought, force would be used, but it was already too late. The people had tasted freedom and without terrible bloodshed it could not be taken away from them. We stayed there most of the night filming a revolution, savouring the moments when every stranger was a friend, when everything seemed possible.

A few hours later thousands of people were queuing to cross into West Berlin. 'We were like children,' said one woman, 'we couldn't wait.' The Party had said passports had to be stamped but on that first day many did not bother. They were just eager to cross to the other side. Some took their cars, their spluttering Trabants, and toured around West Berlin. At times the crowd was so dense I put Lex Tudhope on my shoulders and we filmed like that.

Some of those crossing to the West said that they still wanted to preserve Socialism, but when they returned, clutching their plastic shopping bags and having seen the stores on the other side, they were less certain. I knew, then, that the idea of two free Germanies existing side by side would not survive and, even though it was premature to talk of reunification, it seemed inevitable to me and I reported it.

That evening the Communist Party held a rally. They were still nominally in power. They stood together, fists clenched, holding up their Party cards, singing the 'Internationale'. They sang with passion, as if to convince themselves it was another time. These were the Party hacks, the apparatchiks, the factory managers, the elite. Instead of the once all-powerful Party they seemed like a small sect wrapping themselves around with the old tunes and slogans.

The General Secretary of the Communist Party and a former

head of the secret police was Egon Krenz. He was a sharp-faced
man, middle-aged and grey-haired, who looked more like a sales-
man than a Party official. As he left the rally I stopped him and a
crowd gathered around us. In other times it would have been
impossible to get to the Party leader. 'Are you prepared to lose
power?' I asked him. He took a step towards me and said, 'When
we talk about power we don't mean political power in the sense of
personal power. We mean the power of the working class which I
have fought for my whole life. That we can't give up.' He was still
clinging on, playing with language, offering free elections but insisting that the working class came out ahead, with the Party as its
standard bearer, no doubt. I asked him whether the two Germanies
might become one nation. A sneer crossed his face. 'I go along with
a Frenchman,' he said, 'who once said I love Germany so much
that I am glad there are two of them.' And so his minders laughed,
the hollow laughs of men who knew deep down that it was over.

Before I left Berlin I went down to the wall and joined the
chippers and the hammerers. I borrowed a tool and prised out a
piece of wall coloured by graffiti. I wanted to play a small part in
knocking it down, and brought a chunk home for my children.

The hammers against the wall echoed across Eastern Europe,
beating out the message that Moscow would not use force to
preserve its empire. So peaceful, velvet revolutions broke out
elsewhere and Communism receded. Only in the Soviet Union
itself did Lenin's successors hold on to power. In August 1991,
I was driving home from Italy with my family. We were in Austria
when I heard on the radio that something had happened to President Gorbachev of the Soviet Union. I could not fully understand
the German station I was listening to but it seemed tanks were
on the streets in Moscow. I pulled off the autobahn and called
London. There had been a coup and they wanted me to go to
Moscow immediately.

We drove hard, without stopping, through Germany, Belgium
and France until we reached Calais and the car ferry home. All the
time I was flicking between the radio stations. Party hardliners had
seized power – men who hankered after the old certainties. They
announced that President Gorbachev was on vacation in the Crimea
because of his health and that a state of emergency was in force. In

Moscow there was resistance to the tanks and armoured vehicles. Boris Yeltsin, the leader of the Russian Federation, said 'it was a coup by criminals' and called for a general strike. People were building barricades around the Russian parliament and some military units were refusing to back the coup. The Soviet Union, it seemed, was on the brink of civil war and the world was holding its breath.

By the time I reached Moscow the coup was faltering. The plotters – some of whom were drunk – had misjudged their own society. People had lost their fear. Thousands of them surrounded the tanks, daring the soldiers to kill them. Some shots were fired but the tank commanders hesitated and, as the hours passed, the will to fight evaporated. Coups need speed, ruthlessness and fear to succeed and the old guard lacked all three.

When I met the people on the barricades by the Russian parliament, the so-called White House, they knew they had won. They remained there beside the burned-out cars, the trucks, the metal poles, but more out of choice than necessity. Many were weary and red-eyed but they wanted to be interviewed, to tell the story again, to claim their moment. They were reluctant to drift home, to resume the ordinary, to let go the bond of standing shoulder to shoulder at the barricades. There was nothing to define these people; they were students, factory workers, women who worked in a bakery, and what the Russians like to call intellectuals. Before this moment they did not know of each other. They had all, each of them, just left their apartment buildings to defend a hope. They did not want a return to Stalinism or the sullen days of Brezhnev. In an underpass or out on one of Moscow's main streets they discovered they were not alone and, having risked everything, they were determined not to be ignored.

The tanks withdrew, the coup leaders fled, and President Gorbachev returned from the Crimea. As he came down the aircraft steps he seemed unsteady, unsure of what awaited him. He wore a pale windcheater, a grey v-necked sweater and an open-necked shirt. Behind him came his wife, Raisa, with a blanket thrown over the shoulder of their granddaughter. In that one protective gesture they seemed vulnerable, like a family that had lost everything in a fire or a tragedy. At the foot of the steps Gorbachev smiled, a coy

half-smile of a man hoping, but not certain, that he would be taken
back.

Shortly after this he re-affirmed his faith in the Communist Party
and its leading role in society, conveniently ignoring the fact that it
was Party hardliners that had staged the coup. I was with Alexander
Yakovlev, who had been Gorbachev's chief presidential adviser and
a close friend. He was in his sixties, a clever man, a survivor of the
system and committed to reform. He was taken aback by Gorbachev's speech. 'Gorbachev,' he said, 'thinks the country and the
people are the same.' He shook his head sadly and said, 'The people
have become absolutely different.' In his heavily accented English
he put all the emphasis on the word 'absolutely' and repeated it.

Gorbachev withdrew behind the Kremlin walls, picking up his
old routine, but he continued to misjudge the mood. The crowds
did not want a shuffling of the Party pack. They blamed the Party
for supporting the coup and when they chanted it was for Yeltsin,
not Gorbachev. On the Saturday night, 24 August, Gorbachev bowed
to the inevitable and resigned as General Secretary of the Party. He
also recommended that the Central Committee dissolve itself. It
was the day that Communism in the Soviet Union ended. After
seventy-four years the Party, that had ruled through terror and fear,
was dismissed in a press statement read on television.

Gorbachev's statement was read by an aide. I caught it on a
black-and-white TV screen in the lobby of the Intourist Hotel.
Someone translated his words for me. I needed it repeated to me
so I could take it in. A man in a flat, emotionless voice read, 'The
Central Committee of the Communist Party of the Soviet Union
should take the difficult but honest decision to disband itself.'
The Party that had launched the Russian Revolution in 1917 was
winding itself up. I looked around for reaction but there was little.
Most people continued chatting or drinking coffee, seemingly unin-
terested in this momentous announcement. I felt like jumping on a
chair and shouting, 'The Communist Party, with over twenty million
members, has given up power.' This was not just any political party,
this was the Party that had controlled their lives and that had
claimed for itself the leading role in society. Now the great
smothering embrace had been lifted.

We went outside onto the street with our cameras ready but this

Russian revolution was to be seen not in great demonstrations, or in the tearing down of a wall, but in countless cameos. That evening a few young men on skateboards and rollerblades weaved in and out of the traffic. They carried Russian not Soviet flags. A policeman blew his whistle and tried to stop them, but they no longer had any fear of authority and in their laughs and whistles and catcalls I caught a hint of celebration.

The morning after Communism ended, two men in their thirties turned up at a country club owned by the Central Committee of the Communist Party. It was an exclusive club outside Moscow, with tennis courts and swimming pools. Only senior Party officials could use it. The two men walked past the red-bricked guard post and headed towards the grass and the courts. The guard shouted at them but they ignored him. Moments later a black Volga came down the drive at speed. A man wearing a tracksuit top jumped out and said to the two men, 'You can't come in here.' He was the manager, with the fleshy face of so many apparatchiks. The two men, wearing blue caps and carrying rackets, faced up to him. 'This is the only place in the area where ordinary people can come and relax,' they said. The manager told them sternly, 'This is for the Party.' And they laughed at him, a long glorious mocking laugh. 'We're just sick and tired of Communism and Leninism and all that rubbish,' said the younger man. And he enjoyed using these words, they still had an edge of danger about them. They were words I felt he had stored up and dreamed of using some day, and this was his moment. The other man did not want to lose out, he wanted some of the manager's anger for himself. 'Yeah,' he chimed in, 'we're off to play tennis.' The manager was taken aback. He had never had to make a case before. Finally, after his threats were shrugged off, he said, 'How could the club be managed if it was open to ordinary people?' 'Just charge ordinary prices,' said one of the men, and together they strode off, a slow loping taunting walk across the Party's privileged turf.

In those days after Communism, there were strange encounters. I met Yuri Prokofiev, the former Moscow Party boss. He had been in the room when the Party hardliners had issued their announce- ment of the coup. He was now in police custody and was being taken back to his office. A short while before I would have struggled to get close to him. He would have brushed me off. He would have been untouchable and powerful. Now he looked caged and haunted. All the swagger of privilege gone. Just a small man in a grey raincoat and a flat grey hat. I asked him why he had launched the coup. 'I tell you,' he said, pointing at me, 'I was simply invited to the meeting. I did not know anything.' He was already lining up his defence. He had been in the room but was not part of the plot. And he rolled out his excuses. 'The coup was a farce,' he told me, 'a piece of theatre designed to destroy the Party once and for all.' I did not really listen to him; I just watched him, savouring a moment I never expected. A Soviet Communist Party boss standing in front of me, pleading and pathetic.

With the Party disbanded no one knew who was in charge or who to refer to. It was a great moment to be in television. We turned up at the Central Committee building in Moscow and asked to go inside. The Central Committee was the most powerful body in the old Soviet Union. A guard just let us in and we wandered its empty corridors, down a long red carpet, past heavy wooden doors. He went to the room where the Party secretariat used to meet. There was a long polished table with twenty dark leather chairs. On the table were glass ashtrays and sharpened pencils in glass jars. The wall had a black-and-white portrait of Lenin. A diary, on a desk, lay open at the date of 19 August, the day of the coup and the hardliners' last desperate gamble. The chair at the end of the table was reserved for the General Secretary of the Party. It had been there since Leonid Brezhnev's day. This was Brezhnev's chair. Andropov had sat there. Chernyenko too, and Gorbachev. I sat down and leaned back. The Communist Party had been so feared and yet here I was in Brezhnev's chair. It was impossible to believe. All that history I had read at school and university. The Lenin Station. The purges. The Great War. The gulags. Stalin. The trigger-tempered Khrushchev. The Cuban Crisis. All that weight of history and I was leaning back in the General Secretary's chair imagining the meetings, the decisions taken here. I had a deep desire to carve my name on the table or to lift Lenin's portrait from the wall and tuck it inside my jacket to preserve a memory, but in the end I settled for a piece to camera.

So we roamed through the holy of holies, opening doors, examining files. In one Party building we went to the encryption room from which coded messages had been sent. In the West there was a huge fear of Soviet might, of the Red Army, of the KGB, but the encoding machines seemed laughably ancient. On the floor was the final message sent to all Party managers informing them of the coup and demanding they follow orders.

Then there were chance conversations. I ran into Andre Kachin, a Party official, who was now unemployed and in shock. Unemployed. He swilled the word around his mouth and spat it out. He told me it did not even appear in the Soviet dictionary. Unemployment was one of the differences between Socialism and Capitalism. Yet he was now without work and sought my advice.

And an older man who remembered a child's poem. 'Winter has gone. Summer has come. Thanks to the Party.' That is what they had been taught. Now the Party was no more. It had been a great father figure, a fixed point in his life, but it was gone and he felt a little insecure; I detected a note of creeping nostalgia for the old order.

We went to the office of the Tass news agency, the mouthpiece of the Party. Alexander Yakovlev, the reformer, was meeting the journalists. They crowded into a smoky room, sullen and demoralized. They were living through one of the world's great stories but did not know how to report it. They were used to being fed the Party line. That was the story and there was no truth outside it. They wanted to know what to do. 'Just give objective information,' Yakovlev told them. They stood there silently absorbing this advice. One of the journalists finally found his voice. 'How,' he asked, 'should we report someone like Saddam Hussein? He has always been a friend of the Soviet Union.' Yakovlev was impatient. 'We must stop this,' he said. 'Let's agree. Tell the truth. That is all.' They looked away, averting their eyes as if in shame. Party hacks without a party to serve.

That week I stood in Dzherzhinsky Square, outside KGB headquarters, and watched five cranes tie a metal noose around the statue of Felix Dzherzhinsky, the first head of the Cheka, the secret police and the forerunner of the KGB. Then, this statue, this figure in a long coat, swung in the Moscow night, lit by camera flashes. And an era ended.

14

The Great Escape from China

Sometimes, but rarely, I have had a scoop. An exclusive. On this occasion it emerged unexpectedly from a chance meeting in a Hong Kong apartment. As I walked away, down the hill to the Jaffe Road and Wan Chai, I felt that rush, that sudden hit, the reporter's high of having an untold story. It burns a hole in your pocket. You are possessive of it, protective of it. You worry about it. And in this case I knew that it would be at least six weeks before I could broadcast it.

It was 1991 and after Tiananmen Square. Just two words but everyone knew immediately what you were referring to. It was one of those events that had entered collective memory. The students occupying the square and unfurling a carnival of protest. The parading of a foam-and-plaster Goddess of Democracy. A twenty-one-year-old student in pyjamas lecturing Communist Party leader Li Peng. It had been a heady, exuberant springtime in Beijing with the square a fairground of speeches and ideas. Then the crushing. Hundreds or possibly thousands killed as the ageing leadership of the Communist Party sent in the army. And the enduring image. A young man, with arms raised, standing in the path of a tank. A last hopeless, reckless gesture. The world watched angry and impotent as China closed the door and waited for memories to fade.

It was less than two years after Tiananmen Square that we decided to go back into China undercover. It had proved almost impossible to report from there openly. We hoped to meet some of the student leaders and discover what had happened to the pro-democracy movement. The project was ambitious, even risky. The very idea of a Caucasian male going undercover, blending in among the Chinese, seemed faintly absurd but I was drawn to the challenge.

I flew alone to Hong Kong. Some contacts in London had given me an introduction to a young man who worked for a group that was campaigning for democracy in China. He did not want to meet in one of the large hotels so I took the Star ferry from Central to Tsim She Tsui and walked to an address in Kowloon. The street was narrow, choking with people, and the signs and awnings kept the light low. Even in the morning the traders hung red-shaded lights over what they were selling. The man had directed me to look out for a tall stack of caged chickens. He had a room above the adjacent shop. It was busy with people and might have been an office but there were few books or files. The man was in his early twenties, had thick hair and wore glasses. He sent the others away and we talked together in English.

I had no choice but to trust him. I said that we wanted to go into China and meet some of those who had led the student protests. We would travel as tourists with small cameras that any traveller might carry. I told him that it was a chance for the students to remind the world of their struggle.

He did not need a pitch from me. He had already given the idea some thought. He knew many of the student leaders, he said. He could travel to Beijing with his girlfriend, which would attract less suspicion, and try to set up some meetings. I agreed to pay all his expenses.

As we talked a plan began to emerge. We would travel to Beijing at the same time but we would never meet. I told him that there was a Chinese woman in London called Jackie who was willing to fly to Beijing and stay in our hotel. We would spend little time with her but she would be our translator when we needed her. I told him that she had worked for the BBC World Service and could be trusted. He said that when he was in Beijing he did not want to meet with me. Talking to foreigners was not a good idea. Jackie would be the go-between.

It was a few days later that another man told me of an underground railroad that was smuggling student leaders and dissidents out of China. Someone had betrayed the network and two leading dissidents had been arrested. I had heard nothing about this operation and was interested. He gave me a name and a number. The name was John Sham, but there was never any reply when I rang. I had almost given up on meeting Mr Sham when, while talking to a friendly diplomat, I asked him whether he had ever heard of this man. As luck would have it, he not only knew him but had his address and phone number. The number I had been trying had one digit wrong.

That afternoon I rang again and immediately the phone was answered. An hour later I was sitting with John Sham inside his apartment. He was a man of fast talking, of energy. He had spent some time in Britain working in television and, as far as I could make out, was an entrepreneur.

And then it happened. The scoop. I asked him about the underground railroad and he told me detail after extraordinary detail. It had been set up within days of the Tiananmen Square massacre. At any one time over forty people were working on operations. They had already rescued some of China's most wanted students, including Wuer Kaixi and Li Lu. They had also smuggled out of China Chen Yizi and Yan Jiaqi, two senior government advisers who had been reformers. Su Xiaokang, one of the most wanted intellectuals, had also escaped with their help. The network used high-powered boats and was helped by the Triads. He described how one of the most powerful dons had agreed to a deal. Undercover teams were smuggled into China to provide false documents and disguises. Sometimes make-up artists travelled with the teams. There had even been armed clashes with the Chinese coastguards.

I asked him whether this operation had a name and he said, 'Yes. We call it, unofficially, Operation Yellow Bird.' 'Why?' I asked. 'There is a Chinese idiom,' he said, 'that says that while a mantis preys on a cicada the yellow bird waits behind.' They believed that even whilst the Communist Party was destroying the democratic movement inside China they could preserve it abroad.

None of this had been reported before and I asked him whether it had to remain secret. There were details, he said, that could not be revealed because they would endanger future operations but he felt it was time to talk about Operation Yellow Bird. After all, China's Public Security Bureau knew about it, he said. It was at that moment I knew I would be able to tell the story of the Great Escape

from China. I asked John Sham about his role. He was a sympa-
thizer, he said, but never elaborated. I asked him whether I could
meet and interview the Triad don.

My story was changing. We would still try and meet the student
leaders inside China, but we would also tell how many of the faces
of the pro-democracy movement had escaped. We set about collecting the details of many of the escape stories so that we could
film actual locations in China. We called former student leaders like
Wuer Kaixi, who had made it to California. His memory was vivid.
In the days after the massacre security police were roaming the
capital with wanted lists. The Beijing railway station was a dangerous place. 'Wherever you looked,' he said, 'was a sea of green, the
uniforms of the police and army. They checked everything,' he went
on, 'and nobody smiled. Everybody had a very cold face.' On the
train he was recognized. A man looked him in the face and said,
'It's a great honour to see our leaders here. And don't worry, all of
the people in this wagon will help you. But face out! Face out so
the guards don't see your face.' All over China people helped him
move south. Eventually he waited three nights on a beach before
contact was made with one of the Triad boats. The boat could not
come in close because of submerged concrete posts and Wuer had
to swim out 500 metres. Then a powerboat with four 250-hp engines
took him to Hong Kong. Later we would interview him and the
others on camera.

Gradually I began putting together a team. I would go into
Beijing with Mike Spooner, a cameraman. We would take two small
Hi-8 cameras. Jackie, our Chinese translator, would meet us there
but we would act as if she was another hotel guest who we
occasionally talked to. The young man from Hong Kong and his
girlfriend would contact the students and other dissidents for us
and would set up meetings through Jackie.

A second team would also go to China. There would be three of
them: Dai Richards, a producer, Ron Keightley, a sound-recordist
who would take the pictures, and a young woman who spoke
Mandarin. She would pose as Dai's girlfriend. They would stay in a
different hotel to us. We would never talk on the phone but most
evenings I would try and meet them in a bar to hear how the
filming was going.

There was one immediate problem. We had arranged to travel on clean passports without any stamps that revealed we were journalists. By mistake Mike had used an old passport when he arrived in Hong Kong. Inside there was a visa for Iran, which clearly indicated what job Mike did. We puzzled over this. He could not use his new passport because the Chinese authorities would ask why there was no Hong Kong stamp inside. I approached a senior British official to see if an entry stamp could be put in the new passport. After some inquiries he told me it would raise too much interest in the Immigration Department and he suspected the Chinese authorities had their spies there.

Between us we came up with a solution. If we could find an Iranian postage stamp we would cover the reference to Mike being a journalist. So we scoured Kowloon for a philatelist shop and, surprisingly, found some current Iranian stamps. We then wrote some words in Farsi over them and decided Mike was free to travel.

John Sham came back to me and said that a Triad don would give us an interview but we could not show his face. We arranged to meet him at the Regal Meridien Hotel in Kowloon. The man was middle-aged, gaunt-faced and lean and could have come from a funeral. He wore a dark tie, a black suit with white socks underneath and black polished shoes. There was nothing casual about him, nothing left to chance. He was careful with himself, careful of how others saw him. His car was official-black and he travelled in the back. This snakehead, this Triad, was polite and chillingly formal.

The Triads are ancient criminal societies with their own initiation rights, hand signals and worldwide networks. Hong Kong's three main Triads are K 14, Sun Ye On and Wo Shing Wo. The man never used the word Triad nor revealed the organization he worked for, but I came to believe he belonged to the Sun Ye On.

They sympathized with the students, he told me, but there was also a business calculation. He felt that some of those expelled might one day end up in positions of power in China. They would not forget who had helped them, he said. He denied it was about money. The Triads agreed to make no profits but insisted that their operatives on both sides of the border be paid. An average rescue cost was $5,000, although moving some of the better-known dissidents cost $70,000. He said that his organization had extensive business networks in mainland China. In fact, they ran lucrative smuggling operations and it made sense to use them.

Before I left Hong Kong the network showed me some of their equipment. They had voice-scrambler phones, infrared signalling equipment and night-vision goggles. It could only have come from a Western intelligence service. The discovery troubled me. If we were caught the Chinese might see us as spies.

Eventually our team of eight was ready to travel to Beijing. On the flight was the young man who would make the vital introductions for us. He ignored us and whenever I saw him he was tightly wrapped with his girlfriend. When we arrived we planned to take a taxi to the hotel, but, as we left customs, a man in a suit stepped forward and said, 'Your car, sir,' pointing to a rather official-looking vehicle. I told him I was looking for a taxi. 'This is a taxi,' he said, 'please,' holding the door open.

Every instinct told me he was a government man, a party hack with links to the Public Security Bureau, but I decided to act the innocent as if we were on holiday and his car was the quickest way of getting to the hotel. He spoke good English and we went through our rehearsed story. We were old friends who both happened to be in Hong Kong and, at the last moment, had decided to snatch a few days' holiday in China. Neither of us had been there before.

'What do you do?' he asked, looking at us in his mirror. Mike was a water engineer and I was a financial consultant. A water engineer. That interested him. What project had Mike been working on in Hong Kong, he wanted to know. It had not been in Hong Kong, replied Mike. He had stopped off there on the way back from Australia. I tapped my passport, wanting to remind Mike he did not have an Australian stamp. I tried to help him by asking casually, 'So how is business going?' 'Er, well,' he replied, and then unconvincingly began talking about various projects. The longer we stayed on water engineering the more strained and halting the conversation became. At times it was comically bad. With a note of desperation I said I did not want to talk about work, I was on holiday; I asked the driver about the Great Wall.

The man dropped us at the hotel and we just hoped we had convinced him we were tourists. The following day Jackie arrived from London. We only spoke to her in the coffee shop or in the foyer and we pretended she was a holiday acquaintance. It was a surprisingly difficult role to play. During most casual conversations people smile. They do not have studied, serious faces. So while Jackie talked about clandestine meetings I occasionally laughed or smiled inanely as if she was telling me about a restaurant or bar. Most days she would go to a pre-arranged meeting with the young man from Hong Kong. Some days he would turn up and on others he would stay away.

Mike and I played the tourist. Around Tiananmen Square and the Forbidden City there were other foreigners with cameras and we felt less exposed there. We arrived early at the square in a cold chill light. It is an immense space, much larger than I imagined. For a moment I just stood there trying to absorb it, to understand it, to place events. To the north stands the Gate of Heavenly Peace and the entrance to the Forbidden City. Above the gate is a picture of Chairman Mao, the Great Helmsman. To the west is the Great Hall of the People with its Socialist architecture, drab and monumental. To the south lies Mao's Memorial Hall and his mausoleum. To the east are the Stalinesque museums of the revolution. The square is China's heart, its centre of power. On 4 June 1989, the People's Liberation Army had attacked the students camped there. There was nothing to recall that long night of terror. No bullet holes, no laid flowers, no inscriptions. Only memory and television pictures. That morning, our first in Beijing, there were just a few old men flying kites. With their long tails the kites soared above the square. Yellows and purples. Spring colours. There was something gentle and innocent about the old men in their Mao hats tugging at the strings. And then it struck me how quickly the recent past fades. It was as if the kites flew to say nothing had happened here on these stones. They flew to forget.

There were many police. Some in olive-green uniforms with whistles. Others in plain clothes but easy to identify: young men, usually in twos, in dark-blue casual jackets and khaki trousers. They tended to roll their sleeves up and, even on a drab day, wore dark glasses. They walked everywhere but nowhere; all primed to pounce at the first hint of protest.

Our plan was a simple one. We needed pictures to go with the interviews. We needed shots of uniformed police, of plain-clothes police; we needed shots of the places of power. We would get them by pretending to film each other but in fact using the zoom to shoot the scene behind. On that first morning I heard whistles blowing and I saw a black limousine with police outriders heading into the square. I could not resist a shot. It might be a senior party official. Mike took out the camera and panned with the car. Almost immediately I heard a much closer whistle and saw a uniformed policeman running towards us. Mike lowered the camera and both of us feigned surprise. The policeman waved us away and we moved to another part of the square, but gradually we began collecting the images.

Jackie told me we had an interview. It was not yet with a student, but with an intellectual who had been close to them and who had been branded 'a 4 June activist'. It would take place early evening in a hotel on the other side of the city. She had booked a room and would stay the night. Finding my way there was less easy than I had imagined. I left our hotel and tried to get a taxi on the street but it was difficult, without a word of Mandarin, explaining where I wanted to go. Even though the hotel had a Western name my pronunciation was strange to the driver. I must have repeated it twenty or thirty times. We went to three hotels before finding the right one. I realized I would have to have all instructions written down in future. I arrived late and walked straight to the lift but the staff at the reception desk stared at me. It was impossible in China to glide through lobbies and neighbourhoods unnoticed.

Upstairs I struggled to ask questions from behind the camera while hand-holding it for the length of an interview. When, later, we replayed the tape through the view-finder there was little that could be used. It was a setback. We could not be sure how many other opportunities there would be for interviews inside China.

I could not tell whether we were being watched or not but we decided we had to behave as tourists so I went to a desk in the hotel and ordered a car and guide to take us to the Great Wall. Our guide was a woman, young, attractive and smartly dressed. She was full of facts that she announced like slogans in a staccato voice. It was like having one of the electronic loudspeakers from a railway station inside the car. She irritated me so much that in the end I asked her about Tiananmen Square. She had her answer, which she delivered in the same unwavering voice. The protestors were not really students. They were mainly hooligans and criminals. It was a lie as big as the square, so immense it could not be argued with without drawing me into a dangerous conversation.

I was not in the mood for the Great Wall as I pushed past the T-shirt-sellers and the trinket-hawkers. The tourists had returned and had been welcomed back. They helped with the forgetting. They told all who noticed them that the world had moved on. With their careless laughter they irritated me. I climbed the wall and left them behind. It is only when you walk some distance from the crowds that you can, in silence, look to the horizon and imagine 5,000 kilometres of brickwork stretching to the Gobi Desert. As I got back in the car I read that some of it had been built by political prisoners. It was a tempting avenue of conversation but Mike, on the way back to Beijing, wisely questioned our guide about dating and marriage.

In the evenings I would go to different hotels for an early evening drink and meet Dai, the producer, and his team. The three of them had hired bikes, which made them less conspicuous. They were cycling over forty miles a day picking up shots across the city. They had managed to film on a campus and in the hutongs, the city's dense neighbourhoods. They had good shots of the old men sitting there with their red armbands. Some of the students who had escaped said these men from the neighbourhood committees were usually informers and a real menace to those who had gone underground. Dai eventually travelled south to Canton and Hainan Island where many of those who escaped were rescued by boat.

One morning Jackie met me at breakfast and told me that students at Beijing University wanted to meet us on campus. I was surprised. The university was watched and foreigners were forbidden to go there. I feared a trap but she said they had prepared the meeting carefully. Her confidence persuaded me. We travelled to a bus stop near the university and waited. After observing us, to ensure we were not being followed, two students took us onto the campus. It was immediately apparent that although the democracy movement had been crushed the students still had an organization. The decision to meet us had been taken by a committee. We sat at a stone table in a garden while all around on benches and under trees sat other students who acted as watchers to ensure we were not disturbed. Occasionally one of them would saunter over and tell us to lower our voices.

A young man in his mid-twenties told us, 'Everyone is depressed.' He gestured forlornly at the half-deserted campus and said, 'It's so quiet here. There is no discussion. All argument is stifled.' They spoke of friends who had been taken away for compulsory military training or had been forced to attend political studies sessions. Friends betrayed friends. Some were made responsible for the ideological soundness of others.

This, however, was not the purpose of the meeting. They had decided to give an open television interview. They knew the risk and the individuals would afterwards go into hiding. I asked them why they were doing this. The face of the young man who was leading the conversation tightened with defiance. 'We do not want to be forgotten,' he said. 'We want to protect the truth of what happened.' That was their real nightmare, that their protests faded from view to the point where they were air-brushed out. He spoke of the importance, in a police state, of the one gesture made without fear.

I wanted these interviews badly but I hoped television would not let them down. I had persuaded people before that speaking out would make a difference. It was not always so. There is so much television it has become harder to be noticed, and events can often drown out the impact of one report. The students risked imprisonment, or worse, and I wanted to be honest with them, but their minds were made up so we made arrangements. We would meet in the Fragrant Hills Park outside Beijing. Two students would talk to us. Both had been on the most-wanted list and both had just been released from prison.

Jackie booked a room at the Xiangshan Hotel. It was close to Beijing but it seemed far away. The Fragrant Hills Park is a place of dreams, of memories, of an older China. We drove up hills, through woods, past temples and pagodas. The Temple of Red Glow, the Temple of Azure Clouds, the Temple of Brilliance, the Glazed Tile Pagoda.

We waited at the hotel for the students to come. An hour passed and there was a knock on the door. It was another student. He explained that our interviewees were in poor health and that they had been unable to walk the last half-mile to the hotel. A taxi had to be found. When finally they arrived they explained that one of them had a kidney complaint and the other was suffering from tuberculosis.

They gave us their names and their numbers on the most-wanted list. One of them had been a hunger striker in Tiananmen Square and had negotiated with Li Peng, the Communist Party leader. He was in his mid-twenties and had been studying law at university. While he answered questions his friend lay on the floor. They both seemed weak. Although they were now out of prison they were confined to the margins of society. 'We have no source of income,' the first student told us. 'We've been expelled from university and can't get any suitable work. No one will take us. Our health is poor. Our very existence is threatened.' Because no one would employ them they did not have access to free medical care. He survived through contributions from his family.

The other student had been arrested trying to escape by train. He was depressed. Colleagues who had been taken for military training had returned subservient. They were no longer interested in democracy.

By mid-afternoon the interviews were over. The two young men became very serious and talked together in an intense way as if they were having doubts about what they had said, but they were discussing where they would stay that night. They had no permanent address. Home was the floor of friends. Often nine or ten of them would sleep to a room. The class of '89 had become untouchables, a caste apart, placed in quarantine.

There was one other person I wanted to meet before leaving Beijing. She was one of the few who dared to speak out openly. We sat on a wall outside one of the international hotels and waited for her. After an hour we gave up and drifted away. As we walked a petite woman in her mid-twenties appeared beside us. She told us to go to another address and then she was gone.

Hou Xiaotian was the wife of Wang Juntao, who had been denounced by the authorities as a 'black hand', an instigator of the student protest. He had been betrayed whilst trying to escape and had just been sentenced to thirteen years in prison.

When we met her later Jackie came with us. Hou Xiaotian's English was not good enough for us to have a conversation. She explained that she had been waiting for us to move away from a man who was watching us before making contact. She, like the students, had nowhere to live and her medical care had been stopped. She was harassed daily, some of it was petty but it was wearing her down. Only recently a video camera had been thrust menacingly in her face and a man had shouted at her, 'Be careful what you say.' Her own freedom hung by a thread and, as we spoke, her mind searched for the invisible line that she dare not cross.

When I asked her to talk on camera about her daily life she was reluctant to answer. 'You see,' she told me, 'if I'm talking to a Chinese person, that would be regarded as expressing an opinion. But if I talk about these things to you, I might be suspected of using your influence to put pressure on the authorities.' And she was fearful how the government might react to that.

As she continued speaking the injustice of it all swept her caution away and her eyes flashed angrily. 'Some people,' she said, 'including our government, believe that human rights are just the basic right to be alive. That's not human rights. It's the same right an animal has.'

She and her husband had been married only a few years and her eyes filled with tears as she said they had not spent much time together. 'A thirteen-year sentence on my husband is a thirteen-year sentence on me.' As I had found elsewhere, there are always the few who will not be silenced. Some have been pushed too far. Some burn with injustice. Some feel they have nothing left to lose. Every day there is pressure like a pain behind the eyes. A phone call. A warning. A nudge in the street. A shop that won't serve. A cold shoulder. The slow drip-drip of harassment. Hou Xiaotian was already older than her years, careworn and isolated.

After we finished the interview she told me the taxi firms to avoid. 'Dong Fang' was used by the Public Security Bureau. Be particularly careful, she said, of the unmarked Citroëns that work as taxis. A large number had been bought by the police and cruised the places where foreigners met. As we left the building there were two taxis outside. The first, inexplicably, could not take us. The second was a Citroën. Hou Xiaotian smiled and Jackie and I got in with her. The two women talked about Chinese hairdressing. Then, suddenly, when the car was stopped at lights, she was gone and had disappeared into a dimly lit hutong. The driver hesitated but he had no alternative other than to drive us to a hotel. We had chosen one where we were not staying.

It was time to leave Beijing. The following morning Mike and I returned to Tiananmen Square and recorded a piece to camera. We walked to the centre of the square and waited until there was no one close to us and then I turned to the camera and spoke for fifteen seconds. I think we got it right on the first take.

We then went back to the hotel and put the tapes in a shopping bag and I headed for a friendly embassy. A diplomat had agreed to put the tapes in the diplomatic bag and take them out of the country. There were Chinese police outside the embassy but when I showed my passport they waved me through. Inside, the diplomat took the tapes and replaced them with cans of Coke so it would not appear as though I had made a delivery.

Mike and I went to Beijing railway station to catch an overnight train to Shanghai. Jackie came with us to the station and she and I stood with our arms around each other as Mike filmed the army and the police over our shoulders. We then said goodbye to Jackie and boarded the train. We used the seventeen-hour journey to take the pictures which would help tell the story of the dissidents as they escaped. We filmed from inside the train as we left Beijing station. We took shots inside the crowded carriages. Mike even managed to film Chinese troops guarding a bridge.

In the middle of the night we stopped at a station and I got out to stretch on the platform. A young Chinese woman approached me. She was attractive, fashionably dressed, and spoke with an American accent. She said she was a musician. I said I was on holiday and going to Shanghai for a few days. She then said to me, 'Whatever you're doing, you are not on holiday.' I asked her what she meant but she would say nothing further. I got back on the train and told Mike. Was the conversation a warning or was it just a friendly observation? We did not know but we did not use the camera again until we reached Shanghai.

I had never been to Shanghai before and immediately it seemed more relaxed than the capital. On the Bund sailors called out to local girls. Traders tried to make money on the streets. People ate as they strolled. During the few hours we had in the city we took a room at the old Peace Hotel and interviewed an out-of-work journalist.

That night we planned to fly to Hong Kong. In the hours that I had left I decided to go to Green Lake Park and the English Corner, a garden where on certain days young Chinese come to practise their English. I knew tourists went there and I was also wanting to talk to ordinary Chinese. Until then I had only spoken to those in the shadows. There were old men hunched over their chequer boards, a table of schoolgirls writing in their English picture books. Within minutes a crowd had surrounded me, eager to try out their phrases. At first it was a heavily accented, 'How are you?' followed by lots of laughter, but then a real conversation started. I presumed there would be security police among the crowd so when they asked me about my job I retained the fiction that I was a financial consultant. That excited their interest. 'How does the stock market work?' asked one man. 'How much does it cost to trade?' asked another. 'Can you trust a company's figures?' asked an older man close to me. And this was the topic: money. They were gripped by the idea. Their faces were alive at the prospect of making it. They peppered me with questions that I could not answer.

And then I asked them about their government. 'We don't believe what our government tells us,' said one young man boldly. I asked them what Socialism meant. There was laughter. Irrepressible laughter that said more than words. These young Chinese were not openly challenging the government but they were cynical. They would never again be persuaded by the slogans. 'Socialist values' had died in the square. I saw it in the girls in their green military uniforms – hats askew, chewing gum and laughing carelessly. I heard it from an intellectual who said his interrogator had befriended him, unconvinced by the questions he was having to ask. I heard it from a man who had been to a karaoke club. The party's propaganda department had slipped 'Our Leader Mao Zedong' into the play list. The crowd had just sat it out and when the vinyl was changed they found their voices to sing along to Abba's anthems.

What the government had done was to offer a deal: make money but don't challenge the party. And there were many who had closed on that. The Communist Party kept its grip on power while the people learned to be capitalists. The leadership talked the party line while sending their sons and daughters to colleges and business schools abroad.

A few days later I sat in the lobby bar at the Peninsula Hotel in Hong Kong. A man who I had never met before came and sat with me and left a package. Our tapes had made it from Beijing.

From Hong Kong I flew to San Francisco to interview some of those who had escaped. There was Chen Yizi, a former adviser to the General Secretary of the Communist Party. Li Peng had been so angry when he heard of his escape from Hainan Island that he ordered the arrest of four thousand people. There was Gao Xing, who had once edited a student paper. He had left China with just the poems he had written on toilet paper and a vest while in prison. There was Su Xiaokang, one of China's seven most wanted intellectuals. Local sympathizers had escorted him all the way to the coast before a speed boat had picked him up. There was, too, Wuer Kaixi, the young man in striped pyjamas who had taken on Li Peng, but who met me in a San Francisco coffee shop unnoticed and without an audience.

They had extraordinary stories but there was a sadness about these men. They had risked everything. Others had risked much for their escape. They had their freedom but, at times, it felt aching and hollow. Exile was its own cruelty. Time diminished their voice.

While I was editing the piece in London I got a message from James Miles, who was the BBC's correspondent in Beijing. The students we had interviewed in the Fragrant Hills had sent word asking us not to use their names or show their faces. It was a terrible blow. We tried to verify the message but it proved imposs-ible and we could not take the risk. So we removed their names and covered their faces and the report lost much of its impact. I never found out what happened. Had the police learned of the interviews and threatened them? With their poor health, had the danger of speaking out seemed too great? Had the message really been from the students? All questions I never answered.

I had still broken a story. Apart from a BBC film I had a front page in the *Washington Post*. It had begun as a story about a great escape but ended up more about memory. The Chinese Communist Party has never given a proper accounting of what happened on 4 June 1989.

I have always remembered the earnest face of the student at Beijing University when he told me, 'We must protect the truth of what happened. We must talk about it every day so that the Chinese people can constantly be reminded of it.'

15

The Beast of Corleone

Gina was our fixer. She was a slight, vivacious, dark-haired Mediterranean girl. We all noticed it the moment she walked in. A love bite. It was red, fresh, not on the neck but just beneath one of her high cheekbones. She had made no attempt to conceal it. She just wore it. The bite had been given to her by her boyfriend while they were in a bar. It had been a form of branding, a mark of possession. Gina had been getting attention from other men when her boyfriend leaned over and publicly laid his claim and demanded respect. She was very aware of the weal and its redness but she was not altogether ashamed; there was a pride in being marked, in being wanted.

This was Palermo, Sicily, in 1993. It was at once Italian and familiar. Life lived outside on the street. The passeggiata, the evening strut and stroll around the main squares. The modern alongside the ancient. Motor scooters racing past time-worn statues in their niches. The men standing, drinking their morning espresso and eating a cornetto wrapped in a napkin. The al fresco restaurants with their fruits of the sea. The carpaccio di spada and the glass of Corvo.

But it was a different place too. The boyfriend hinted at it. There was no greater shame than to be a *'cornuto'*; to be cheated on, betrayed, cuckolded. 'Cornuto' was a much-used term of abuse. People were given not just the finger but a sign of two horns. This was a place of honour, of respect, of codes and rituals. In Sicily there was a front of house which visitors saw and returned for; but there was, too, an interior, rarely seen and impenetrable.

I had come to Palermo because of an arrest on 15 January. A man in his sixties had left a gated compound in the city and had been driven away in a Citroën. At the next traffic lights, undercover police surrounded the car and pulled the older man out. Shortly afterwards the police paraded passport-size photos of him like some trophy. They could scarcely contain themselves. They had arrested the head of the Mafia, of Cosa Nostra, the Capo di Tutti Capi, the boss of bosses.

The man was Salvatore 'Toto' Riina, from the hill-town of Corleone. Because of his medieval brutality he was known as la Belva di Corleone, the beast of Corleone. After his capture he was very polite and respectful. Colonel Mario Mori told him formally that he was under arrest and that a judge would read out the charges against him. 'Riina got to his feet,' Colonel Mori told me, 'and saluted me formally in the typical manner of an old Sicilian peasant.'

Shortly after his arrest I had flown to Sicily. If true, this was a major event: the arrest of the head of one of the most secretive and feared criminal organizations in the world. So much had been written about the Mafia that truth had merged with fiction. The Mafia was *The Godfather*. The Mafia was a film. Everyone, it seemed, had heard of Corleone but it was a town made famous by a book. Along the street from where I was staying was the Teatro Massimo where, in the film, Michael Corleone is shot on the steps. People took pictures there. It had become a tourist moment and the closest most outsiders got to the Mafia. We all thought we knew the Men of Honour. We had absorbed the images, the dialogue, the faces; but they were fiction. Now they had the real man.

Early one morning I queued at the gates of Ucciardone prison, where Riina was being held. The Mafia was so feared that the authorities had built a court room inside the prison. I was fortunate to be allowed inside. The room was spacious, modern and bright. It reminded me of a sports centre, except at the back of the court were a line of cells.

Riina was escorted by about eight or nine carabinieri. He was aged sixty-three, a small, squat paunchy man with salt-and-pepper hair. He wore a brown check jacket with a green shirt and a white vest underneath. He gave a triumphant wave. He scanned the room for his wife and daughter but when he went to wave again a carabinieri officer held his arm down. They were fearful that even from inside prison he might send a signal to his organization. His was not an educated face; he looked like a man from the hills who had spent long periods living rough. As he passed close by I noticed first his stubby fingers and then his sunken eyes, hard and alert. Everything I had heard told me I was staring at an evil man and I searched his face for signs, but all I came up with was the ordinary, someone who could pass for a small-town shopkeeper.

I looked across at his wife and daughter. What was it like to have a father who was head of the Mafia? They gave no clues. His wife, Ninetta Bagarella, wore large-framed glasses and simple earrings. Even if she had dressed down for the visit to the prison she was not a stylish woman. There was no money in her clothes. His daughter had long black hair and dark eyebrows and leaned forward, trying to catch the eye of her father.

Riina nodded to the platform where the judges were and sat down. He was then asked a simple question. *'Conosce Cosa Nostra?'* Do you know Cosa Nostra? Riina replied in a slightly high voice. 'I have never been part of any criminal organization.' The judge reminded him that that was not the question. Riina was half-apologetic, even deferential, and then replied, 'No I have never heard of it.' It would have been surprising if there was a Sicilian alive who had not heard of the Mafia or Cosa Nostra but Riina believed in the old code of silence, of *'omertà'*. There was a Sicilian proverb: 'He who is blind, deaf and mute will live a hundred years in peace,' and that was Riina's world.

Still some found Riina hard to believe. He came across as a semi-literate man from the hills. His false identity card had him down as a Sicilian farmhand and that is how he appeared. There was not a trace of wealth about him. It was difficult to accept that he commanded an organization with worldwide tentacles, yet the authorities insisted this was the man.

I struggled with how to make a television report about the Mafia. Yes, there was Riina and his picture, but I could not imagine anyone, with knowledge, wanting to talk about the man or Cosa Nostra. A starting point was the small group of investigating magistrates who were leading the fight against the organization. Two of them, Giovanni Falcone and Paolo Borsellino, had been killed. They were two of the best-protected men on the island but the Mafia had got to them with well-planned, almost military, operations.

The first magistrate to see Riina after his arrest was Roberto Scarpinato. He lived in an apartment above a busy shopping street close to the centre of Palermo. Outside the door were two soldiers with automatic weapons. I waited while they phoned the apartment. Inside were other men in jeans, blue shirts and body armour, with pistols in shoulder holsters.

Roberto Scarpinato sat amidst a pile of court documents, his cigarette smoke curling around him up into the angle-poise lamp. He had a beard and frizzy hair that reminded me of a 1970s footballer. He did not come across as a magistrate but more as a university lecturer. I looked around the room. There was not a hint of a life outside his battle with the Mafia.

As he spoke he told me he was under a kind of house arrest. 'I have given up living a normal life,' he said. He could not go for a walk or take a holiday trip. He had been in Palermo for seven years. During that time he had seen only his apartment and his office at the court building. When he made that short journey he travelled in an armour-plated car with eight bodyguards. He drew on his cigarette. There may have been two occasions when he had been able to shop but that was all. 'This is a price I am willing to pay,' he told me, 'if it leads to the defeat of a criminal organization that has stopped our democracy from developing into a mature one.'

Even whilst preparing this major case, he had time for me. He wanted me to understand the Mafia and its head. 'Riina,' he said, 'is a man of extraordinary self-control who has an exceptional ability for camouflage. His ability was not to seem what he was.' Scarpinato thought history would judge him a great criminal genius, a man crazed with power.

Salvatore Riina belonged to the Corleone clan or family. During the 1980s he had ruthlessly gained control over other families, often through murder. Over eight hundred people had been killed. The authorities were learning, in chilling detail, what life was like inside Cosa Nostra. 'Riina was like Jesus Christ,' said one magistrate, 'since he had supreme power. With a sign he could take away life or save it. He was the first person to invent a system of inviting people to lunch before killing them.' The savagery had persuaded some Mafiosi to break their vows of silence and begin talking. They were known as the *pentiti* or supergrasses. Riina had been betrayed by such a man who feared so much for his life he had gone to the police.

Riina was not driven by greed or money or the desire to own villas and estates. He wanted power, the power that decided who would live and who would die. Men feared him and there was no greater respect than that. He had changed the Mafia and in killing the magistrates he had ended up challenging the Italian state itself.

Scarpinato was very precise with his language. This was his life's work and the details mattered to him. Men like Riina had survived only because they had been protected, he said. The Mafia delivered the votes and the politicians returned the favour by giving the Men of Honour public-works contracts. When they were arrested they had judges in place to reduce the sentences. One judge was known as 'the sentence killer'. The influence of the Mafia had reached into the highest levels of power. Scarpinato paused to extinguish his cigarette. One of the Mafiosi who had turned informer and who had been close to Riina had told them how the head of the Mafia had met with the politician who on seven occasions had been Italian prime minister.

So they were actively investigating Giulio Andreotti. Even as I sat there I struggled with the idea that this rough-hewn man from Corleone had actually sat down with a prime minister and international statesman. The story was irresistible even though I did not know how I would tell it. Scarpinato and some of the other magistrates gave us documents which contained compelling first-hand accounts of life inside the Mafia. Working with me was Peter Molloy, one of the most imaginative documentary makers. He felt that we should take these Mafia stories and reconstruct them. My Italian was halting but each morning for several weeks I got up, read *La Repubblica* and then translated the files.

The stories were medieval: bodies being dissolved in barrels of acid; a prisoner being clubbed to death with an iron grille; a man strangled with rope at a lunch table. This was not fiction, although it read like it. These were the real-life stories from men who had never spoken before, who had been at the very heart of Cosa

Nostra. We had two main difficulties; one was how to find people in Sicily who would be willing to play Mafiosi. The other was how to get to Giulio Andreotti, the former prime minister.

We heard of one man, a Mafioso, who might actually talk to us. His name was Rosario Spatola from Campobello, and he had been a member of Cosa Nostra for twenty years. He had volunteered to talk to the magistrates, fearing his life was in danger. He agreed to meet us at the expensive Excelsior Hotel on the Via Veneto in Rome.

Spatola did not want to be filmed openly but would give us a back-to-camera interview. He was very careful about the arrangements. We would book a room and then at a certain time he would call us. The phone rang and Spatola asked for a room number. Moments later he was at the door. He had used the back stairs, he told us. He behaved like a man on the run, taking precautions so that he was not followed by former Mafia colleagues who were out to kill him for his betrayal.

I shook hands with a man who I suspected had killed. He was a 'made man' and it was likely that the price of joining Cosa Nostra would have been to take someone's life. I had expected a hard man, a thug, but Spatola was not like that. He was tall, straight-backed, formally polite and fashionably dressed in a checked olive jacket and tie.

He talked about growing up in Sicily. There was a mystique, an aura about the Men of Honour. 'You listened in awe,' he told me, 'when you heard about certain people. I could see these men were honoured and respected.' So he was initiated into the Mafia. In those days, he claimed, it was almost a gentlemanly secret society. 'When a Mafioso passed in the streets heads would bow,' he said. And that is what he still craved, I felt – the nod of respect, the tilt of the head. It was more important than money.

Spatola had met Salvatore 'Toto' Riina and feared him. He talked about how the Mafia had gone to war, turning on its own. 'Riina was a Man of Honour,' Spatola said, 'a classic Cosa Nostra type.' He paused and then said, 'In Cosa Nostra we were all wild beasts.' It was a moment of reflection. This was a man who wanted to believe he was more than a criminal but he had lived in a world of betrayals, rivalries and murder. He had cheated his Mafia bosses in a drugs deal. Even for men who had seen honour in killing, the

Riina years had been too much. 'You were frightened to go for lunch with friends,' he said. 'You doubted your own Mafia family; you rarely slept at home. You never knew when the decision had been taken to finish you.'

Back in Sicily an officer from DIA, an undercover anti-Mafia unit, had offered to drive me into the hills and to show me some of the Mafia's houses. We met in a police compound in Palermo and got into a unmarked Fiat Croma. The driver had a pistol, and the man next to him wore body armour and had a machine pistol on his lap. The officer in the back beside me carried an automatic weapon. Another car with three men came behind us. This was the island of Taormina, of Agrigento, of escape, but the men around me were at war.

We drove to San Giuseppe Iato, a little-known town in the hills between Palermo and Corleone. The Mafia family here was controlled by Bernardo Brusca and his sons. They were allies of Riina and the Corleonesi. Even though this was a small place an expensive highway was under construction. It straddled the hills, supported by tall white concrete columns. But in sight of the town it stopped, suspended in mid air. My police guides said it was a typical public works project where the money had run out, siphoned off into the pockets of the Mafia.

They took me to the house of Giovanni Brusca, the Mafia boss who was still on the run. They approached cautiously, pushing their weapons out of the window. The old honey-stoned Sicilian farmhouse was boarded up, the green shutters down. I had to wait in the car while the police searched the grounds then, while I took some pictures, they stood beside me cradling their weapons. They were edgy, impatient for me to finish so they could move on. Two older people, a man and a woman, walked past. They never looked over or acknowledged us. 'The Mafia will know about our visit,' said the officer with a smile.

They wanted to show me another building on the other side of town, then we had to leave. It would be dangerous to stay longer. We stopped outside a half-finished villa that was being built by Baldassare di Maggio, the man who had betrayed Riina. Money had been spent here. The house had a commanding view across the valley, a helicopter pad and escape routes built underground. The police were not confident waiting outside; they treated this as Mafia territory. The officer took out a map of the island. He pointed out districts in Palermo, from Uditore to Brancaccio, and then named the family that controlled them. The island, too, from Catania in the east to Trapani in the west had been parcelled up between secret criminal societies.

We were still having difficulty finding actors who would play the Mafia for us. While our fixers worked their contacts the film crew and I went to Corleone, the seat of Riina's power. It was surrounded by rocky outcrops, fingers of stone that climbed out of the land-scape. The town itself almost seemed to grow out of the rock. It was a heavy-set place of solid stone, of small shuttered windows, of sturdy oak doors – a place turned in on itself. The streets were steep, mainly in shadow, out of the sun. The fronts of the medieval houses were cluttered with balconies, railings, washing lines and telegraph wires. The older men wore flat hats, suits and open-necked shirts. A stranger stood out and was rarely acknowledged. In the 1980s and earlier few outsiders had visited the town and even fewer had dared to ask questions about the Mafia, but that was changing. The guidebook writers had begun to arrive and, behind them, the independent travellers. It was too soon for the coach parties. The people were used to journalists and film crews and knew how to turn their backs.

Riina had grown up here but no one knew him. It was impossible to find anyone to talk. They retreated into dialect and a shake of the head. Riina's wife, Ninetta Bagarella, lived there, as did his son and daughter. I rang their bell and asked if they would see us. 'No. That's not possible,' said a woman's voice through the entry-phone. And no one rings twice or pesters the family. I wanted a picture of Ninetta and we waited in the main square with a camera hidden in the car, hoping to catch her shopping, but she never came. We ordered espressos, drank cans of aranciata, studied maps and acted as if our interest was in the local church. Never had tourists stayed so long looking at so little. It may have been coincidence but I suspected that we were seen for what we were and the word was put out; and we left empty-handed.

Even in Corleone there were people who had spoken out against the Mafia. They were the courageous few. The majority saw nothing and knew nothing. There was Dino Patternostro, an awkward, stubborn newspaperman who would not be cowed. We met others on the island, people like Gabriella Sicuro, who had refused to pay pizzo, protection money. Part of her family's machine-tool business was burned down. Normally that persuaded most people to pay up but she turned defiant. 'They can't kill us all,' she said. In Palermo we met Vincenzo Agustino. His son and his pregnant wife had been shot by the Mafia. Agustino had long grey hair and a straggly beard. 'I have sworn on my children's grave,' he told me, 'that until I have truth and justice I will not cut my beard and hair.' He looked eccentric, as if turned by tragedy, but he spoke out fearlessly. 'We want to be free,' he said. 'We no longer want to be suffocated. We want the air we breathe to be pure. We've had enough.' We met, too, Maria Falcone, the sister of the murdered judge. She spat out her scorn at Riina. 'A beast,' she said, 'exactly that. A bloodthirsty beast.' These people were the few but their voices were the stronger for that. I had seen it elsewhere – in the Soviet Union, in the terrors of Uganda, in Saddam's Iraq – that, however great the threat, not everyone could be silenced. And when you met these brave people it was always the same: you left a little bit humbled and the mood of the day lifted.

One of our fixers had found a man who could supply actors for our reconstructions. We now had a location, a farmhouse just outside Palermo. The man came to the hotel with two colleagues. He wore a leather jacket and reminded me of the men who used to sit in the lobbies of Soviet hotels. They were either spooks or pimps and you did not want anything to do with either.

We were desperate to start filming the next day and the man smelt our desperation. I explained that we wanted to shoot some scenes in silhouette or back-lit, based on accounts given by Mafiosi. 'Why not?' he said. 'It's possible.' He had the men, the actors. 'How many you want?' he asked me. 'Five,' I said. He said something, which I did not follow, to the man beside him who then went off to make a call.

The man saw the BBC as a major studio and wanted thousands of pounds for a day's work. I explained that this was a report for a news and current affairs programme, but he chose not to under-stand that. I told him that the BBC was a public service broadcaster and did not pay large fees, but he did not believe me. So we argued and haggled while I struggled to make my case in Italian. 'You want real Sicilians?' he asked me. 'Yes,' I said, 'but not at any price.' After three hours we arrived at a deal and he agreed to bring men to the farmhouse the following day.

The house was in Ciaculli, a district run by the Greco family. It was a classic Sicilian building from the nineteenth century. There was some basic furniture inside but that was all. It was dusty, cool and unused. I wondered who owned it and who knew that it was empty.

Peter Molloy, the producer, wanted to begin by shooting the scene when Baldassare di Maggio was initiated into the Mafia family. He dressed the room like a crypt, with a ring of small squat red candles and statues of the virgin. Becoming a 'made man' was intended to be solemn, a blood commitment sealed with religious symbols. On the rectangular table we laid out an open knife and a .38 pistol just as di Maggio had described it.

The actors, when they arrived, could not have been more authentic. I caught Peter's eye. It was what he wanted. The men were aged between thirty and fifty. They wore grey and dark ill-fitting suits. They fidgeted inside them, trying to get comfortable. These were not men who had been to acting school or had spent time in Rome or Milan. As far as I could tell they were from the poorer districts of Palermo.

Peter selected one of them to play the Mafia boss Bernardo Brusca. He went through the lines. Brusca had asked the man about to be sworn in, 'Are you sympathetic to these people?' Further questions followed. 'Have you ever been unfaithful to your wife with a married woman or any other woman?' One of the actors pointed out that was not the second question. He was right and I explained that I had edited the account, but I began to wonder about these men and their knowledge of Mafia customs.

We then read out what happened next. 'I was invited,' said Baldassare di Maggio, 'to prick my right index finger with part of a needle, drawing blood. Bernardo Brusca put a card in my hand bearing the image of a crucifix, like those found in church. I then cupped my hands like a bud while the godfather set fire to the holy image, inviting me to repeat the oath.'

We had brought a needle and a number of small cards with pictures of saints on them. The actors became animated. They took the needle and showed exactly where it was to enter. When we said we wanted to light the card in one of their hands they said it was not done that way. The card was lit by the boss and then placed in the cupped hands. The man must not flinch, they told us, and the card must burn to ashes.

We asked them whether they had filmed a scene like this before. No, they had not. None of us asked them whether it was usual for ordinary Sicilians to know the details of Mafia initiation ceremonies. But in this isolated farmhouse, in a half-lit room, the Mafia suddenly seemed very real.

We had to shoot the scene several times to change the angles and get the close-ups. On each occasion the men were faultless. As the saint's image burned the actor playing Baldassare di Maggio said, 'May my flesh burn as the image now burns if I ever betray my family.' He delivered the lines without seeming to learn them.

In the middle of the day the man who had found the actors appeared and wanted to renegotiate. I did not have the energy for another argument and put up my hands to stop him, saying, 'We have a deal and I don't want to talk about it.' There was anger in his face. He felt rebuffed and I thought he might withdraw his men. He went over to Gina, one of our fixers, and I saw him talking animatedly, his hands expressively making the points.

After the initiation the new Mafioso kissed the others. There was a way to do this, the actors explained. Their hands slapped the back of the shoulders of the men opposite and then they kissed each other on both cheeks. They all did it the same way. The next scene involved the strangling of Rosario Riccobono, a boss whom Riina had invited to lunch. The actors too had their views on this. It would involve more than one man. Two men would have held Riccobono in his chair from the front while a third tied the rope around his neck. By the end of the day we all felt we had been with the Mafia.

The following morning we were due to shoot another reconstruction on the streets of Mondello, a coastal town near Palermo. The man with the actors arrived late and we had a further argument. He again wanted more money for the previous day and wanted us to hire more actors for that day. We insisted we only needed two. He drove away, angry.

I then made a terrible misjudgement. We wanted to reconstruct the killing of a man called Salvo Lima. He was regarded as the link between the Mafia and the politicians and, in particular, the former prime minister, Giulio Andreotti. Lima had been killed the previous year by a man on the back of a motorcycle who had drawn alongside his car and shot him. His murder had been ordered by the Mafia because he had failed to arrange a reduction in the sentences of convicted Mafiosi.

We had hired a red Honda bike and brought it to a quiet street in Mondello. Two actors, with dark visors, would ride on it. The plan was to put the camera inside our minibus and to film the bike as it drew alongside. The actor on the back of the bike would pull out a gun and point it at our vehicle. What I had failed to do was to notify the local authorities and the police.

Just as we began shooting the scene a police car came into the street behind us. In a flash I could see a tragedy unfolding. The police, at war with the Mafia, would see the gun being drawn by the pillion passenger and would open fire. We began waving at the bike to stop but there was no way of contacting them. With the police car closing on us, I could see the man on the back preparing to pull the gun. I shouted at our driver to stop. As I looked out of the back window I saw the police stop and level their guns, using the car doors as shields. The bike stopped, the riders unaware of the police behind them. I jumped out of the minibus and ran towards the police waving my arms in the air. I distracted them enough to prevent them firing.

They were furious that we were using a replica gun on the streets without telling the local police. It was inexcusable and for days I felt almost sick as I replayed the moment. I also learned something about the way Sicilian society worked. The police had been tipped off that there was a motorcycle with two men and a gun. Most likely that had come from the man who had supplied the actors. I had not, in his view, shown him respect and he had taken his revenge.

Sometime later, after the report had been shown, Giulio Andreotti agreed to see me in his apartment in Rome. Eight Mafiosi had accused him of 'not occasionally, but continuously favouring

Cosa Nostra'. They called him 'the Uncle' and charges were being prepared against him. I was uncertain what to expect. Here was a former prime minister who counted Reagan, Gorbachev and Thatcher as friends, and yet I was going to ask him whether he was the Mafia's man.

The room was spartan, the furniture dark and forbidding. In the background hung a crucifix and on the table was a picture of Andreotti with the Pope. For one and a half hours he never moved his body. He sat there, a very still man with a large head on hunched shoulders. As he spoke I noticed his belt buckle. On the front was a large 'G'. His cufflinks were gold-crusted. His blue shirt was monogrammed with a 'G' just above the waistline. It was as if he was sponsoring himself.

It was like watching an artist as he weaved his defence, gently destroying his accusers. He admitted to almost being driven mad by the allegations. The Mafia kiss, he told me, was absurd. He had not been in Palermo during that time. No one apart from the Mafiosi had seen him. How was it possible for a prime minister to travel without anyone seeing him? I mentioned that eight Mafiosi had identified him as the Mafia's man. 'You would trust the word of a Mafioso before mine?' he asked me. These were all criminals, he said, telling the magistrates what they wanted to hear. Several times he drew a distinction between the older Mafia and the organization run by Riina. As he spoke I wondered, if back then, he had had links with Cosa Nostra. I asked him directly but he deflected the question.

He wanted me to know that when he travelled he was still received. He listed names. Yasser Arafat had met him, so had the Israeli prime minister, Shamir. President Assad too. This attention mattered to him. Now it only happened abroad. The US president he admired most, he said, was Richard Nixon. Even after Watergate he was still consulted. Andreotti wanted this for himself too.

He spoke of his faith. Every morning at six o'clock he attended Mass. His fellow believers had shown trust in him. His contacts, friends in power, called him to say he was still believed. That mattered to him too. He was a hurt man who craved respect. As I left it was impossible to form an opinion beyond the sense that here was a consummate politician steeped in the deals and compromises of power. One of his comments stayed with me. 'It was important,' said Andreotti, 'to be esteemed.' Like the Men of Honour, he still wanted heads to bow.

Salvatore Riina was given a life sentence and developed heart problems in prison. Land confiscated from the Mafia was given to young farmers who grew grain for pasta. They called it 'anti-Mafia spaghetti'. A mansion with a gold-plated door handle, that used to belong to Riina, was turned into a school. For all of that, Cosa Nostra remains undefeated. Giulio Andreotti was acquitted of association with the Mafia. However, the judges in Palermo ruled that he appeared to have had closer links than he should have done, but they had ceased after 1980.

In the film *The Godfather*, Anthony Corleone asks his father Michael, played by Al Pacino, 'What makes this beautiful country so violent?' Michael replies, 'History.' And tradition too, with its warped sense of honour. 'The hidden evil of the Mafia,' said the magistrate Roberto Scarpinato, 'was not thirst for money but thirst for power and, with it, respect.'

And that was the Sicily we had found.

16

Sweating to See the Prince

I knew I was in a competition, a high-profile race. I had not wanted it that way but the headlines in the paper told me it was inescapable. It was Friday, 23 October 1998, and the *Daily Mirror* ran a large headline: 'Dimbleby too scarred to interview Charles at 50'. The first two paragraphs of the story reported that the television journalist Jonathan Dimbleby was still feeling wounded after his interview with Prince Charles four years earlier. There had been, apparently, a cooling, a souring of relations between the two men after the prince had admitted on camera to being unfaithful to Princess Diana.

Now, according to the paper, there was a new battle to interview the prince on the occasion of his fiftieth birthday. In one corner was ITV and I was in the other. 'Gavin Hewitt is heading *Panorama*'s bid,' the article reported. I was not considered the favourite. I had a good 'journalistic track-record' but the BBC had not been forgiven for allowing Princess Diana to use *Panorama* as her confession box.

A final comment caught my eye. 'Charles,' an insider was quoted as saying, 'was going hot and cold over the interview. One day it's on and the next day it's off.' That I knew to be true. We had approached St James's Palace in April, eight months before the prince's birthday. It was like a months-long audition. Sometimes we were given briefings and filming opportunities. On other occasions calls were not returned and we felt the distinct chill of disapproval. The interview hung in the air like an unanswered question.

The prince was undecided about what to do about television and his birthday. Four years earlier his advisers had persuaded him to drop his reserve, to go unplugged and pour out the agony of his personal life; but it had all backfired. There was little sympathy out there for his adultery. His instinct now was to retreat behind the veil of public engagements and to avoid interviews, particularly on television. And yet if he was to rebuild his popularity he needed exposure. So while he decided, we waited. We had our own dilemma. There was a diminishing audience for bland royal profiles. We needed access to the man himself.

Until the previous year I had had no experience covering the royal family. It had always seemed a fenced-off enclosure where credentials were checked and rules followed, and I had never been drawn to that. Only a few years before, BBC journalists had not been allowed to approach the palace directly. All inquiries had to be channelled through a BBC bureaucrat in charge of royal liaison. This person was not there to facilitate reporting, but to keep all but a trusted few outside the gate. A colleague had once phoned this person to see if she would check with the palace a detail on a story about Prince Charles's marriage. She dismissed the inquiry as 'impertinent' and 'in bad taste' and slammed down the phone.

I had first reported on the royal family after the death of Princess Diana. On the morning of her crash I had been called at home at 6.30 by Steve Hewlett, the editor of *Panorama*. He asked me to come in and present the BBC's obituary of the princess. A short time later I was in the office. The obituary had been found in the library. It consisted of twelve minutes of pictures randomly edited together without commentary. We all swore, paced up and down demanding to know who was responsible. The unexpected had happened and the BBC had been caught out. So teams began scouring the film library for clips whilst others phoned anyone who knew the princess and begged for interviews.

I settled down to write about a woman I had met only twice. Some correspondents have a royal-tone button that they turn off and on – a cadence, an inflection coated with the unmistakable lilt of deference. I could not do that. It was a massive story but I could only report it like any other.

As the pictures were edited I wrote to them quickly, instinctively. While producers urged me to write faster I struggled to find the words with which to end the sixty-minute tribute. I wrote, 'She was an icon for a world fascinated with fame and celebrity. With her youthful vitality she became the human face of an ancient institution and changed for ever the public's perception of the monarchy.' That will do, shouted the producers. We ended with a clip in which Princess Diana expressed her desire to be the people's Queen of Hearts.

I learned then my first lesson about covering the royals. The tribute went out and everyone sighed with exhaustion and relief. Shortly afterwards I was told of a plan to sell the tribute to raise money for a fund that had been set up after her death. But I was told my tone was not quite right for the market. 'It had too much edge.' It needed to be softened. What they wanted was the coffee-table book, glossy and air-brushed. History without the rough edges was not for me and I refused to rework the tribute, but I understood then that not everyone wanted reality intruding on their magic.

I was helped in having as a producer Frank Simmonds, one of the best documentary makers in current affairs. He knew instinctively where the money was, what worked on TV, and he was never satisfied with less. He was also amusing, vivid with his language. He once told me that he had 'just filmed Prince Charles covered in road-kill'. On closer questioning it turned out this was his way of saying he had filmed the prince wearing a particularly furry-looking sporran.

We began with visits to St James's Palace to meet the prince's inner circle. There was Sandy Henney, his press secretary. She was in her forties, blonde, and, unusually for a palace official, sometimes wore an ankle bracelet. She was hardbitten from her years of dealing with the press but, for all of that, she was a straight-shooter and we liked her. Mark Bolland was in his early thirties, boyish, conspiratorial and the prince's key adviser on public relations. Then there was Stephen Lamport, his private secretary. He was a former foreign office man, discreet, effortlessly polite, establishment-smooth and difficult to read. These were the people we had to convince that the prince should talk to us.

Our pitch was a simple one. A fiftieth birthday was a natural moment to profile the prince. We assured them the report would not just focus on his private life but be a balanced portrait. Sandy Henney tried to close the door. The prince wanted no attention on his birthday. We replied that articles would be written and films made whatever his wishes. She said that they could not stop us attending public occasions. The problem with that, we said, was that it would seem as if the prince was trying to avoid the cameras. We thought it would be in his interest to seem open, relaxed and cooperative. There was the slightest hint of a threat in all this, but these were early meetings in what would turn out to be a long negotiation. We told them the film would be made anyway and that it would be a major BBC documentary shown at prime time, and that was our strongest card.

And so we circled each other warily. As Frank observed, 'They want you to go away and you start turning up.' We quickly concluded that the key aide was Mark Bolland. His task was to relaunch the prince after the death of Princess Diana. He was less dismissive. Nothing had been decided, he told us. He accepted that it would be damaging to the prince to appear withdrawn, stiff, cold and formally polite. That was precisely what his critics accused him of. So we started filming without any promises being made, but gradually there were exclusive moments when only our camera was present. One of the first was on a farm in Stratton-on-the-Fosse, which was part of the Duchy of Cornwall.

The prince arrived in rain, in a mud-splattered Land Rover. He wore a flat hat, green wellington boots and a brown oilskin. He had four men with him including his estate manager. They dressed in the country camouflage of greens and browns. Even amidst the gunk of the farmyard they all wore ties. They leaned against a rail, easy with each other, and watched a calf being born. The prince was certain of those around him and he lingered, discussing some tongs he had heard of that could ease the birth of calves.

During the visit I was introduced to him. We had not spoken before. Sandy Henney said, 'This is Gavin Hewitt. He's making the film about you for BBC 1.' 'How absolutely frightful for you,' he said as we shook hands. I did not know how to take the comment. After all, he was the subject of the film. I concluded it was intended as irony and laughed. 'It's not that bad,' I replied. 'I can think of worse things.' 'Is it properly funded?' he asked. 'Or do you have to raise money?' Again the unexpected question. I explained that it was a BBC production and funded by the corporation. 'Well, very good luck with it,' he said as if he had no influence on the project. He gave not a hint as to whether or not he would give us an interview or cooperate further. And it remained that way for much of the summer.

While we were on the farm we all went inside one of the tenant's cottages. The estate manager and some of the tenants were there. One of them had a birthday, a fiftieth, and Prince Charles wished him many congratulations. The man, in his brown-checked jacket and tie, laughed nervously. The prince said, 'I'll leave that for you,' and placed a red box with a whiskey bottle inside on the table. The man continued to laugh with the rest of the room but somehow missed the fact that he had been given a gift by his landlord, the Prince of Wales. And then it dawned on him that this, indeed, was a present for him and he had ignored it. 'Are you serious, sir?' he blurted out, laughing now more loudly. The prince replied, 'If you really want to know, it's an empty bottle.' At this moment the man stepped forward and said, 'Oh sir, that's very good of you.' The word 'sir' was elongated and contained all his embarrassment. But he was not finished. 'Oh sir, thank you. Thank you. You took me by surprise.' Then another man to my right chimed in, 'And I think, sir,' he said, raising his glass towards Prince Charles, 'that we should wish you a happy birthday.' The prince, I was told, wanted people to behave naturally with him, but time and again they did not.

The prince's circle was careworn. For too long they had been playing defence. There had been so much criticism that I felt they wanted to retreat behind the palace walls, to spool back history to another time when they did not have to explain. They trusted no one in the media. 'We've been mugged too often,' said Sandy Henney.

While we waited on the prince we were invited in for briefings. Stephen Lamport, the prince's private secretary, talked the big themes. The prince, he said, saw the monarchy as representing 'timeless principles'. His views on 'kingship' were very private but he saw the Crown as a continuum in the nation's history. But no one is really interested in this, he said, with a sigh of resignation.

That was also the mood of friends who were sanctioned to talk to us. Weary and defensive. People who knew the prince never spoke without permission. They knew that a word uttered out of place would lead to exclusion, and the invitations so important to them would dry up. They talked of a man misunderstood, who carried his hurts. His former teacher Eric Anderson was allowed to talk to us and spoke of the prince's 'great capacity for being wounded'. Nicholas Soames, one of the prince's oldest friends, thought his treatment had been 'unspeakable'. The former Tory minister Chris Patten spoke of a man 'scarred by intense, brutal, unfair criticism'. 'He has had a much less happy life than he deserves.'

Self-pity clung to the prince. We noticed it more, the more time we spent with him. At public occasions he was often self-effacing. His left hand would slide inside his jacket pocket and he would fiddle with his tie. His speeches were low-key, conversational, almost throwaway, as if he doubted anyone was seriously interested. Self-deprecating clauses were dropped in. When he was discussing architecture in Aberdeen, he said, 'For well over a decade I have tried, for what it's worth, to get a debate going...' His confidence was low. 'For what it's worth' was followed by 'if anyone cares what I think'. When he visited some older people who were being looked after by Age Concern he began with an apology 'I hope my visit hasn't meant too much trouble for you.'

His staff were even apprehensive about his appearance at the Party in the Park concert in Hyde Park. It was in aid of the Prince's Trust, his charity that worked with young people. It would be the largest crowd he had faced since Diana's death.

We waited at the back of the VIP stand that had been built to one side of the arena. The prince arrived in a dark-green Bentley. He wore a grey double-breasted suit, a blue shirt and a silver tie. The two aides who were with him also wore suits. He was met by Tom Shebbeare, the Trust's director, who was wearing a beige suit and an open-necked blue shirt. He was an articulate, thoughtful man but when he met the prince his face creased in worry. 'Oh sir,' he said, 'I'm so sorry, I seem to be improperly dressed.' And here I noticed it again: the prince's office repeatedly said he wanted less formality and yet those close to him could never quite drop it.

We waited beneath the stage for Stephen Fry, the actor and friend of the prince, to take the microphone and ask for applause for 'the good old Prince of Wales'. On cue the prince appeared on the stand. This was not the casual event it seemed. It had been decided that the prince should not appear alone but with David Duchovny, the actor from the TV series *The X-Files*. The crowd turned towards the VIP stand and clapped the man behind the concert they were enjoying in the summer sun.

The other key moment was the photo call. The previous year it had been with the Spice Girls and every paper had carried the picture. The palace wanted the same again. Their man at ease with popular culture. This time it was the all-girl band All Saints that had been chosen. We walked with the prince to the tent where the picture was to be taken. One of the band, Melanie Blatt, was five months pregnant. The prince asked her whether she found it difficult being on stage while pregnant. 'No,' Mel replied. Nothing more. Conversation over. The prince stood beside the girls, who threw their arms around him. 'This won't do any good for your reputation,' he said. 'You'd be surprised,' shot back Shaznay Lewis. There was something easy, free-souled and spontaneous about the way the band treated him.

While I watched all this Ronan Keating came up to me and said, 'Are you doing anything?' At that moment I was just standing close to my cameraman as he took pictures of the prince so I replied, 'No, not really.' 'Well, just hold this, mate,' said the lead singer of Boyzone, handing me his beer. So I just stood there with Ronan Keating's half-empty glass. The prince walked by and said, 'You seem to be enjoying yourself.' Rather defensively, I replied, 'It's Ronan Keating's beer. I'm just holding it.' I could see in the prince's face that he did not know whether or not to believe me.

Discussions continued about the interview. The prince was just not persuaded it would help him. I suggested that we make it less formal and that on certain occasions I might ask a few questions while he was in his car or helicopter. They would put it to him, but I could see they were unconvinced and time was running out.

Over the summer I spent time on Prince Charles's organic farm with David Wilson, the manager. Richard Aylard, the prince's former private secretary, showed me around the gardens at Highgrove. After all the artificiality of public occasions this is where I felt closest to knowing the man – amidst the Cotswold stone, the fountains and the pergolas. The gardens were not just an indulged interest. They were a belief. The thyme walks and wildflower gardens were almost an act of defiance, as if to say, 'See what has been lost, what has been abandoned and thrown away.' It was a garden full of yearning for another period, timeless, untroubled and enduring. His friends told me that he was tired of all the 'froth' of modern life and Highgrove was his place of retreat, his place of safety.

As the weeks went by Mark Bolland increasingly became our point of contact. He was an assistant private secretary but in reality he was in charge of public relations. He could talk to the prince like few others. Most of Bolland's energy was spent on the 'coming out' of Camilla. He and the other aides were driven by a fear that if the prince and his lover appeared together the public would turn against her and the prince himself. Bolland told me, with anxiety etched on his face, about a recent journey the prince and Camilla had taken from Scotland to Highgrove. They had stopped twice at motorway service areas. It would have been so easy for someone to take a picture. He shuddered at the thought.

So he spent his time agonizing over the 'coming out' of a middle-aged woman. There was something eighteenth century about it all. The question was 'What would society accept?', as if she was a shamed, fallen woman and the community had to decide whether they could accept her back or not. Bolland calculated when she should be seen. In what context? Should she be alone with the prince? They had not been seen together since the death of Princess Diana and that was the heart of the problem.

We wanted to film Camilla and I felt she should not be a figure in the shadows. He agreed that it was not a sustainable position. He said there may be an event where, if we had our cameras in a certain position, we could glimpse her from a distance. The idea did not appeal but it was better than nothing. Then we were told it might just be possible to see her at the Osteoporosis Society charity event. We waited for a call and it never came.

Bolland was focused on a wedding in late October between Santa Palmer-Tomkinson and Simon Sebag-Montefiore. Both the prince and Camilla would be attending. At one point we were told to be ready with our camera to see them leaving St James's Palace together. Then, without explanation, that was cancelled. In the event the prince arrived twenty minutes behind Camilla. They sat two rows apart. The prince left three minutes ahead of his lover. All of this was scripted, laid out in a battle plan. It was too soon for the 'coming out'.

As an outsider I had presumed the prince's office at St James's Palace and Buckingham Palace would speak with one voice. They did not. They briefed against each other. So I found myself moving between two separate groups of officials, without either side knowing. I would meet Mark Bolland and then the Queen's press secretary, Geoff Crawford. He was an Australian and a former diplomat. He could pass as a typical courtier but when he said, 'Let's have a drink, mate,' you knew he, too, was something of an outsider and refreshingly direct.

The two men had their restaurants. Bolland liked the gilded Byzantine dining room at the Criterion. Crawford preferred the Avenue with its modern, clean lines and New World wines. Over lunch Bolland would make the case for Camilla. 'Whenever the prince is at Highgrove,' he said, 'she's there.' The take at the Avenue was very different. 'The Queen hasn't met Camilla, and won't.' There will be no Queen Camilla. Back at the Criterion: 'They're spending more time together than ever. She often appears at meetings at Highgrove.' But at the Avenue, 'Charles is not ready to be king. He needs time to resolve issues in his life.' In the Criterion Bolland could scarcely conceal his irritation that Charles had not been given more responsibility. 'It's not how we conduct official occasions; it's just that we're not asked.' Bolland was the more difficult of the two men to read. He was dismissive of the officials at Buckingham Palace. At one point he opined that he would get rid of them all. They were opposed to modernizing the monarchy and they were resisting Prince Charles having more responsibility. It was difficult to know who was talking here. Was this Bolland or was it his master's voice? I was never sure.

None of this was on camera but here was part of the real story; the tension between the palaces and within the family. We had resigned ourselves to not having an interview with the prince but during October I got a call. There would be no interview on camera but I could spend half an hour with him. It would be sometime during a visit to the Balkans at the beginning of November. The meeting would be private and I was to tell no one about it. Somehow I had to use that half-hour to find a story.

So I flew to Bucharest, the capital of Romania. It was a down-at-heel, worn-out city just emerging from Communism and President Ceaucescu's criminal fantasies. As soon as I arrived several royal correspondents asked me directly whether I had come to interview the Prince. They could see no other reason for me to be joining this low-key tour. I avoided answering their questions directly, which only increased their suspicions. I still did not know when I would see the prince. I talked to Sandy Henney, who would only say, 'It's going to happen,' but not when.

I had dinner with Kent Gavin and Mike Forster, two of Fleet Street's best-known stills photographers. We found a low-lit restaurant with long burgundy curtains and ate schnitzel and drank Hungarian wine. The best days of royal reporting were behind them, they thought. It was hard to get pictures in the paper. They were still in mourning for Diana. It had all been so different then. They had been shooting for the front page. Now, with Charles, they waited for the unexpected, a gaffe, an incident, a ridiculous hat, a snatched kiss.

We came to the end of the visit to Romania and I had still not seen the prince. On the way to the airport we drove past Ceaucescu's monstrous palace. Houses and districts had been torn down to make way for it. I boarded a chartered 757, with wide leather seats, for the short flight to Sofia, the capital of Bulgaria.

When we touched down Sandy Henney told me that during the day I would have my time with the prince. I had to stay close and she would tell me when it was going to happen. It had to be done in great secrecy otherwise all the royal correspondents would complain. I also felt she wanted deniability. The prince's first public engagement was a visit to a children's cancer ward. While he was talking to patients the office called me. They had just seen a press release. ITV, who were preparing a rival programme on Charles, were claiming that the prince would be 'privately delighted' if the Queen abdicated soon. It was a sensational story and it meant that ITV's programme would steal the headlines and all the attention. It made it even more important that I get something out of the meeting with the prince, otherwise our film risked being ignored.

Late morning Sandy Henney told me that during the afternoon the prince would lay a wreath at the Memorial to the Unknown Soldier. During the brief ceremony and while the other reporters were distracted she wanted me to climb into the back of a British embassy minivan which would be parked behind the prince's car. We would then drive to the ambassador's residence and we would have our meeting.

Over lunch the prince came to the Sheraton Hotel where we were staying. From there he would travel to the memorial. I had been told to avoid the reporters' bus and to make my own way there. I had been to Sofia once before, just after the overthrow of Todor Zhivkov, the Communist dictator, and was confident I knew the city. While I waited at the hotel I called the office and spoke to Peter Horrocks, the editor of *Panorama*. He stressed the importance of asking the prince about Camilla. I could tell from his voice that it had become more important because ITV had such a strong headline. I sat over a coffee and worked out how I would ask the prince about his lover. I wrote in my notebook the words, 'How would you like your relationship defined?'

I left the hotel and walked towards the Alexander Nevsky Cathedral, the largest Eastern Orthodox church in the Balkans. I was certain the memorial was there but as I got close I noticed there was no crowd, no police and no cameras. It was uncomfortably quiet. With a rush of dread I realized that I had turned up at the wrong place, that I did not know where the Memorial to the Unknown Soldier was and that I risked missing the one meeting that we had been waiting months for.

I stopped passers-by. Anyone. Old people. Students. Kids. I rushed from one to the other asking them where the memorial was but none of them understood me. I could not find anyone who spoke English and the minutes were passing. There was only one place where I could be certain I could get directions and that was back at the hotel. I ran through the streets, pushed past guests who were checking in, and breathlessly asked where the memorial was. I could feel the crowd in the lobby staring at me. The concierge explained that it was not far away, but I knew the prince's car would leave in ten minutes. I ran out of the hotel. There were no taxis and, in any event, the streets were clogged with traffic. I started running, hard running. There were too many people on the pavements so I ran between the cars, my arms pumping the air. People stopped and pointed at this figure in a charcoal-grey suit but I ignored them. I could feel the sweat working its way down my back.

And then I saw it. A small crowd standing in a half-circle. I spotted the prince's car and the dark-blue minivan but they were on the other side of the police lines. The ceremony was drawing to a close. A military band was playing an anthem. I tried to push through but the police would not let me pass and I could not make myself understood. To my right I noticed a gap in the police lines and I ran through it, vaguely waving a pass. One officer tried to stop me but I calculated that if I could reach the minivan one of the prince's aides would explain that I was part of the official party. So whilst everyone was standing to attention during the national anthem I made my run and reached the van. The driver was expecting me and I jumped inside.

Moments later the prince's aides and embassy officials joined me in the van. They each in turn stared at me as I gasped, 'Hello.' My hair was wet. Sweat still trickled down my face. There was not a dry patch on my white shirt. There were even damp stains on my jacket and trousers. Every so often, as we drove to the ambassador's residence, a face would look back at me, scarcely believing that I was the man going to meet the prince.

When we arrived at the residence I could sense there was tension. The prince grimaced as an aide spoke earnestly to him. I guessed that he was being briefed about the story that he wanted the Queen to abdicate. I was taken to the drawing room and the door closed. I was then told I had to move. The prince needed to make a call. I was then put in the nursery and this door closed. For a long while I waited there alone. Nobody came to see me. I just sat on a chair and looked at the toys that were scattered over the floor. I began to fear that the prince had changed his mind or that I had been forgotten.

Then Sandy Henney came in and told me the prince had phoned the Queen. A statement had been issued in London branding the suggestion that he wanted her to abdicate as 'outrageous, deeply offensive and hurtful'. She said the prince would see me shortly and I was taken back into the drawing room.

I could feel his irritation the moment he came in. He was slightly red-faced and he fiddled with his cuffs. He clearly did not want this meeting. I began by talking about Ceaucescu's palace. What had he made of it? This was a subject he liked and he relaxed a little. He thought the people's housing complexes 'dreadful'. It was what he had been going on about for years. Soulless housing estates. 'I've been trying to undo the legacy of the fifties and sixties. You can't just remove the soul,' he said. 'I believe the spiritual is very important.' I mentioned that I liked some modern architecture, particularly in the United States. 'We've got nothing to learn from the Americans,' he snapped. It was more than just an irritation. I could sense he did not like the country that had so embraced Diana.

I asked him about the monarchy. He believed it could change. 'After all,' he said, 'it's defined by the people involved.' He wanted it to be less formal. 'I'm forever breaking protocol,' he said. I suggested that many people wanted a slimmed-down Scandina-vian-type monarchy. 'Those who advocate it,' he said, 'have they seen it?' His voice was full of scorn. 'Most of those countries have a population of two million. We're a population of sixty million.' I questioned whether the royal family needed so many palaces. He sighed. He had no intention of moving out of Buckingham Palace if he became king. 'That's what people come to see.' Neither was he in favour of reducing the ceremony of the State Opening of Parliament. 'It's what makes us uniquely British. It's what people come to Britain for. It's what makes us unique.' He believed in the quirkiness of the British. It was one of our national traits.

I asked him about the selling of the royal yacht *Britannia*. He thought it was a dreadful decision. 'It's the Treasury,' he said. 'They can't see beyond a balance sheet.' He noticed that the Spanish were spending £12 million on a royal yacht just as we were getting rid of ours.

I looked at my watch. I still had not approached the Camilla question and I had only ten minutes left. So I asked him, 'How would you like your relationship with Camilla Parker-Bowles defined?' He stiffened. 'I don't see any reason why I should define my private life.' I pointed out that it was a matter of public interest. He screwed his face up at this. 'Even royals are entitled to some privacy,' he said. I countered that he had to accept that it was legitimate for the public to want to know about the personal life of the heir to the throne. 'All my life,' he said with real intensity, 'people have been telling me what to do. I'm tired of it.' I went to interrupt but he had not finished. 'I thought the British people were supposed to be compassionate. I don't see much of it.' He was flowing with quiet rage. 'My private life has become an industry. People are making money out of it.' He continued, leaning forward in his chair. He was being 'tortured' by people over his relationship. He never once referred to Camilla by name. And then he almost pleaded, 'I just want some peace.' He told me that he would decide things in his own time. Then he turned on the BBC, accusing it of dumbing down. Even the BBC, he said, was engaged in competition, trying to beat rivals. There was a strong vein of resentment running through him. As I sat there I could see why he so loved Highgrove and its escape from the modern. I was with a man who wanted to be left alone but knew he never would be.

And then my time was up. Sandy Henney came back in the room and said the prince had to leave. I stood up and we shook hands. There had not been much warmth in the conversation. As I left I could only regret the meeting had not been filmed but, as so often happened, without the camera I had learned more. He would never have spoken in the way he did with a lens pointing at him.

Back at the hotel I read the statement about the 'abdication story' that had been issued in London on his behalf. In it the prince had said, 'I begin to tire of needing to issue denials of false stories about all manner of thoughts, which I am alleged to be having. Some stories are so preposterous that they barely warrant a denial. However, others are both so outrageous and hurtful to my family, to the monarchy and me personally that they demand response.' It was the same tone of the man I had just spent half an hour with.

Two days later our film was broadcast. It got a bigger audience than ITV but they had the headlines. I felt dissatisfied, that I had only scratched the surface and that a better story lay untold in my notebook. The story of my meeting leaked to the papers. One article even had me and the prince meeting in the back of an embassy van.

Twenty years before, I could never have imagined sitting down with the prince and asking him about his love life. So much had changed in such a short time. The lives of public figures were dissected and laid bare. There were many reasons for this but for me the start of it all was Watergate. As a journalist I was breastfed on the hearings. The president lied and was forced from office. The lesson was that people in power could not be trusted. They had to be harried, hounded, probed, investigated, their feet held to the fire. That view still ran in my blood, that those born to privilege and power should be accountable. I still believed it, but the light we shone on others was often harsh, relentless and unforgiving.

In the years since my meeting with Prince Charles it has only got worse for him; the accusations, the perceived betrayals. Even servants and butlers joined what the prince called the 'industry' and made money out of him. His uncle once said, 'Realize how fickle public support can be. It has to be earned over again each year.' And that is the prince's burden.

17

The Day I Didn't Make It

I **knew the night** would be long and sleepless, fighting off the weariness until we both declared we had it. The images. The story. It was 10 September 2001, and for some days cameraman Hedley Trigge and I had been planning this shoot. That afternoon we had visited a hypermarket outside Calais and bought a large Mag-Lite torch and food: bananas, biscuits, power bars. I felt like a cop piling up high-energy snacks for a stake-out.

We were in northern France and close to the Red Cross refugee camp at Sangatte. During the previous nights scores of would-be asylum seekers had left the camp and tried to storm trains heading for England through the Channel Tunnel. It had been a kind of break-out, desperate and dangerous. Despite the surveillance cameras, the barbed wire, the high metal fences, they had found a way onto the track. Train services had been suspended and the operators of the tunnel were about to go to court to demand the closure of the camp.

Sangatte was a small neat French coastal town from where, when the light was right, you could catch a flash of white. The cliffs of Dover. That white smudge across the water was what drew the refugees to the town. It beckoned, visible from the hill above the camp. It taunted them, played on their minds until they made their break. Everyone in Britain knew of Sangatte. It was not just a place but a word, loaded with meaning and fear. Sangatte was the hordes at the gate, a clamouring mass, incoherent and threatening.

We decided to tell the story of one night beside the tracks, exactly as we found it, and we had hired a night-vision lens. While it was still light, we identified all the farm tracks and paths that ran around the twenty-mile perimeter fence. Our plan was to cruise for most of the night, driving to the various vantage points, switching off the engine and watching and waiting.

It was close to midnight when we saw movement in the freight yard at Frethum. Dark figures running. It was like watching a jailbreak – ten or twelve men, darting in different directions. Many of them did not share backgrounds or languages but in the camp they had learned to work as a pack, splitting up, making it difficult for the gendarmes and the Eurotunnel security guards to catch all of them. Those who were not immediately discovered hid and waited for the moment, twelve or fifteen seconds of opportunity. They lay still in the gloom until the driver climbed into the cab and edged his train forward. And those were the seconds when a train could be boarded, before it picked up speed. And in those fleeting moments men ran across the tracks and clung to whatever part of the train they could reach, knowing that in half an hour they would be through the tunnel and in Britain. We saw those who failed and were caught. They were put in police vans and returned to the camp only to try again another night. This was the nightly ritual and, from a distance, we caught most of it on camera; but I also wanted to talk to some of the asylum seekers, to travel a distance with them and hear their stories.

At about two in the morning we were parked in the shadowed corner of a field where the glow of the sodium lights of the yard did not reach. Beside us was a bank, some undergrowth and, beyond, the metal fence bordering the tracks. With the night-vision lens Hedley picked out two figures coming towards us. Their hands were thrust deep in their pockets and they looked like two friends lost in conversation, but every so often they stopped and examined the fence as if looking for a hole. Even through the lens I could scarcely make them out and I knew they had not seen us. As they got closer I became nervous. Some of the refugees had recently thrown stones at the cameras and had attacked cameramen. They understood – and the news was passed around the camp – that cameras brought publicity and publicity brought more gendarmes. And more gen-darmes delayed their journey to Britain. So as these two men came towards us I slipped the heavy Mag-Lite torch into my pocket. I am not sure what I was going to do but I liked its weight and felt safer. In the night silence we could hear their voices. When they were just a few feet away they saw us. They recoiled, drew back a few steps, deciding whether or not to run. I called out to them, 'It's OK – we're the BBC.' They moved closer, suspicious and curious. I took my hand off the torch and offered it to them.

They were from Afghanistan, fleeing the Taliban. Their English was poor but it was good enough for us to understand they wanted to go to Britain because they had friends there. Others had made it before them and word had been passed down the line that, even if caught in Britain, almost no one was ever deported. I told them I had been to Afghanistan; that caught their attention and we shared memories. Places, buildings. And here in the blackness, in a field in northern France, was another echo, a tremor from the past. Between us, the Soviets and the West, we had played our game in Afghanistan, we had had our way with them and then left them behind to fall back into obscurity; but now, in this shrunken world, they were on our doorstep like an acquaintance who had unexpectedly turned up.

They agreed to talk and to be filmed as long as we did not show their faces. They knew of a hole in the fence and hoped to be in Britain the next day. So Hedley and I followed them as they pushed through the bushes, holding back branches so they would not scrape the camera. We did not go all the way with them; they threw a wave back and disappeared into the rail yard. It was hard not to wish them well. After all I, too, in a very different way, had been an immigrant. At about five o'clock we got to bed and woke late morning. Hedley had viewed the pictures and we were looking forward to editing a report for that evening's news.

It was a short breathless call from a producer in London. 'Turn on the TV,' she said. A plane had flown into the World Trade Center in New York. I flicked on the television and there was one of the Twin Towers with smoke pouring from it. I sat on the edge of the bed trying to read what I was seeing. My first thought was that our report would be pushed down the running order that evening. My mind flooded with questions – numbers of casualties, what kind of plane, how did a pilot fly into a skyscraper? I stepped away from the television to clean my teeth and then opened the door. Hedley was in the corridor and could hardly get his words out. Two planes had hit the World Trade Center. Every instinct told me his infor-

mation must be confused or wrong, but in seconds I had phoned
Mark Popescu, the editor of the *Ten O'Clock News*, who just said,
'Go to New York.'

That was it. Sangatte no longer mattered. Erased in a phone call.
The fickle finger of daily news. Hedley, like most cameramen, was
meticulous in caring for his equipment but he threw items into his
camera boxes and twenty minutes later we were driving to Paris. I
had booked seats on an Air France flight to New York. We had
driven for no more than ten miles down the autoroute when we
heard on the radio that all flights from Paris to New York had been
cancelled. We turned around and headed for Brussels airport
instead; their flights, they told us, were still flying to the United
States. We drove fast, spurred on by radio reports of more planes
being hijacked. Then it was announced. North America's airspace
had been closed. Four thousand planes were told to clear the skies
and land at the closest airport. One of us said, how about Canada?
We could drive from there to New York. We began checking on
flights to Toronto and Montreal but before we could make a
booking we heard that the closure of North America's airspace
included Canada.

So we slowed and drove almost casually to Brussels, listening to
the radio in disbelief and a little fear. I knew that from this moment
the world would be a different place and that most probably it
would affect my life too. The attack would not go unavenged. Even
in Brussels there was tension. The roads near the American embassy
were being cordoned off. Police with automatic weapons were on
the streets. All over the world people hurried home, seeking out the
security of friends and family as they watched the news.

As we sat in the traffic, thousands of miles from the story, I
burned with frustration. Not only was I not in America or on the
way there but I was not involved in that night's coverage. I debated
with the editor returning to London but we decided that getting to
New York was the priority. None of us knew how long America's
airspace would remain closed. So every hour we were calling the
airlines and making fresh reservations on flights from Brussels,
Paris and London.

Wednesday, 12 September, and I was sitting in the autumn
sunshine at a street café drinking coffee and eating a croissant. We

worked the phones; it eased the frustration. Hedley ordered an NTSC camera, which was compatible with the format used in America, and his wife, Carolyn, brought it over from London. Rumours of flights came and went. North American airspace was opening later, then it was postponed. We were concerned that even when flights resumed it would be difficult finding a seat so we decided to charter our own plane across the Atlantic. We thought that Canadian airports might open first and that we should fly to Montreal and drive from there to New York. The BBC's Brussels bureau found a 737 and chartered it. Hedley and I had too much time on our hands and we worried over every detail. I worried that a 737 could not cross the Atlantic and found myself questioning Privatair, the charter company. The 737, I was reassured, had extra fuel tanks. The plane was in Switzerland and I wanted it moved to Brussels so we could leave as soon as we got clearance.

The waiting continued into the Thursday. The plane, chartered at over £100,000, had arrived in Brussels. As the hours passed the crew ran out of their flight hours and another crew had to be flown in. I, and a handful of colleagues, paced impatiently in the VIP lounge. At about seven in the evening we were told we had clearance to fly to Canada. Boarding the plane was like entering a hotel suite; there was a table with beige leather chairs arranged around it and a sofa with reading lights. There were only about ten rows of seats. At the back of the plane was a bathroom, a double bed and a kitchen. The plane was luxurious and was normally hired by heads of state and royalty. It was bewildering, somehow inappropriate to be travelling like this to a tragedy. When we finally took off, I toasted our departure with a glass of Corton Charlemagne Grand Cru 1997. At last we could begin working. I was determined, more than I had ever been, to get to Ground Zero for the next night's news.

In London there was a similar drama unfolding. All the British TV networks and agencies had got together to hire a 747. It had been waiting on the tarmac at Stansted airport for clearance. I knew that if the 747 reached Montreal before us there would be several hundred journalists and camera crews waiting at immigration, unloading crates of equipment, hiring transport and queuing at the border crossing into the United States. To arrive second was to risk losing an hour so we persuaded our pilot to try and reach Montreal first. We were airborne first and as we flew through London airspace he told us that the 747 had just lifted off. We flew a few miles apart across the Atlantic but were already at Canadian immigration when it landed.

Back in Brussels I had made a mistake. I had asked someone in the bureau to book cars for us at Montreal airport. Because of our equipment I had said, 'Just get us the biggest car you can.' I had not been specific. When we arrived we found a line of limousines waiting with drivers. There could be no more useless a car for a television crew than a low-slung, slow-paced limousine. It had a tiny boot space and so we had to pile the camera boxes on the floor inside. The driver complained and boxes were moved in and out as we tried to spread the load. As soon as we left the airport the bottom of the limousine scraped the road whenever we hit a bump. The driver announced we could not make it to New York and diverted to his depot on the outskirts of Montreal. The boxes were shifted again. It was four in the morning and I had my first doubts that we could file a report for that evening's news.

US Customs and Immigration were helpful. They waved us and the small army of reporters and television crews through, even ignoring the fact that some of them did not have carnets to import equipment into the United States. In our limousine we dawdled through up-state New York, our driver slowing for every dip in the road. As we neared New York City he, for some reason, came off the main route and drove into the suburbs. More time was lost. I knew New York well and ended up directing him into Manhattan, but the hours were slipping away.

We left the editing equipment at the BBC office on the Upper West Side and took a taxi downtown towards Ground Zero. It was 11 a.m. local time and just six hours before the *Ten O'Clock News* in London. I was curious about the exuberant city I knew so well, how it wore its trauma, how it lived with tragedy. At first I could not see it. The place was unchanged: the street energy, the vendors, the hustlers, the joggers off to Central Park. Only at Union Square did the immensity of it intrude. There were people, with faces that had not slept, walking around holding up pictures of those who had gone missing. There was a field of candles. Three days on there were sudden, unashamed tears and strangers embraced and held each other. And all this we saw as the taxi, almost in slow motion, moved through the crowds. And then on the streets further south more photos pasted on walls, black-and-white pictures, fading Polaroids. Street galleries of the lost. So many faces, so many lives upended.

The taxi could not drive further south than Canal Street, which was where they had established the police cordon. From Canal nothing could be seen, not even the smoke rising. We asked a police officer to let us through but he directed us to Canal and the West Side highway. 'That's where they're letting the media in,' he told us. We walked the half-mile to the petrol station on the corner and spoke to the officers but they said we needed a city press pass to be allowed beyond the barrier. 'Where do we pick one up?' we asked. They directed us back to the corner of Broadway and Canal where we had just come from. So we picked up the tripod again and threw the bag with its heavy batteries and tapes on our shoulders and retraced our steps. But the officers at Broadway knew nothing about passes, they had been drafted in from outside the city. Over an hour passed walking up and down Canal Street. There were images to be filmed – the ambulances departing, the huge cranes arriving – but this was the periphery and we ignored it. Finally a police officer told us the passes were being issued at Police Plaza, at the other end of Canal Street.

We pushed our way along a pavement crowded with rescue workers, shoppers, and the curious. A light rain was falling and wind swirled through the streets kicking up the uncollected garbage. We reached the corner of Bowery and Canal and a policeman opened the cordon to allow us to walk the couple of streets to police headquarters. Outside the building was a line of perhaps a hundred journalists. The word in the queue was that only one officer was processing passes and there were people ahead of us who had been waiting two hours already. We had a dilemma. Without the pass I doubted we could get close to Ground Zero and yet, if we waited for one, we would film nothing that day.

As we stood there, tired and worn down by the frustrations, I noticed there was an exit at the back of the police building. There was a single barrier across it operated by an officer in a booth, like a highway toll. Police vehicles were coming in and out. As I watched I realized that if we got beyond the barrier we would not only be inside the cordon but we would be less than half a mile from the site of the World Trade Center. Hedley and I discussed it and decided it was our only chance. We left the queue and walked towards the barrier holding the camera down and hiding the profile of the tripod. As we got close to the booth a white van pulled up and the driver began talking to the officer. While he was distracted we walked through and kept walking. Both of us expected to be called back, to hear a shout behind us, but we never turned around.

We walked beneath an underpass, turned left and then right into Beekman Street. It was quiet here, evacuated. There were soldiers, clusters of the National Guard, but they ignored us. It was the police we were wary of. We followed the billowing smoke, which we could now see clearly. At each corner we stopped and checked for police patrols. In that way we zigzagged through the streets, back-tracking when we saw police officers, but all the time edging towards the site of the disaster. Eventually we found ourselves on Liberty. At the end of the street there were more people, firefighters, soldiers and rescue workers in their yellow hard hats. We realized it together; that was Ground Zero. In our way was a metal cyclone fence, an inner cordon. As we stood in a doorway and planned how to get around it we saw a rescue worker lift a corner of the fence and walk through, and we followed him. There was now just one street to cross to reach One Liberty Plaza. On the corner there were police officers. We waited for them to move but as one group walked away another appeared. Then after five minutes they turned their backs, their attention elsewhere, and we walked across Broadway and into Ground Zero.

For a few moments we stood there, staring at the enormity of it. A towering smoking waste tip of twisted girders and concrete, taller than a six-storey building. There were groups of men working on it, like scavengers, small figures, amidst the immensity of the rubble. They used drills, spades, mechanical diggers and hands. And everywhere the throb of generators. Gusts of wind caught the smoke. It was in our eyes and in our throats. It was an acrid smoke laced with fibreglass and asbestos that left a chemical taste. The scene was bewildering, overwhelming, daunting, almost defying a camera to capture it. We stood like this, without talking, for half a minute and then we started working, expecting that at any time we would be excluded. Every second was precious. I told Hedley to film while I deflected questions from police officers or firefighters. Hedley worked as if he had only five minutes. First the establishing wide shot, revealing the scale. Then the mid-shots with the rescue workers in the rubble. Then the close-ups, the dirt-stained faces of men tearing at the rubble.

A firefighter shouted at us. 'Watch yourselves,' he said. 'That building is about to come down. We're getting out of here.' I looked up. We were standing right under One Liberty Plaza, a fifty-four-storey building. Small pieces of concrete, of hardened ash, of what seemed like paper were falling from it. It was swaying in the wind and the rain and one of the firefighters thought he had seen the top floor buckle. They had formed a line and were evacuating their forward base, moving out their rescue equipment. They had posted watchers to look for the signs that the building was coming down. Hedley and I agreed that at the first shout we would abandon the camera and sprint to the corner of Greenwich and hope that the surrounding buildings would shield us. There would be no debate. We would run for our lives.

The firefighters ignored us; they were all absorbed, working with red-eyed intensity. Hedley filmed close-ups as they passed their equipment down the line from one man to the next. I took the microphone and asked one of them, 'What does this mean to you?' He did not pause or hesitate. 'Freedom,' he said, 'freedom for our country.' He did not say it was about rescuing colleagues or saving lives, it went beyond that, to something primal and fundamental. And all of them were like this, eyes glistening with patriotism.

We almost had enough material for a report. I just needed to record a piece to camera, to place me at Ground Zero. There was no time to carefully craft what I was going to say. It was instinctive. I was dirty, my hair matted with rain and dust. Off the top of my head I talked of the dangers faced by the rescue workers and the risk of another building falling. We knew then we had the story even if we were thrown out. Hedley relaxed and began working closer to the mound of rubble, building sequences rather than just shooting news shots.

A rescue worker in a yellow hat approached me. He spoke quietly and said he was a photographer working undercover. 'I can't talk to you for long,' he said, 'or they'll be suspicious and my cover will be blown.' He had some stills that he wanted delivered to his magazine. He did not want to leave the site or he would never get back in. I agreed to help him. Immediately after the towers had collapsed he had bought a hard hat and gone to Ground Zero, and had stayed there ever since. This was a moment of history. The firefighters wanted it recorded. The public wanted to see it, not just long shots, but to look into the eyes of the men working at the face. But to get those images required subterfuge and deception.

We moved closer still until we were at the foot of the mound of rubble. The rain had turned the dust into a grey paste and some of the rescuers had drawn angry graffiti in it. The men beside us all wore face masks and I wished we had thought of that. A senior fire officer stopped us and said, 'Are you with the city?' I did not answer his question but said, 'Can we help?' He told us it was unsafe where we were standing but he did not ask us to leave. Neither did the police officers at the site. Once inside the inner cordon everyone assumed we had permission to be there. Neither Hedley nor I wanted to leave but we had just three hours to get back uptown, to edit the story, and satellite it. But we could have stayed, perhaps for days, and I wish we had.

We retraced our steps through semi-deserted streets. It was like being in a city on a holiday or a Sunday morning, except there were no lights in the buildings and there were soldiers and military vehicles. We walked through the cordon and stood on the corner of Canal and Bowery but there were no taxis. Eventually I stepped into the traffic and waved down drivers. In those days after 9/11 the normal rules of the city had been suspended; strangers made eye contact and people connected. A white van pulled over and the back door opened. Inside were some young volunteer workers who were going to mid-town. We climbed in and sat on the floor with them. They were in good spirits, laughing, throwing comments out of the windows at those on the street. It was the worst of times but they felt good about themselves; to be involved, to belong, to have a cause.

We arrived back at the bureau with an hour and a half before the satellite feed. It would be a tight edit but not impossible. We were the first BBC team to have reached Ground Zero and we were the lead story. Even though the time was short we fast-viewed the pictures, noting down the time code of the best images. Then I wrote the script and recorded it and Hedley edited the pictures to the words. The minutes flew by. With fifteen minutes to our deadline we learned that we would have to convert our pictures to NTSC, the format used in the United States. We had been told that they could feed PAL, the UK format. The converter had been set up incorrectly and more minutes were lost but at five minutes to five, five minutes to ten in London, we had the tape in the machine ready to play. London, however, could not see the pictures. There were frantic calls. Ten o'clock came and went. I just sat there silently, my head in my hands. There was nothing I could do. There was a problem with the downlink. Then we lost our slot on the satellite and it could not be restored. And the minutes passed and the programme ended. Hedley and I could not look at each other.

The journey that had begun with a fast pack in Sangatte, that had taken us across the Atlantic on a private jet, through the night from Montreal, across police lines in New York, had ended in failure. This was the day I did not make it. In silence we picked up our equipment and went to the hotel, drained of energy. The adrenaline was gone and in its place was a great weariness. In that instant I knew what it was like to lose. It was a kind of defeat and for a long period afterwards it was too painful for Hedley and me to discuss it. The report ran the next day but it was not the same. The weather had changed and the newsreader had to explain that the report was shot the day before, but with a story that changed by the hour, yesterday was history.

We got close to Ground Zero again but never as close as on that first day. The cordon tightened. Every journalist wanted to go there. One day we watched as a well-known ITN correspondent approached the police lines. He was dressed as a rescue worker with a hard hat. His cameraman carried a shovel and had a small camera inside his jacket. The police turned them back; they had wised up to the ploys of reporters. In the days that followed there were major events: Wall Street reopened, heads of state visited, the president attended services and made his military plans. These were the top lines of a day but just beneath the surface a country was changing. The attack had unleashed something – a wave, a current, an energy. I felt it one night when I sat at Nino's, a café where some of the men came for food when they left the site. They knew they would not find anyone alive there but it made no difference to them. Many of their faces were vacant, absorbed, far away. It was like watching men at devotion. The cause had become sacred to them. Most of them did not want to be disturbed or to have to struggle to find the words. Some would begin talking and then stop mid-sentence and just shrug, as if talking were somehow to belittle the endeavour.

And outside the cordon, on their way home, crowds lined the West Side highway cheering them, waving banners, telling them they were heroes. The poster-holders waved as much for themselves as for the firefighters. They had a need to be part of this, to feel connected. And as I watched and reported during those days I felt again the power of the myth. The firefighters who died had been heroes and within days had been folded into the country's story and what it stood for. The image of the firefighters raising a flag above the rubble became iconic. It drew upon past images – the marines raising the flag at Iwo Jima – and so became a reaffirmation of who they believed they were. People everywhere wanted to sign up. In those days and weeks it was easy to offer a life, to lay it down. Flags flew from car aerials, were worn in lapels; football fields were painted red, white and blue. It was inescapable, this great stirring, this enormous patriotic outpouring, and I wondered then what would be done with it, where it would lead.

In a tragedy the cameras are often an intrusion, a violation, seeking out the tear-stained faces that plead to be left alone. It was that way, too, after 9/11. But there were others who found comfort in an interview, who found strength in publicly sharing what they were going through. The symbol of loss were the firefighters. Over three hundred had lost their lives. Approaching the families was difficult; many were inundated with calls from reporters. Thea Fairley, a producer on the *Ten O'Clock News*, found Jean Fischer, who lived on Staten Island and whose husband, John, had died inside the North Tower of the World Trade Center when it collapsed. She actively wanted these, the most painful days of her life, to be shared. She had three children and invited us to film at the memorial service for her husband. She said we could film outside the church and inside during the service. We were invited to the wake afterwards and she agreed to be interviewed in her home. So, in a very short time, this family was no longer an image, a news clip. They were Jean and her three children Timothy, Laura and John junior.

The service was held at the Sacred Heart Church in West Brighton, Staten Island. The firefighters have their own rituals and traditions. They are more a band of brothers than workers. Buddies who shower, sweat, cook and eat together. In the cramped fire-houses, the outer shell, the bull, the lines that all of us shoot, are broken down. In a short time they get the measure of each other, who will be standing beside them when they enter a burning building. The families know each other. Sons follow fathers. This community has its way of saying farewell to colleagues.

Hedley and I waited outside the church. The coffin had been placed on an old pump-and-ladder engine, its age a linking back to others who had died on duty. The engine came up the hill slowly, silently. As it got closer to the church the firefighters on either side of the street lined up. The engine passed under a giant flag strung between the raised ladders of two fire trucks. Behind, in cars, came the family.

The service was informal. Friends and colleagues remembering a man, the quirks and stories of a life. There was the manner of his death. John Fischer was on the thirty-fifth floor of the tower when the order came through to evacuate the building. He noticed two of his men had continued up. He could not reach them on the radio so he walked up to tell them and was never seen again. There were the memories of an ordinary life; the teenager working in a deli, the local man, the soccer coach, the cooking at the firehouse. His widow, Jean, recalled that when they were dating the heavens would invariably open up. Simple moving stories. And the final call. He had left a message before heading to the World Trade Center. 'I called you back but got no answer,' she read out. And then her final tribute, words trailing off: 'Everyone calls you a hero ... I always knew it.' I recalled words from another time: 'We are always saying goodbye in this world – always standing on the edge of loss attempting to retrieve some memory, some human meaning from the silence – something which is precious and gone.'

I was standing on the church steps when the service ended and the coffin was carried to the back of the engine. Beside me were a group of ten-year-olds; John Fischer had been their soccer coach. As the coffin passed they saluted and tears streamed down their faces. As I stood there at this stranger's funeral I cried too, real tears that could not be disguised. Over the years I had attended and covered countless funerals but had always been detached. Even at my own father's funeral I had shown no emotion. Maybe it was the boys next to me, maybe it was my brief meeting with the family, maybe it was memory and the loss of my own father, maybe it was a weariness at having witnessed so much, but on this Staten Island street there was a breaking point and I was no longer immune.

Later we went to the wake but did not take the cameras inside. The following day I interviewed Jean. She was relieved that the ordeal of the memorial service was behind her. The house was busy and she liked it that way. They were off to stay with family. In my notebook I had jotted down the obvious questions. What was it like to lose someone in so public a tragedy? What had been the effect on the children? How do you explain it? She had been helped by the community: friends calling; strangers sending food parcels. The children knew their father had died trying to save others and there was comfort in that. The hardest part was that there was no escaping 11 September. It was everywhere. In every paper, on TV, in speeches, on the radio. It was a reference point, the day that everyone would always remember where they were. TV channels replayed the pictures of the planes going into the World Trade Center and the towers collapsing. There was no respite. I met a man whose wife had been a flight attendant on the first plane that had flown into the towers. Every time he saw the image he broke down. Sometimes, as journalists, we talk of people 'coming to terms with', of 'closure', of 'moving on'. Glib, easy, banal words. In my experience 'moving on' is a much harder road to travel and here I met people who were trapped by the kind of arresting images that I struggled so hard to produce. Later some TV networks locked away the most disturbing images of 11 September and maybe that was right.

So much of news involves tragedy – thousands of lives lost in a 9/11 or an earthquake, or just the pain of individual families. When I started reporting the cameras were kept away or stayed wide, leaving some space between us, the viewer, and the horror of the event. Not any more. We are in close. After the Bali bombing officials unzipped body bags to identify victims from their rings and watches in front of our cameras. After the attacks in Madrid there were cameras inside the morgues. Private space has shrunk.

In August 2002, less than a year after 9/11, I was sent to the village of Soham in Cambridgeshire. Two ten-year-old girls, Holly and Jessica, had gone missing. Their fate had become a huge story. Every moment that followed – the search for them, the false trails, the discovery of their bodies, the arrest of their murderer – was reported in detail.

Soham is a village: a main street, a church and a few roads running off. A small community violated by murder, by child murder. Then there is the media. No longer is it just a few television reporters. It is an invasion. Satellite vans. Twelve or fifteen of them parked up, their dishes extended. (In America I have covered events where there are fifty to sixty satellite trucks.) Then the foreign camera crews all seeking images and interviews. People are stopped, questioned, then stopped again.

On the Sunday, after the girls' bodies had been found, I was parking my car when a woman recognized me and screamed, 'Why don't you just leave us alone?' Shops and pubs put signs on their doors: 'Media not welcome.' Eventually the local priest asked us to leave town. Yet that night, the village, along with millions elsewhere, watched the news.

A few months later, in November 2002, there was an earthquake in southern Italy. The tremor, measuring 5.4 on the Richter scale, had not been large. In the hill-town of San Giuliano di Puglia, most of the buildings had held firm but part of the school had collapsed, trapping dozens of children. That made it a story: the rescue of the children. Hedley and I flew to Naples and arrived at the village at two in the morning. There was no electricity and the village was dark except for floodlights illuminating a pile of concrete and twisted girders. On top were rescue workers and firemen. We filmed from a distance but gradually moved closer. Clustered around the school were the families waiting for news of their children. Occasionally there was a shout and a small girl or boy would be lifted alive from the rubble. There were cries of 'viva, viva' and then applause. Other families sat on chairs yards away from the rescue workers. One mother clutched her missing child's stuffed toy. Another woman, beside us, gave out a long despairing cry and then called her child's name, 'Antonio, Antonio.' It was a harrowing, haunting cry that split the night. And we were right in beside them, at this the most terrible moment of their lives. I was not certain that we should be there, to see a family hear their child was dead. The angry cry of denial, the uncontrollable howling, and the mother collapsing on the ground in front of us. The grief was unbearable. During that night there were moments when we kept the camera on the ground but others did not. Over the years we have moved in closer and closer. It is a different time now, a period of little restraint. Lives are laid bare. The lenses are unsparing – if not ours, then the ubiquitous digital camera.

Time and again the irony strikes me. We want to see, we expect to see, to be taken there by the cameras and yet, when people see news-gathering in operation, they are offended by it and resent it.

18

Boot Camp

I felt apprehensive and edgy as I drove down I-95 out of Washington. It was one of those February days when the world was just a drab place. The sky was leaden, the trees stripped bare, and all the cars were caked with a dark-brown slush.

I was on my way to boot camp at Quantico, the headquarters of the United States Marine Corps. A kind of journalistic call-up was under way. For the first time in half a century the Pentagon was planning to integrate reporters into its war machine on a large scale. Quantico was intended to break us in, to prepare us for war: some basic training, some safety lessons and a light flick of discipline.

I had spent long summers in these parts, biking to Mount Vernon or sitting with a beer and a hotdog in the stands at Camden Yards. These places suddenly felt beyond reach; every familiar signpost only underlined what lay ahead, what had to be gone through before I could return. I was on the other side of normality. It was as if all the dreams and plans that go to make up hope had been withdrawn. In the way stood war, inescapable and unknown.

Quantico was both familiar and strange. As I drove past the guardpost there was a column of marines doing their shuffle-jog behind a flag. Everywhere there were young men and women, scrubbed clean with idealism, books under their arms, walking between classrooms. Cinema had made all this familiar. And yet here I was with a large Northface backpack reporting to a marine officer, and that seemed strange.

I had agreed to a week of boot camp because I was going to be 'embedded' with an American unit. It was a clumsy, bureaucratic word. Microchips were embedded and not much else. The dictionary definition was 'to place in a mass of matter', which seemed a pretty harsh judgement on the American military. To most people it sounded like 'in bed with' and that was a problem. As friends never tired of pointing out, when you go to bed with someone you have already expressed a preference. So I was due to be 'embedded' and to some I was already compromised.

It was not essential to go to Quantico but we were on a diplomatic offensive. The Pentagon owned most of the front-row seats for the forthcoming war and I wanted one. So I had spent the weekend running myself ragged ticking off the marine checklist, searching the Washington malls for a lensatic compass, a watch cap, foot powder, hand-sanitizer lotion and thermal undergarments.

There were about sixty of us. More men than women. Average age, thirty-five. I was older than most but confident in my fitness. As we queued for our room keys I recognized a few faces from my time as a correspondent in Washington but I was the only person from Britain.

I walked across to one of the barrack blocks. The corridors were long, dimly lit and battleship grey. There were four bunks in the room, a washbasin, toilet and shower. There was already a backpack on top of one of the bunks. I threw my bag onto the other top bunk, preferring to be closer to the ceiling than to have someone sleeping above me.

We gathered in a classroom. As the officer in charge of the basic school entered the chairs of our marine escorts flew back and they stood and saluted. Not a journalist moved. We all sat on our hands but you knew what everyone was thinking. We were close enough to the military just by being there without standing to attention.

In the past a little bit of fear, a little bit of loathing, had marked the relationship between the military and the media. In 1991, during the First Gulf War, the Pentagon had gone out of its way to exclude reporters. Some commanders preferred it that way. Some journalists, too, were happier with a stand-off, with mutual suspicion.

9/11 had changed all that. You could not avoid the new patriotism in America. Flags were worn in the lapels. Firefighters, soldiers, marines. All were heroes and untouchable. There was a new conformity. The Republic was under attack and it was a time for respect, for the old values. God had not withdrawn his blessing and the sceptical reporter trod carefully.

Even so, marines and journalists watched each other warily. Neither could quite believe the other. The captain, who took the first class, began by saying, 'We like to practise being miserable.' He spoke about cardiac hill and the five-mile road march. There was nervous laughter.

I had two roommates: Brian, a cameraman from Fox News, and Jeff, a young magazine reporter out of New York. So much seemed random. Brian's name had just appeared on a list and he was due to go 'somewhere in the Middle East' but he appeared to have little say as to where he would end up. Jeff was a feature writer. He had never covered a demonstration before, let alone a war. Someone on the magazine had suggested he do some stories on an American unit. So here he was, sitting on the edge of a bunk, trying to make sense of it all. I had, at least, chosen to cover the American campaign but from that moment on it would be others who would decide where I would go and the unit I would travel with.

The wake-up call was at 5.30 in the morning. On the first day a marine knocked gently on the door. Brian, the cameraman, was unimpressed and asked rather too loudly, 'You call that a wake-up call?' The following morning the door nearly came flying off its hinges as it was hammered from the corridor. Marines were not to be mocked.

At Quantico the past breathes. Marines are shaped by it. It stares down at them from the walls in the expressionless faces of men who made the ultimate sacrifice. It's in every painting and photograph. Marines had participated in all of America's wars going back to the Continental Congress. A continuum of bright, shining moments. All to be lived up to. Every corridor asked the same question: 'Do you measure up?'

A few months earlier I had visited the military academy at West Point. They were running classes on character. 'You are not fit to lead men and women,' said the major, pacing the front of the class like a small-town preacher, 'until you've looked inside, really looked inside and established your code.' Lies were out, even the small ones you tell your girlfriend. The soldier who tells a lie cannot be trusted in conflict. 'I want to ask you,' said the instructor, 'do you have the courage to do the right thing?' What was expected of the soldier was a higher standard than was found on the street.

It was the same here at Quantico. Take away the guns and the uniforms and you just might be at a seminary. The higher calling even extended to the breakfast line. 'Two eggs, ma'am,' they would politely tell the catering staff. A marine never passed me without saying, 'Good morning, sir.' I wanted to know what happened to these values when men and women were frightened and confused in battle.

The Vietnam era with its screwballs and dissent seemed but a memory. There was a new earnestness not seen since the paranoia of the Cold War. Out there was a real enemy. The military was standing tall, sure of itself, basking in public affection.

Our days were filled with classes. Maps, contour lines, military grids. True north and magnetic north. We shot the azimuth. Without pausing we were on to cotton undergarments and moist towelettes. The women were shown how to straddle ditches and piss; how ponchos gave them a shot at privacy. Then it was on to abdominal wounds. Tourniquets and pressure points. The M40 field protective mask followed. So did the instructions. Stop breathing. Close your eyes. No facial hair in the desert. It breaks the mask's seal. No contact lenses.

Horrors were rattled through. Chemical agents. Nerve. Blood. Blister. Choking. VX. Severe muscular twitching. Respiratory failure. Or did Sarin cause that? I flipped back a page but we had moved on to Atropine pens. An auto-injector to be used after nerve-agent poisoning. Press the green-capped needle into the upper part of the buttocks. Hold for ten seconds. Then all six at once. Could that be right?

'Surface-to-surface missiles give little warning before they detonate.' I was with that. I was back in the zone. I wrote it down. How did this bite help me? I was not quite sure. We were on to high-explosive, incendiary rounds and chemical munitions. 'Never drive towards the direction of impacting rounds.' I was on to that. Smart advice but the instructor was already on to ambushes and the wedge formation.

I sat cross-legged on my helmet and listened as words and

phrases flowed over me. I focused intently. This, after all, was about my survival; but as the hours went by I tuned out. I could never be ready for war in a week. I kept thinking of what 'Che' Guevara had said: 'Death may surprise us.' Much the better question was, 'Did I feel lucky?'

At night, after dinner, we dropped by the bar. The instructors were often there. Most of them wanted to be in Kuwait. Iraq was the next big game and they itched to be on the field. Not all of them. Some had seen enough. We were not what they expected, they told us. They had imagined a class of the unaccepting, the cynical, the ever-questioning, row after row of stony-faced sceptics.

The strange thing was we never discussed the forthcoming war with Iraq. Not in terms of whether the case had been made, whether it was justified, whether it was right or wrong. It never came up. It was as if by coming to Quantico we had moved beyond that. We had just accepted war was coming and our part in it.

It was hard to pin us down, hard to know what had brought everyone to Quantico. We were all so different. It felt as if across America every editor wanted their take on the biggest story of a generation and the Pentagon was offering a ride-along. So there was a woman reporter from *People* magazine with an eye to the Scud-stud and the GI hero; a photographer from the *Rocky Mountain News* who wanted to snap some of the local boys in the desert. There were snappers and writers from papers I had never heard of, all signing up as war reporters.

Then there were the network correspondents. Bob Franken from CNN. He would never get too close to the military. He was an old-fashioned prickly reporter who liked to stay on the outside, enjoying the occasional face-off with authority.

David Bloom from NBC was a network correspondent like myself. He co-opted me as his table-football partner. He put me in defence, coaching me through every game. Every goal mattered. 'I'm a very competitive guy,' he told me. There was no point in playing if you did not want to win and we were never beaten by the marines.

He had resolved his doubts about the war. He wanted to be there in the frontline. He wanted his network to be first and had put all his energy into devising the equipment that would give his coverage an edge.

Occasionally, news would reach some reporter as to which unit they had been assigned to. My roommate Jeff heard that he was heading for an airbase somewhere in the Gulf. He would be able to fly on missions into combat. What his paper did not know was that he hated flying. We lay on our bunks discussing this. 'How can I tell the paper that I can't do this?' It was gnawing away at him. During the middle of the week we were put in a helicopter for a ten-minute ride to a landing zone under fire. Jeff hated that, too, and was sick inside his helmet. The fact is he did not have to do any of this; but reporters find it almost impossible to walk away from a major story.

On the Thursday we were taken to the gas chamber, which the marines use for their chemical and biological training. The plan was to enter the chamber wearing a mask and then CS gas would be released. We were supposed to use two fingers to let some of the gas seep inside the mask and then practise clearing the mask without inhaling any of the gas.

I had just about worked out how to get my mask on in nine seconds but on this occasion, instead of holding my breath, I took a gulp of gas. My eyes stung, my chest tightened and I began coughing, drawing in more CS gas. I could have signalled for help and one of the marines would have taken me outside, but I was determined to avoid that. Somehow I hung on, only for my mobile phone to ring. I tried to silence it but hit the wrong button and answered it instead. Through the mask I tried to explain that I couldn't talk, I was in a gas chamber. We came outside and all of us laughed about the phone call but I knew that I wasn't ready for a chemical or biological attack. Most of us felt that. If the Iraqis used chemical weapons, few of us would survive. You practise and you hope. That's how people get by.

Late in the week we were visited by Colonel James 'Jay' Defrank from the Pentagon. He was an older officer, sharp-faced and intelligent. 'The intent,' he told us, 'is to allow you to be there in live combat operations.' It was a simple statement, made with no great emphasis. The lecture hall was quiet. We were being told we would be going not just to war, but to the front. I looked around. Every face was taut with concentration.

I knew his words would be met with some scepticism. There were many reporters who had been promised on previous occasions that they could report a war, only to be kept back. Daily briefings were as close as they ever got to the action. Defrank, however, was a precise man. There had been, he said, 'a significant shift in thinking on behalf of the military'. The Pentagon was committed to providing 'the greatest degree of access consistent with the security of the mission'.

He did not want there to be any misunderstanding. If a television team was with a unit that saw combat then that team would be able to film whatever was happening. We would be taking the same risks as the troops. There would be no censorship although there could be some blackout periods just prior to engagements.

We were, he told us, to be 'embedded for life'. We all laughed. 'What does that mean precisely?' asked someone. 'From now until the victory parade,' replied the colonel, 'you will eat, sleep and live alongside the frontline troops. Once assigned,' he went on, 'you can leave your unit but you won't be able to return.'

Suddenly it was all happening fast. Breathtakingly fast. The Pentagon was making the final decisions on assignments. We would be moving out to the desert as soon as possible. The Pentagon wanted us with our units several weeks before war started. Some reporters would fly on military planes directly from the United States.

So this was it. Everyone was talking. We crowded around the colonel in the corridor. We could not get enough detail. I recalled those queues outside recruiting offices, of young men lying about their ages in order to join up. What we were being offered was dangerous but there was an excitement about it. For a moment we were all caught up in the drama of units and times of departure.

The following day was our last at Quantico. It had snowed all night and the trees sagged under the heavy fall. The base was quieter, the sound deadened. There was something reassuring and disturbing about the snow. It linked back to childhood memory, to a magical, safe place of dreams, and yet it was a reminder of what so easily could be lost.

We were due to go on a march through the woods where we would be attacked by marines. They would simulate a chemical attack and, under fire, we would have to put on our masks. It turned out this was also 'media day'. I had never imagined anyone would be interested in our training but there was a line of cameras. TV stations and reporters would be able to film us and ask questions.

The original plan had been for us to wear uniform as we headed off into the woods. Suddenly voices were raised against. It was as if we had all woken from a sleep. There was no way I was going to be filmed in a marine column, in combat gear. I realized then what a delicate line we were treading. I saw myself as just preparing to cover a war, but to others we had joined up.

So I wore my grey fleece, but I felt uncomfortable in the column as TV cameras filmed me. I felt on the wrong side of the line and found myself trying to avoid the lenses. Away from Quantico this was going to be a controversial war and as an 'embedded correspondent' I would be under suspicion.

The fresh snow was too tempting. Soon we were pelting the marines with snowballs. The cameras recorded everything. After a while I stood aside, unsure what the people of Denmark or Saudi Arabia or any place else would make of this. Were these the games of buddies, of enlistees? I didn't know.

We lined up for course photographs in front of a large yellow-and-orange sign for a landing zone. Most of us wore ski hats. We looked like any group of hikers except for the few marine instructors standing with us. We were all smiling. A carefree moment in the snow. In a short time many of us would be in the Gulf. We would meet again briefly but some lives would end out in the desert.

We embraced and made promises that we would buy each other drinks in Baghdad. Then we were gone. I drove back to Washington. It was late afternoon and I went to the Daily Grill in Georgetown and ordered a vodka. It was not a drink that I normally had but I wanted to stop the world for half an hour and try to regain control of my life. Then my phone rang. I had been assigned to the American Third Infantry Division and in a short time would be heading to the Gulf.

19

The Desert Days Before War

On Thursday 6 March, I left London for Kuwait. There was no way of disguising it or spinning it. I was going to war. To family and friends I had played down the risk, but you cannot do that to yourself. Joining the American Third Infantry Division was as much a call-up as if I had been in the military.

I was aged fifty-two and putting myself in harm's way. No one was forcing me. It was not the thrill of seeing combat. I was way past that. I knew war was capricious, that in a moment lives were changed. Those who returned were often damaged. I had colleagues who lived with flashbacks, the recurring images of people close to them dying. Even so, something powerful was drawing me towards Iraq. It was partly reporter's pride, partly ambition, but mainly it was the pull of the biggest story in years and I had to be there.

I found myself constantly calculating the odds. Would the Iraqis fight? Would they use chemical weapons? These mind games were like a loop of piped music that I could never quite escape. They were a search for reassurance, something to cling on to, but the answers changed from day to day and so did my mood.

The flight stopped at Larnaca, a holiday destination. Here, as in London, the sun was shining as the first of the season's package flights parked beside us on the runway. The normal world was continuing around me but I felt disconnected, no longer part of it.

The following day I woke up in Kuwait, in a chalet beside the Gulf. I was in a resort hotel, although why anyone would want to lie on an artificial beach and gaze out at an oil terminal was beyond me. War seemed much closer here. The hotel was full of American and British officers, the media and a few Kuwaiti families who believed the hotel was beyond the range of Iraqi Scud missiles.

We had to register for war. In the past reporters would hitch a ride to the front and report what they saw. This time it would be different. Everyone who wanted to cover the war had to get an ID card from the Coalition Forces, which meant the British and the Americans.

We were divided into two groups: 'unilaterals' and 'embeds'. The 'unilaterals' would operate independently, crossing into Iraq after the war started and taking their chances. The Americans did not really want 'unilaterals' floating around the battlefield. 'Listen,' said one captain, 'no one is going to stop you but if you approach one of our units and we don't know who you are bad things can happen.' So hundreds of reporters from all over the world were queuing for passes. For them registering was relatively simple; but for 'embeds' like myself it was a long and sobering process.

The Americans wanted family names, next of kin, blood group and phone numbers of relatives. We had to be measured for chemical suits. Letters had to be signed indemnifying the United States government from any responsibility in the event of our death or injury. There was also a list of ground rules that had to be signed. If these were violated military police would evict us from our units.

I read the fifty clauses fairly closely. Some were simple. I could not carry firearms, 'consume alcoholic beverages' or 'possess pornography'. I could not disclose details of future operations or the size of American units, or reveal the effectiveness of Iraqi tactics. Live broadcasts from the battlefield had to be authorized by the local commander. I did not have too much difficulty with any of that.

I noticed at the top of the document that these rules were 'not intended to prevent release of derogatory, embarrassing, negative or uncomplimentary information'. I underlined that and tucked the rules in my pocket, knowing I might have to fall back on this piece of paper if I fell out with any American commander over my reporting.

By the end of my first day I had a yellow pass, with my photo, that read: 'Gavin Hewitt "embedded: 3ID"'. That is what the military called it – '3ID', not the Third Infantry Division. Underneath my name was a motto: 'We will not falter. We will not fail.' I had never had a press pass with a motto on it before. I noticed that I had been assigned to the division for over a year, until May 2004. I just hoped this was not the length of campaign they were expecting.

We met the commander of the Third Infantry Division. General Buford Blount was a slightly hunched fifty-four-year-old. He was grey-haired, softly spoken and courteous. He came into the room and shook hands with each of us who would be travelling with his forces. He was not what I had expected. There was not a trace of aggression about him. He was unhurried, a man with time.

It was different when he spoke. He was precise, very direct. 'The goal,' he said, 'is to set conditions for regime change in Iraq.' There was no mention of United Nations' resolutions or weapons of mass destruction. We were off to 'get' Saddam.

The general gave us a brief history of the division known as the 'Rock of the Marne'. It had its own celebrities. The movie star Audie Murphy had fought with the division. As at Quantico I was struck by how much the past matters to the military. It is what they measure themselves against. He listed, in great detail, his equipment. It reminded me of visiting an American historical site where the guide reels off statistics. 'When we cross the LD [the line of departure],' he said, 'we will be carrying a million and a half gallons of fuel.' Ten thousand vehicles would be travelling with the division.

The general told us, in his same low-key, measured way, that it would be 'austere' and 'pretty rough'. 'We've been told to be ready,' he said, 'and all systems are loaded.' If the attack happened the division would be the lead element and we would be on the frontline. He acknowledged that the fear of chemical attacks was causing some concern to the soldiers but he personally 'slept pretty good at night'.

Most stories are about other people's lives. As a reporter you are detached, a breed apart. Often it seems we travel with immunity. Now, more than with any event I had covered before, I felt exposed. There was no special pass, no safe place for reporters to escape to. The general was not talking about some other group, he was talking about what could happen to us.

After he left everyone began staking out how much risk they would take. A CBS correspondent told me that he would not go into Baghdad if there was street fighting. A reporter from *Time* magazine was worried about being held back by his unit if Baghdad was falling. He was prepared to break away and head up the road himself rather than miss the fall of the Iraqi capital. In my experience you never know what you will do.

I had a more urgent problem. Officially the Pentagon had told us that we could bring what we could carry. That would include clothes, body armour, helmet, a sleeping bag and any equipment, but for the major television companies that would not work. We had slimmed down our equipment but we still had sixteen boxes. You had to expect technology to fail in the desert. So we had a camera, a smaller hand-held videocam, an edit pack, two small satellite dishes, two laptops, a videophone, a night-vision lens, two satellite phones, as well as batteries, chargers and a tripod.

General Blount wanted television coverage so he had agreed that a few networks, including the BBC, could bring their own vehicles. This had to be done in great secrecy. The Pentagon must not learn what was being planned – nor other reporters, or else they would demand the same and Washington would end up vetoing the whole idea.

The ideal vehicle was a civilian Humvee, similar to the standard four-by-fours used by American forces. Its wide wheels were excellent in the desert and it had the great advantage that if it went wrong the unit would be carrying spare parts. We moved late, far too late, to find a Humvee. There were none left in Kuwait or anywhere else in the Gulf. The Americans had also insisted the vehicle run on diesel. All the military vehicles used diesel and so it would be easy to refuel us. Petrol was too flammable, too dangerous in war. We had people scouring the Middle East for diesel-powered four-by-fours but they, too, had all gone.

So here we were, just days before we joined our unit in the desert, without a vehicle. A diesel Land Rover Discovery had been found in Luxembourg but it was electric blue. It was now being sprayed in desert camouflage before being flown to Kuwait. If it was delayed our whole plan for covering the war would be in jeopardy.

The American networks were way ahead of us. Parked outside the Sheraton Hotel, the other main media hotel, was a row of modified Humvees. Some had sophisticated satellite dishes on the back, which would enable them to broadcast pictures 'live' on the move. I found it very depressing. The war had not started and

I already knew we could not compete. Even if all our equipment worked we would not be able to broadcast 'live' pictures. I had made a promise that I would put myself in danger only if I was able to compete with the best. Already that promise felt empty. It was my recurring nightmare that we would take all these risks only for our reports to arrive behind the other networks'.

We had been told that often we would be driving at night, without lights, sandwiched between tanks and fighting vehicles. The driver would have to use night-vision goggles and we had some flown in from California. We decided that we needed a driver who had been in the military. A friend recommended Jimmy from Scotland, who had just finished a long career in the Special Forces.

Even from a distance you would not mess with Jimmy – and that was, later, the view of the soldiers. He had little hair and what he had was cropped short. It was the shoulders and arms which, even under a shirt, looked as if they had been worked on. He was a tough, no-nonsense Scot with an immense pride in having worked in the Special Forces.

We were to be a team of three: me, Jimmy and Peter Gigliotti, a cameraman who went by the name of Jig. Everyone thought Jig looked Australian even before they knew it. He was in his early thirties and always looked relaxed, as if a beach and a beer might not be far away, but he had been in conflict before and knew about taking pictures when bullets were flying.

It was now Monday, 10 March, and the following day we were due to join our unit in the desert. We were not ready and were running out of time. Jig was wrestling with new satellite equipment, which he had been trained on only days before. Jimmy and I left him at the hotel trying to send video data by satellite.

We met up with Ali, a Jordanian who lived in Kuwait. I had met him in January and had taken him on as a fixer. He was a restless, energetic man who liked the challenge of proving he could deliver the impossible. Ali, Jimmy and I now raced to a shipping agent's office. We shook hands, we drank tea, we pleaded for the papers that would allow us to import a Land Rover into Kuwait. We then argued our way into the cargo area at Kuwait International Airport. There we found our sand-coloured Land Rover Discovery strapped to a pallet. Ali somehow persuaded the cargo workers to release the straps for Jimmy to drive the vehicle off the ramp. After we had paid various taxes we left the airport and drove to the only Land Rover dealership in Kuwait City.

We wanted the vehicle serviced, a roof rack fitted, and sand filters added. We needed the vehicle alarms removed because we were afraid that in a moment of tiredness we could set off the alarm in the desert and alert the Iraqis to our position. All this would normally take over twenty-four hours but we needed it done in four. In the end a deal was struck. We paid four hundred dollars and picked the vehicle up late afternoon.

While the vehicle was being serviced the three of us headed into a district of workshops and hardware stores. We bought shovels, tow ropes, filters, fan belts, battery chargers that could run off the engine, cargo netting, luggage straps, desert-jacks, blackout material for the windows. Ali knew a souk that usually sold jerry cans but a war was coming and by the time we got there they had all been sold. We were now having to rely on bribes. Ali put out the word that we would pay over a hundred dollars for a jerry can. Later that night three mysteriously turned up. We visited a vast supermarket that looked like a hangar. Jimmy threw toilet paper, power bars, water containers, juice for the water and bananas into the trolley. 'These,' he said with a smile, holding up packs of baby wipes, 'will become some of your best friends in the desert.'

Early evening we picked up the Land Rover and drove to one of the few men in Kuwait who knew about fitting a satellite-phone antenna. I wanted to be able to broadcast 'live' on the move even if it was only for radio. For three hours two technicians worked on fitting a microphone to the front windscreen, a cradle for the phone, a speaker phone and a magnetic plate to the roof, which would be the antenna. There was a problem with the software but we had to return to the hotel to pack the vehicle.

It was late evening by the time we drove the forty kilometres back to where we were staying. The three of us worked into the night preparing our vehicle for war. It was soon apparent that we could not bring everything with us. We settled on one medical kit, not three. A car charger was coming but not the diesel generator. Head torches like miner's lamps were in, Magnum Lights were out.

Two plastic water containers were packed, the water filter was not. Spare clothes were discarded. I settled for seven T-shirts, five shirts and two pairs of light chinos. Smaller items like sand goggles and compressed-air cans were slotted in under the seats until, as Jimmy said, it looked 'like a tinker's caravan'.

Before leaving London I had had my first anthrax vaccination. I was supposed to have two more within a month. A doctor gave me needles and the vaccine but in the race to leave the hotel I left the vaccines in the fridge. I would have to take my chances.

Tuesday, 11 March was the day for 'shipping out', for leaving civilization behind. One American commander had told us 'to think of the worst camping trip you can imagine' and he would be right. At 7 a.m. we formed a line in the hotel car park and collected our chemical and biological suits. So much of what we know is formed by cinema that the unusual seems common. I had watched scenes like this in war movies; new recruits – strangers to each other – lining up. The tennis courts, the palm trees, the low humidity could so easily have been Californian. It was hard to digest, as I moved onto a court to have my mask fitted, that this was real and I was part of it.

We were shown how to assemble the gas mask and how to check that it was not leaking. I kept telling myself that all I had to do was to stop breathing, close my eyes and fit the mask. The mask was held in a pouch on your left hip and the trick was to be quick to the draw. Several times I managed, with my eyes closed, to put it on in under nine seconds but I knew I would be very lucky to repeat that if we were under chemical attack.

I wondered whether anyone around me was apprehensive, whether anyone was sweating inside. It did not seem that way. For some the war was a chance to live out a fantasy. There was one French reporter dressed in Special Forces black down to his skull cap and military boots. He seemed far away, withdrawn and possibly dangerous. There were others in military uniform for whom covering the war was the next best thing to joining up. Others wore the war reporters' uniform of khaki trousers and a waistcoat full of pockets. Many had keffiyehs tied around their necks even though we were in the lobby of a five-star hotel. They sat around reminiscing about Afghanistan, Kosovo or the Gaza strip; their lives were defined by other people's conflicts, with adrenaline as their drug of choice.

I desperately needed a few moments to myself. I found some rocks overlooking the Gulf and sat down. It was a beautiful day. The water was calm. The searing heat of summer was still weeks away. There was no way back now, not that I was looking for it. The route home, and to all those people I loved, lay via Baghdad and war.

The Third Infantry Division had insisted that the deception about the vehicle must continue until we were with our unit in the desert. Jig and I would be driven out in a bus along with other journalists and photographers. Jimmy had to drive to a rendezvous point just north of the Mutla Pass from where he would be taken to one of the American base camps.

At 3.30 in the afternoon a fleet of buses pulled up at the hotel. About forty journalists, weighed down by huge backpacks, began boarding. My rucksack was embarrassingly small for an indefinite stay in the desert. David Bloom from NBC smacked me on the back and said, 'This looks like a man who has a vehicle driving up the road to meet him.' We laughed. I knew he not only had his own vehicle but had tested it to enable him to broadcast live from the battlefield. He could not wait to get out into the desert and begin reporting.

We still had not been told which units we would be joining. The division planned it that way. They did not want endless negotiations about who was going where. We would be told our unit when we got there and when we could do little about it. All Jig and I had learned was that we would be with the 3rd Brigade. It was a major anxiety. One senior British television correspondent had already told me he had been assigned a Patriot-missile company based south of Kuwait City. Unless he could get it changed his war was all but over.

We swung in a huge arc around Kuwait City before joining the highway north towards Iraq. After an hour and a half we left the road and headed west on a desert track. All around us was a vast plain with military encampments. The light was already fading as we crawled behind a long convoy of army supply trucks. The bus moved from one base to another dropping off photographers and reporters.

Even though we had a military escort we lost our way amidst the convoys and the swirling dust. Everyone on the bus was hot and frustrated. 'Maybe the Iraqis stand a chance after all,' someone called out. It was about one in the morning when the bus stopped for Jig and me and a handful of others. We walked between two lines of barbed wire and entered a briefing tent. We were met by Colonel Daniel Allyn, the commander of the Third Brigade. I still had my civilian mind and expected a coffee, bed and a briefing the following day.

It might have been the middle of the night but briefing us was part of that day's task and it was not going to wait until morning. Colonel Allyn launched into a detailed breakdown of the 3rd Brigade Combat Team, including its call signs. His was Hammer 6. The structure was difficult to follow because normal units had been raided to form task forces. Jig and I were told we were being assigned to Task Force 1-30 Infantry.

Even here, during the night, Colonel Allyn wanted us to know something of the history of the brigade. He rattled off World War One battles like Aisne, Champagne–Marne and Meuse–Argonne that the brigade had taken part in. We moved through the history of the last century but I lost him when he explained that the 3rd Brigade was actually the same as the 197th, which was deployed in the First Gulf War as part of the 24th Infantry Division.

There were more ground rules. All interviews with soldiers were on the record. The media had to consult with the commander upon receipt of any 'perceived rumours from soldiers or speculation about future operations'. I could be removed from the unit if I was not physically fit.

Colonel Allyn wished us good luck and we were introduced to Captain Mike Shultz, our liaison officer with Task Force 1-30. He told us to throw our backpacks into his Humvee and then slowly we weaved our way past the silent rows of military vehicles parked in the desert.

We were taken to a communications vehicle. An awning had been stretched over the back of it and inside a few canvas cots had been laid out. The captain said we could sleep there for the night.

Just as he was leaving us he said, 'One other thing – you can't piss in the desert.' He took us in the moonlight to what looked like a piece of piping sticking out of the ground. 'You piss down the pole,' he said. In a military camp there were strict rules about hygiene.

I slept fitfully for maybe a couple of hours. Soldiers kept coming and going and just a few feet away there was endless radio chatter with those on watch. Two soldiers were sitting by the radio thumbing through *Stud* magazine. Behind them was a large pin-up on the wall of a girl with tumbling hair, legs apart. In just a few hours sex had become an intrusion. Somehow it did not belong in the desert. Jimmy had already told us that it was best to forget what had been left behind. Do not waste your energy thinking about bars, beds with sheets, women, good food. Survival is about 'letting go'. 'The desert floor is now your friend.'

I woke shivering, but within two hours the heat was burning. We were surrounded on four sides by a sand berm, a mound that even a tracked vehicle could not drive over. Inside the berm there was a vast army laid out in the desert. At the south end of the encampment were tanks and infantry units. At the north end more tanks, a line of perhaps forty or fifty that had just arrived from Fort Riley in the United States. They had not even been painted in desert camouflage. Then there was the bulldozer park. There must have been a hundred of them. Then the bridge builders. The multiple-rocket launchers. The recce units. The fuel tankers. There were over 250 of them. And so it continued – and this was just one brigade. None of us had seen anything on this scale before.

We were given further training for chemical and biological attacks; how to stick atropine needles in muscle, how to check masks. We were also shown how we would be decontaminated after an attack, how we would run a gauntlet of troops who would spray us with water and then help us to remove our chemical suits without exposing our skin to any nerve agents.

We met the commander of Task Force 1-30. Lieutenant Colonel Wes Gillman came out of a tent with a guidebook to Iraq in his hand as if he had been researching a holiday location. He was a tobacco chewer who interrupted every sentence with a spit. He was tough and unsmiling and did not want to bond. We would be briefed at the last moment. It was not encouraging.

Later in the day we joined Bravo Company, the actual unit we would be travelling with. Captain Darin Nunn was a tank commander, about forty years old, with wrap-around shades and a small cigar that rested in the south of his mouth. Under his command he had ten Abrams tanks and eight Bradley Fighting Vehicles. He wanted us with his unit and had ideas about how to get us close to the fighting.

We were a welcome distraction to the soldiers. Most of them had been out in the desert for three months and their training was over. They were battle-ready and bored. Jimmy arrived with our Land Rover having spent the night at Camp New York, one of the permanent American bases out in the desert. We did not know how long we would have to wait before the war started so we decided to put up two tents. The soldiers sat idly on their tanks watching us, watching what kind of people we were. Jimmy wanted to give a good impression, to let them know that we would not hold them back or put them at further risk. In his strong Scottish accent he shouted out instructions to Jig and me as we put up the tents.

'Where are you guys from?' asked a soldier off the captain's tank.

'He's from Scotland,' I said, pointing to Jimmy.

'Where's that?' said one of his mates, who had also come over to us.

'Sean Connery,' someone shouted out. That was it. No one was very sure where Scotland was but a movie star made them feel they had located it. They knew more about Australia, a land of beaches and open spaces, and several of them planned to visit as soon as they got out of the military.

Most of them were from small-town America and were as different as the places they came from. Sanders was aged twenty and from Oklahoma and the Bible belt. 'You can't get a drink where I'm from,' he said. He was a driver of the M88, the tank recovery vehicle. The two best things in life were 'pussy and food' and he was not getting either out in the Kuwaiti desert and could not wait to get home.

Sergeant Steve Waddell really wanted to be in a tank but had ended up driving the captain's Humvee. He, too, just wanted to get the job done and go home. 'No one gets left behind,' he would like to say as a way of reassuring himself.

Lieutenant Brandon Kelley was an African-American who you could sit out with and just pass the day. He was open, positive and matter of fact about the war. 'Let's just get it done,' he would say.

Sergeant Sean Morrow was different. He loved being a soldier and above all loved leading his platoon of Bradley Fighting Vehicles. He could not imagine a better job in the military. He was a believer in the mission and there were not many like that.

These were some of the men who I would travel with from Kuwait to Baghdad. Most of them were nineteen or twenty, had left high school and drifted into the military. None of them had much curiosity about Iraq. It was a place, a job, nothing more. This was a task not a cause. Almost no one felt passionate about it. Most had a simple explanation for the war. Saddam was a bad guy 'and we're here to give the Iraqi people back their freedom'. It rarely got more complicated than that. None of them was spoiling for a fight.

I was here to report on their war but I would also be dependent on them for my safety. As we spoke I realized I was no longer entirely neutral in this war. My reporting could still be honest, even critical, but I had a personal interest in these soldiers fighting well.

I wanted to send a report that night, to establish with the audience that we were with a frontline American unit. There was only half a story. The American defence secretary had said that it might not be necessary for the British troops to actually fight. This was intended as a helpful gesture to Tony Blair who was facing strong opposition to the war. I spoke to some of the soldiers about it. They liked the fact that British units were based a few miles away. They were all supremely confident in American power, but they did not see why it should be just them against the world and they wanted the British to fight alongside them.

That evening we began editing inside the Land Rover. It was cramped and uncomfortable. I had to sit in the front seat and could not even see the pictures Jig was editing behind me. Out of nowhere a sandstorm tore through the tanks around us. Within minutes the lights of the camp had been swallowed up in dust. The vehicle was buffeted and eddies of sand ran down the windows. Even inside, with the doors closed, there was sand in the air. It got in the mouth, in the nostrils and within minutes a film of sand covered the editing machine. We feared that on our first night in the desert we would lose some of our equipment.

When the editing was finished the pictures had to be sent to a satellite, but not in real time. Our system compressed the data but it took, on a good day, twenty minutes to transmit one minute of pictures. We had to cling to the two satellite dishes to stop them blowing away as the sand whipped into our faces and even got inside our goggles.

When we finally reached the tent it, too, had filled with sand. The weave of the canvas was no protection against fine grains of dust. I tied a scarf over my nose and mouth and finally slept with exhaustion.

It was Thursday, 13 March. All night the canvas had flapped in the sandstorms. We were woken at 5.30 by the whine of an Abrams tank engine starting up. The soldiers emerged with plastic bottles of water, which they warmed by the tank engine. The exhaust was hot and the trick was to warm the bottle without melting the plastic. I shifted the bottle from hand to hand and used the water to shave in the wing mirror of the Land Rover. The storm had abated but I wondered how long we could exist in these conditions with just a few hours' sleep.

After breakfast the wind returned. You could watch it picking up the sand, swirling it around until it formed a dust cloud that obscured the sun. The vehicles drove with lights and the soldiers huddled together in the lee of the wind. They were on two hours' notice to leave for Iraq, they told us. A few were excited at the prospect of war but they were the minority. Most just wanted to get it over with. They wanted to get to Baghdad but only because the way home lay via the Iraqi capital. These men could never be real imperialists, I felt. They had little or no curiosity about the country they were about to invade and had no desire to stay there.

After thirty-six hours the wind subsided and the sky cleared. Apache and Blackhawk helicopters began flying again in formations of five or six. The sound of the blades was like an incessant soundtrack to war.

Late afternoon, as we were filming the helicopters, a young soldier jumped off his Abrams tank and ran towards us. He was from Louisiana and an enthusiast. His tank had a plough in front and his job was to clear minefields. He could not stop talking. He had been training for three years and wanted to show us what he could do. 'Come and find me,' he kept saying. 'I want my folks to see what I'm doing.'

We edited a story about the sandstorms, about the harsh, unforgiving conditions, but we could not find space on any satellite. We stayed up until one in the morning trying to make a connection. The engineers in London told us we had, apparently, failed to block-book space on the satellite at a time when every news organization was trying to feed material. We all felt low and exhausted. We were only two days into this and already we were ragged. None of us said it but we were potentially going to war for nothing.

The nights were bitterly cold. Even inside a sleeping bag under canvas I shivered. I may have got four hours' disturbed sleep but no more. All night helicopters had been taking off, using the clear night sky. I had a cold shave and walked across the desert to the tent where they were serving hot 'chow'. I stood in line and a soldier slapped some ham, reconstituted egg and a slice of cake onto a paper tray. Outside we were given coffee. We stood eating at some tables surrounded by soldiers from several companies. They were all talking about the 'goddam delay'. 'It's to help Blair get a second UN resolution, said one soldier.' These men were tired of waiting.

When I returned to the company Captain Nunn came over. He said the men would be given twenty-eight hours' notice of the invasion. We would get twenty-four. 'You will be travelling in the centre of the brigade at the front,' he said, 'at the tip of the spear.' We will, he reassured me, have a front-row seat at the war. It was what part of me had wanted from the moment war with Iraq became a possibility and yet I would be taking the same risks as the soldiers. The only difference was that they were protected by armour. We were in a four-by-four that would scarcely save you in a motorway crash.

There was another reason that the captain wanted us at the front. One of their first targets in Iraq, he told me, was a place with bunkers. There might be weapons of mass destruction there and he needed me to verify whatever they found and tell the world.

Friday, 14 March, and the brigade was given a down day. The soldiers saw it as a sign that war was close. Across the camp groups of soldiers played touch American football. They played hard, shouted, swore and sweated as if that was the only way to forget what lay ahead. Others played softball, kicking up the sand in the warm evening light. For a moment the war receded and the Kuwaiti desert was like a college campus with the promise of long, summer days stretching ahead.

The commanders were summoned to a meeting and were told, 'We're waiting for Tony Blair.' The White House had decided to see if more international support could be found to help its closest ally. The men knew the invasion had been delayed and did not like it. They were asked to check back in their ammunition. Morale sagged. The captain called together the sergeants and told them the delay would be brief. He shared with them some of the invasion plans 'to keep them focused'.

The night sky was clear with a bright intrusive moon that picked out the shapes of the tanks. Nothing could be hidden on such a night. The soldiers sat on their vehicles and speculated in low-level murmurs.

Saturday, 15 March, began with another cold night. Even though I was in a sleeping bag I had put on my fleece. I had almost got used to the whine of the early morning Abrams as it started up and summoned the company. On this morning a voice sliced through the canvas, 'It's a great day, let's go fuck Saddam.'

In a matter of days we had developed our own routine. Wake at 5.30. Shave in the mirror of the Land Rover and then listen to the radio news, sweep the dust from the vehicle and test the equipment again. There was a wooden makeshift shower where water had to be poured into a bucket with holes. It dribbled out slowly, just enough to wash with, but we would shower only once until the war was over and we had left Iraq. We relied on moist baby wipes to – as the soldiers liked to put it – 'do maintenance on the undercarriage'.

At breakfast we ate a hot meal but for the rest of the day we had MREs – meals-ready-to-eat. They came in tan-coloured plastic parcels. Each had a main meal such as beef and mushrooms, pasta with alfredo sauce and jumbalaya. There were twenty-four varieties and every soldier knew what to look for and what to avoid. The meals were cooked by putting them in a heater bag. When water was added it reacted to a chemical and started boiling. Ten minutes later there was a hot meal. Each parcel had peanut butter or jam or cheese spread. These meals were calorie-rich and full of preservatives and chemicals but, in the desert, you do not think about that.

Part of the pattern of the day was that at about ten o'clock a detail of soldiers would empty the latrines. They were three wooden huts bonded together, with a bowl and a tray underneath. The soldiers would open a flap at the back of the latrines, remove the tray and burn the contents. We referred to them as the 'shit burners'. That day I had gone across to the latrine and used it without realizing that the soldiers had not replaced the tray. A short time later a soldier shouted at me, 'Hey, you – did you just use the latrine?' He told me there was shit on the floor. I could see other soldiers watching. It was an important moment. I told him it was my mistake and I would clear it up. I went to the back of the latrine and cleaned up. Jimmy, with his career in the military, said I had seconds to do the right thing or the men would have frozen us out.

Sunday, 16 March, and I woke having had my longest sleep since being in the desert. I had had the tent to myself after Jig had slept in the vehicle. We drove off early in the morning around the camp perimeter. Most soldiers were resting or writing letters home. Everyone was marking time. At the multiple-rocket launchers, the MLRSs, a young sergeant with teeth stained from chewing tobacco came over. He feared we were civilian engineers and that more work on the camp meant further delays. He was an enthusiast for the MLRS. 'Awesome power,' he said, shaking his head. 'Can destroy every living thing in a square-mile radius. Come back when we're firing at night,' he went on. 'Makes a pretty picture.'

Everyone here was trained out. They were bored with live fire, with the ranges. They were tired of the desert, tired of waiting. The temperature had risen. It was now 30 degrees during the day. Even without the wind our lips cracked and everyone walked around with a stick of lip balm.

The next day, Monday, 17 March, it was hotter again. I was able to stand outside and shave and shampoo with my shirt off. The desert was coming alive with insects, ants, birds and large green lizards.

17 » Chipping pieces
out of the Berlin Wall

18 » Carrying camerman
Lex Tudhope on my shoulders
as East Germans crossed
to the West

19 » Talking to students in China after Tiananmen Square

20 » Prince Charles with his tenants

21 » Going 'live' in New York City

22 » Rescue workers evacuating Ground Zero after 9/11

23 » Ambushed by Marines at Quantico in mock chemical attack

24 » Colleagues in the Iraqi war: Jimmy Grant, ex-Special Forces, and cameraman Peter Gigliotti (Jig)

25 » The team with Captain Darin Nunn

26 » The Land Rover Discovery abandoned in the desert

27 » Escaping the sun

28 » The last piece to camera before the outbreak of war

29 » Travelling on the back of an 88 into Baghdad

30 » Trapped in the mud after sand- and rainstorms in the Iraqi desert

31 » At one of Saddam's bases

32 » Sharing a cage with a tiger

33 » Meeting John Kerry during the 2004 Presidential campaign

We went to see Colonel Allyn, the commander of the 3rd Brigade, who told us we would be attacked with chemical weapons when we entered Iraq. He said this without qualification. Just a short time ago this news would have been shattering and disturbing but we knew there was no turning back. I made a mental note to keep my mask closer and to keep it clean, but already I was finding that I was thinking little about the future. The world outside the berm had begun to fade and, like the soldiers, I was learning just to worry about the moment.

Late afternoon there was the sound of hammering as the sleeves on the tank barrels were fitted back on. It was just a way to pass the time. Cleaning, checking, re-checking. At five o'clock in the evening the sergeants and the lieutenants were told the location of the fuel and water points inside Iraq, and when the supply vehicles would come to the front. They were subdued as they took notes. Privately, some of them admitted to feeling tense.

Captain Nunn fitted thermal strips to our Land Rover so that we would be identified by the tanks as friendly. Jig climbed into a tank to verify that they saw it the same way. The captain drew a diagram in the sand to show where precisely we would be in the column. We would be 200 metres from the front in a soft-skinned vehicle.

Then suddenly, without any announcement, the camp began to be torn down. The camouflage netting came off the wooden showers. The latrines were dismantled. The sandbags were removed from the urinal pipes. Bulldozers dug large pits and everything that was not coming to Iraq was carried there and set alight. All over, campfires were burning. Earthmovers began punching holes in the berm so the brigade could easily move to the border. There had been something secure about living behind a ten-foot-high sand wall. Now we could look out and see the dust trails of military convoys on the move.

Tuesday, 18 March, and the soldiers crowded around my radio as President Bush gave Saddam Hussein forty-eight hours to leave the country. This was the final countdown to war. We were told that we must have all our water and fuel packed by the next morning.

For the first time the men seemed edgy. There were arguments at the food tables. A soldier who had been talking to us was picked on. 'What the fuck do you know about anything?' he was asked. A black soldier pointed his plastic knife at the man and shouted, 'Why don't you shut the fuck up?' We all noticed it. The men were restless, tense and were needling each other.

Captain Nunn drew a map with rope and blocks of wood on the desert floor. The wood blocks were bunkers. One of the first objectives would be to seize Tallil airport. The operation would be at night and the men were told to memorize the plan, to go over it again and again in their minds.

On Wednesday, 19 March, the sandstorms returned and the visibility came down to a few metres. We were summoned to a final briefing by General Blount at his desert headquarters. Although we were escorted the soldiers lost their way and we arrived late.

General Blount was in a large tent. Inside it could have been a city dealing room except that everyone was in uniform. There were rows of officers, men and women, sitting in front of their laptops. Huge air-conditioning units were cooling the desert air and protecting the computers. In the corner a television was showing Fox News with Oliver North acting as cheerleader. For a moment we had stepped out of the desert and could have been back in America.

I turned to Jimmy and Jig and said they should never forget this scene. It was a moment in history. Here we were, getting the battle plan from a general on the eve of a major war. The Americans were taking a huge risk in briefing us. If any of the details had leaked the invasion would have had to be delayed and the plans revised. There was an anxious moment when a Japanese reporter had clearly misunderstood that this was all strictly embargoed.

General Blount stood in front of a large-scale map of Iraq. There would, he said, be a massive bombardment from the air, from multiple-rocket launchers, from artillery. This would, in his words, 'set the conditions for the ground attack'.

The 3rd Brigade, which we were travelling with, would race 120 kilometres to the outskirts of Nasiriyah in about six hours. I asked him what we would face as we crossed the border. There were just a few outposts and some minefields left over from Desert Storm. Outside Nasiriyah was the Iraqi Eleventh Division but he did not expect strong opposition.

1st and 2nd Brigades would swing wide into Iraq's western

desert and move north towards Najaf. Within forty-eight hours they would be halfway to Baghdad. 3rd Brigade would link up for the push into the capital. The plan was to by-pass the cities along the Euphrates. 'When the capital falls, it's all over,' said General Blount. 'As we get closer to Baghdad we will have to go into the cities,' he said, 'and we expect some heavy resistance.'

He was quietly impressive, a thoughtful soldier who smiled a lot. He commanded immense power but would use it reluctantly. 'The Iraqis,' he said, 'will be given every opportunity to surrender.' They were dropping leaflets explaining to the Iraqis how to capitulate. Their tanks had to be parked in a square with turrets facing backwards. Their commanders would be allowed to keep their weapons. His confidence was high. 'If the regime capitulates,' he said, 'there is a plan for an air-drop into Baghdad.'

As we left his headquarters the army was already moving. We had to sit for forty-five minutes by a desert track as 2nd Brigade headed for the border. It was a military rule that you could not interrupt a convoy. You had to let it pass. The visibility was so poor that sometimes all we could hear was the whine of a tracked vehicle; then, at the last moment, a 70-ton Abrams tank would sweep by, its driver relying on thermal imaging to tell him where the other tanks were.

We returned to the base camp and at around 4.30 in the afternoon the company got the order to form up at one of the holes that had been made in the berm. We were going to war. The soldiers came to life. 'Yeah, let's go,' shouted one man on top of his tank. 'Let's roll,' shouted another. Men were high-fiving each other and embracing. One man grabbed me by the shoulders, looked into my eyes and wished me luck. This was the World Series, the big game, and everyone seemed up for it. Not a doubt surfaced. One black American said to me, 'We're coming home. We're going home.' He pointed into the camera as if he was delivering a promise to a faraway family. So this was war. Not to liberate Iraq but to get home. There was not a man in the company who expected the campaign to last more than ten days.

20

Hajis Don't Surf

We were going to war but not fast. Before we could break camp we were stalled by a military traffic jam. As far as we could see there were convoys, dark shapes with dust trails, snaking through the desert, moving up to the Iraqi border. We sat for three hours as an artillery unit and a column of marines crawled past us.

The convoys, which had been moving all day, had left deep gullies and trenches. The vehicles coming behind were snared in the ruts and, as they churned the sand, they sank up to their axles. One soldier said it reminded him of Michigan in a snowstorm.

I was impatient, demanding to know why we could not just by-pass these stranded vehicles. Part of our problem was that we needed a three-hour window to unpack our equipment and edit a report and satellite it. Waiting, not knowing whether we were about to move, was the worst of all options for us and I could see another evening passing without being able to file a story.

The soldiers were bemused by my irritation. 'What's the hurry, man?' shouted one sergeant from inside a Humvee. 'We're only going to fucking war.' I heard laughter in the background. Hanging out, running their mouths, smoking, picking over the meals-ready-to-eat was part of a soldier's life. Time lost its meaning. The only date that mattered to them was the date of going home. So we watched and waited as tank-recovery vehicles fixed tow ropes and pulled trucks laden with supplies to where the crust was firmer.

Night fell and the convoys switched on their lights. The vehicles were bunched close together and from a distance it looked like rush hour with its long fluid streams of white light. The commanders were confident the Iraqis had no way of seeing us.

Our convoy had about three hundred vehicles led by Abrams

tanks. When, finally, we moved forward the tanks threw up large dust clouds. It was like driving through patches of fog where vehicles suddenly disappear. We were tense, scared of driving into the tracked vehicle in front or of being rammed from behind by a 70-ton tank. Sometimes we stopped, waiting for the dust to settle, only to find we had lost the tail-lights of the armoured vehicle we were following. We hoped General Blount was right when he said his tanks could see through the dust. War already seemed a dangerous environment even without any fighting.

I sat looking out of the passenger window, a scarf covering my nose and mouth, trying to pick up the tracks for Jimmy, who was driving. There was little to be seen except the occasional large sand hill and a pipe running through the desert. We passed broken-down vehicles – a Humvee with a flat tyre, a Bradley without its track. The general had told us he expected to lose two hundred vehicles during the invasion. I could see why.

Convoys, like slow-moving traffic, often paused and in those moments the night cleared and we could see the line of silver lights curling back for two to three miles. For the first time I used our radio satellite phone and broadcast 'live' on the move. The agreement with the American military was that 'embedded' reporters like myself could describe what we were seeing but not much else. I could not say where we were or where we were heading. On this occasion I got in a tangle on air. I boldly described being in an armoured column on the move. Not surprisingly the news presenters wanted to know the significance of this. I tripped over my sentences as I tried to explain that this was just part of the preparations for a possible invasion.

We stopped on what looked like a small plateau. The lights were turned out and we were told for the first time to black out the windows of the Land Rover as we worked. Jig edited a report but once again we could not find a satellite.

The next morning, Thursday, 20 March, I woke cold, with a headache. I had fallen off my bedroll onto the hard sand. The war had started with a cruise-missile attack aimed at killing Saddam Hussein. Captain Nunn told us that we were on standby to enter Iraq in two hours.

I was so tired I did not have the energy for fear. Within two hours of dawn the heat was intense. Jig tried again to satellite our story but we failed to make the deadline for breakfast news. We were hot, sapped, covered in dust and angry. Our equipment was failing and we were about to risk our lives. At one point I heard Jig shouting at his computer, 'Listen, you piece of shit.' We all felt like that, worn down with frustration. We briefly considered turning the vehicle round and heading for Kuwait City, but a return, for what-ever reason, would have been a retreat and a humiliation and we had come too far for that.

The tank crews were strangely silent. They reminded me of animals conserving energy. They were neither awake nor asleep. They just lay there. No one wanted to talk. They knew what was coming and wanted to be alone with their thoughts.

For hours we stayed like this, two long parked columns of armour. Just occasionally we would shift positions, following the shade, as the sun moved. There was nothing much to be said. Nothing I did would change anything. I had given up my choices when I joined Bravo Company. Like the soldiers around me, my future would be determined by unknown men in faraway places like Washington or Qatar or Tampa, Florida.

In the middle of the afternoon we were ordered to put on our chemical suits. All around us, on top of tanks and on the lowered ramps of the Bradleys, men began breaking open vacuum-packed plastic bags. Once exposed to air the suits were effective for only forty days. The first hours of the war were considered dangerous; it was one of the moments when Saddam might use chemical weapons. I asked several soldiers how it felt to be putting on the suits. 'Not too bad,' said Sergeant Craig; 'they're a little cooler than the older ones.' They spoke in flat, neutral, emotionless voices like company spokesmen. Outwardly none of them seemed troubled about a chemical attack. Way back they had learned to shut down their imaginations. These were men who existed in the present, and in that way survived. The future, with all its potential horrors, was unknowable, and they spent little time thinking about it.

The Americans had four levels of alert for chemical and biologi-cal attack. They called them Mopp levels. At Mopp level 4 you were fully zipped up, breathing through masks and wearing gloves and boots. We had moved to level 1. The suits had to be worn at all times but we did not have to put on our masks. They were worn on the hips like holsters, to be drawn at the first shout of 'gas, gas, gas'.

I was now in uniform. For a few moments I studied myself from every angle in a wing mirror as if I was trying on an outrageous coat in a fitting room. But this was not going to be returned to the rack. To the Iraqis I would be an American soldier. I did a piece to camera explaining why I was wearing a combat suit. I wanted the viewers to know this was not my choice, that I had not gone off into the desert, thrown off my independence and joined up. Even so, I was becoming less of an outsider; the uniform was a blending in, blurring the distinction between myself and the soldiers.

Late afternoon, and we were told to line up. 'We're going into Iraq,' said Captain Nunn without any sense of drama. There were no speeches, no pumping up, no huddles of soldiers steeling themselves for the big game. The order had been so long in coming that it was received almost with a sense of relief. At the front of the column were most of the tanks, then a few Bradleys, then, sandwiched in between them, our Land Rover. This time we travelled without lights. Jimmy wore night-vision goggles, which picked out an infrared panel on the tracked vehicle in front. We drove slowly, silently, up to the border.

Then the war started. The terrible beauty of shock and awe. Salvo after salvo of rockets launched into the night sky trailing arcs of brilliant white light. Sometimes we could pick out the rockets before the heat exhausts faded and they continued their journey in the darkness. There were flashes, orange flashes as the artillery fired. And the sound, the rumble from the multiple-rocket launchers and the sharper crack from the guns of the Paladins.

The convoy stopped and started with no reason given. Sometimes the men got out and stood in clusters by their vehicles. They made comments like 'awesome' and 'hello, Iraq', but there was no laughter. No excitement. No high-fives. No kick-ass talk. In the first moments of war these were preoccupied, focused, closed men.

In London the BBC was 'live' on air. I was one of the few correspondents in a position to see anything. It was like being on a viewing platform, describing a giant fireworks display. The more descriptive I became the more I was in danger of sounding like a cheerleader. The fact was that the ground war had begun, it was happening in front of me, but I did not know who or what was being fired at beyond the low horizon of the desert. War was like this. You had a frontline seat but, even so, you ended up partially sighted. Weapons were fired but you rarely saw where they landed.

None of the soldiers used any light. They felt secure in the darkness. With their night-vision technology they believed they owned the night. We were a potential threat to their safety. However careful we were, we needed pencil lights to operate our equipment. When we edited, the screen lit up the back of the vehicle. Jimmy had cut burlap strips to cover the windows but the light often seeped through. And I was filing report after report on a satellite phone, my voice carrying through the night. Although the men were friendly to our faces some felt we were a risk not worth taking.

The convoy was stalled and I could not find the captain's tank to ask what the delay was. I switched off the phone and lay down exhausted in the desert. My mind was too active to sleep. At around 3 o'clock in the morning the engines around us started up again. Through the goggles I could see barbed wire. In the darkness an American soldier with a night stick was guiding us through a gap in the fence that marked the demilitarized zone separating Kuwait and Iraq. I leaped out to record a piece to camera, marking the moment of invasion. The soldiers were edgy and kept turning the turrets of the guns.

At the Iraqi end of the zone we passed a huge anti-tank ditch but US Army engineers, operating ahead of us, had already bridged it. As the light came up we were driving through desert scrub, the first time we had seen any vegetation for nearly two weeks, but it was a desolate, empty landscape with no sign of any Iraqis.

An hour and a half inside Iraq the American 3rd Infantry Division, the Rock of the Marne, with its thousands of vehicles, was forced to a crawl by a huge camel train. There were hundreds of camels moving stubbornly across the desert. The Bedouin herder was unhurried, waving in a nonchalant way as if the sight of hundreds of tanks and armoured vehicles was a normal part of desert life.

The train took time to pass. Captain Nunn later told me he had considered driving his tank into the camels or even opening fire at them. I was shocked; I still had a civilian mind that would have let these animals pass. War was not like that, as I would learn. The commanders were unsentimental. From the moment the order to invade was given they changed, and would change more the deeper we got inside Iraq. In the soldier's mind the camels had caused the tanks to bunch up, creating a potential target for the enemy. It was the same with the few isolated people that we saw on that first morning. They were mainly nomads living in tents. I, perhaps naively, thought the soldiers might wave. Instead a Bradley would detach itself from the main column, move in close and traverse its gun.

We drove onto a gravel plain and the column fanned out into a giant formation a mile wide. In the front line were eight Abrams tanks. Falling in behind them, stretching back for miles, were the fighting vehicles and supply trucks. It was one of the most dramatic and possibly the last great tank charge in history. At times we were travelling at forty miles an hour. We were about eighteen vehicles from the front and in each direction all we could see and hear were tracked vehicles churning through the desert. I felt a strange high. My weariness was ebbing away. This was an invasion, a declaration of war. We were riding into battle with speed and power and all the arrogance of the invader. I knew that on this morning the world was focused on this barren place and I was glad to be there.

I was often interviewed on the satellite phone. The one question the presenters wanted to ask was how far inside Iraq we had travelled; that was the one answer I could not give. When I said we had been driving for five hours John Humphrys of the Radio 4 *Today* programme asked me, 'So what speeds are you travelling at?' It was the right question but I hedged the answer, fearful that the Iraqis, like the listeners, would make the calculation and work out where we were.

Sometimes the terrain was rutted or the sand too soft and then we slowed. Occasionally the desert looked like an Iraqi military scrapyard. There were the rusting hulks of armoured personnel carriers that had been left out in the desert from the 1991 Gulf War. Other sites had been attacked more recently from the air. Munitions lay scattered across the sand. These bases were always approached warily but the Iraqi army had gone.

After seven hours' driving we stopped, got out, stretched and opened our meals-ready-to-eat. Almost immediately fuel tankers drew alongside. I had imagined these giant bowsers, laden with five thousand gallons of fuel, bringing up the rear but they had been bouncing across the desert close to us. As soon as they braked, the tanks and Bradleys lined up on either side as if they were at a desert petrol station. Each of the tanks swallowed a gallon every mile. Just to turn on its engine consumed ten gallons.

As soon as they were refuelled the tanks resumed their position in the formation. 'What's the hurry?' called out a soldier sitting on a tank that had 'Buffalo Soldier' on its sleeve. 'There's gold in the banks in Nasiriyah,' someone shouted back. The mood had lightened. The waiting was over.

We moved forward again, faster than before. We had been told to hold our formation, to keep a hundred metres from the Bradleys around us. Just occasionally a vehicle would break free as if we were in a desert car rally. At one point the column was overtaken by a tank carrying a folded bridge. Everyone laughed. 'Shit, a bridge is going to take Baghdad,' said someone over the radio.

Mid-afternoon and pylons emerged from the heat shimmer. Shortly afterwards we were crossing the Basra to Baghdad highway. An Iraqi truck had stopped on the tarmac. There was a look of utter bafflement on the driver's face. It's possible he had not even heard that the war had begun. He got out of the truck and just stood there, dressed in a blue-grey djellaba, hands on his hips. At one point he took a few steps forward, waving his arms as if demanding that the highway be cleared. Then somehow it dawned on him that this was an invasion and he fell back, leaning against the front of his vehicle and wiping his brow.

We were close to the city of Nasiriyah when the formation broke up. Bravo Company stopped. There were reports that an Iraqi tank unit was heading towards us. Some of the Bradleys tucked in beside sand mounds. The men were tense. To our left, multiple-rocket launchers began firing towards the city. We could see the outline of buildings. A few of them were on fire. American tanks drove towards a bridge over the Euphrates, which we could see in the distance.

The company pushed down a paved road towards the city outskirts. I imagined we would be in the city before dark, being welcomed by the Iraqi people. That was what the soldiers around me expected. But we did not drive far. We sat on the road and watched artillery firing at Iraqi positions. We began hearing that there was strong resistance around one of the bridges over the Euphrates and that surprised everyone.

Darkness came and we were told to extinguish all lights. Only with the night-vision goggles could we make out the shapes of tanks and other tracked vehicles. Close to us I could see houses, warehouses and schools. I found myself scanning the buildings for movement, for Iraqis. I was not an invader but I had come with them and was as edgy as the soldiers around me.

Most of the tanks in our unit moved off. We had been told that our Land Rover had to stay behind the executive officer's tracked vehicle, a 113. During the evening we lost them. We not only feared we had lost contact with our company but we realized that to other American soldiers the Land Rover might be mistaken for an Iraqi vehicle. We argued about whether it was too dangerous to move but in the end decided that we had to search for Bravo Company. We drove along the column and had a moment of luck. Using the night-vision scope we spotted the executive officer. We had to make it clear that they could not just drive off without us. Their coopera-tion was grudging. Some soldiers felt that now the war had started we might hold them back and increase their risks.

Before leaving Kuwait we had been told that the company's first objective was to seize Tallil airport on the outskirts of the city. It was an Iraqi garrison with three thousand men. The Americans wanted to land their own planes there as soon as it could be secured. The plan was for three companies to take the airport during the night.

Through our goggles I could see American armour lined up on either side of a two-lane highway waiting for the attack. Then we stopped and for a period there was only silence broken by the occasional sound of firing in Nasiriyah.

I had watched fighting before but usually from the relative safety of a building or a ditch. I had never been part of a night attack. We were going into battle in a thin-skinned vehicle. I wrapped my body armour tighter but this blacked-out airport, with light rain falling, seemed an easy place to lose a life.

We heard the sound of planes at high altitude and then the ground shook as the bombs fell. We were so close we could feel the vibration, the rush of air, the smell of explosives. Balls of flame burst out in different parts of the airport. Some died away at once. Others burned brightly, spewing out exploding ammunition. Sometimes the explosions were deeper and we speculated that the bombers were attacking the bunkers.

The attack continued into the night, hour after hour. It was difficult imagining any Iraqi surviving this. I had hardly slept for two nights and, even though I was frightened that we might soon be in the middle of a firefight, I fell asleep in the back seat of the Land Rover.

When I awoke there were the first traces of dawn and we were driving across a ribbed landscape inside the airport perimeter. In the half-light we seemed to be riding over irrigation channels or sand berms baked hard by the sun. Every rut we crossed violently jolted the Land Rover. Jimmy, who was driving, swore at the tracked vehicle we were following for taking such a difficult route. 'More of this,' he said, 'and the vehicle will be wrecked.'

We were in a wasteland, a pulverized land, pitted, cratered and rutted. Smoke from the fires drifted past hangars and bunkers. On the ground there were the twisted casings of the bombs. Unexploded ammunition lay everywhere. As Jig filmed I became a spotter for Jimmy, shouting every time I saw a bomb lying in the earth. This was more dangerous than the long bursts of automatic fire.

The soldiers leaped out of the Bradleys and ran towards the buildings, providing cover for each other as they kicked down doors. We drove out onto the runway. There was little sign of the Iraqis. Some of the Bradleys were firing into the airport buildings. There were brief, sharp firefights but there were few bodies and almost no prisoners. The Iraqis had decided not to make a stand here. They had blocked the runways with rusting vehicles in a half-hearted kind of way.

As we stood around with the soldiers there was a sense of anticlimax. The troops went from bunker to bunker hunting for Iraqis. Sometimes they shouted at the doors, 'Come out, with your hands up, or you'll be killed.' There was a brief pause then the bunker doors were blasted open. Grenades were thrown down air vents but few Iraqis were found.

The Americans seemed deflated. 'It's a shit-hole,' said one. The airport buildings were dilapidated. Even without the overnight bombing there were holes in the roof and the walls were crumbling. The doors to the bunkers were rusting. The first impression of Iraq was of a broken-down society. The men were disappointed. They had not been in a real fight. It was as if the weakness of their opponents had taken the edge off victory.

Outside one of the bunkers there was a debate as to who would get the chance to fire a tank shell at the door. The tank commanders felt deprived. They had been unable to use their main guns. The fighting had been scrappy. Just Iraqis with rifles sniping and running. To blast open the rusting doors of a bunker was a kind of consolation and they all wanted it. In the end it was Captain Nunn who got to 'loose one off'.

Later we heard that the colonel in charge of the 3rd Brigade was critical of the operation. It had taken too long. The soldiers on the ground had been too cautious. The bombing had been excessive. Within the unit there was a sense that they had let themselves down in their first major action inside Iraq.

As we drove away from the airport I recalled that I had been told that I might be needed to verify the existence of weapons of mass destruction at the site. I had never been clear how I would do this. I had visions of myself prising open a barrel and turning to the camera with confidence and saying yes, I could confirm there was Sarin here. However, the searches seemed cursory and I presumed specialist units would come behind us. But, having taken the airport, no one ever mentioned weapons of mass destruction again. It was as if they had been dropped from the agenda.

We drove to a government building and the tanks lined up and parked outside. The building had not been bombed but it was wrecked and abandoned. Fittings had been torn out. Glass from the windows lay on the floor. There was a pile of discarded gas masks. Only the wall painting of Saddam had not been disfigured. The soldiers were exhausted after three nights on the move and they broke open their canvas cots and lay down wherever they could find the shade.

Late afternoon, and the unit began sending out patrols. One of the tanks, which had the name 'Braggin Rights' on the sleeve of its barrel, surprised a group of Iraqis about to attack an American convoy. There was a firefight and the Iraqis were killed.

The men from 'Braggin Rights' were elated, euphoric. 'Blew the mother-fuckers right away,' said Edwards, an African-American. Others crowded round as they told their story. They wanted to know what it was like to go up close, face to face with the enemy. 'Just wasn't those fuckers' lucky day,' explained one of the crew. 'Those guys looked up to see a fuckin' Abrams coming round the corner.'

Everyone in the unit wanted a moment like this, to have a story they could take home with them. They did not necessarily want to kill but, deep down, they wanted to find out about themselves in those long moments of dry-mouthed fear.

I had got one of my first reports wrong. Standing in front of a picture of Saddam I had said the Americans expected that Nasiriyah would be fully under their control within twenty-four hours. That is what a commander had told me, but members of Saddam's militia, the fedayeen, had entered the city. Unlike the regular army they were fighting fiercely.

There were other signs that troubled Bravo Company. They stopped a white Toyota Land Cruiser; two men were inside with rocket-propelled grenades and guns. They were stripped to the waist and forced to lie on the ground at gunpoint. They insisted they were moving the weapons to a safer place to prevent them being used but the soldiers were convinced they were planning an ambush. None of us had expected a hit-and-run war.

It was Sunday, 23 March, and the order came to move north. Nasiriyah had not fallen but that was now up to the marines. The plan was to by-pass many of these towns and cities and head for Baghdad. The Americans believed that once the capital fell the rest of the country would follow. We headed towards Al-Batha and for the first time saw ordinary Iraqi people.

At first it was mainly kids, excited, with broad innocent smiles, jumping and waving, running beside the tanks. Some did the thumbs-up, which they clearly thought was an American gesture and would go down well. Others shouted, 'Hello, mister,' or 'Water,

water.' What they most wanted from their invaders was clean water. Occasionally the troops would toss a plastic water bottle out of a Bradley and the kids would scamper after it.

Many older people also came down to the highway. One man, in a white djellaba, carried an American flag that somehow had been hidden away and preserved in Saddam's Iraq. Another had cut out a photo of President Bush from a paper, cradling it in his hand like a saint's picture. These were the few. The brave. They had come out early whilst Saddam's men were still in the villages.

A greater number of people hung back. I saw sullen, withdrawn, inscrutable faces; faces that turned away, that did not want to meet the eyes of the foreigner. Even in liberation there can be humiliation.

The soldiers were on edge, too wary to wave back. Even then, in these early days of the war, they did not want to get close to any Iraqis. They were just a backdrop, a crowd scene that filled out the picture. The ordinary GI was only too happy to return home having never spoken to an Iraqi. Sometimes, when I was not broadcasting 'live', I waved out of the window. I was just an outsider but to those by the roadside I was an American too. My wave was a guilty, sentimental gesture. Guilty because we were invaders. Sentimental because looking into those faces – daring to hope – I did not want them to take back to their houses just the stony-faced stares from the men on the tanks.

Our task that day was a bizarre one that irritated the soldiers. We were heading north but we were to collect broken-down vehicles left behind by units that were now ahead of us. When we stopped I leaped out to record a piece to camera. The column was soon ready to drive on but when I got back inside our Land Rover it would not start. The engine had died.

The tanks at the front were moving and were not going to pause for us in the middle of what they saw as enemy territory. We could not be left behind and so the 88, the giant tank-recovery vehicle, hooked up a tow chain.

We were on a track that led through derelict kilns and furnaces. The soil was black and fine like coal dust. In places it had been whipped by the wind into large mounds. The 70-ton 88 drove straight over these black hills, dragging the Land Rover up the slopes, crashing it down on the other side. Sometimes the vehicle tilted dangerously.

'We could die here,' said Jimmy as he fought with the wheel. It was almost impossible to steer. The driver of the 88 could not see behind him. He was focused on keeping up with the rest of the column. Our vehicle could tip over and be scraped along on its side for miles without the driver in front knowing anything about it. Jimmy had been in a mobility unit in the military and knew everything about desert driving but he was scared. Every time the tank took up the slack we were jerked forward violently. As we were dragged up the ridges we threw the weight of our bodies from one side of the vehicle to the other to keep it upright.

We travelled like this for nearly two hours until the light faded. We rejoined Highway 8, the main route for the convoys heading north. It was congested with military traffic, fuel tanks, ammunition trucks with tank shells, trucks with water and food, signals units, bulldozers. All engines straining. All pushing north in the choking dust.

Occasionally, as we slowed, we would hear a shout and then laughter from a group of soldiers beside the road as they spotted the 88, this mammoth of a military vehicle, pulling a Land Rover. 'What the fuck's that?' we heard more than once. Men peered in at us as if we were a piece of loot scavenged from an Iraqi compound. Jimmy, who had lost none of his pride from having fought in one of the best units in the world, hated the humiliation.

We finally pulled off the road and parked for the night on a deeply rutted piece of desert. We were covered in dust, battered, shaken, and vulnerable. If Bravo Company was attacked or had to move out suddenly we would either be left behind or have to be towed. The mechanics came over and in the darkness tried to recharge the battery, but without success. We were now a drag on the company.

In the midst of this I had to report the war. None of us felt like working, unpacking the equipment and editing a story. Just surviving was draining us. We all wanted to lie down in the sand and forget the day but we were here to file stories. Before we could view any of our material Jig had to squirt compressed air at the computer and edit pack to disperse the dust. So while the soldiers slept we blacked out the windows of our broken-down vehicle and went to work.

I took the satellite phone, stepped out of the Land Rover, and talked to the editor in London. As we spoke, I walked, without thinking, beyond the outer circle of the encampment. When I returned an angry soldier shouted, 'You step outside here again and we'll shoot you.' The editor heard everything and asked me if I was all right. 'Sure,' I said, 'you nearly got to witness a friendly fire incident on a mobile phone.' Everyone was frayed. The whole company knew that the fighting back in Nasiriyah was tough and that convoys were being attacked.

At around 12.30 I lay down in the sand beside a tank. The nights in the desert were freezing. I put on three T-shirts and a balaclava and pulled up the hood of my chemical suit and still shivered. I was just falling into an exhausted sleep when a soldier shook me. 'Gavin, is that you?' It was a lieutenant from one of the Bradleys. Earlier in the day I had said he could use the satellite phone to call his girlfriend in the States. It was her birthday or their anniversary and I had promised him a call.

I could hear parts of the conversation. It was strained and difficult like most of the calls. Two worlds jarring under the pressure of a five-minute conversation. He promised her the war would soon be over, a promise we all made. She clearly had her own problems, the irritations of an average day. 'I can't deal with that now,' I heard him say. The commanders did not like these calls home. They were often unsettling. It was almost better to forget what had been left behind until this war was over. I heard him say, 'I love you,' and he handed back the phone and walked off into the night.

Monday, 24 March. I woke cold and tired. Four hours' sleep had barely taken the edge off my exhaustion. I stripped to the waist and washed my face with bottled water then shaved in the wing mirror of the vehicle. I felt low but bloody-minded, as if standing there half-naked in the morning cold was an act of defiance that somehow would improve my mood.

Captain Nunn and Rocky, one of the medics, came over. They could not have been more different: Nunn, around forty, military-hardened, a stogie at the edge of his mouth; Rocky, a small man in his late twenties, open-faced, and the conscience of the unit. They wanted to talk about Nasiriyah. American soldiers, the captain said, had been captured. Among them were female soldiers including Jessica Lynch, although none of us knew her name then. The captain said, 'If necessary, 499,000 people will be removed and the city emptied.' Other men joined us. The marines, they all agreed, would play hardball. 'If anything happens to those POWs they'll raze the city,' said one of the men. The mood and the language were hardening. The faces taut and strained. Rocky did not like what he heard. 'This is serious shit,' he said, before walking back to his vehicle.

A short time later some Iraqis walked down the road close to the company. 'Get those fucking hajis away from here,' shouted the captain. Every Iraqi was now a potential terrorist and had to be waved on. Even friendly Iraqis were told to keep walking. Others were ordered to lie face down on the ground while they were searched. I felt the battle for hearts and minds was already under strain.

The mechanics had located a new battery in a unit down the road and were hopeful we would soon be driving again. As we waited the senior officer in charge of Task Force 1-30 dropped by. Colonel Wes Gillman was dusty, wrinkled, his face bone dry. He was a hard, tough, seasoned officer, sparse with words. He was proud of the push from Kuwait. 'You saw history, Gavin,' he said, clapping me on the shoulder. He was defensive about the taking of Tallil airport. He said his men could have carried out the attack without the air-strikes but it would have meant firing every weapon and tank shell. I wanted to ask him how many Iraqis he thought he was facing there, but he changed the subject.

He wanted to talk about 'terrorists', 'irregulars'. 'Who are these fedayeen?' he asked me. I told him the little I knew. They were a militia, loyal to Saddam. In the battle plan no one had given them any thought. Most of the regular Iraqi army had faded away and returned to their homes, as the Americans had advised them. The colonel told me we were heading for the north-west of Baghdad but he was extremely reluctant to enter the capital. The Americans did not want to fight street by street. It was their greatest fear.

A battery had been found in the field trains, those long supply columns that make up the tail of an army on the move. The mechanics fitted it but the engine still did not turn over. They hunched over the engine and talked quietly to each other and finally announced, 'The alternator has jammed.'

The band of mechanics were a breed apart from the ordinary soldier. They were grease-monkeys who loved engines. They had worked in auto-repair shops or breaker's yards, often in small-town America. The military had been their means of escape. They had their pride; they believed that they could fix any problem. One of them thought they could repair it if they got the right bearings. They knew a kid from West Virginia in another company who had a way with engines. 'The kid would do it,' they all agreed. But if we could get a spare alternator they would fix it in minutes.

The captain suddenly received an order to move with the rest of the task force to Samawah, another town on the Euphrates. There were reports that large numbers of fedayeen were using the city to attack American convoys. We suddenly did not matter. We were left behind, sidelined. This, after all, was a war. All the soldiers we knew, and who had been part of our lives for two weeks, mounted up and drove away. Captain Nunn did not even say goodbye. Everyone wanted to fight the Iraqis and they were not going to wait for us. We were stranded beside a desert road.

A few supply vehicles were left behind with us and some medics. There were certainly not enough soldiers to fight off any major raid by the fedayeen or any other Iraqis. Even the men in the supply vehicles told us they would soon be making deliveries to a unit up the road. We could be stranded in the desert without a vehicle, wearing American military uniform.

I phoned Mark Popescu, the editor of the BBC's *Ten O'Clock News*, who immediately understood what a potentially dangerous position we were in. We agreed on the phone that we could not allow the last Americans to leave without us even if that meant abandoning more than £100,000 worth of equipment. We would have to get on their trucks even if it meant riding on the roof.

Within minutes of the call ending the BBC was phoning Bryan Whitman at the Pentagon, the official whose idea it was to embed reporters with military units. The BBC's position was that we had left Kuwait with the 3rd Infantry Division and it was their duty to protect us. There was, however, a slight problem. The agreement that we could bring our own vehicle had been made secretly, at local level. It was against Pentagon policy and they had been by-passed. Whitman wanted to know what we were doing with a Land Rover at the front. He was unsympathetic when told about failed alternators. 'That's why we did not want television teams driving their own vehicles,' he said, but he promised we would not be abandoned.

This conversation was passed on to us but London thought it a good idea to see if we could find another alternator. Jig and Jimmy shook their heads in disbelief. We had nothing else to do so we called the dealer in Kuwait City, but they had no spares that would fit a Discovery. We heard of another BBC Land Rover that was in a compound run by the US marines. We asked our office in Kuwait whether the part could be removed and flown north. They laughed and we gave up. The Americans were fighting a war and the chances of someone putting an alternator on a helicopter and delivering it to us in the desert were non-existent. 'It's not going to happen,' said Jimmy and he was right.

I lay down in the shade of the vehicle. I felt the story slipping away, moving north without us. I was burning up with frustration. We were all ragged, drained by sleepless nights and failing equipment. I could see our war ending on some churned-up piece of desert miles from the front line.

Later that day remnants of Charlie Rock Company pulled in. With them was the kid from West Virginia who had a way with engines. He was young, eighteen or nineteen, un-lined and softly spoken. He cradled the alternator gently in his hand, like a collector, and then unscrewed it. He nodded quietly to himself and then said, 'Sir, you gotta problem with your bearings. They've worn clean away.' He thought he could rebuild the alternator with spare bearings but they were in a truck in one of the field trains. It was a lifeline – a slender one. 'Where is this truck?' I asked, but the kid was poor on the details. 'What is the unit?' I said. He was a little vague about that too.

In the late afternoon a Bradley arrived with Major Jim Desjardin. His black-rimmed glasses with a sports strap made him look like a civilian. He was in his mid-thirties and had the easy confidence of a man out of officer school. He was part of Colonel Gillman's staff and wanted a favour. He knew we had a satellite phone and needed to call his family back in the States. I agreed but said we had a problem too. I told him about the bearings in the field trains. He gave me a slightly quizzical look as if to say, 'Do I need to hear this?' There was an absurdity about my pitch to him. Here was I, in the early days of a war, asking a US major to find a ball bearing in the midst of his huge supply columns. 'I'll do what I can,' he said, 'but don't count on it.'

He had an offer to make of his own. If we could not fix the Discovery then we could use his personal Humvee and his driver. It was almost empty and we could load most of our equipment inside and rejoin Bravo Company. 'Take it all the way to Baghdad,' he said. 'That's where I'm heading.' I agreed at once. 'Let's try and fix the Land Rover, but if that fails we'll transfer to the Humvee.' He said he would tell his driver to join us later and as soon as we had an escort we could return to the front. It was the best we could hope for, although we knew that without our own vehicle it would be much harder breaking away from the unit when we got to Baghdad.

A small unit of scouts arrived with their turtle-backs; armour-plated Humvees with TWO missiles on top. They were staying the night and would be our protection. At first they said little. They were few in number but immediately set up a perimeter. Jimmy sauntered over and spoke to their captain. It was not long before his Special Forces background had got their attention. Jimmy's view was that they were the best troops we had met so far and would be as effective as a whole company.

Tuesday, 25 March. There was no news and no Humvee. A vicious wind buffeted our vehicle. During the morning the storm strengthened, kicking up the dust. It swirled into a vortex, reducing visibility to a few metres. It was a storm unlike any other we had seen. The wind tore into the desert floor, driving before it rivulets of sand. It stung our faces and got inside our goggles.

Most of the convoys on the highway stopped. I tried to do some radio reports, crouching behind the vehicle in the lee of the wind. As I spoke my mouth filled with fine sand and between answers I spat it out. At times it was as if the flying sand had sucked out the air and we had difficulty breathing. At midday the dust reddened into an eerie dark-burgundy cloud. The sand raked the Land Rover like pieces of hail. Even inside there was a mist of dust. The storm was a story. The American advance had halted. I wanted to report this and asked Jig whether we could film any of it. 'If we get the camera out it will never survive,' he said, and so once again we were denied, unable to work.

In the middle of this storm we heard we were moving north. The major's Humvee arrived driven by Rick, a young Californian. The plan, he shouted to us through the wind, was for the Land Rover to be pulled by the Humvee. With our faces swathed in shemags – Arab scarves – we connected a tow rope and were pulled up an embankment onto the main track. We crawled in low gear, unable to see to the end of the rope. Beside the road were stalled convoys, with guards posted and their crews hunkered down against the storm.

The Iraqis used the storm as cover and out of the murk attacked Bravo Company. From the back of a pick-up truck travelling in the opposite direction to the unit, gunmen opened fire. The sound of the shooting was initially muffled by the wind. Some of the soldiers did not realize they were under fire until they heard bullets pinging off the armour around them. Many of the American guns jammed, clogged up with sand. 'The Iraqis hopped out, opening fire with AK47s,' said Lieutenant Brandon Kelley. 'It felt like minutes before the 50-cal gun on top of the Bradley destroyed the truck.' In the half-light it was hard to know how many Iraqis had escaped. There were no American casualties, but the storm was the great equalizer where technology did not count and it was just man against man. Some of the Americans were elated to have been in combat but most were subdued. This was not the war they had come to fight.

We pulled off the road and waited. Late evening there were violent flashes that lit up the sandstorm. The flashes were frequent and, at first, we thought it was guns firing but these were flashes of lightning. Rain followed, a driving, torrential, tropical rain that cleaned the air but turned the desert into a quagmire. It was like walking through sludge, a coagulating clay that clung to our desert boots. With each step we sank three to four inches, our boots coming up heavy with a thick layer of wet sand.

It meant that we had to sleep upright inside the vehicle. Jimmy thought he would get a better night curled up on the bonnet. I threw a sleeping bag across the front seat, propped my head against the steering wheel and arched my body over the gear stick. It was a terrible night for all of us. The rain and wind swept Jimmy off the bonnet and he lay in the mud.

Wednesday, 26 March. The storm had passed leaving a cold, damp day. The desert was pockmarked from the heavy rain. Jimmy's sleeping bag and bedroll were caked in mud. Walking was like wading through treacle. Even the Humvees, with their high wheels, were stuck. This was day three of being stranded without a vehicle. We all felt low and frustrated. The phones did not work. 'We can't take much more of this,' said one of us. We sat trying to kick the mud off our boots, watching a pack of stray dogs pick through the discarded meals-ready-to-eat. A young camel, with a low haunting moan, circled the camp having lost its family in the storm. The wind picked up again but the sand was too wet to fly.

Major Desjardin arrived and told us we were going to be towed to the outskirts of Samawah. He had a lieutenant with him who was losing his faith in the mission. 'It's just like Vietnam,' he told me. 'You don't know where these guys are coming from. I look at every bush or ridge of sand ready to fire.' The attacks had spooked and unnerved him and he wanted to talk. 'My father was in Vietnam and had told me never to go into the military. He would turn in his grave seeing me here. How the hell are we ever going to get out of this?' Already they were looking for the exit. I nodded but said little. I looked across at Major Desjardin who was sitting on the lowered ramp of his Bradley. I did not want the officers to think I was bad-mouthing the war.

I walked across to see Rick, the driver, who was now part of our team. He was nineteen or twenty, olive-skinned and too slender to look like a soldier. He seemed detached from the war; content to stretch out in the back of the Humvee whenever he could. He had drifted into the military before deciding he really wanted to be a cop. In the rim band of his helmet he carried the pictures of two high-school girls. 'Both are my girlfriends,' he said with a smile. And that was about as much as you got from him. But increasingly we would depend on Rick for our safety under fire.

Samawah was another Euphrates town; it was dusty, with low-rise buildings and factories on the outskirts. In the battle plan the

Americans had not expected to fight here. They intended to put in a small 'fixing force' that would allow the rest of the division to go north. General Blount and his staff had been led to believe that the town's people would welcome them. What American intelligence had not picked up was the number of fedayeen fighters who had come down from Baghdad. There were several thousand of them and they were forcing some local residents to fight too. The fedayeen were not only blocking the bridge over the Euphrates, they were also coming down to the highway and attacking the convoys.

Thursday, 27 March. It was about 9 o'clock in the morning when the ambush began. Firing started and the soldiers began running. No one had time to explain anything even if they knew. I saw little puffs of white smoke coming from buildings close to the highway. Captain Nunn shouted, 'Let's get going. Mount up and get out of here.' All around there was the sound of engines starting up. On the radio Bull Company said they had identified where the enemy was. It was a two-storey building close to the road. The Bradleys opened fire with their .50-calibre guns; their tracer bullets streaked across the open ground. The sound of firing intensified. Most of it came from the Americans. Black smoke rose from the edge of the town; an Iraqi taxi had been caught in the fighting. It was still burning when we passed it. There were bullet holes in the windscreen in front of the driver. We could not see any bodies. So much in war was unexplained.

American helicopter gunship hovered above us. Outside the gates of a factory, which had a large wall painting of a suited Saddam, a crowd of Iraqis gathered to watch. The Americans did not want people on the streets and the unit fired warning shots. Every Iraqi was a potential enemy. The workers scampered back inside, denied a viewing seat at their own liberation.

The radio crackled with rumours: 'There are some bad guys down at the railway yard.' When Bravo Company checked it out it looked eerily deserted. Just lines of rusting trains. Someone believed they saw something and a tank fired at one of the freight cars. Later, some ammunition was found and an old Russian-made T52 tank was destroyed, but the Iraqis who were fighting were not using tanks that were no match for the Americans. They were elusive, operating in small bands. This was the war of the flea.

Some Iraqis were suicidal. Two ran at a Bradley firing AK47s and were shot down. 'They were crazy,' said Sergeant Sean Morrow, 'why do they do it?' When the company drove through the market a man had drawn his finger across his throat. The captain had seen it. Outside the protective walls of the tank it felt dangerous and unpredictable, surrounded by faces that could not be read. The Iraqis became one, a lumped-together mass that soon everyone in the unit referred to as 'hajis'. It was not intended as an insult or a slur. It was just easier that way. You did not have to think of them as individuals, just as 'hajis', an amorphous, shapeless, voiceless people that would be liberated whether they liked it or not.

After three hours the mission was declared over and the tanks and Bradleys returned to the desert on the edge of town. The Iraqis had been pushed back from the highway and the convoys resumed their journeys north. But the Iraqis had not been defeated. We could still hear firing from the centre of Samawah. They could not be rooted out by tank units or gunships but only by troops on the ground.

Late afternoon we edited a report on the battle for Samawah. Most of the company had gone out on another patrol. A sergeant walked over and told us that the tanks and Bradleys might be away all night. That would leave just a few of us, some soft-skinned vehicles, three half-tracks and a supply truck. We were close to Samawah and the soldiers were afraid we would be mortared during the night. While Jig was editing I was drawn into discussions about how we would defend ourselves. The vehicles were driven into a defensive ring, the crippled Land Rover forming part of the circle. There was a plan. When the first mortar landed we would jump into the nearest vehicle and drive into the desert, and later, some- how, we would meet up again. After we had satellited our report I lay down close to one of the Humvees, my Kevlar helmet beside me.

It was a beautiful night; the sky was milky with stars. For a moment I forgot the war. Captain Nunn arrived back in the early hours of the morning, tired and stressed out. 'Turn that bitch off,' he shouted at a sergeant who had the engine of his Humvee running. Close to where I lay they were monitoring a radio. It was full of anxiety, a stream of raw information. A prisoner had told the

Americans the fedayeen were planning an attack and tanks were moved to defensive positions. Nights were often like this; an hour here, an hour there of interrupted sleep.

Friday, 28 March, and day nine of the war. I woke at 5.30, cold as usual. The soldiers gathered round to listen to the BBC news at 6 o'clock. It had become a kind of ritual. A US general was reported as saying the advance had stalled because of the guerrilla attacks. The war might go on for weeks and months. The men listened intently, silently. Each knew what the other was thinking. The war was not going well. Home – going home – once again was receding into the distant future.

'What do you think?' I asked Captain Nunn. 'It's not what I hear,' he said. 'We're moving out today, leaving this place behind.' 'What about the fedayeen?' I said. 'They're still running around.' 'Not my problem,' said the captain with a half-smile. It was hard to know what he really felt. 'Anything that takes us closer to Baghdad sits fine with me,' said Lieutenant Kelley. Away from the ears of the officers I could hear the soldiers talking. 'What the fuck is going on?' I heard one asking. One stopped me and asked, 'Do you think the reports are true?' I had no idea and I found myself not wanting to depress the men who, whether I liked it or not, were now responsible for my safety.

I got a call from David Willis, a BBC correspondent travelling with the US marines. He was somewhere on the other side of the Euphrates. A question was nagging away at him. 'How long do we stay out here if this turns into a long siege?' I did not know. The sandstorms and the snipers were eating away at his men too. All I knew was that we were bone-weary, living off adrenaline and high-calorie snacks. That could not last for ever.

The captain told me we were pushing far north to the outskirts of the holy city of Karbala. 'It's a long drive,' he said, 'and I ain't having you towed.' So that was it. We had lost track of the kid and had heard nothing more of the ball bearings. Our £15,000 Land Rover Discovery was to be abandoned in the desert. We transferred our bags to two Humvees but we could not take everything with us. So we held a desert car boot sale, except that we did not intend to sell anything, but in a company there were always men who wanted ropes and cans and wipes.

The tanks were going to be loaded on what they called 'hets' for the 150-kilometre journey to Karbala. 'Hets' were heavy-equipment trailers or transporters. All over this makeshift camp there was the sound of drilling and banging as the soldiers and the mechanics made repairs. The war was close – the other side of the highway – and yet in their minds the men had moved on. The talk was easy, relaxed, time-filling.

A first lieutenant reckoned his rank was the best in the military: 'No responsibility and you're not a cherry.' The cherries just laughed. A sergeant working on the breaker chimed in. 'I just gotta get myself a rag-head,' he said, as if we were on some hunting trip and the body of an Iraqi was a trophy. I could not tell if he was serious. There was a half-smile on his face but the talk was changing. The Iraqis were either 'hajis' or 'rag-heads'. The more we were delayed, frustrated and shot at, the harder the men became. 'Why don't we just waste the mother-fuckers?' said one of the soldiers who could not understand the restraint of the commanders. This was a desert locker room, full of sounding off and cursing, a 'shit' and 'fuck' world that was amusing and scary at the same time.

There was no privacy. The toilet was the desert. A few steps with a short-handled shovel and some baby wipes. You hunt for privacy out there, some slight dip in the sand. All of the men do it, choosing one piece of arid dirt over another, but you are never out of sight from the men on the tanks. You dig a hole, squat, and face out into the desert. A half-snatched moment alone. Once I walked too far and saw an Iraqi. The executive officer balled me out. 'You're going to get your ass shot off,' he told me, 'and we ain't coming to get you.' So you stayed close in, tight on the camp.

There were more delays. The transporters had not arrived. They, too, had become victims of the attacks on the supply route. Fighting continued around us. Bursts of firing then a pause. Bravo Company blew up an ammunition dump and a large black cloud hung over the horizon. Helicopters and planes attacked Baath party buildings in the town.

Captain Nunn said the 101st Airborne, the 'Screaming Eagles', were going into Samawah. I wondered whether the battle plan was changing. Tank units, like Bravo Company, were no good at securing cities. The Americans did not want to fight a house-to-house campaign, but in this town 'boots on the ground' had become the only option. 'I think these guys are going to keep coming out and harassing us,' said General Blount. 'I think eventually we're going to have to go in there and kill them.'

Many of the transporters, when they arrived, were driven by women. None of us had seen a woman for weeks. They were shapeless in their chemical suits and Kevlar helmets but the men changed. They were parading, shooting the lines, making plays. 'Hey, honey, can I ride in your cab?' one soldier shouted at a woman directing an Abrams up the ramp. The women were used to it. Most of the men were respectful in an old-fashioned kind of way, falling over themselves to help. Some, the following day, would claim they had got a name. Another said that when the relief driver had taken over, one of the women had rested her head on his shoulder in the tight warm fug of the cab. For some of the men this was a little bit of a dream, a night-thought to summon up and cling to amidst the noise of guns. A few of the soldiers ignored the women; they found them intruders, disturbing, reminders of what had been left behind.

As we lined up for the journey north, news came in of a suicide attack on the road ahead. American soldiers at a checkpoint had been killed. This was the first suicide bombing of the war and the story flew down the line of vehicles. We were now travelling in a Humvee with a flapping canvas door. We were the weakest link in the convoy, without any protection if we were attacked.

The incident delayed us yet again. The whole task force was moving to Karbala and Colonel Gillman now wanted every vehicle in a very precise order. The afternoon wore on as he swore and yelled at the men to get them in position. We were tired before we even started. The convoy finally left in the early evening, inching up the highway, endlessly stopping when a suspicious light was detected or an Iraqi vehicle seen.

We were on what the men called 'main supply route Jackson'. It was not much of a road, more of a track chewed up by convoys. I sat in the back of the Humvee scanning the darkness through the flapping perspex windows, panning from side to side, seeking reassurance. There were reports that the Iraqis were singling out the soft-sided Humvees for attack. I put on my body armour and helmet and tried to sleep, but it was cramped with our equipment. My feet, which rested on a battery, pushed the body armour into my chin. I sat huddled like this waiting for the night to pass.

We continued hour after hour. Sometimes we would pause and men would leap out and urinate. Then we rolled forward again. By dawn we were in green fields. There were mud-baked houses with women in black carrying coals or grinding corn. Some were living under animal skins that had been stretched over poles. They did not wave or even stare. They just ignored us as if the battles ahead would have no impact on their simple lives and the daily grind of survival.

Rick said little. During the night he had driven with goggles and by first light he was clearly spent. His head would loll forward and the Humvee would drift off the track. Jig and I took it in turns to watch him and shout when he succumbed to another wave of exhaustion.

The terrain changed. There were flat-topped mesas and large rock formations rising vertically out of the desert. A pass ran between them and as we climbed we could see the long military tail stretching back behind us. It seemed as if we had travelled to another country; but then the land flattened again and the old drab featureless desert returned. There were a few signs of war. Iraqi anti-aircraft trucks lay crumbled and disabled by the road having been attacked from the air.

After twelve hours' driving we stopped beside a field of sand-coloured bunkers. They were unlike any other military buildings we had seen. They were modern, recently built, and looked after. 'Saddam kept his Scuds here,' said someone, but I had no way of finding out whether or not any missiles had been stored there. 'Engineers will blow the buildings later,' said the captain. I thought it a bad idea and spoke up. 'Who knows what chemicals might be released?' I asked. The captain told me the engineers would take care of that, but I was not so sure.

Monday, 31 March, and day twelve of the war. After the overnight drive this was a down day. Men giving each other haircuts. Dominoes slapping down on tables. For the first time since leaving Kuwait we got a cooked breakfast. A truck, with a kitchen trailer, pulled up out of nowhere and began serving food. We ate grey-looking scrambled egg and sausages with ladles of ketchup, and it tasted good. We stood around in the morning sun drinking coffee and talking easily. The food was reassuring, a flashback to the old normal world that we had left behind.

After a while some of the soldiers began to question the meaning of this breakfast. I knew there were stories in London that American forces were running out of food because of the overstretched supply lines. I briefly thought this delivery might be aimed at me, so that I would go on air denying the stories of shortages. The soldiers had their own theory. This was a last breakfast, a last supper, before they went up against the Iraqi Republican Guard.

Some of the men tried to find their own space, a little patch of privacy amidst the scrub. They sat down, leaned against the tank tracks and faced away from the camp. I did the same. I called London but there was pessimism everywhere. The papers were full of it. The advance was stalled. Units were short of food. The commanders were considering a pause in the campaign to allow the supplies to catch up. The war might last two months.

I could not survive another two months, I knew that. The cold, the dust, the heat, the sudden ambushes, the failing equipment. They all wore you down. Time no longer defined a day. There were no fixed points that measured out one twenty-four hours from another. Sleep was random, snatched, and disturbed. With the military there was no time alone, no quiet and no escape. Even now, with everyone around me resting, the turbines of the tanks were still running. It must have been like this, I thought, in previous wars – but far worse. Campaigns had lasted for months, extending into years. But if this advance stalled there would be no easy exit, no passes home. I would get to leave only when the war was over, and there was little point in imagining otherwise.

Suddenly we were driving. The orders had changed. It was a short push. Twenty kilometres. Not more. I was glad to be moving again. Thinking time did not work out here. We arrived at another piece of desert where some army had been before us. Probably the Iraqis. Scattered across the ground were unexploded shells and grenades. The captain ordered some of the men to collect the ammunition from around the camp and blow it up.

Late afternoon two bulldozers built a high sand wall around us. We were close to Karbala and less than five kilometres from the Iraqi Republican Guard. The berms were to protect us from mortar or shell fire. We had a long discussion about where was the safest place to lie down. I lay half under the 88. Only a direct hit by shell fire would destroy the tank-recovery vehicle, I guessed.

Tuesday, 1 April. At 8 o'clock in the morning Bravo Company lined up for an award ceremony for Staff-Sergeant Morrow, whose promotion had been posted on the Internet. Colonel Wes Gillman joined us. 'You are truly the professionals,' he told the men. 'The whole free world is real proud of you.' He asked Sergeant Morrow to step forward and said, 'I present to you the newest Sergeant First-Class in the United States Army.' Morrow was a shy man. 'Glad to be here. Glad to get out of here,' he said. He gave a couple of grunts – 'Wo. Wo.' – which some of the men echoed and then said, 'That's all I got.' The executive officer took over and shouted at us, 'Shake his hand – even if you hate his guts.'

The colonel told us the battle for the Karbala Gap would begin that night. So much for a pause in the campaign. The intelligence was poor. The colonel did not know whether the Medina Division of the Republican Guard had dug in or retreated closer to Baghdad. At some point the Third Infantry Division had to cross the Euphrates to get to the capital. There were two options. They could cross at Hindiyah or go through the Gap, a choke point that lay between the city of Karbala and the Razaza lake to the west, and cross the river higher up. Some units were moved to Hindiyah but that was a feint intended to mislead the Iraqis. The next day the division would squeeze through the Gap.

While waiting for the attack to begin we drove across the desert to visit the 'MLRS boys'. They were the unit with the multiple-rocket launchers and were pleased to have company. 'Hey, look at this, man,' said a young fair-haired lieutenant, lifting a couple of rucksacks out of the back of the Humvee. 'Ran over a damn mine. See this,' he said, pointing at the sacks. 'That's shrapnel. We're lucky to be here.' They had their story and they wanted to tell it as they would when they returned home. They did not have a take on the war. They shrugged as if it had nothing to do with them. 'The phone rings in the launch vehicle. They give us the coordinates. We punch them in and the rockets are launched. That's it,' said the man, as if describing a job on an assembly line.

Close by, Iraqis were working in green fields that looked incongruous in the desert. They had water pumps and irrigation but the crops they were growing were spindly, withered plants engaged in their own battle for survival. I had not spoken to an Iraqi since the war began. I put my grey fleece over my chemical suit and walked over alone towards a farmer with his three children. He wore a dark-blue djellaba and a black-and-white keffiyeh. I smiled as I got closer. 'I speak no English,' he said remarkably clearly. His son wrote some Arabic in the dust, which I could not read. Using sign language, I asked him about the war and the firing of guns. He indicated that he could not sleep at night and gestured towards a group of women who were watching us. I took it to mean that they too were frightened. Then he drew his finger across his throat and I could not quite make out the target of his hate but he was coldly polite and I felt no welcome.

I walked back to the Humvee which we had parked a hundred metres away. As I looked back I saw his eldest son was following me. When I stopped he paused or crouched in the desert as if he did not want to be seen. When I reached the vehicle he came closer. He could have been no more than thirteen or fourteen. He put two fingers to his mouth and made a gesture as if he was drawing on a cigarette. His father may not have liked me but he did not want me to leave without handing over a gift. I gave the boy a bottle of water but I sensed cigarettes were what he was after.

A blood-orange sun hung low and full in the sky. Apache and Blackhawk helicopters circled in front of it, gathering for the attack, their rotor blades a soundtrack to war. The battle for Karbala began in the early evening with the whoosh of rockets fired towards the city, each a flaming parabola. Artillery and bombers followed. We heard the planes high in the sky, B1s and B2s, and then the ground shook as the bombs fell. B52 bombers joined the attack, dropping their payloads with their signature tune of rolling thunder. It continued relentlessly, a barrage of terror intended to break the enemy's will. We watched and filmed until we lay down in the desert and drifted in and out of sleep.

The soldiers woke at 4 o'clock in the morning and, against a crepuscular sky, edged towards the city, with rockets fired ahead of them. Overhead we could see the contrails of the last B52s before they began their long journey back to bases in England. From a distance Karbala slept. No people, just wisps of smoke drifting in front of low-rise buildings fringed by palm trees.

The city outskirts were cratered; it was a terrain pitted with ditches and channels. Some of this was the work of the overnight bombers, but not much. The desert was a giant backyard, a land-fill site where the people dumped their rubbish and the desert wind carried it away. There were brief firefights. Bursts of fire then silence or shouting. The soldiers ran over to a ditch pointing their weapons. More shouting: 'Get your hands up.' Then a line of Iraqis emerged with hands held high. None of them wore uniform. These were stragglers, irregulars. There was no determined resistance. The Republican Guard had not yet made its stand.

Huge American bulldozers moved in and built sand barriers across the roads, preventing Iraqi forces from coming in or out of the city. This was the plan. The Americans did not want to shoot inside a holy city. They wanted to hem the Iraqis in while the Third Infantry Division poured through the Gap and headed north. This was the moment when the American campaign regained momentum. Bravo Company stopped just north-west of the city with a mission to enforce the blockade of Karbala for a couple of days before joining the push on Baghdad.

Late afternoon we saw an Apache helicopter, which was hovering close by, fire two short bursts with its machine gun. Minutes later Captain Nunn ran towards Rocky and the other medics and shouted, 'Get your shit together. We've got casualties.' The Apache had fired on an American Humvee. This was 'blue on blue', friendly fire. Everywhere people were running. A soldier I had never seen before yelled at us that they needed the lights of our Humvee. A mini-operating theatre, lit by a circle of vehicle lights, was set up in minutes. We held back, with the camera hidden away. There was a different mood among the men, raw and angry. I had the certainty that if we intruded they would turn against us; but the injuries were slight and the stretchers and drips were packed away.

As we edited a report on the battle for Karbala we were interrupted by one of the Bradleys opening fire. They had seen two Iraqis moving towards where we were dug in. The men dropped to the ground and were captured. None of us spoke any Arabic but the men seemed to be saying they wanted to surrender.

As we put away the satellite dishes I noticed a group of soldiers pointing to the north. 'See that?' said one of them. 'The lights of Baghdad. Now ain't that a pretty sight?' There it was, unmistakable, the faint glow of a large city at night. The men stood watching it, drawn to the light pollution as if it were a beacon signalling the way home.

At dawn we could see the two Iraqi prisoners being guarded at gunpoint, their arms and legs tied with plastic cuffs. One of the two, a man in his mid-thirties dressed in a dark-blue shirt and grey trousers, had an inquisitive face. He kept leaning forward, examining the line of armour backed up on the highway. Later, they were given water and meals-ready-to-eat. The company took other prisoners. They were all the same: out of uniform and of military age with the impassive faces of the defeated. I tried talking with them but they turned away. These were mystery men, silent ghosts from an army that had evaporated before us. We did find a new Mercedes ambulance that was ferrying rocket-propelled grenades but these were for ambushes.

Some of the men did not like feeding the prisoners. One shaven-headed soldier talked about 'confirmed kills'. It was something he aspired to, rather like a medal or a badge of honour. 'I could get myself a confirmed kill right now,' he said, shaping his arms into a rifle and pointing at the prisoners. I could see how it could happen, how easily the ties that bind men into orders and rules could be broken. The prisoners were loaded onto an open-backed truck and driven through the camp. The captain shouted at them, 'Hajis off for mine clearing.' The soldiers laughed. The Iraqi prisoners were not badly treated, they were just despised, inferior men without names or identity.

Later that day we drove into Karbala, the burial place of Hussein, a revered Shi'ite martyr. I rode in the turret of a Bradley alongside Lieutenant Brandon Kelley. Hundreds and hundreds of Iraqis came out to see us. Families stood together. Parents with their hands on their children's shoulders. Families stood apart. Men outside the front gate, women in black on the rooftops. They were inside, secluded, off the streets, but they were not to be denied a glimpse of their invader.

'Look down the alleys and at the back of the crowds,' said Kelley, handing me binoculars. I was not just part of an army taking control of an Arab city, I was panning rooftops and dark streets for snipers and ambushes.

To most of these people we were liberators. Karbala had felt the lash of Saddam's cruelty. Many waved, some jerked their thumbs up, others had their hands spread in welcome. One man held up a small baby towards a tank, almost an offering, as if to say his child would now be growing up in a different world.

We patrolled. They waved. But there was a space between us. The American soldiers did not want the people close. They were liberated but not trusted. The people also held back. They were restrained, guarded, a half-smiling crowd. No outpouring. This was not like other liberations when soldiers and people hugged, sure of each other. Here there was a gulf of uncertainty. The men on the tanks had the power and the street knew that. What they did not know was what the Americans would do with their power. Red-and-white taxis darted in and out of the column as if to say it was their city and they had fares to collect. Sometimes I caught the eye of one of these drivers. I got a cursory nod and that was it. In their bustling impatience they were saying these were their streets and we, the outsiders, were clogging up the traffic.

In the midst of the wariness I saw a US medic's vehicle. On one side was written, in large black tape, the words: 'Do I make ya horny, baby?' I gave a gut-laugh. It was so absurd, so out of place. The idea that here, in this holy city, a man, a foreign man, might score. It was so insensitive but not by design – just two different worlds colliding on a dusty street. Space between us. On the other side of the vehicle, in equally large letters, were the words: 'Hajis don't surf.' That was the point. They were being freed but they were out of the loop. The hajis did not get it because the hajis could not see the joke. They had not seen the film, the acid-craziness of *Apocalypse Now*. And so we sat atop the tanks and fighting vehicles and smiled at each other and the space between us went unfilled.

We reached a square, not the main square of the city, but an open space in front of a blue-domed mosque. Standing on a small plinth was a sand-coloured statue of Saddam Hussein. The soldiers decided to topple it; it was a gesture intended to tell the people that the old regime had gone. A crowd watched from the pavement in front of the mosque as an Abrams tank knocked over the statue, reversed, and then crushed the face and head.

We expected applause but there was silence, stunned silence. The armoured column continued its patrol before returning to base. 'What's with those people?' asked Kelley as we climbed off the Bradley. 'They seemed none too happy about us knocking down that statue.' Another tank man joined us. 'Hey, did that statue look like Saddam to you?' he asked. 'Might have been a young Saddam,' said another. 'I think we hit the wrong man,' said Kelley. We all laughed, imagining the people of Karbala sitting around, shaking their heads and wondering about those Americans who drove into their city, knocked down a statue of a local poet or religious leader, and then left. The space between us.

That evening, 5 April, we were told we could remove our chemical suits. Captain Nunn smiled. 'You don't need to wear them any more.' 'Where did that come from?' I asked. 'Brigade HQ,' he said, used by now to his orders being met by my questions. It was like a release, a sudden lifting of fear, but I could not quite believe that the threat of chemical attack had passed. The outskirts of Baghdad had always been the 'Red Zone' where the regime might play a last desperate card. The captain did not have the answers.

The soldiers shouted to each other from the top of their tanks, 'No more chem suits.' Almost at once they began peeling them off. There was a bubbling, party mood. Silent withdrawn men found their voices. Taunts and curses flew. This was more than the lifting of one threat; this, to the men, was the first sign that the war was drawing to a close. After two weeks I was out of uniform, back in a crumpled blue shirt and chinos.

We then got the order that we all wanted. We would be moving into the heart of Baghdad. We headed north-east, following a rugged, bone-crunching track. It was much hotter here, with temperatures in the nineties. When we were overtaken by fast-moving scout vehicles our faces and hair were matted in sand. Dust flew in through every crack in the Humvee. We drove past hard-scrabble, patchy-green fields with farmers trying to eke a living out of a dust-bowl.

The column lost its way. 'We passed here an hour ago,' I said to Jig. We drove around in circles until we stopped in the middle of the desert. Everyone was hot and frustrated. I had never seen the officers so angry before. They picked up maps and avoided me. I could hear raised voices. We were delayed again. For the first time I heard open criticism of the colonel. 'You should have been with 269 Armor not Task Force 1-30,' one soldier said to me. We were not far from Baghdad but I felt a fraud broadcasting about the push on the capital when we were still behind the front line.

Sunday, 6 April, and we woke at 5 o'clock. At last we were going to Baghdad and on a paved road. We saw the evidence of recent fighting: a crumpled, blackened Iraqi anti-aircraft gun. A motorcycle with a mortar tube – which looked like a World War Two leftover – lay on its side. We passed a Humvee on fire, with soldiers taking cover in a ditch. There was the sound of shooting but it might have been exploding ammunition. We skirted around and kept driving. I was now impatient to get to the capital and willing to take some risks.

We crossed the wide Euphrates at Musayyab. American soldiers guarded the bridge. There had been a real battle here. The air was acrid with burning diesel and ammunition. There were the charred remains of Iraqi tanks and artillery that had been dug in around the palm trees. They had been clinically taken out. A few were still on fire or smoking. The Iraqis had lost a company's worth of equipment here, or more.

The roads were clogged with American armour. It felt as if a decision had been taken to seize Baghdad and bring the war to a close. We overtook stalled convoys, swung up a steep motorway ramp and drove onto Highway 8. The plan was to head west before turning into the city. Beside the road were pyramids of concrete, perches for Iraqi anti-aircraft guns. Most had been destroyed from the air. Fifty metres off the highway were blackened trenches that had been filled with oil. Some had been set alight and the air smelt of burning oil. The Iraqis had thought that these curtains of fire would distract and mislead the American missiles and bombers.

We stopped briefly and Captain Nunn said he wanted to divide the column. The tanks and Bradleys would go ahead; the soft-skinned vehicles and some of the supply trucks would follow about a mile behind. The captain wanted the armour to clear the way before exposing his more vulnerable vehicles. Jig decided that he would travel in the front column and use the turret of the 88 to film from. Sometimes we both travelled in the tank-recovery vehicle but on this day I stayed with the rear column.

We took a left-hand exit and joined the main highway that runs from Jordan into the city from the west. Under the first motorway bridge was a disabled tank. An Iraqi soldier lay dead, spread-eagled in the road. His foot, still in its army boot, was twenty metres away.

Across on the other side of the highway, two cars had collided with the crash barrier. Another two, with their doors open, had been abandoned, skewed across two motorway lanes. A red bus, with its windows shot out, had stopped close to the kerb. Behind them were other cars and trucks pockmarked with bullet holes. All had stopped suddenly, frozen in the moment of attack. Some bodies were still slumped in their seats; others were hanging out of the doors as if they had been trying to escape. There were a couple of women at the back of one of the cars, killed as they had tried to take cover. Other bodies lay in the verges. We drove by slowly with none of us speaking. All around us was death, gruesome and unexplained. These people had been caught up in the random violence of war – perhaps driving down the highway at the moment the Iraqi tank was attacked from the air.

As we approached youths had run off to the side of the road where they stood waving. They were looters, picking over the vehicles and the bodies like motorway crows feeding off road-kill.

Shortly afterwards there was a loud explosion, different from what we had heard before. The column stopped, every vehicle taking up defensive positions, facing outward in all directions. 'What was that?' I asked Rick, the driver. He did not know. We moved forward again and there was another explosion followed by a plume of black smoke off to our right, about a hundred metres away. I heard machine-gun fire but I could not see who was firing. The road dipped between two high-sided concrete walls that supported a small bridge. There was another ear-splitting bang with fragments of concrete torn from the top of the walls. 'That was incoming,' I said. 'Is that incoming?' I asked Rick, hoping he might reassure me, but he did not know and his face was scared.

Jimmy was in the Humvee in front and came running back. 'We're being shelled,' he said, 'from the right-hand side of the road.' Fear is instant, neural; it envelops you before you have even thought of it. You are hard-wired to run and hide but we were trapped, hung out on a highway with few exits in a canvas-sided vehicle that offered no protection from shrapnel.

As we emerged from the underpass another round fell and we watched a column of smoke rise. This round had dropped closer than the others. The column paused again. Jimmy was getting agitated. 'They're bracketing the highway?' he said. He could not imagine an easier target than a paused convoy sitting on a slightly elevated road. I, too, was shouting out of fear. 'Why don't we just get the hell out of here?' I demanded, as if somehow it was Rick's decision. The fact is we were all frightened, but there was nothing we could do. We were in a military convoy and under orders.

We could not understand what the lieutenant in charge was doing. It was almost as if he had frozen under fire. 'If we don't get off this fucking motorway some of us are going to die here,' continued Jimmy. He knew he was right and was tempted to get out of the Humvee and argue with the officer in charge. I sat there helpless, wrapping my body armour tighter and trying not to think where the next round would land.

After several minutes we moved forward but went only a short distance before we found a hole in the central barrier and joined a slip road. It was less exposed than where we had been but we dawdled as if they were map reading in the lead vehicle. I was shouting again with frustration and helplessness. The fact that my life was in someone else's hands was eating away at me.

The convoy then took a left turn away from where the shelling was coming from. It was not a regular road, more of a track that ran through some waste-ground. We had driven only a few metres when soldiers started jumping from their vehicles with their rifles. One of them ran to my window and screamed, 'Wheel 360.' His face was taut with panic and fear. 'What the hell does that mean?' I said, but he just waved us on. Rick stopped the Humvee close by a wall. I shouted at the nearest soldier, 'What's up?' 'We're under attack,' he said. 'The Iraqis are coming.' He pointed across some black mounds that might have been coal heaps. There were shots and shouting. No one seemed in command. I crouched between the vehicle and the wall.

Another shell landed nearby. I could hear what sounded like falling rain as the shrapnel shredded the palm trees. Jimmy was trying to find out who was in charge but no one seemed to know. He grabbed one soldier and shouted, 'We've got to move from here.' The soldier tried to shrug off this interfering man who was not even an American soldier. I joined in. After all, this was my life. Jimmy was insistent. 'If we stay here we die. They're walking those shells towards us.' He had been in these situations before and was certain that the Iraqis had spotters and sooner or later they would drop a round on top of us.

There were soldiers running everywhere, some crouching, some firing. I said to Rick, 'We've got to get out of here.' I could see he was tempted to drive. Then the men began running back to their vehicles and everyone was shouting, 'Go, go, go.' I had not heard an order; the idea just seemed to have taken hold, to have caught men up in it, and they ran for their lives. Convoy discipline broke down. Trucks and half-tracks and Humvees all jostled for the narrow exit, away from the shelling. A truck with a trailer squeezed in front of us. I shouted, but the driver did not listen. In those few moments we cared only for ourselves.

We drove over a railway line and into a dusty street of houses and small factory buildings with some open land behind. There was a burst of fire and the convoy stopped. The soldiers leaped out and took cover behind their vehicles. Jimmy told me to crouch behind the engine mount. 'It's the strongest part of the vehicle,' he said. Again there was shouting and firing and arguing. Some of the men believed the shots came from a house; others said they came from the opposite direction. There was a shot close to me and I rolled on the ground. More shots followed. Jimmy thought it was an accidental discharge. The soldiers were spooked by their own shadows and the shots from their own weapons. Most of them were not frontline men and had never seen any fighting before.

I thought of Mogadishu and *Black Hawk Down* and the men surrounded in a strange city swarming with gunmen. I felt trapped in nameless streets with maps that told us nothing and Iraqi snipers circling us.

The convoy moved forward again. Rick ripped off the door of the Humvee so that he could shoot better. He drove with his M16 cradled on his lap. We stopped again. More shots. And then a Bradley appeared with an officer in the turret. He had been reached on the radio and had come back to lead us to where the other tanks and Bradleys were.

We drove to another neighbourhood. I saw a car with bullet holes and a man lying in the middle of the road. Jimmy went to look. The man had been shot in the back. Just another unexplained death. Close by there were explosions, tank rounds being fired. An Iraqi armoured personnel carrier had been spotted, edging out from behind a warehouse. There were more explosions and the guns on top of some of the Bradleys opened fire. There were plumes of dark smoke and the crackle of ammunition exploding. The battle swirled incoherently.

Our convoy drove past three blackened Iraqi tanks. Two were smoking, one was burning fiercely. A charred body lay on the ground. Jimmy spotted that another blackened Iraqi soldier beside the road was still breathing. We wanted to tell the medics but the radio was congested with the urgency of fighting. Beyond the Iraqi tanks was a civilian truck, perched on the side of an irrigation canal. The driver was still in his cab where he had been shot. On the other side of the road were three cars. They too had been raked with fire. The dead were slumped at the wheels or lay on the ground. On the back seat of one of the cars a tray of eggs was unscathed.

Beside the road a man cowered in a drainage ditch with his hands raised. A family stood under a makeshift white flag as if transfixed by the destruction around them. 'What happened here?' I asked no one in particular. There were no answers. I could only guess. The Americans had attacked the Iraqi armour with over-whelming force and anything in the way of that terrible fire was cut down. A truck driver, an old man out foraging for eggs. War, when it came to the cities, was rarely clinical.

We were in a neighbourhood of irrigation canals and sand banks and scattered housing. The land here was fertile, with woods and patches of green cultivated land. The column turned along a ridge,

passing more civilians, women in headscarves, men clutching possessions. They were trying to flee the fighting. They had no welcome
for us, just harrowed looks as they trudged to safety under white
pieces of cotton tied to poles.

We passed another Iraqi vehicle burning fiercely and then drove
into a field. There was a steep berm on one side, with trees and
buildings on the other sides. It was decided that we would stay the
night here, it being too dangerous to link up with the rest of Bravo
Company. There was a half-hearted attempt to form a perimeter.
Our Humvees were pushed out into the field facing a line of trees.

There was little armour with us. We were a back-of-the-line
crowd, supply trucks, soft-skins, medics and a couple of ageing
armoured personnel carriers. A soldier came around with a clipboard and took names for guard duty. These men were casual,
slack, careless and disengaged; the tail of an army, not its fighters.
These were the 'remfs': the rear-echelon mother-fuckers. Jimmy
knew all about 'remfs' and thought we were in much greater danger
here than with the tanks.

I sat down, leaned against the back of the Humvee and wrote a
script. This had been an important day. The battle for Baghdad was
not yet over and I was troubled by the number of civilians who had
been killed in the fighting. I wrote that the war needed to end soon,
before the Iraqi people judged the price of their liberation too high.

I went round to the front of the Humvee, took out my satellite
phone and dialled the BBC in London. The number put me through
to 'traffic' – a clearing system that alerted all BBC programmes that
I was on the line. Editors and producers could listen in as I filed my
report. Unusually, for during the war, I had written down what I
wanted to say. Halfway through my broadcast there was a loud,
close burst of gunfire from the woods. My voice wavered as I was
torn between just falling to the ground and continuing the report.
The shots were clearly audible in London. I hurried my last breathless sentences and said, 'I've got to get out of here,' and rang off
abruptly. Iraqis were firing at me from the trees. I lay flat on the
ground and, using my elbows, dragged myself under the Humvee
until I reached the relative safety of the other side.

I was trembling, my hands shaking, but I was also angry. It was
something instinctive, irrational, knee-jerk, like a fist clenching after

a violent push. There was nothing brave about it just a wild, blind desire to strike back, to take a gun and go after these people. In a flash it had become personal, disconnected from my role as a reporter. And then the moment passed, my breathing slowed and once again I was the detached observer. But I had felt it, what the soldiers felt – that under fire killing was possible, if not easy.

Two hours later I decided to call London again, to reassure them that I was safe and had not been injured. I also wanted to file another report without the shooting in the background and my scared voice. It would be less upsetting to my family and friends. This time I decided to phone from a different position, from the back of the other Humvee, which I judged to be better shielded from the woods. I was halfway through this fresh report when an Iraqi opened fire again. My voice fractured. You could hear the fear in it. As soon as it was over I turned off the phone and lay on the ground. I had taken too many risks for one day.

We were very exposed. There were Iraqis around us and it would be easy for them to fire rockets or mortars at us during the night. On the drive in we had noticed a ditch and decided to lie down there for the night. I was too wound up, too strung out to sleep. There was still the sound of firing and, occasionally, the much louder thump of American artillery.

As I lay there I felt cramp in my stomach, which I tried to ignore but it would not go away. In the dark I could not hunt for a bit of privacy and dig a hole. There were Iraqis in the trees and the American soldiers on patrol were nervy. I crawled along the ditch, as far as I could from a sleeping Jimmy, and then scrabbled in the dirt to make a slight dent in the ground. I was violently ill with all the tension of the day. I clawed at bits of rock, soil and weeds to cover up where I had been before returning to my sleeping bag.

Monday morning, 7 April. We drove the short distance to join Bravo Company and the tanks and Bradleys. The area was still unsafe. Rockets had been fired at the company overnight. Jig had been grazed by a ricochet as it flew off the side of the 88. It had hit him on the thigh, leaving an angry purple-blue bruise. He did not really want to talk about it or for me to mention it to London but I could see, like the rest of us, he wanted this to be over.

The captain's Abrams tank had had to be winched from a ditch while Iraqis had fired at him. The soldiers were red-eyed, short-fused, their skin grey with exhaustion. Kelley said to me, 'You happy now? You got what you came for?' I did not know how to answer him. I had never wanted the killing or the danger but I had wanted to be there at the end of this epic journey, when the American forces went into Baghdad. 'Guess it's a case of be careful what you wish for,' said Kelley. There was not much more to be said. I had wanted to cover this war and here, on the outskirts of Baghdad, we had found it.

Bravo Company moved on, closer to the centre of the capital. For the better part of the day we patrolled amidst the dykes and canals, picking off Iraqi tanks that had been hidden there and had now been abandoned. So much armour was destroyed that the captain was told to spare any equipment that might be used by a future Iraqi army.

The Iraqi soldiers, as they had before, melted away, withdrawing into the more tightly packed streets downtown. Their uniforms lay strewn beside the roads, cast off and discarded as they fled the American forces. There was now no uniformed Iraqi army to fight.

The next day, we were told, we were driving into the heart of the capital. That evening we stopped on open ground surrounded by houses with fenced yards and unkempt gardens. Rocky, the medic, sat down beside where we were editing on the concrete stoop of a half-finished building. A tank commander, to whom I had spoken several times, joined him. The commander, with dark-rimmed glasses, was a tall, lanky, sensitive man. He was troubled and chose to confide in Rocky. 'Why are we killing so many civilians?' he wanted to know. Some of the men were talking. He accepted that most did not care; their minds closed over events almost as soon as they were past.

The commander poked a stick into the soil. He wanted a war that he could be proud of, not an edited, sanitized version that he would tell his friends back home. He wanted to be at ease with himself and his own values. He sat there, a disconsolate figure, and there was nothing much Rocky could say to him.

They were interrupted by a woman in a headscarf who approached the company under a white flag, with her husband and children beside her. The soldiers ran for their guns. 'Get her away from here,' shouted one of the officers. 'Go, go,' he waved at her aggressively. The woman was persistent. 'She speaks English,' said one of the men closest to her. 'I know,' said the captain, 'but the last time some mother-fucker pregnant lady showed, she blew up a car load of guys.'

The woman said she had found a gun. 'They have a gun,' said one of the soldiers, misunderstanding her. 'Put the gun on the ground,' shouted another man. The encounter was tense and confused. No one seemed to be listening to her and I feared there could be a tragedy. Every Iraqi now was mistrusted, to be kept at a distance. It was what the suicide bombers wanted.

The soldiers ended up by shouting, 'Leave. Go. Anywhere – just leave.' 'Where we go? What we do?' the woman pleaded. Later, after she moved away, Sergeant Morrow spoke to her. She, in fact, was a supporter of the invasion and led the troops to four truck-loads of ammunition that had been abandoned by the Iraqi army.

On 9 April, we drove into residential neighbourhoods. I travelled in the back turret of the 88. There were ammunition boxes everywhere; some had been broken open, leaving rocket grenades strewn on street corners. It looked as if they had been dumped there deliberately; street arsenals for what Saddam Hussein hoped would be a fierce, last-ditch defence of the capital.

Most people stayed in their houses, which is where the Americans wanted them to be. When figures darted between buildings one of the Bradleys fired down the narrow streets. There was gunfire but I could not tell from where. One of the tanks destroyed an Iraqi tracked anti-aircraft vehicle and it burned fiercely.

We drove up a ramp onto a wide road with dense housing either side. There was the crackle of gunfire and the company stopped. 'They're shooting at us from the left,' said Sanders, who was the driver of the 88. 'I can't see them, I can't see the mother-fuckers,' shouted the gangly black American who was on the .50-cal. There was more shooting. 'Shit, the gun's jammed,' the soldier shouted. Sanders was passed an M16 but it, too, did not fire. 'Can someone give me a weapon that fuckin' works?' he shouted. Another M16 was unclipped from the rack and he fired from the front turret.

I lay on the floor, enclosed in a steel box, with people outside trying to kill us. It was hot, claustrophobic. The soldiers were frightened of a stray round that might come through a turret and kill a couple of us. I wondered whether this vehicle would withstand a direct hit from a grenade. I lay there, just wanting the convoy to move on, to leave this place. The crew were finding it difficult to locate where the shooting was coming from. Someone thought it was the roof of a building. Another thought it was a tree. They had seen a flash. Sanders thought that was the glint of sun. No one was certain but they fired all the same, a random, raking kind of fire.

The main gunner finally clipped in the rounds and opened fire with the heavier gun. He stood on a round stool almost on top of me. His trousers were only loosely fastened and bizarrely he kept trying to hitch them up whilst wrestling with the .50-cal. One of the soldiers shouted, 'To hell with your trousers, man.' The gunner let them fall and all I could see was the shaking naked butt of a man a few inches from my face.

Then the convoy drove on. It was often like this. There was shooting but nothing was resolved. The gunmen retreated and the company lost interest. We passed through the district of Shula and stopped beside an electricity sub-station. Next to it was a half-finished housing estate. Abandoned beside the houses were thirty to forty trucks, many piled high with ammunition. As we drove I heard a 'whoosh' and an explosion. 'RPG,' shouted someone. The rocket had passed just above our heads.

Sergeant Morrow surprised some men unloading rockets from a truck and killed them. The city crackled with gunfire and explosions. The captain ordered the company 'to circle the wagons', to form a ring, with the Abrams tanks on the outside and the more vulnerable vehicles closer to the centre. This felt a much more dangerous place than out in the desert. We were on a building site surrounded by roads and houses beyond. The soldiers felt vulnerable and kept their weapons close.

I heard the captain talking to a young soldier. 'Don't look at them as humans,' he said, 'think of them as vermin.' The comment shocked me. 'Vermin' was a word laden with history, memory and flashbacks. The previous century had been scarred by the cleansing of 'filth', 'vermin' and 'rabid dogs'. What if the camera had been running? Would I have used it? Probably not. The word tainted this war that I and the others were risking our lives for.

The comment unnerved me in another way. The captain was firing up his men because he felt surrounded by hostile territory. I picked up that anxiety. I was sitting on top of the 88, panning the buildings with my binoculars. It was then that I noticed a blue truck. What made me pan back was the movement of the men around the truck. They were hurried, furtive, looking around as they pulled back a tarpaulin and unloaded something heavy. Close to them a man seemed to be studying us with binoculars. All my instincts told me we were about to be attacked. I tried to argue with myself to stay out of it, to stay uninvolved – but, sitting on this tank, I was involved and could die here as easily as the soldiers around me.

I shouted over to the captain, 'You should check out that truck. They could be planning an attack.' I expected him to order an Abrams or Bradley to take a look. Instead he ordered a Bradley to open fire. Orange tracer flew across the open ground. Some struck the buildings behind. The captain shouted, 'Keep it low, keep it low.' All I could think was that people, innocent people, could die out there because of me. Then the truck exploded in a ball of flame. Moments later there was a second, louder explosion. 'That was ammunition going up,' said one of the soldiers. Then a third, car-splitting explosion that destroyed the truck. The men around me had no doubt. The truck had been full of grenades and I had saved the unit from attack. Soldiers embraced me, thanked me, high-fived me. One African-American soldier, who had never spoken to me before, came up and said, 'You're the man.'

For the first time I felt accepted, that I was part of this unit and that these men would fight for me too. Much as I struggled to hold it at a distance, part of me wanted that warmth of belonging. While the truck was still burning Captain Nunn walked over. The incident had only confirmed to him that we were in harm's way. This was like Vietnam, he said, although he had never been there. In his mind this was the same. We were surrounded by an elusive enemy in a strange land. 'If we're attacked during the night,' he said, 'we'll take out that whole neighbourhood.' He spoke of passing on the coordinates to the men with the multiple-rocket launchers. I was afraid about what we were getting into, but inside I knew I would accept the bombing of a neighbourhood if I could walk out of there.

Early morning, 10 April. As I was standing talking I saw an object with a faint trail of smoke fall close by. We looked at it with curiosity before someone shouted, 'RPG.' I dived behind a tank but the grenade failed to explode. That was another thing. I was growing used to risk and danger and the sounds of shooting and bombing.

The tanks and Bradleys headed closer to the Tigris, the river that divided this city. In the narrow streets men ran from buildings firing shoulder-held rockets. This was street fighting, close and personal. About thirty rockets were fired. The men from Bravo Company screamed into their radios, warning each other of where the enemy was. 'Light 'em up,' they shouted. 'Smoke the mother-fuckers.' This was something else. Kill or be killed. The language of restraint had no place. Captain Nunn shouted, 'I've been hit, I've been hit.' A rocket had struck a grille just under the turret of the Abrams where he had been standing. For a moment he could not see, his eyes blinded by the explosion. The other tanks rushed to his side but he was uninjured.

In the midst of this I got a call from London. The statue of Saddam Hussein had been toppled by a crowd and the Iraqi leadership had fled. The war was over. 'It's not over here,' I told them, but they were no longer interested. The images of a falling statue were being beamed around the globe and the fall of Saddam Hussein was a fact. I told the captain. 'I wish someone would let these guys know,' he muttered.

Later, on the west side of the city, the fighting subsided. The company returned to its base amidst the half-finished buildings. The men listened to the radio and began talking of home. They believed at last that the campaign was over. The consensus was that they would be back by May. One of them began talking of Shannon Airport in Ireland. The plane stopped there on the way home to the United States. They were allowed two drinks but they intended to drink the bar dry and they knew no one would stand in their way. Others spoke about girlfriends or just 'getting pussy'.

The following day the mood of the city had changed. The men with the guns had gone. Crowds lined the streets waving at us as we patrolled the neighbourhoods. A man ran beside the tank we were riding on. 'Thank you, thank you,' he shouted, his hand raised, emphasizing the point. 'Thank you, Mr Bush, thank you, Mr Blair.

Saddam killed my family.' The man could not say thank you enough. He jumped in his battered white Mercedes and drove after us shouting 'thank you' through his sunroof. 'This is what we came for,' said Sanders, who was driving the 88 again. The soldiers wanted to feel they were the good guys and to return home with heads held high.

This was liberation day, bright, shining – but incomplete. There were people on the streets, but half the population ignored us. On the right side of the road was a straggly line that waved with coy half-smiles, whilst on the left side men pushed carts piled high with chairs, cupboards and televisions, which they had looted. Cars followed our victory parade but many were weighed down with rugs, boxes and electrical goods on roof racks. Many of them were looters impatient to get home and store what had been seized.

When I spoke to General Blount about it he was relaxed; he saw the looting almost as a release, a cathartic moment, a cleansing – the action of a people who were taking back what had been stolen by Saddam's regime.

But it did not seem like that to me. One soldier had shouted out of a Bradley, 'You're free now,' but the puzzled man in the street had no idea whether this was a good thing or not. We spoke of rebuilding Iraq but the people had no sense of society or community. We had a vision for them but they could not see it. We spoke of the future but it was hazy, an indistinct concept that meant little. All they saw was the chance to grab something, even if they did not need it.

In one street close to where Bravo Company was based, every window in every house was smashed as looters stripped neighbourhoods bare. Looters ambushed looters. People returned home with their spoils only for their own homes to be raided. At night the shooting returned, but it was mainly home-owners driving off the bands that were moving across the city.

We all felt deflated, denied the buzz of victory. The looters took care of that. Some of the soldiers felt the Iraqis had shown no gratitude. There had been flashes of celebration, like the man running beside the tank, but they were few. Initially the unit just watched as if this was someone else's fight. The Americans had taken the capital but, within hours, had lost control of the streets.

In those first few hours and days the soldiers who had won a war went some way towards losing the peace. They had not brought freedom but insecurity. At company level there was no plan for running neighbourhoods and so the ruthless and the hard men filled the vacuum.

The soldiers sat in their newly acquired base, detached from the chaos of the city. They had fought but had invested little in it. They felt nothing for the Iraqi people. They had no ambition for them. From the start they did not really want to meet them. All they really wanted to do was to see the mission through and 'get out'.

Later that week we decided to leave, to cross the Tigris and report from the east side where the large hotels were. We said goodbye to Bravo Company. Some of the men envied us; envied the ease with which we could pack up and leave. We shook hands and embraced. Sergeant Waddell was disappointed that he had not seen more fighting. 'Make sure you get home,' I told him. Rocky, the medic, had never adjusted to being a fighting man and was counting the days to finding a new career. Sergeant Morrow was a pure soldier for whom the cause continued to burn brightly. There were the men in the 88 who cursed and argued their way through the campaign and whose company I would miss. There was Rick, with the pictures of his girlfriends inside his helmet; his mind was already on California and his new life as a cop. Lieutenant Brandon Kelley was a bright, impressive man whose future, I guessed, would lie outside the military. I had come to like Captain Nunn, a tough career soldier determined to bring his unit home.

Our two Humvees drove to the airport where we hoped to pick up an escort to take us to the other side of the city. We met Major Birmingham, the press aide to General Blount. He took us to one side. There was a military flight leaving in the middle of the night for Kuwait City. Did we want to be on it? The three of us looked at each other. Leaving was not on our minds, but as soon as the offer was made the war for us was over. I could see it in Jig's and Jimmy's eyes and it would have been there in mine too. As soon as we were given a choice it was as if all the weariness, the sagging exhaustion, the dirt and the fear rose to the surface. In that moment my will to stay was broken.

Before we left I spoke to General Blount in the VIP lounge that
was now his office. There was nothing triumphant about him. He
remained as I had found him at the start of the campaign, reflective
and thoughtful. His first concern was that I did not portray him as
a General MacArthur figure. He did not want any of that. The war
had lasted only a few days longer than the battle plan envisaged,
despite all the setbacks. There had been, among the Iraqis, more
casualties than he had expected. More civilians had died and that
troubled him. I asked him how many. 'I don't want to get into that,'
he said. That remained the unknown, the unmentionable subject:
the human cost of winning and taking Iraq.

Sometime later, in the middle of a black cloudless night, we
were taken to the edge of a runway. I heard the distinctive engines
of a C130. The plane landed in darkness, its pilots using night-
vision goggles. On the runway soldiers from the 101st Airborne
raced ahead of the plane on quad bikes; the infrared strips on the
back of the bikes guided the pilots to a stop. They kept the engines
running and lowered the ramp. Within minutes we were strapping
ourselves to the red netting along the inside walls of the plane.
Then the ramp was shut and we sat there in the obsidian black,
unable even to see our hands. The plane accelerated and banked
sharply. I tried to count to seven minutes when, for some reason, I
thought we would be out of missile range. There was a flash when
the pilot emitted anti-missile flares. It was my last moment of
sudden fear and it passed within seconds. In less than two hours
we were back in Kuwait. It had been only a few weeks but it was a
lifetime. We went to the Sheraton Hotel and I sat under a shower
for half an hour until my skin began to flake. I then climbed
between crisp white sheets and phoned everyone I knew.

I arranged to meet Jig and Jimmy in the coffee shop. As I was
getting out of the lift I ran into a journalist who had been at boot
camp with me in Quantico. 'How was it?' I asked. 'Out of this
world,' he said. 'We had been driving close to the centre of Baghdad
in a Humvee with our M16s.' He did not seem at all concerned
about revealing that he had carried a weapon. 'The soldier up top
had shouted, "Enemy to the right,"' he went on. 'We turned around
and just hosed those guys down. Fucking great.' Iraq, for this man,

had been a shooting gallery where, without fear of arrest, you could 'loose one off' and 'hose' guys down. I was too shocked to argue with him, but ran to the coffee shop to tell Jig and Jimmy.

Bravo Company did not get to go home in May. They stayed until late summer and resented it. It was more than most of them had signed up for. Many of them, when they returned to the United States, left the military. It had just been a job and they were not prepared for year-long rotations. A few I have stayed in touch with, but most dispersed into the vastness of the United States and got on with the rest of their lives.

When I returned home friends stopped me and said, 'You had a good war.' I always looked away, uncomfortable. War may be necessary but it was rarely good. I had told it how I had found it, but once again I thought television had captured only part of the story. It was I who had said to Jig that we should be careful about showing bodies. As a result he had pulled wide when we saw dead Iraqis, so the viewers got a cleaned-up, sanitized, prime-time war. They were spared the horror, and in that sense I never shared the war I lived through.

This time I had not been an onlooker. I had lived the story. I had been with good men, but even good men can waste lives. It is that easy in war. I knew, too, that when we were under attack I was no longer neutral. You cannot be neutral about your own life and I knew that in the battle for survival I, too, could have picked up a gun.

21

Strangers in a Clinch

In the late nineties I had presented two programmes on the disappearing tiger. It was a change for me, a different pace. With news, time is always an enemy, but with natural history programmes it is the opposite. They thrive on patience and the long empty hours of waiting. Wild animals or insects are impervious to television's deadlines. They live outside modern time. I was flown to India to record some pieces to camera, but they decided to shoot the opening to the programme in London. The producer wanted me with a tiger and it was difficult to arrange that in the wild.

I have never been that confident with domestic animals, let alone tigers, but reluctantly I agreed to the shoot. I was working with producers who had made a landmark series on the planet and I trusted them. The location was a warehouse in west London. The tiger got there before me. She was already inside a large cage which had been built for the day. I was introduced to the trainer who assured me that the tiger was a veteran of fashion shoots and TV commercials. 'In fact,' he said, 'she's probably done more television than you.'

The producer outlined the plan. I was to go inside the cage – and that came as something of a surprise. The cameras would stay on the outside, shooting through the bars. The trainer would coax the tiger to leap onto a stool behind me and roar. And that would be my cue. A roar. I would then turn to the camera and deliver my lines. I had doubt written across my face. Whether it was true or not, it had lodged in my mind that staff at safari parks were regularly mauled.

There was no reason to worry, said the trainer. This tiger had been with him since a cub and she feared him. The key to working

313

with tigers, he assured me, was that they must never discover a
human's true strength and how strong they themselves were in
comparison. The tiger had to remain afraid of us. 'The whole thing
is a con,' said the trainer, who was clearly enjoying my unease. And
I was nodding at his words while hoping that this was not the day
that the tiger realized that for all these years she had been had.
I vowed to stay inside the cage for the briefest time possible. So I
paced up and down learning my lines. This was not a moment to
fluff and stumble. Before they unlocked the cage I checked with the
two cameramen and their sound assistants that they were ready.
'I don't want to hang around in there,' I said with a nervous smile.

A door in the iron grille was opened and I went inside the tiger's
cage. She looked bored or preoccupied. I could not tell which. I
breathed deeply, trying to control my anxiety. I swivelled my body
to face the tiger but avoided looking her in the eye. The trainer,
holding a long pole, shouted a command and the tiger leaped
towards me, giving a roar as she landed on a stool close by. I then
turned to the camera and, in a slightly tremulous voice, said, 'What
a magnificent creature . . .' and delivered the opening lines to the
programme. The words came out but I was not relaxed enough.
The producer wanted me to 'enthuse' over this animal as if she was
my pet. So the tiger was sent back for a second take. Next time the
tiger fluffed it by forgetting to roar. On the third take the cameraman was not happy with the pull back from the tiger to reveal me
and I was still struggling to find the whispering intimacy of natural
history presenters. I could hear the tiger breathing and could even
smell her stale, meaty breath. After a dozen takes I felt certain we
must have a usable version but still not everyone was satisfied.
Then the tiger gave up. The trainer shouted his command but the
tiger just sat there looking agitated and they opened the cage for
me.

The producer still needed some pick-up shots of the tiger but
the trainer said there was a problem. He went back inside the cage
and a short while later announced that the tiger was pregnant and
might be unpredictable so he planned to move her to a cage in a
truck and to bring on instead a stand-in tiger.

'Pregnant,' I said. 'Didn't you know this?' 'It's nothing,' said the trainer, with a dismissive shrug. I followed him, demanding to know what he meant by 'unpredictable'. I could not get an answer. The producer was amused by it all and tried to reassure me that we had a couple of usable takes. And that was it. I was ushered out of the warehouse. The television moment was over. Ironically, when the programme went out they ran some footage of a tropical forest behind the tiger and no one believed that the animal and I had been in the same place. They thought it had been staged.

The incident reminded me of interviews done down the years. However many phone calls are made or question areas agreed there is always the chance of the unexpected, the bizarre, the off-camera comment, the confession, the guard dropped. A television interview is artificial. Two people meet. They may know each other but more often they do not. And shortly after shaking hands this stranger has to come alive and perform. A few minutes later it is done and they are strangers again.

It is February 2004 and I am waiting and hoping to interview John Kerry, who is the almost certain Democratic Party candidate for the American presidency. We are in New York and it is a typical day on the stomp. The before-breakfast scramble for that day's accreditation. Boarding the campaign bus. Cameras slung over shoulders. Bagels and muffins in hand. The short ride to a community hall in Harlem. The jockeying for a camera position. The inevitable arguments with the secret service about where we can stand. Then, in the age of security, the long wait for the candidate. Just before his arrival the secret service decide on a new rope-line and the jockeying resumes.

The speakers pump out music from Coldplay and John Kerry is in the room, hand shaking, back slapping, embracing, thumbs in the air. Endorsements and introductions follow. Local members of Congress. Councillors. All get their thirty seconds. Yesterday's campaign phrases fly. Frontiers, tomorrows, beginnings, dreams. They are all trying to capture a spark. Then a few words from the candidate, his campaign riff, and we are piling out, off to Jamaica in Queens. And it is the same again. The security sweep. The fight to get in or to stay out of the press pen. And all the time we are negotiating to talk to the candidate. It is a difficult pitch. Although

BBC News is shown on a number of cable stations in the States we reach a relatively small number of voters but, for some reason, on this day John Kerry agrees to talk to us.

The haggling begins. We can have only five minutes with him. No more. Then it is slashed to three. We are told to go to the back of the stage and wait. Kerry will do two interviews, one with NBC and the other with us. After the American interview Kerry shakes the correspondent's hand and walks away and his shoulders slump. Almost immediately an aide rushes to his side and the two of them whisper together. Then Kerry whirls around, walks after the correspondent, throws an arm around him and wishes him 'happy birthday'. It's a nudge from an aide. An after-thought.

He's weary, glazed-eyed with connecting, his voice strained from speaking. There is no energy for small talk; he even hesitates over the handshake with me. He just wants to deliver his bite, his sound-bite, and be gone. The producer says she has met an old friend of his and his eyes flicker into life. Then he waits, his mind elsewhere, as the final adjustments are made to the camera and the lighting. I then ask him whether he now thinks the war in Iraq was a mistake. He puts on his television face, animated, authoritative, engaging, pleading to be liked and trusted. After a few moments it is over. There is hardly a goodbye. In a second we do not exist. He is far away and another aide briefs him about his next public moment. It is clinical, cold, a clip requested, a clip delivered. The unexpected, the probing supplementary question all but ruled out. Just a clinch between strangers.

Sometimes these chance encounters have been bizarre. In 1984 I flew to Bombay to interview Moraji Desai who, a few years earlier, had been India's prime minister. I wanted to talk to him about Indira Gandhi and her son Rajiv. She was in her fourth term as prime minister and her son was emerging as a future leader. We climbed the stairs to his apartment. Desai was sitting in an armchair, a small, imperious man, with a closely shaven head and large dark-rimmed glasses that dominated his face. Beside him on a table was a glass with a straw-coloured drink. Over the top he had placed a saucer. We all saw it and we all knew what it was. Desai drank his own urine, believing it improved his health. It was the one detail about the former prime minister that had fascinated the camera crew but they had not expected to see it. And then Desai asked the inevitable question. 'Can I get you a drink?' The crew shot back a 'no thank you'; it was the swiftest rejection of a drink that I can recall. I was now struggling not to laugh. Then, when Desai was distracted, the cameraman took me aside and asked me in a conspiratorial voice whether I wanted the urine in the shot. He could pan off it, he assured me. I shook my head in bewilderment and said the interview was not actually about urine-drinking.

The interview began and we talked about India. He liked scathing one-liners. To my first broad question about his country he replied, 'It's a totally wrong idea.' To the second question he snapped back, 'Only those who are ignorant of politics can say this.' His response to the third question was, 'I don't understand what you're driving at.' He was dismissive and acerbic. Mrs Gandhi, he said, only wanted to 'keep herself in power'. Rajiv 'has not the capacity to be prime minister'. I asked him about the millions sleeping rough on the streets just a short distance from his apartment. They were not his concern, he said. That was the way of things. He was an old man who had become more certain with age. I had in my notebook a favourite quote of his. 'Hypocrisy,' he had said, 'was the main failing of mankind. Fortunately I gave it up many years ago.' Then, as I continued with my questions, he took a sip. Not a gulp, but just a little taste. And he did it without the slightest inhibition. Age had given him the right. We ended the interview and left him to his certainty and his drink and he lived to be ninety-nine years old.

Once, during the same period, I went to interview a leader and ended up praying with him. In 1984, although she denied it, Prime Minister Indira Gandhi of India was again manoeuvring to secure her political dynasty. Her father, Jawaharlal Nehru, had been India's first prime minister and she had been the country's leader for fifteen years. She had wanted her son Sanjay to succeed her but he had died in a plane crash four years earlier. Now she was nurturing her son Rajiv. I wanted to interview him and he suggested I join him on a campaigning trip to Rajasthan.

There were no motorcades or outriders or armoured cars. All of that would come later, after the assassinations. Rajiv travelled in a white Ambassador car. Another one, with the police, came behind.

He was a reluctant campaigner. He did not really want to meet the people and was slightly embarrassed by their attention. He was a man made powerful because of his name. He was a Gandhi. For the visit he wore a white tunic and a white collarless shirt underneath. He had wrapped a red turban around his head. It was curiously ill-fitting and lopsided, as if he had tried to tie it correctly but had lost patience with it. As soon as he stepped from the car there were crowds pressing in on him, handing him flowers. He held his hands together in front of him in the traditional gesture of respect and he wore a string of yellow marigolds like bracelets. Then he tossed them back into the crowd and was amused to see the people scamper after them. These rural people danced for him; they had painted their faces for him; they whirled for him. He did not have a speech. He just waved, smiled coyly and left. For a couple of the campaign stops he asked me to ride with him. He wanted to talk, to eat up the time. He was softly spoken, even self-effacing. He was interested in ideas and how technology was shaping the future. It was like travelling with an intellectually curious colleague. As we drove through the villages there were faces at the window staring inside. Most of them smiled, hoping for something back, a flicker of recognition or a wave. Rajiv gave little: a slight movement of his hand. Some politicians feed off a crowd's affection; he wanted to damp them down, to keep some distance from them. He was hesitant about seeking power while knowing it was inescapable. He had enjoyed being a commercial airline pilot. Sanjay, his brother, had been the political son but he was dead. Now destiny was dragging Rajiv centre stage.

At the campaign stops we got out and the crowd thought I must be someone – I had flowers around my neck and I was bowing, with my hands together, following Rajiv. The crowds wanted to touch me, to break my reserve and see me smile. Part of me wanted to own up, to throw my hands in the air and to admit I was a fake, but I was also enjoying the farce of it. It was as if there had been an extraordinary mix-up and I had ended up being an Indian politician. And it amused Rajiv, who chuckled every time he looked over at me. Then we were back, cocooned inside the Ambassador with hundreds of faces gliding by. I had come for an interview but, strangely, I was now working the crowds, shaking hands with local officials.

Then we came to a Hindu temple in the region of Kishangarth. Rajiv said he was going to perform puja, ceremonial worship, and asked me to join him. I said, rather obviously, that I was not Hindu but he said it did not matter. So we walked down steps to a sacred pool. Petals were dropped on us as if we were a married couple. We crossed a tiled floor and then sat cross-legged on a rug while a crowd stared. There was a priest with straggly grey hair and a slash of red paint between his eyebrows. He daubed a red spot on Rajiv's forehead and did the same to me. I bowed slightly, guessing this might go down well, but the priest was stony-faced. Rajiv was handed a round ornate box of purple and saffron. 'What's in the box?' I asked. 'More petals,' he replied. Beside us on the floor were small baskets with what looked like spices. 'Just follow me,' said Rajiv. So I sat there with my hands together, as if in prayer, watching him out of the corner of my eye. He then dropped a few petals in the temple waters and shortly afterwards, having prayed together, we sat down and I interviewed him.

Having spent the day with him it was hard to change the tone of the conversation. We had been chatting like friends. I asked him whether he actually wanted to be prime minister and he replied, 'It would be a challenging job, yes,' but I knew he was uncertain. I told him that I had spoken to his mother and she had said she did not want him to seek India's top post. I asked him why he thought she had said that. 'My God, I don't know,' he said and laughed. Neither he nor I believed her. I asked him whether India needed a dynasty. 'I think what we do need in India,' he said, 'is what we've always needed and that is a binding . . . and if the country feels that our family is a binding force then it does serve a purpose for the country.' Then we parted. A few months later his mother was assassinated and he was prime minister of the world's largest democracy.

Sometimes an interview gets stolen, hijacked, and you realize you are no longer in charge of the brief embrace. It happened in 1984 shortly before I met Rajiv Gandhi. In Amritsar the Golden Temple had been taken over by Sikh extremists. They wanted a

Sikh homeland and were led by a firebrand preacher, Sant Jarmail Singh Bhindranwale. Some called him the Khomeini of the Sikhs. He and his heavily armed followers had occupied a building adjacent to the temple, and violence was growing in the Punjab. There were fears for the unity of India and the Sikh unrest was becoming a major story.

Bhindranwale kept us waiting for days. Sometimes we glimpsed him and his followers striding through the temple grounds. They wore white robes and had black beards. A few had saffron turbans but most of them, including Bhindranwale, wore blue. He carried a short silver spear in one hand and at his waist was a leather holster with a pistol. All of them carried swords, which was the Sikh tradition. They walked with intensity, with swagger, with the fundamentalist's certainty. When they went to pray, others stood aside. Some fell to the ground in front of Bhindranwale, trying to kiss his bare feet. He was slightly taller than his followers and always walked a few paces in front.

His court was a rooftop. There he would sit, surrounded by his men, reading out the names of policemen, politicians and political opponents. 'There are sixteen or seventeen men who are drinking the blood of the Sikhs,' he would say. Then the names would follow, and most of them would end up dead. It was a hit list, whether he intended it to be or not. We flattered him by being there. It enhanced his status. People had come across the world with their cameras to talk to him. For hours we sat by the Pool of Nectar while the hymns and readings wafted across the water like an aroma. Bhindranwale wanted us there and to be seen waiting for him.

Then we were called to the roof. On the way up the stairs we passed boxes of ammunition, automatic weapons and rocket-propelled grenades. Windows were sand-bagged and had been turned into machine-gun emplacements. His men insisted I wore a turban. Bhindranwale sat in a chair. He ignored us while we set up the camera. Behind him stood his followers. We asked them to move but they refused. He liked to speak surrounded by his men. I asked him about the killing of policemen. 'I do not care about the police,' he said. 'We're prepared to fight them. We are all prepared to die as martyrs.' He spoke in riddles with a smile at the edge of his mouth. 'I have never praised anyone,' he said, 'for killing a human being, but the killing of a cruel man I do praise. A Sikh never kills,' he continued, 'he only asserts his rights.' He spoke in a soft voice and rarely looked at me. When I challenged him about the violence he responded with a calculated insult. There was a silence as he studied me and then he announced, 'You are a Sikh but you have a deformed face.' His men laughed. They laughed the loud laugh of subordinates. They liked the fact that their guru was playing with me. 'You should be wearing a beard,' he continued, 'and then you would be accepted here.' I thought it was my interview and tried to bring him back to answering the questions, but I had become the man with the deformed face and, once mocked, it was easy to toy with me. A few months later the Indian army invaded the temple and Bhindranwale was killed.

Then there are the hard men, the reviled, the outcasts. Men like Mugabe, Milosevic and Saddam Hussein. They are always difficult to interview. The viewers have already made up their minds about them. What they expect is a confrontation where the leader is challenged about crimes and abuses, but the advantage lies with the person being questioned. In the space of a short interview it is easy to lie, in the certain knowledge that the reporter has not the time to summon the evidence that will contradict them.

I have interviewed Robert Mugabe of Zimbabwe twice. He was superficially friendly and formally polite but he always wore a mocking half-smile. He was a leader who survived by creating plots and enemies. Although he attacked the Western press he liked giving interviews, certain he would always come out on top.

I first interviewed him in 1983. At the time his notorious Fifth Brigade was terrorizing Bulawayo and the Matabele. His aim was to crush Zapu, the party of his political rival, Joshua Nkomo. I had witnessed the troops going into the townships, had seen the beatings and had spoken to eye-witnesses about the killings. Mugabe liked to sit forward in his chair during an interview, constructing his defence with his hands and his long fingers. When I asked him why he was silencing his opponents he said, 'We believe a multi-party democracy is a luxury.' He was brazen, bare-faced, unflinching, without the slightest trace of an apology. If challenged, he fell back on attacking the West, Britain and the colonial past. It was always the card that got him out of trouble. Evidence was dismissed with a wave of his hand. The violence was always the work of dissidents. Joshua Nkomo was a 'wily creature' who was plotting against the government.

At the time there were reports that Mugabe had brought in North Korean troops to train the Fifth Brigade. One of Mugabe's aides had told us that they had already left the country and Mugabe had said it had been no more than a small fraternal gesture. A few days later we were interviewing Emerson Mnangagwa, the head of Zimbabwean State Security. While we were setting up the camera for an interview we noticed a red folder marked 'Secret' on his desk. I could not resist glancing at it. The documents were about Mugabe's travel plans. In a couple of days he was travelling to the east of the country. There would be a rally and afterwards a visit to an army camp. What caught my attention were the names. The officers he would meet all had Korean names.

We chartered a plane, hired a car and turned up at the rally. Afterwards, flashing our press passes, we tagged along behind the official motorcade and when we arrived at the army camp we were waved inside. It was full of North Koreans. Mugabe strode to the platform and said, 'I would like to pay tribute to our comrades in arms, the instructors from the Democratic People's Republic of Korea . . . once again we have an example of the splendid generosity and cooperation of our brother, the great leader, Comrade Kim Il Sung.' During the speech we had moved closer to the stage until we were right in front of it. As he spoke I stared into Mugabe's face until he caught my eye. I wanted him to see me there, to recall our interview. He looked at me with cold fury.

Some years later I was back in Zimbabwe when President Mugabe had a new enemy: the white farmer. It was a dangerous and unpredictable time. White farmers were driven from their properties. Some were killed, although the worst suffering was that of African workers and the political opposition. In the midst of all this Mugabe went to the town of Bindura to address a party rally. He mocked Tony Blair and the British government, the old colonial power, for interfering in the country. After he left the stage I wanted to snatch an interview with him, to challenge him about the violence. As he came close I threw a question and he could not resist answering. We tried to slow him down and positioned ourselves between him and his car. As I pressed my questions I felt a heavy blow to my head and I fell to the ground, dazed. One of his security men had a weight inside his sleeve, which he used to stun anyone who got too close to the leader. As I was struggling to my feet Mugabe's black Mercedes drove by with Mugabe waving and smiling.

It is always interesting to meet a leader who is widely hated and despised, to see how he carries himself. In 2002 I interviewed the French far-right politician Jean-Marie Le Pen. This was his moment and it had arrived unexpectedly. He had just come second in the French presidential elections and had even beaten the Socialists. His success had sent a tremor across Europe. In a few days there was to be a second round of voting and France would face a choice between Le Pen and Jacques Chirac. On the streets of Paris there were daily demonstrations with Le Pen denounced as a Nazi and fascist.

I wanted to interview him and he asked us to meet him at a television station early one morning and then go with him to his party headquarters. He arrived in a modest car with just one bodyguard. He was quite tall and held his shoulders back, clinging on to his ex-paratrooper's stride. The swagger remained but he was now overweight and his face fleshy. He knew that everywhere he went there were people – perhaps even the receptionist from North Africa who had to greet him – who did not just disagree with him but hated him. None of it touched him. The greater the outrage, the greater his conviction.

We sat down in a cramped office. He spoke some English, though not as well as Jacques Chirac, but he insisted in speaking in French, and I expected that from a French nationalist. Usually before an interview I try and relate to the person I am going to be talking with by making an observation or a friendly remark. Le Pen was not interested in small talk and that suited me. It is always difficult to interview a man whom many people regard as a fascist and a racist, and I had spent the evening before planning the interview.

I asked him a soft-ball question to start. He expected me to attack him so I decided to try and settle him, to tease him out. I asked him why so many people had voted for him. 'The real earthquake,' he replied with surprising honesty for a politician, 'was not so much the rise of Le Pen. It was the collapse of the country's established parties.' I could tell he liked the question but I had ready a second, which I thought might create difficulties for him. I mentioned France's brilliant soccer players Thierry Henry and Zinedine Zidane. Both men had North African roots. 'When you see them playing for France,' I asked Le Pen, 'do you have pride in their skills?' 'Yes, absolutely,' he replied. He saw the trap immediately; there were political risks in going against these popular players. He explained that they came from countries that were close to French culture, which meant that they could be assimilated and integrated easily. What he was against was a 'generalized melting pot'.

I was forced to rethink my line of attack and asked him why so many young people denounced him as a fascist. 'They are being manipulated by their Marxist teachers,' he replied. 'Everybody knows that ninety per cent of French teachers are Marxist support-ers.' Such sweeping statements pose a dilemma for an interviewer. You suspect the answer is a wild exaggeration but you cannot challenge it without being drawn into the opacity of the French education system.

I was still hunting for a searching question. I could not find it and ended up asking what I thought was another easy one. 'What place in France,' I said, 'do you see for immigrants if you become president?' He leaned forward. He could not resist it. 'I think our entire continent is threatened by an invasion stemming from an overcrowded world and if we do not take every measure to defend our territory, our population will be reduced to slavery by the waves of foreign people.' It was not coded. It was what he believed.

I had a hint of the man but I wanted more. I wanted to tempt him out further. I told him that Tony Blair found him repellent. That got to him. The world 'repellent'. 'I advise Mr Blair to mind his own business,' he snapped back. 'I tell you that if I become president of the Republic the first thing I will do is to send him the refugees from Sangatte [a Red Cross holding centre] on a special train.' It was the brawler, the political bruiser in him. It was not the language of a future president but that did not concern him. It would play well in France's poor white neighbourhoods. A slap at the British prime minister and a simple solution to the immigrant problem. Refugees packed on a special train. I had my clip for the *Ten O'Clock News*.

Shortly after the interview we went with him to his heavily guarded headquarters in Paris. Le Pen invited us to film the opening minutes of his daily strategy meeting. He sat at the head of a rectangular table with his closest advisers around him. They were all in good spirits, savouring their success, enjoying the political tension. I was focusing on picking out shots with the cameraman and missed the start of it but one of them was telling a story which made the others laugh. To my utter amazement it was about a concentration camp. We caught a little of it on tape. I puzzled over the episode. How could it be, at the moment crowds were shouting 'fascist' on the streets, that Le Pen's inner circle were telling a story about a concentration camp with the cameras present? It seemed a gift to his enemies. As I watched him, his shoulders shaking with laughter, I realized that outrage was part of his appeal. He did not want to bite his lip, to encode his comments like other politicians. He knew that in France there were people who felt insecure, fearful and that their identity was threatened. They were drawn to him precisely because he was politically incorrect.

After a long interview there is often a brief unrecorded conversation. Having been debating for maybe half an hour it is hard to stop abruptly and walk away. Sometimes the discussion just keeps going, and with the cameras switched off there is the temptation to open up, to become less guarded, and to make a small confession. In 1985 I was reporting on the Palestine Liberation Organization. Three years earlier it had been driven out of Beirut after the Israeli invasion. There was a new Palestinian diaspora as they scattered throughout the Middle East. We wanted to interview Yasser Arafat but he was constantly on the move, changing his plans, fearful of his security. His people asked us to fly to Jordan but he had left by the time we arrived. Finally we sat down with him in Baghdad.

It turned out to be a long interview. His English had improved although it was still heavily accented. What he had learned to do was to finish his point despite interruptions. He was fired up and combative. I asked him about the killing of Israeli women and children. He said it was against 'our religion, our principles'. Nevertheless, I said, it was happening. He grew irritated and asked me why I did not talk about Israeli attacks on Palestinian families in Lebanon. 'Resistance,' he told me, 'is not a picnic but it is our destiny and our right.' I wanted to know what armed resistance had achieved. 'The Palestinians,' he said proudly, 'have become a key factor in the Middle East.' I asked him, 'Who is the real Mr Arafat? Gunman or peace-maker?' 'Both of them,' he replied, 'because I am carrying the olive branch and the gun to protect the olive branch.' What he would not do was to give up the armed struggle. That was capitulation.

I wanted to pin him down. 'Are you prepared to recognize Israel's right to exist?' I asked him. 'Simply and clearly,' he said, 'I'm ready to accept all the United Nations resolutions.' 'Why can't you answer that question clearly?' I demanded to know. 'I have cards,' he replied. 'I have small cards. I haven't many cards to play with.'

So the interview stopped but he wanted to keep talking. I had to understand, he said, that the Palestinians would not accept him if he recognized Israel. 'It is one of our best cards. If I give it away they will kill me.' There was sweat on his face. He was edging closer to me, trying to make me understand. Sure, he said, the Israelis wanted to destroy him but there were people on his own side who could kill him just as easily. He moved from place to place not so much out of fear of the Israelis as out of fear of other Palestinians. He was frightened of taking risks for peace. The cost of compromise, he told me, might be his life. That was his confession and that is what stayed with me. Not the interview but a man who wanted me to understand his dilemma.

In 1984 we were invited to a garden party at the Pakistani president's house in Islamabad. It was a left-over: a colonial occasion without colonial masters. The white bungalow-styled building. The lush gardens and archways draped with fairy lights. The food delivered by men in red tunics and shining gold buttons, their white turbans finished off with fantails that stood proudly at attention. One had only to close half an eye to be back in another time. Even some of the voices and their idioms drew me back to an imagined past.

Our host was President Zia al-Haq, Pakistan's military leader.

He practised an old-fashioned courtesy. He was dressed all in white in a long jacket coat and collarless shirt. Even out of uniform he was a military man. Parade-ground turned out and immaculate. The parting down the middle of his hair was wide and straight. Not a hair strayed to the wrong side. His greying moustache was carefully trimmed. His dark-rimmed eyes made him look severe but he had a wide smile that revealed comic-book buck teeth, and some people mocked him but that was a mistake.

During this period he was giving the mullahs their head. Islamic laws were being strengthened. We had seen women lawyers dragged from the streets in Lahore after demonstrating for women's rights. When I began the interview he defended the new laws with lofty explanations. 'Here we have the three fundamental principles of an Islamic society. Freedom of speech. Freedom of thought. Freedom of choice.' I reminded him that Pakistan was a military dictatorship where democracy had been suspended. He was an astute man who soon wrapped me up in long explanations about what 'choice' and 'freedom' meant. I said to him that there were demonstrations on the street demanding greater democracy. He dismissed them as mere 'agitations'. 'In a military regime,' he told me, 'you can only overthrow a military regime with a military person.' I was not sure about that and so the interview meandered to its conclusion.

Afterwards, when the camera was switched off, he wanted to talk. He spoke with energy, confidentially, as if I was an old friend. It was a confession of far greater interest than the interview. He wanted to talk about the Shah of Iran. 'The Americans made a great mistake in not standing by him,' he told me. It had sent a message to the region that the United States would not stand by its friends. 'What you have got in his place,' he said, 'is Ayatollah Khomeini.' So he had swung Pakistan down a more traditional Islamic path. 'If I had not done this I am doubtful I could have survived.' And this was the confession. These changes were born less out of belief and more out of necessity. I asked him about the women whose dem-onstrations were not tolerated. 'They have to be sacrificed,' he said with a pleading note in his voice; a pleading to be understood. 'I am standing in the way of Khomeini here.' This was the real story. He had seen how America had abandoned one ally, the Shah, and so had tilted towards the fundamentalists. Then the confession was over and he walked along a red carpet to the entrance. A harsh, courteous man who had confided in a stranger.

Just before he became prime minister I interviewed Tony Blair at his home in Islington for BBC *Panorama*. It was a long interview. Towards the end I insisted repeatedly that in order to fund his social programmes he would have to raise taxes. As I refused to let the subject go Tony Blair suddenly said, 'Sorry, did you hear that?' Taken aback I said, 'What?' 'That noise in the corner,' he replied and pointed towards the sound-recordist who was sitting on the carpet. Tony Blair turned to him and asked, 'Did you make a noise?' The recordist took off his headphones and shook his head, just a little baffled. It was a device that broke the line of questioning from a man who would go on to become one of the most expert politicians of his generation in handling questions.

And so I have always loved the interview. It is a kind of blind date tinged with uncertainty, where the moment can be broken by a noise in the corner or a sullen tiger. And afterwards to walk away knowing you have been in a clinch with a stranger.

22

And Finally

In news-speak 'and finally' signals a change of mood or tone. The final story is often trivial, sometimes humorous but nearly always human. It comes after the main events, the images of conflict and the words of politicians. It is often a story apart. When I returned to London after the war I wanted to put Iraq aside for a while, to breathe different air, to pick up the rest of my life, but the war continued to intrude. There were media debates about 'embedding' and a BBC film to be made about our journey from Kuwait to Baghdad.

I felt I had lost some fitness out in the desert and returned to the gym and my old routine: twenty-five minutes on the exercise bike; six minutes rowing 1,500 metres; fifteen minutes of jogging, followed by a few circuits of aerobic weights. On Wednesday, 7 May, after nearly two months away, I got back on the bike. After a few minutes, as I increased the resistance, I felt a tightening across my chest as if I had indigestion. I had never experienced anything like it before. I continued cycling and eventually it subsided.

That evening I decided to see my doctor. I felt sure it was nothing but I was troubled too. I saw him the next day and he could find nothing wrong with me but felt, as a precaution, I should see a cardiologist. Within twenty-four hours I was sitting in a consulting room. The cardiologist asked whether I suffered from indigestion and I shook my head. My blood pressure was high but he thought that might partly be explained by 'white-coat syndrome': the fear of doctors. Then he asked me about my family history and I told him that my father had died from a coronary thrombosis at the age of fifty-five. In that instant his whole attitude changed and I felt my first fear that I might not easily walk away from this. He wanted me to have immediate tests and over the next few days I had an echo sound and an electrocardiogram stress test. I walked on a treadmill at various speeds while the electrical activity of my heart was recorded as a graph. While I waited for the results I went back to the gym, hoping the tightness had gone, but it was still there.

The following Monday I returned to see the cardiologist in the early evening. Most of the results were good but he wanted me to look at the graph from the stress test. Each of my heart beats was shown as a spike. As they subsided the base line should have been straight but, with me, it fell away slightly. In his view I had a blocked artery and he delivered his judgement with chilling certainty. I immediately summoned up counter-arguments as if somehow I could get him to change his mind. He had met people like me before and was firm in his response. He wanted me to have an angiogram as soon as possible; he had already checked with the hospital and there was a vacancy in two days' time.

An angiogram, he explained, was an X-ray of my arteries. A thin tube, or catheter, would be inserted through an artery in my upper thigh and go up to my heart. A dye would be injected into the tube which would enable a picture to be taken of my heart and arteries. I wanted to slow everything down, to try and regain control of what was happening to me. I explained that I was going on holiday at the end of the week and would think about the angiogram after that.

And then he hit me with it. 'Most probably,' he said, 'you have coronary artery disease and if you fly at 30,000 feet you could die.' Professionally, he said, he had to advise against it. Those three words – coronary artery disease – were like a sentence. You feel your whole life changing, slipping away from you. I was not yet ready to agree to an angiogram and promised to give him an answer in the morning. I drove back to Television Centre. I was doing the main story for the *Ten O'Clock News*. It no longer mattered. On that evening nothing did. I dragged myself through it with the help of Dan Kelly, an excellent producer and a friend.

I alerted my family that I had bad news. I felt a flicker of shame as if, in some way, I had let them down. That night I tossed through the long hours, scared of this procedure and what it might find, but in the morning I knew I had to face it, that I could not walk away. I recalled what James Baldwin had once written: 'Not everything that is faced can be changed but nothing can be changed until it is faced.' While I waited I became separate from the rest of life. I was on the outside as if behind a screen. Others continued going to work, visiting a store, slipping out for a drink, but I no longer belonged with them.

Wednesday, 14 May, came and I was in hospital for the first time in my life, waiting my turn in a queue. I was offered a shot of valium and took it. I lay still as the catheter moved inside and images were taken of my heart. Within twenty minutes it was over. I had a thirty per cent blockage in my left circumflex artery. The consultant thought it was genetic and that it had been developing over thirty years. He wanted me to have an angioplasty in which a stent would be inserted into the artery to keep it open. We agreed that I would have the procedure three weeks later and, having discovered that I was not in immediate danger, he declared me free to go on holiday.

I was, at first, relieved. I had a problem but they seemed confident they could fix it. So a few days later I flew to Bermuda. This was to have been my escape after the desert and the war. Books, beaches, water sports. But everything had changed for me. I tiptoed around the island. I shied away from riding motor scooters or wind-surfing. Long Bay Beach, next to Horseshoe Bay, is one of the world's most beautiful beaches. A stretch of unspoilt pink sand, a churning turquoise sea, rocks and coves. It was the kind of place where you wanted to jog along the beach or body surf or throw yourself against the waves. I now sat and envied the freedom of others. I was forever checking myself, holding myself back, on guard for signs of chest pains. Whilst on the island I made a call about the timing of my angioplasty and the assistant let slip that thirty per cent of patients developed further problems, and that unsettled me.

When I returned from Bermuda I worked normally. I did not tell my colleagues; I just hoped I could quietly have my angioplasty and resume work a few days later without questions or explanations. On the surface, angioplasty seemed quite straightforward. My artery would be widened by a balloon inflated through a catheter and a stent, or tube, would be inserted to keep the artery open. When I got to the hospital the consultant told me he had examined my X-rays and he thought it advisable to stent a second artery. This was the first I had heard about a problem in another artery and I was very uncertain as to whether or not to agree to it. These were decisions about my life but, beyond asking questions, I could not make a judgement; in the end I went along with the consultant.

During the procedure I was awake, looking at a monitor where I could see my arteries and someone working on them. I preferred to look away. The consultant needed me still but when the balloon was inflated I felt my chest tightening and they increased the valium. The first stent went in easily and the consultant joked that it must be nothing compared to the war in Iraq, but at that moment I would have swapped any part of the desert for the operating theatre.

When it came to the second stent there were difficulties. I could hear it in the tone of his voice. A tension. An anxiety. A slight fear. I lay there pleading for it to be over as I felt a man struggling with an artery to my heart. At last, after nearly an hour, it was done and I returned to a room to lie still before being released from hospital the following day. Sometime later the consultant came to see me and said it had gone well, but he spoke rapidly and dropped into the conversation that I could always have another stent. I wanted to believe I was free of this but I knew the man who had done the procedure did not believe it himself.

A few days later I resumed normal life; the only restriction was that I could not travel for a few weeks. On 29 May 2003, the editor of the *Ten O'Clock News* asked me to follow up an item on that morning's Radio 4 *Today* programme. Andrew Gilligan had reported that there was unhappiness within the intelligence services over the government's September dossier which set out the case for acting against Iraq. The report had also said that the government had inserted a claim that Iraq could deploy its weapons of mass destruction in forty-five minutes, probably knowing the information was wrong. Gilligan quoted his source as saying the government had wanted the dossier 'sexed up'. There could not have been a more damaging allegation, accusing the government of taking the country to war under false pretences. I agreed to follow the story up, but only if I could stand it up myself through my own conversations.

On previous occasions I had met some of the weapons inspectors who had been in Iraq – men like Ambassador Richard Butler. I also knew that there was a highly respected British inspector who was an expert on Iraq's weapons programmes. I did not have a number for David Kelly, so I called Tom Mangold, a friend and former colleague on *Panorama*. Kelly had been a source for one of his books and he passed his number to me.

I reached Kelly on his mobile. He was in New York. I told him at once that I wanted an off-the-record conversation and he agreed to speak on that basis. He immediately gave me confidence. He was measured, analytical and authoritative. He told me that he had been consulted over the dossier and that, in his view, some spin from Number Ten had come into play. I wrote the words boldly in my notebook. Kelly went on to say that in the week before the dossier was published, material was being put in and taken out, and the document was being sent backwards and forwards between the intelligence services and Downing Street. That interested me too.

He personally believed that Saddam Hussein had weapons of mass destruction, but he had doubts about the language in the dossier, the way it had been presented. I could tell that he was on the move and that the conversation would be short. I mentioned the claim that Saddam could use his weapons within forty-five minutes. He said that he could not entirely go along with that, but we did not have the time to fully explore what he meant. I knew I had a story; here was a highly respected scientist, in a position to know, who had doubts about the dossier that had made the case for war. Later that day I spoke to a former head of the Joint Intelligence Committee who confirmed that at the time the dossier was published she was picking up unease amongst her former colleagues in the intelligence community. What I had was not as dramatic as Andrew Gilligan's report but I had a story; there clearly was some concern within the intelligence community about the dossier.

I mentioned Dr Kelly's name to Mark Popescu, the editor of the *Ten O'Clock News*. I had long felt that on very sensitive stories my editor should know my sources. I had come to this view after a meeting at the *Washington Post* in 1990. I had written an article, which was heavily dependent on unnamed sources. David Ignatius, who was editor of the Outlook section of the paper, took me to see the *Post*'s editor, Ben Bradlee, a legendary figure, made famous by the Watergate scandal and the subsequent book *All the President's Men*.

As soon as he had read my article he asked me who I had spoken to. I hesitated because I had never been asked to reveal my sources before. And in that second of doubt Bradlee said he would not run the piece if I did not tell him. It was the editor's right, he said. In his view the rules of the confessional applied to reporters and their editor. I was persuaded and, ever since, have been open with my editors about the people who have passed me information.

I did not take the story of the Iraqi dossier further. I watched from the sidelines as Downing Street demanded that the BBC accept that the Gilligan story was wrong. There have been many arguments between the BBC and various governments but this was different. It was a high-octane battle with neither side prepared to back off. The more the government demanded an apology the less able the BBC felt to give one. In Whitehall the hunt was on to find Gilligan's source and gradually David Kelly's name emerged. I was very surprised to realize we had spoken to the same person. I was also puzzled at a question put to David Kelly at the Foreign Affairs Committee by an MP, Gisela Stuart. She asked David Kelly, 'Have you had any conversations or meetings with Gavin Hewitt?' Dr Kelly replied, 'Not that I am aware of. No. I am pretty sure I have not.' I have never discovered what prompted that question, but from that moment onwards I was drawn into this unhappy affair.

On 17 July, David Kelly took his own life and a political row ended in tragedy. I knew at once this would be a major crisis for the government and the BBC. I was asked to report the story for the *Ten O'Clock News* but that afternoon there was a reference in the *Evening Standard* to the fact that I, too, had spoken to David Kelly, and it was impossible for me to go on covering these events. Over the weekend most of the papers reported that David Kelly had also been my source. On the Monday I left for Washington just before a photographer from the *Sun* knocked on my front door.

Before I travelled I had heard more bad news about my health. I had not felt well. There were no obvious signs, just a sense that something was wrong. I had another echo sound and stress test and the results showed that there was still a problem with one of my arteries. My cardiologist did not regard it as a serious problem. I was off to America and he was going away and we arranged for a more detailed test later in August.

When you know you have a heart problem the thought never leaves you. It's always there in the background, like a hand on the shoulder. The future is denied to you. Plans cannot be made because there is always the uncertainty, the question mark. Nothing can be fully enjoyed. Friends, laughter, restaurants, walks. I was there but always elsewhere. I went to the gym, but the tightness in my chest was back.

Shortly after I arrived in Washington I was contacted by the Hutton inquiry. I would be called as one of the first witnesses and would have to fly back to London in the middle of August. I was very confident of my reporting, but I knew that this would be a high-profile cross-examination.

I was due to appear on day three of the inquiry. I had watched some of the other witnesses arrive at the Royal Courts of Justice in the Strand. Some stopped in front of the banks of cameras; some did a turn as if this was the red carpet at a movie premiere. Others arrived by car and shrank from the camera lenses. I did not want to do that. I had no reason to hide away, but neither did I want to parade for the cameras. I also did not want to arrive alone. The BBC had suggested I went to Bush House and walk the short distance to the court. A BBC lawyer and the head of public affairs for news agreed to come with me. I had also invited my daughter, Becky. I had hoped that we would get close to the court before I was spotted, but that is not the way the modern media works and I of all people should have known it. As soon as we left Bush House there was a crew from *Panorama* tracking back in front of me. One camera attracts others so within seconds there were more. Some of the stills photographers ran through the traffic, desperate not to miss the shot. The running caught the attention of the tourists, an entire bus-load of Japanese visitors. They saw the cameras and imagined we must be famous. So they joined in, bumping against each other to get the shot. Some took two pictures: one of me and the other of my daughter, who could more easily pass as a star. And then, as always, moments of farce. The lawyer tripped on the edge of the pavement and fell, and they wanted a shot of that. My daughter's heel got caught in some grating and someone flashed that. There were so many people in the road that the traffic stopped. Drivers were curious. Something was happening, but they could not make out what it was. The stills men were shouting my name, all of them trying to get me to turn their way. A young woman tried to sell me an ice cream – possibly a stunt, possibly a product launch.

For one of the few times in my life I was on the other side of the camera. I was the hunted. And there was a dangerous edge to it. Two photographers barged Becky out of the way. As I walked across the pedestrian crossing towards the entrance to the Royal Court I had the same sensation I had had in the gym. It was unmistakable. A tightening in my chest. An attack of angina. I was suddenly afraid I was going to have a heart attack going into the Hutton inquiry. Inside the entrance to the court there was a metal detector and an X-ray machine. I stood there, breathed deeply, and the pain subsided. I said nothing and we went upstairs to a room close to the court. My mind filled with negative thoughts. Say I had another angina attack while being questioned? Would I have to tell Lord Hutton I was unwell, and what would the papers make of that?

Gradually I cleared my mind and when I entered Court 73 I was calm and confident. After the first few minutes I knew I would get through it. A page of my notebook was shown on the computer screens. Everyone has their own way of taking notes. It is personal, but here all the oddities of my note-taking were being shown to the world. My notes are sparse. I write down only what I need. I have my own abbreviations and some teeline, which is a form of short-hand. It means my notes are very difficult to decipher. So I was asked by the inquiry to read my own notes. To my slight embarrass-ment I was asked what 'lot p' meant. I had a stab at it but eventually conceded, 'I am afraid I cannot even read my own writing.' It was the only uncomfortable moment.

Then it was over and Becky and I left the court by car. As we turned left out of the gates some of the photographers saw us and chased after us down Fleet Street, the lenses pressed against the windows. I dropped Becky off near Ludgate Circus and the driver turned to me and said, 'So who was the blonde, then?' It was that kind of day.

I knew I was in trouble with my health, and was frightened. Two weeks later I went for a thallium scan at the Royal Brompton Hospital. This was nuclear medicine. A radionuclide substance was injected into me and a special camera recorded the blood flow in and out of my heart. Afterwards Professor Underwood took me aside and said I should contact my cardiologist. It was the way he said it that prompted further questions, but he insisted that I get the details from my cardiologist. He dropped into the conversation that he knew airline pilots who had had bypass operations and were still flying. It was the first time that anyone had mentioned major surgery.

I was working the next day and it was not until twenty-four hours later that I got to speak to my cardiologist. There was, he said, a severe narrowing in one of my arteries and he wanted me to have another angiogram. A few days later the catheter was again inside me, exploring my arteries. Shortly afterwards the cardiologist came in to see me and said, 'We're into bypass territory, I'm afraid.' He had a picture to convince me. There is a key artery, the LAD, the left anterior descending, and mine was ninety per cent blocked. I was bewildered. Only a few months before it had been clear, but I had been unlucky. When the second stent had been inserted it had caused a lesion and scar tissue had built up around it, narrowing my main artery. At the time I had questioned the need for the second stent but, although I had finally agreed to it, the procedure had gone wrong and my life was now at risk. Part of my mind wanted to lay blame, to rail against the injustice of it, but none of that helped.

It was a different kind of fear to being in conflict. In war, danger is sudden and can recede just as quickly. This fear was deeper, more fundamental. Part of me protested. How could someone who had been so fit be in this position? Surely they had the wrong man. I wanted to claim the journalist's immunity, that I reported on what happened to others; that we were a breed apart.

I asked whether I could have another stent rather than surgery and an appointment was made with the consultant who had done the original angioplasty. He thought it would be very difficult and dangerous but he was willing to try and I agreed to it. As I was leaving he said to me that every time he had seen me on television he had said to himself, 'Thank God.' I realized then that he feared all along that the original treatment had not worked.

It was a Saturday morning in September and we agreed that I would come in for an angioplasty the following week. If it failed I would have to have a bypass. That evening I ate out and went to bed. I woke at about 4.30 in the morning and realized that what had woken me was a tightening of my chest. I was having an angina attack in my sleep. I was as frightened as I had been in my life, and the more anxious I became the more the pain increased in my chest. I phoned the hospital and they called my cardiologist. Moments later they told me to 'come in'. And so a drive through the night's end, through empty streets, wanting every light to turn green, counting down the moments to the hospital. This was not the Green Line or a Baghdad suburb but London's terraces, reassuring and familiar, and yet this was a dash for my life as serious as anything I had lived through before.

Once I was in the hospital the pain subsided. I was told I would not be leaving until I had had an operation. I had unstable angina and it was too risky. That afternoon – a Sunday – they decided to attempt the angioplasty. The consultant told me that they would stop it and pull back if it looked too dangerous. So, once again, I was lying under lights, surrounded by monitors, receiving shots of valium. The catheter was inserted but after two minutes I heard the doctor talking to a heart surgeon. They both agreed it was too risky to continue. I was wheeled back to my room knowing that heart surgery lay ahead.

The operation was set for four days later, 11 September. Time slowed. There were hours to fill and I finally told the BBC that I was facing a serious operation. For those few days you live without a future. There are no plans to be made or dreams to have. There is nothing beyond that moment, 8.30 on the Thursday morning, when I would be taken down to the theatre. I called friends and skated over the details. Then there was the conversation that has to be had. What happened if I did not make it? Things had to be said.

Practical questions addressed. And then there were the calls that lift you. A friend called and said, 'If you don't make it, can I have your car?' And I loved that. The sparkle of life. The life I wanted to reclaim.

As I waited I felt a cussedness, an obstinacy, a refusal to lie down. Where it comes from you do not know but the closer I came to the operation the more defiant I became. A doctor asked me to speak to an older man in the room next door. He was about to have an angiogram and was very nervous. For a moment it seemed absurd, the idea that I would be reassuring others, but when I spoke to the man and saw him relax and smile I caught some of his hope.

The evening before my operation my body was shaved as I watched television. The anaesthetist offered me a Scotch but I turned it down. Drinks belonged elsewhere. A nurse asked me if I wanted a sleeping pill but I said no. I wanted those few hours for myself, to savour them in the quietness of the night, to prepare myself. And then they came for me. You have a pre-med and you drift into unconsciousness. Six hours later I woke in the same mood, desperate to get on with my life. Although I could not speak because of the tubes in my throat I signalled that I wanted to write a message. The cardiologist handed me a clipboard and I scribbled, 'Did it go OK?' and he laughed and said it had.

The following day I took my first steps. Then I had to walk to the end of the corridor. Then it was the corridor four times a day. Then the stairs. And in my mind these were circuits and I was back in training; the future returned and, with it, that indispensable hope.

The hospital physiotherapist asked me to attend a therapy session. She would be going over some basic exercises. In the room there were three other men. Much older. In their late seventies or early eighties. Frail white-haired men. And we were the class and we stretched and breathed together. The phsyio asked us to throw a ball to each other. The men threw and their faces lit up. They were alive, gloriously alive. They threw hard, mischievously. And we laughed and all of us, in that moment, felt life returning. As I sat with them I felt that if I had been covering this, here was the story.

Not the operation. That was the surface of it; but here my camera would have captured something else – the human spirit, irrepressible, fighting back.

Later I met with the surgeon. The operation had gone well. He told me to see what had happened as 'an episode' and nothing more. There had been no damage to my heart. I had not had a heart attack. I was told to resume my life. So, a week after my operation, I was out of hospital breathing, exercising, walking; I was on the long slow climb back to health.

It was as beautiful an autumn as I could remember. Each day, as I walked just that little bit further, the sun shone. The colours were deep and vibrant. Straw-yellows, copper-reds, russet-browns and auburn. Maybe it was because I had time that I saw more or maybe I just appreciated what lay around me. It had been there all the time, taken for granted, unappreciated, but was now restored like some old painting with the grime removed and in its place a startling beauty.

A major operation leaves a doubt, that intimation of mortality. Mostly it lies there dormant but then, like a tug on the sleeve, it takes you back, reminds you that you are not immune, that, in some way, the odds have shortened.

Then I was back working, slowly at first. Friends and colleagues stop you. They have heard stories, rumours, snippets and you have your version ready. The fifteen-second version. The minute. Just enough and no more. Then there are those who are that little bit too interested in the detail and you see the unspoken fear and you know that they, too, have had a scare. You matter for a day or two but no more. Your story fades much as those we cover. So very quickly the slack is picked up and life resumes. Guantanamo Bay; the Madrid bombings, the Kerry campaign; the funeral of Ronald Reagan.

Looking back I have covered two major stories; the Cold War and the War against Terror. They have defined my period, filled so much air-time, and dragged me across the globe. At the time the events seemed clear, easy to read, but, in truth, we rarely know how they will turn out, and more often than not the consequences are unintended. The Soviets invaded Afghanistan to widen their influence, and ended up losing their empire. The CIA backed the mujahedin and ended up with Osama bin Laden. The West stuck with the Shah and got the Islamic Revolution. We sided with Saddam Hussein only to have to destroy him later.

And that's what so much of my reporting became, a cycle of returns and revisits, picking up the echo, the past's haunting beat and often its terrible consequences.

Graham Greene had warned me about learning to put my soul on ice. It happened but not by choice. An outer shell forms, a carapace, a hardening that lets you be there but stand apart. And just when the only laugh is cynical a human story rescues you. The fireman's widow; the unknown man in front of the Chinese tank; the patients in the cardiac ward; the stubborn sculptor carving the mountain; the dissident's lonely courage; the embrace when the wall came down. They are banked up in the memory. And, from all the images and places, it is their stories that retrieve some human meaning from the pans, the close-ups, the cut-aways and the torrent of phrases and words. And tomorrow, when we find ourselves living through one of history's moments, I will feel the same irresistible pull. To be there.

Index